Dedicated to Professor James Hankins, complatonico

Also in the Variorum Collected Studies Series:

MICHAEL J. B. ALLEN
Plato's Third Eye: Studies in Marsilo Ficino's Metaphysics and its Sources

NELSON H. MINNICH
The Decrees of the Fifth Lateran Council (1512–17)
Their Legitimacy, Origins, Contents, and Implementation

THOMAS MORRISSEY
Conciliarism and Church Law in the Fifteenth Century
Studies on Franciscus Zabarella and the Council of Constance

H. LAWRENCE BOND AND GERALD CHRISTIANSON
Reform, Representation and Theology in Nicholas of Cusa and His Age

TIMOTHY J. WENGERT
Philip Melanchthon, Speaker of the Reformation
Wittenberg's Other Reformer

THOMAS M. IZBICKI
Reform, Ecclesiology, and the Christian Life in the Late Middle Ages

F. EDWARD CRANZ
Reorientations of Western Thought from Antiquity to the Renaissance

PAUL F. GRENDLER
Renaissance Education Between Religion and Politics

JAMES D. TRACY
The Low Countries in the Sixteenth Century
Erasmus, Religion and Politics, Trade and Finance

ANTHONY BLACK
Church, State and Community: Historical and Comparative Perspectives

MORIMICHI WATANABE
Concord and Reform
Nicholas of Cusa and Legal and Political Thought in the Fifteenth Century

F. EDWARD CRANZ
Nicholas of Cusa and the Renaissance

VARIORUM COLLECTED STUDIES SERIES

Studies in the Platonism of Marsilio Ficino and Giovanni Pico

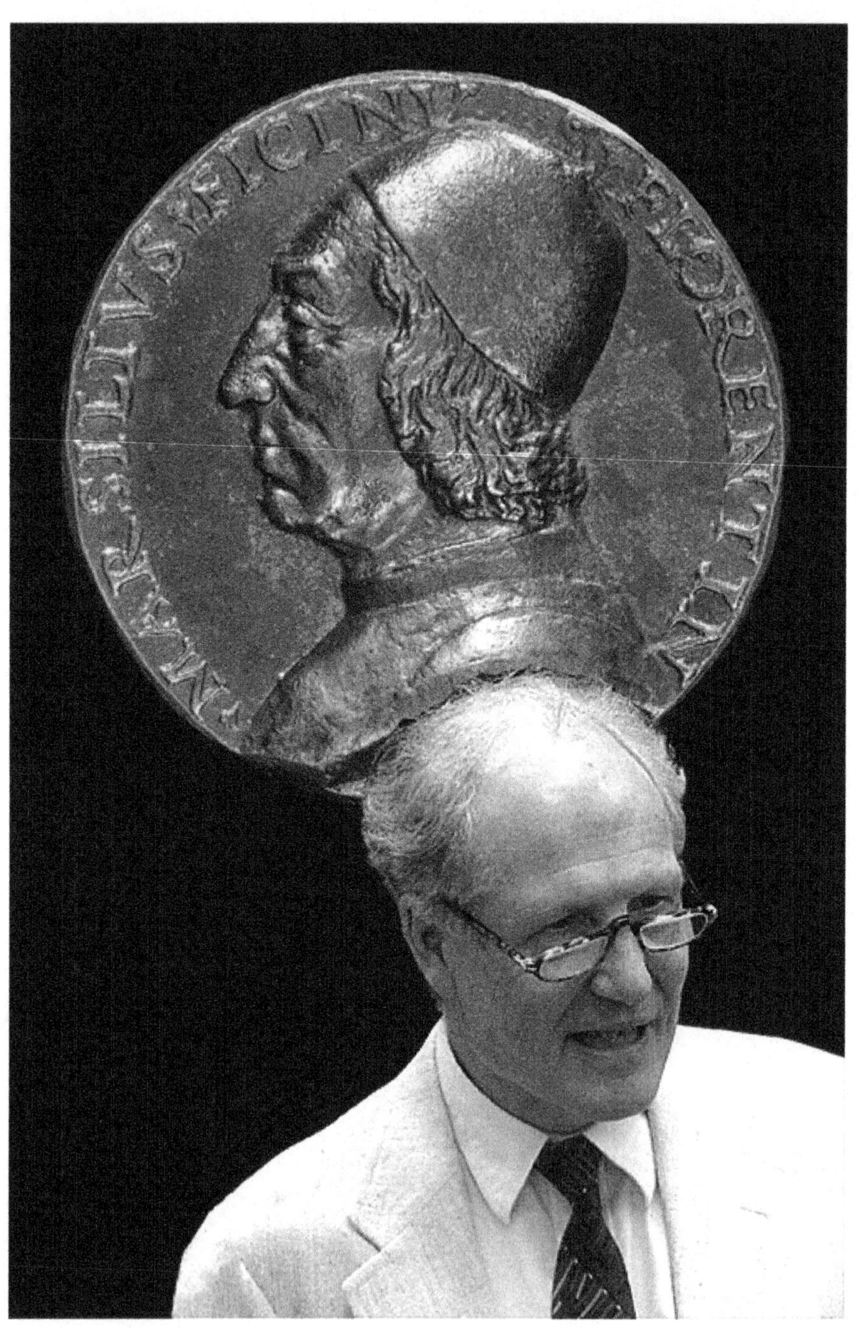
MARSILIVS FICINV FLORENTINV

Michael J. B. Allen

Studies in the Platonism of Marsilio Ficino and Giovanni Pico

LONDON AND NEW YORK

First published 2017 by Routledge

2 Park Square, Milton Park, Abingdon, Oxfordshire OX14 4RN
711 Third Avenue, New York, NY 10017

Routledge is an imprint of the Taylor & Francis Group, an informa business

First issued in paperback 2018

British Library Cataloguing in Publication Data
A catalogue record for this book is available from the British Library

Library of Congress Cataloging in Publication Data
A catalog record for this book has been requested

ISBN: 978-1-4724-4838-5 (hbk)
ISBN: 978-1-138-33020-7 (pbk)

VARIORUM COLLECTED STUDIES SERIES CS1063

Printed in the United Kingdom
by Henry Ling Limited

CONTENTS

PREFACE

This second volume of Ficino essays consists of eighteen pieces written over the last two decades. Except for the introductory account of Renaissance Platonism and more particularly of Ficino's formative role in its articulation in the first essay—which is, alas, misattributed in the *Columbia History of Western Philosophy*—the other seventeen essays are specialized studies of aspects of Ficino's thought, or in the case of essays II and X of Pico's thought. They were variously written for conference or commemorative volumes or for collections devoted to a particular work or theme as in the case of XVIII's concern with the *Epinomis*. I cannot here do full justice to the cascade of essays by other scholars that have appeared since my first Variorum volume of 1995. Instead I must refer interested readers to the Ficino bibliography that appears periodically in *Accademia*. I would like to take this occasion, however, to mention the interpretive and historical work of a *catena aurea* of scholars who have enriched my own understanding of Ficino: James Hankins, Valery Rees, John Monfasani, Chris Celenza, Jacomien Prins, Stéphane Toussaint, Pasquale Terracciano, Maude Vanhaelen, Carlos Steel, Guido Giglioni, Wouter Hanegraaff, Guido Bartolucci, A. Neschke-Hentschke, Sebastiano Gentile, Fosca Mariani Zini, Sergius Kodera, Paola Megna, Anna Pace, Thomas Leinkauf, Anna Corrias, James Snyder, James Coleman, Denis Robichaud, Teodoro Katinis, Simone Fellina, Valerio Sanzotta, Grantley Macdonald, Tamara Albertini, Dilwyn Knox, Stephen Clucas, Peter Forshaw, Sarah Hutton, Douglas Hedley, Jill Kraye, Paul Richard Blum, Letizia Panizza, and for both Ficino and Pico, among other Piconians, my beloved colleague Brian Copenhaver. Secondly, I must adduce the important editorial work by Sebastiano Gentile on the second book of Ficino's *Letters*; by Maurizio Campanelli on Ficino's Hermetic *Pimander*; by Daniele Conti on Ficino's sermons, and, forthcoming, on the St. Paul Commentary; and by Maude Vanhaelen and separately by Francesca Lazzarin on Ficino's *In Parmenidem.* For Ficino's Commentaries on the *Mystical Theology* and *Divine Names*, see the editorial work of Pietro Podolak along with my own work on the 2 vols I Tatti edition with accompanying translation. Of signal importance to the Anglo-phone world has been the succession of stimulating sessions on Ficino at the annual Renaissance Society of America meetings lovingly organized by

Valery Rees, who has herself written authoritatively on Ficino's angelology and on various issues raised in and by Ficino's letters.

I am hopeful, given friends' encouragement, that these essays continue to stand on their own merits, or at least that they retain some of their original vigor and interest. Gathering them together, certainly, means in a number of instances that they now reference and serve each other. Eight more essays not included here for various reasons are:

"Life as a Dead Platonist," in **Marsilio Ficino: His Theology, His Philosophy, His Legacy**, ed. Michael J. B. Allen and Valery Rees, with Martin Davies, Brill's Studies in Intellectual History, vol. 108 (Leiden: Brill, 2002), pp. 159–178.

"Plato's *Gorgias*, Ficino and the Poets," in **Commenter et philosopher à la Renaissance: Tradition universitaire, tradition humaniste**, ed. Laurence Boulègue (Villeneuve d'Ascq: Presses universitaires du Septentrion, 2014), pp.135–147.

"The Proclus of Marsilio Ficino (1433–1499)," in **Interpreting Proclus: from Antiquity to the Renaissance**, ed. Stephen Gersh (Cambridge: CUP, 2014), pp. 353–379.

"Pythagoras in the Early Renaissance," in **A History of Pythagoreanism**, ed. Carl A. Huffman (Cambridge: CUP, 2014), pp. 435–453.

"Marsilio Ficino's Last Great Achievement: his Commentaries on the *Mystical Theology* and *Divine Names* of Dionysius the Areopagite," **Rinascimento** 54 (2014/16), pp. 51–67.

"Attica and Atlantis: Marsilio Ficino's Interpretations of the *Menexenus* & *Critias* of Plato," **Rinascimento 55** (2015), pp. 3–33.

"Glory, Transfiguration and the Fire Within: Marsilio Ficino on the Metaphysics and Psychology of Light" in **Lux in Tenebris. Selected Essays from the Third Conference of the European Society for the Study of Western Esotericism**, ed. Peter Forshaw, Boaz Huss & György E. Szönyi (Leiden: Brill, in press).

"Marsilio Ficino on Power, on Wisdom and on Moses," forthcoming in a Brill **Festschrift** for Jill Kraye.

For my earlier work on Ficino, see the bibliography in *The Rebirth of Platonic Theology*, generously edited by James Hankins and Fabrizio Meroi (Florence: Olschki, 2013), pp. 1–4.

ACKNOWLEDGEMENTS

For permissions to reprint the essays in this volume I am grateful to the following publishers: to Columbia University Press, New York; for "The Renaissance: Platonism"; to the Cambridge University Press, Cambridge, for "Renaissance Neoplatonism" and "The Birth Day of Venus: Pico as Platonic Exegete in the *Commento* and the *Heptaplus*"; to the Massachusetts Institute of Technology Press, Boston, for "Marsilio Ficino, Daemonic Mathematics and the Hypotenuse of the Spirit"; to Harrassowitz Verlag, Wiesbaden, for "*In principio*: Marsilio Ficino on the Life of Text"; to the University of Notre Dame Press, Notre Dame, Indiana, for "The Ficinian *Timaeus* and Renaissance Science"; to the Italica Press, New York, for "Paul Oskar Kristeller and Marsilio Ficino: *e tenebris revocaverunt*"; to Droz's Cahiers du Gagdes, Geneva, for "Marsilio Ficino, Levitation, and the Ascent to Capricorn"; to Springer, Dordrecht, for "At Variance: Marsilio Ficino, Platonism and Heresy"; to Wilhelm Fink Verlag, Munich, for "Sending Archedemus: Ficino, Plato's Second Letter, and its Four Epistolary Mysteries"; to Fabrizio Serra Editore, Pisa & Rome, for "Marsilio Ficino on Saturn, the Plotinian Mind, and the Monster of Averroes"; to Bibliopolis, Naples, for "*Ratio omnium divinissima:* Plato's *Epinomis*, Prophecy, and Marsilio Ficino"; and finally to Leo S. Olschki for the following six essays: "*Cultura hominis*: Giovanni Pico, Marsilio Ficino and the Idea of Man"; "Marsilio Ficino and the Language of the Past"; "*Quisque in sphaera sua*: Plato's *Statesman*, Marsilio Ficino's *Platonic Theology* and the Resurrection of the Body"; "To gaze upon the face of God again: Philosophic Statuary, Pygmalion, and Marsilio Ficino"; "Eurydice in Hades: Florentine Platonism and an Orphic Mystery"; and "Prometheus among the Florentines: Marsilio Ficino on the Myth of Triadic Power."

I am also much indebted to the editors of *Rinascimento* and of *Bruniana & Campanelliana*, and to the editors of the various collections. Finally, I am deeply grateful to Michael Bourne in Oxford and to Hillary Gordon in Los Angeles for their scanning and preparation help.

1

THE RENAISSANCE: PLATONISM

* * *

PLATONISM

Whatever their attitudes toward Aristotelian philosophy, Renaissance readers knew it as a various but familiar institution, part of the ancient intellectual heritage passed on to them by the many medieval scholars who had studied Aristotle since the twelfth century. Plato's recovery, however, was distinctly a Renaissance achievement and mainly the work of a single person: Marsilio Ficino, the most accomplished Hellenist of his time. Earlier Quattrocento work on Plato had begun with a few dialogues and letters Latinized by Leonardo Bruni, the translations of the *Republic* by the Decembrii (father and son), and the *Laws* and *Parmenides*, badly, by George of Trebizond. But these pioneering humanist attempts bore full fruit only with Ficino's rendering of the complete canon, published in 1484 with commentary and introductory material under the generous patronage of Filippo Valori, a member of a Florentine family hardly less celebrated than Ficino's other patrons, the Medici.

In the centuries before Ficino restored Plato, Europeans had known very little of or about him. They had only part of the *Timaeus* in the fourth-century Latin of Chalcidius; unreadably literal versions of the *Phaedo* and the *Meno* done in the twelfth century by Henricus Aristippus; and sections of the *Parmenides* embedded in the commentary by Proclus and translated—again literally and often unreadably—in the thirteenth century by William of Moerbeke. Platonic concepts were also known, of course, from such authorities as Cicero, Pseudo-Dionysius, Augustine, and Boethius and from the numerous cosmological works that drew upon the *Timaeus.* In this way, "participation," "recollection," and other key terms had entered the philosophical lexicon not only in the Platonizing Bonaventure but even in the Peripatetic Aquinas. Nonetheless, the impact of new and direct access to Plato's complete dialogues and letters in Latin was vastly greater than the influence of the few and fragmentary bits available before the Renaissance. Plato's presence in a reclassicized Latin was all the more appreciated by a learned culture awakening to the importance of Greek, of which Plato is a paradigmatic stylist.

One might have supposed that it was the story of Socrates' death that most captured Plato's new admirers. Early on, Bruni had chosen the Socratic drama of the *Apology, Crito,* and *Phaedo* for his first translations, and eventually the fascination with Socrates grew into an obsession in the sixteenth century. It was Erasmus and later Rabelais and Montaigne who gave Socrates his Christian apotheosis, even though Ficino and others had sketched the main lines of accommodating argument: that Socrates, like the heroes of the Bible, was a type of Christ; that his passion resembled the Lord's passion (including silver, a cup, a blessing, a cock, a turning of the other cheek); that his piety and justice had at last been divinely vindicated; and that he had set the health of the soul over all bodily comforts, even the very life of the body (*soma*) punningly described as a tomb (*sema*). But the example of Socrates, however much the humanists honored him, was not the main reason for reviving Plato. To the contrary, the early Socratic dialogues were generally neglected in favor of later works where Socrates appears and speaks, but often in a role subordinated to other figures with Eleatic or Pythagorean authority. In these texts, the insistent Socratic questioning, defining, and discovering of distinctions—largely for ethical ends—has given place to the exploration of metaphysical doctrine and a new complex dialectic. The attraction of these later works of Plato for early modern readers lay close to hand within the prevailing Christian tradition.

One of the supreme testimonies to the Christian life of faith is the story of Saint Augustine, in many ways the fountainhead of medieval spirituality and an eloquent witness to the experience of conversion and belief. His probing theological analysis of freedom and necessity, grace and free will, was a primary stimulus, too, for the innovations, preoccupations, and divisions of the Reformation. Augustine was a philosopher of great depth and originality—many would call him the father of Christian philosophy—and his compelling account of the part played by Greek metaphysics, and signally by Platonic metaphysics, in returning him to the faith of his mother and his youth had special meaning for Renaissance thinkers. While many had grown sceptical of the methodological and terminological elaborations and fixations of late Scholasticism, they remained committed to the rational defense and understanding of faith and were still possessed by the medieval desire for a *summa*, for a rational system comprehending all questions in the light of divine truth. Early modern intellectuals who shared this spiritual vision called each other *ingeniosi* (loosely, the "spirited" or perhaps "the gifted") and it was they especially who looked to the great North African Father, as Petrarch had looked to him on the summit of Mount Ventoux.

In the *Confessions*, Augustine tells a graphic story about the summer when he obtained "through a certain man, puffed up with overweening haughtiness . . . a few books of the Platonists," including Latin translations by Marius Victorinus of some, if not all, of the *Enneads* of Plotinus and probably of two works by Porphyry. It was these books that drew Augustine into the world of the Platonists and resulted in an integration of Plotinian metaphysics into his mental world. Later in life, Augustine repudiated this encounter with the pagan Platonists and no longer advocated their study as the natural prelude to conversion for a Christian intellectual. But his retraction lacked the rhetorical force of his *Confessions* and of other works that spoke to Plato as a Gentile prophet, an Athenian voice from the world of the Old Testament with the implication that one could interpret biblical revelation by way of Plotinus and his successors. The same hermeneutic motivated and legitimated the study of Plato's predecessors as well, those who had adumbrated the ancient theological wisdom that Plato himself perfected.

The notion of a pre-Platonic succession of sages in possession of Platonic truths was an ancient one that long antedated Augustine's strategy of "back-reading." The Greeks often claimed Egyptian, Chaldaean, Lydian, Persian, Thracian, or some other "barbarian" ancestry for their gods, cults, and mysteries. Plato himself, speaking through Socrates, intimated that many of his ideas derived from others, most notably the Pythagoreans. At the end of the *Republic*, for example, he credits a Pamphilian named Er with a visionary journey to the afterlife; his *Laws* are presented as the wisdom of the Cretans; his *Sophist* as a vehicle for the visions of an Eleatic, a follower of Parmenides. Throughout his works, Plato quotes verses from Orpheus, the mythical Thracian bard, and accords him greater authority than he accords Homer and Hesiod, who are severely criticized in the *Republic*. By late antiquity, the Platonists had worked out a pre-Platonic genealogy of wisdom stemming from Zoroaster in Persia and Hermes Trismegistus in Egypt and then passing through Orpheus and Pythagoras down to such sages as Aglaophemus and Philolaus and on to Plato. Loosely associated with this wisdom "tree" were other *theologi* such as Heraclitus, Empedocles, and, above all, Parmenides, the founder of the Eleatic school and author of a philosophic poem describing the soul's chariot ride up through the gates of night and day to the feet of an anonymous goddess. Parmenides was famous for his radical monism and for maintaining—in the teeth of apparent contradictions—that nonbeing cannot be in a world of absolute (and, according to him, spherical) being.

In the opinion of the Platonists of antiquity, Parmenides was the most important philosopher before Socrates because the dialogue Plato had named after him presented them with their greatest philosophical challenge. Slighted by the Middle Platonists as an eristic exercise, the *Parmenides* came to be seen by the Neoplatonists as the apex of Plato's work and the repository of his highest mysteries concerning the ultimate ground of being and nonbeing, of the One that Plotinus put at the summit of his metaphysical hierarchy. The first part of the dialogue criticizes Plato's theory of Ideas and discusses the kinds of things that do not have Ideas. The second part sets forth what the later Neoplatonists determined were nine hypotheses: a set of five positive and a subordinate set of four negative hypotheses. The first set they saw as treating the five *hypostases* (roughly, levels of being or reality) in what for them had become the standard pentad of the Platonic metaphysical system: the One, mind, soul, Forms in matter, and matter (or matter in extension as body). The four negative hypotheses establish the absurdities that would follow if the one were not to exist, and these correspond to the last four positive hypotheses.

The effect of this subtle Neoplatonic analysis was to make the *Parmenides* into a summa of Plato's "theology" and the capstone of his thought; the other dialogues were deemed tributary to it. Once the *Parmenides* was understood, argued Proclus, Plato's other works became essentially unnecessary. In any case, they could be fully understood only in terms of the *Parmenides*. Hence the decision to make this work the climax of the Neoplatonic teaching cycle, the supreme test of an initiate's dialectical and exegetical training. The Neoplatonists saw the *Parmenides* as the crown both of the ancient theology of pre-Platonic Platonism and of Plato's own meditation on the One and the good. Parmenides of Elea becomes Plato's spiritual grandfather, if you will, and Plato presents his dialogue as a sublime and filial tribute to the metaphysics learned at the feet of the disciples of this Pythagorean, above all Melissus. Significantly, the most authoritative presentation of this exalted view of Parmenides and his eponymous dialogue, namely the incomplete commentary on it by Proclus, was selected for translation by William of Moerbeke and thus made available to a few medieval readers. Moreover, when Parmenides presented the ultimate metaphysical truths, he had also defined his absolutes by way of negation in the dialogue's last four hypotheses. In Christian eyes, then, he had anticipated the apophatic (negating) theology of Pseudo-Dionysius the Areopagite, a thinker revered in the Renaissance as Saint Paul's first Athenian convert but later exposed as a late fifth- or early sixth-century follower of Proclus.

Whether William or other medieval readers really plumbed the depths explored by Proclus is doubtful. In the West at least, Ficino was the first since antiquity who clearly achieved a mastery of Proclus's complex works. As an authority on the Platonic tradition, he became indeed supreme in his day, remaining so for centuries to come, and he is listed among Europe's most accomplished Hellenists. Who taught him Greek is still in question. His father, a court physician, intended a medical career for him, but we have evidence of his youthful interest in philosophy, specifically in the Latin Platonic tradition, both pagan and Christian. From the late 1450s, when he was in his mid-twenties, examples survive of his paraphrases and translations of difficult Greek texts, treatises by Iamblichus, and the hymns attributed to Orpheus. In 1462, the aging Cosimo de' Medici, having purchased a complete codex of Plato's works and anxious to learn what was in them, ordered Ficino to translate them. Hardly had he begun than Cosimo gave him another manuscript that contained the first fourteen treatises of the Hermetic corpus, which he wanted to read or hear in Latin. As Cosimo lay dying in July 1464, he requested that Ficino read him the ten Plato dialogues that he had already managed to translate, including two masterpieces: the *Parmenides* and a cognate work concerned, they thought, with the supreme, not just human, good, the *Philebus*.

Under Cosimo's son Piero, and his grandson Lorenzo the Magnificent, Ficino worked through the entire canon with extraordinary accuracy, penetrating insight, and not a little eloquence. He composed a long and brilliant commentary on the *Symposium*, which he called the *Symposium on Love*; a first version of a commentary on the *Timaeus*; and introductory epitomes or arguments for all the other dialogues and for the *Letters*. These were published together in Florence in one of the great monuments of early printing, the 1484 *Complete Works of Plato*, reprinted in 1491 in Venice along with a massive work of original philosophical speculation called *Platonic Theology: On the Immortality of Souls*, a name suggestively compounded from titles by Proclus and Augustine. Ficino's enormous labor built on earlier humanist efforts to a degree and where available, but he produced independent renderings throughout based on his unrivaled understanding of the Greek text and of the ancient scholarship devoted to it. Later Renaissance versions corrected him on a few things while adding errors or tendentious readings of their own, but they never supplanted Ficino's Plato. Samuel Taylor Coleridge (1772–1834) read and annotated a copy of it in his youth, and Ficino's work remains the supreme Latin version to this day.

Having put Plato into a language that educated Western Europeans could read, Ficino turned immediately to Plotinus in the fervent belief that Plato's soul had been reborn in his third-century disciple and, following Augustine, that Plotinus was at times even more profound than his master. Ficino's esteem for Plotinus and his school explains why Ficino's philosophy has often been called Neoplatonist, a term he would have rejected on the grounds that the Platonic tradition is unitary. Moreover, even as Plato's works constituted for him a unified whole, so did the works of Zoroaster, Hermes, and other ancient theologians bear witness that the highest truths had long been revealed to the Gentiles in a revelation parallel (and, one suspects, barely subordinate in Ficino's eyes) to the revelation of scripture. Once again, Ficino accompanied his translation of the enormously difficult *Enneads* of Plotinus with explanatory materials amounting to a running commentary. All this was published in 1492, and, like the Plato volume, preceded the first edition of the Greek text by several decades. Ficino also published a number of translations of later Neoplatonist works by Porphyry, Iamblichus, Proclus, and Pseudo-Dionysius; the Pythagorean *Golden Sayings*; the brief treatise attributed to Alcinous; Athenagoras on the resurrection of the body; Synesius on dreams, and others. In its totality, this work of translation and interpretation emerges as a monument of energy, sustained intellectual commitment, and formidable, authoritative learning.

But translation and commentary were only part of Ficino's labors. He also proselytized for Platonism through an immense web of influential correspondents in Italy and abroad. Among the epistolary commonplaces in the twelve books of his published letters are many penetrating Platonic formulations and analyses, some of the letters being in effect small essays. After he was ordained a priest in 1473, he prepared an eloquent treatise in defense of the Christian religion and, presumably, to advertise his own orthodoxy.

In a less orthodox mode, he also wrote *Three Books on Life,* dealing with physiology and psychology as well as the pharmacology, astrology, and demonology involved in prolonging human life, especially the life of the scholar; it became the most influential statement of a philosophical theory of magic since antiquity. In it he reappraised Aquinas's comments on magical talismans and symbols in light of Neoplatonic theories of cosmic sympathy and antipathy, taking particular notice of a work by Proclus, *On Sacrifice and Magic.* Essentially a therapy manual—seen by some in our own day as a foundational text of Jungian psychology—it nonetheless stirred opposition from the papal curia, even a threat of formal investigation. The threat came to nothing, but the incident shows that Ficino was treading a fine and possibly unorthodox line when he raised controversial issues concerning natural and demonic magic governed by the harmonies and ratios he derived from the mathematical and musicological treatises of antiquity and the Middle Ages.

For Ficino was an accomplished performer on his "Orphic lyre"—a lute designed to reproduce what were thought to be the Greek chords—to which he sang Platonic hymns with magical intentions. More important, he was learned in the theory of harmonics that, together with his medical training and his study of the *Timaeus,* helped him to formulate an integrated view of cosmic and human nature and to center it on twin notions: that the spirit (*spiritus* or *pneuma*) making up the soul's vehicle or chariot is the link between the sensible and intelligible realms; and that the world is governed by the world soul, the soul of the all, by way of harmonies, ratios, and correspondences—that is, by musical "powers" and relationships.

The *Parmenides,* the *Philebus,* and the *Sophist* were the three dialogues that supplied Ficino with the core of his Plotinian metaphysics, as apparently they had Plotinus himself. The *Timaeus*—with its cosmological and biological concerns, its striking numerology of the triangles making up the four elements, its master image of the demiurge, and its equally effective concept of ruling proportions—provided the material for his speculations on the world soul. Other dialogues dominated his anthropological and ethical thinking. The *Symposium* and the *Phaedrus,* two of Plato's greatest mythopoetic works, provided him with his theories of love, divine beauty, and the soul's origin in, descent from, and eventual reascent to the world of Ideas. His youthful commentary on the *Symposium* is an iridescent elaboration of Plato in light of Plotinus on love and beauty and a powerful though often preliminary statement as well of his own most cherished thoughts. Remarkably free of Christian allusions, it rarely invokes the erotic themes of the Psalms or the Song of Songs or the love imagery of the Christian mystical tradition.

Central to Ficino's analysis is the soul's ascent toward its own unity and thereafter toward union with the One, a controlling vision supported by the Neoplatonic metaphysical system. The *Phaedrus* gave him an account of beauty couched in Plato's most memorable series of images, those of the chariot's ascent to the outermost rim of the intellectual heaven, thence to gaze afar at the eternal Ideas in the "supercelestial place" before returning to pasture its twin horses on nectar and ambrosia in the meadows we temporally call home. This imagery suffuses many of the arguments of Plotinus and Proclus, and Ficino draws on it repeatedly. The same is true for another passage in the *Phaedrus*: the description of the four divine furies culminating in the *mania* of love. This has long served as a corrective to Platonic intellectualism and helps to account for Ficino's vacillation in the Scholastic debate on the primacy of the intellect or the will in our fallen condition. From the *Phaedrus*, therefore, he assembles a complex portrait of the sage as a philosopher-poet-prophet-lover-priest—a magus, even—enraptured by a divine fury and swept up to Saint Paul's "third heaven" into paradise to hear "unspeakable words" (2 Cor. 12:2–4). Because it is hard to imagine a conception of philosophy more remote from post-Cartesian norms, it is all the more important to understand the ubiquitous presence of Ficinian Platonism in the sixteenth and early seventeenth centuries.

For Ficino personally, as for the eclectic Neoplatonism that he revived, the *Symposium* and *Phaedrus* are complementary texts. Moreover, they have to be reconciled both with the cosmological speculations of the *Timaeus* and with the metaphysical dialogues that lead up to the *Parmenides*. Creation is the overflowing of the One, which is the source of being and yet utterly beyond being. First born of the One is mind, the supreme being, in whom all things are contained in their prime unity as the Ideas. Below them are their images in soul, the source of all motion and life, and in unitary soul are all other souls, beginning with the world soul. Unity is still present in matter in extension as the forms of bodies. Even matter—absolute nonbeing in Plotinian terms—is one and therefore dependent on the One. Ficino's achievement was to open up this whole lost realm of Neoplatonic ideas and images, to recover and illuminate its grand ontological hierarchy in which soul occupies the pivotal center among the five Plotinian hypostases, the concern of the first five hypotheses in the *Parmenides*, what G. W. F. Hegel was to call Plato's *Kunstwerk* and Ficino "the inmost sanctuary" of his thought. Even more important was Ficino's success in accommodating (if not fully integrating) this vast and intricate system with Christian dogma concerning the Trinity, the soul's resurrection and immortality, and redemption through Christ as the logos incarnate.

Even so, tensions remained, arising especially from Ficino's demonology and from his Platonic conviction that a few philosophers at least can return to the divine condition, can make themselves like God (*homoiosis theo*, in the famous phrase of the *Theaetetus* 176b). This puts Ficino in a Pelagian or semi-Pelagian position that aligns him with the ancient opponents of Augustine in maintaining that the soul is not irredeemably corrupt but for Christ's free gift of grace. In essence it is a true spark of the divine, a fallen star, god or demon, imprisoned in the body but able in a divine frenzy to rise by its own intellectual powers of contemplation to the realm of its fellow gods, the planetary souls who circle beneath the angelic minds that exist in motionless intensity in an intelligible realm profoundly different from the heaven delineated by traditional Christianity. To a degree, Ficino reenacted the first encounter between Christianity and Greek philosophy in late antiquity, recapitulating positions taken by Clement, Gregory of Nazianzen, Gregory of Nyssa, Origen, Marius Victorinus, and other patristic authorities. Even so, his enthusiasm for a lost Platonism; his sense of its stretching back to a distant origin with Zoroaster; his belief that Christ had come to fulfill the Platonic promise and that in its fundamental truths Platonism was another way of presenting Christianity to a wise person—Plato, John, Paul, Pseudo-Dionysius, and Plotinus all being witnesses to the same religious wisdom: these assumptions are not those of the apologists of the early Christian centuries. When we recall besides that Ficino knew Augustine and other Church Fathers and that he read Scholastic philosophers including Avicenna, Avicebron (Ibn Gabirol), and Averroës as well as Aquinas; when we consider his preoccupation with the principles of astrology, music, and humoral therapy (if not the mundane practices of them) then a picture emerges of an original thinker of genius, one who spoke to the historical circumstances of his age, who indeed helped define the self-conception of the Renaissance, and who produced some of its most complex and visionary formulations by way of a rigorous presentation of a largely novel and perennially difficult body of ancient materials.

Not all Renaissance Platonists subscribed to the elevation of the Plotinian *Parmenides*, however, nor did they all give way to Ficino's authority. Curiously, Ficino seems not to have known the work of his predecessor Nicholas of Cusa (1401–1464), who certainly had nothing like the huge impact on the thought of his time that Ficino achieved through his network of correspondents. Indeed, Nicholas seems to have worked in intellectual isolation, despite his busy life as an influential cardinal, his role in the conciliar movement, his encounters with Italian humanists in Basel, Ferrara, and Florence, and his assembling of a famous library. Moreover, he died before he could profit from the wide diffusion of learning made possible by the new print technology, Ficino being the first major philosopher to win fame in his lifetime through the press.

Nicholas anchored his Platonism in the *via antiqua* (old way) of Thomism and in medieval Dutch and German mysticism, "the way of negation." His original thinking owes more to that Northern spirituality and to the Catalan visionary Ramón Lull than to any particular texts of Plato, since he lacked Ficino's expertise in Greek and had nothing like his massive scholarly ambition to reveal Plato to the Latin world. His most important works—*On Learned Ignorance, Concerning Conjectures,* the *Idiot,* and *On the Vision of God*—toy brilliantly with arithmetical, geometrical, optical, and other conceits whose aim is to evoke rather than to define the intelligible world and to disclose our mental limitations by conceptual play and paradox, which is Socratic in spirit but not at all Socratic in form. While he created some of the most arresting images ever fashioned by a philosopher, he worked—like Erigena before him and Vico afterward—strangely apart from the mental world of his contemporaries.

The opposite is true of another brilliant Renaissance philosopher profoundly influenced by Platonism but deeply engaged in the life and culture of his contemporaries, Giovanni Pico della Mirandola (1463–1494), an aristocrat, a publicity seeker, a comet who flamed across the Italian firmament for a brief decade before succumbing to Girolamo Savonarola's renunciatory spell and dying a premature death, possibly murdered by a disgruntled retainer. Like Milton after him, Pico della Mirandola set out to dominate the cultural terrain of his time, immersing himself even more in Aristotle than in Plato. He knew a number of Scholastic texts more intimately than Ficino did and felt intellectually closer to the schools, so much so that we can think of him as a late Scholastic, rather than a Platonist. Ficino described him revealingly as an eminent Aristotelian in the preface to the Plotinus translation that Pico della Mirandola urged him to complete.

But Pico della Mirandola also ransacked the pre-Platonic sages, the Orphic hymns, the Pythagorean *dicta*, the "Chaldaean" oracles, and the Hermetic *Pimander*, at the same time preparing himself to study the Kabbalah in the Hebrew and Aramaic originals, armed with translations by a converted rabbi who taught him Hebrew and salted the kabbalist texts with the trinitarian clues that he knew his student wanted to find. Without becoming an independent expert in this new arena, Pico della Mirandola mastered enough of it to cull the propositions needed for his grandiose scheme of defending nine hundred theses taken from the whole range of his philosophical reading, including Plato, Plotinus, Iamblichus, Proclus, and other Platonists. He planned to stage this medieval spectacle—a scene familiar to the Parisian doctors with whom he had briefly studied—in the heart of Renaissance Rome. A curial commission asked him to reconsider just thirteen of the nine hundred propositions since they dealt with the real presence in the Mass, the nature of Christ's bodily form after resurrection, and other delicate issues of Christian dogma. The hotheaded young count's refusal provoked the condemnation of his entire enterprise. Further defiance forced him to flee to Paris and caused his brief imprisonment.

When he returned to Florence at the instigation of the Medici and of friends such as Ficino, he presented his own version of Neoplatonic metaphysics in a commentary on a friend's Italian love lyric, using the occasion to attack Ficino's understanding of the *Symposium*. His flashes of Platonic insight are on a par with Ficino's and deeply indebted to them, but he presented them in a haphazard series of glosses. Here and elsewhere, Pico della Mirandola writes like one in haste, a brilliant and animated lecturer who knows his subject better than himself and who speaks without notes and without restraint. Some of his disagreements with Ficino are curtly phrased, in the manner of an aristocrat trained by French Scholastics to score in argument. At the very end of his meteoric career, he was still battling authority, whether it was the wisdom newly established by Ficino's Platonism or the doctrines long proclaimed by the astrologers whom he refuted in a huge, unfinished work of amazing erudition. His scorn for much of what passed as astrological prediction—unlike Ficino, who had been reluctant to reject all astrology—was not in itself Platonic or Aristotelian; its main philosophical ancestry was the scepticism that was on the verge of being revived (by Pico della Mirandola's nephew Gianfrancesco) when Pico della Mirandola died. Plotinus had declared in *Ennead* 2.3 that the stars are signs, "letters perpetually being inscribed on the heavens," but not causes of earthly events, yet he wrote movingly of the cosmic dance of sympathy that binds us to the stars, the "enchaining" of all things. And even before Ficino produced his Latin Plotinus, the *Timaeus* had that the heavens obey and transmit the primal ratios that govern the lives of humans, of their institutions, of nations, and of nature itself. In the context of the Platonic tradition, Pico della Mirandola championed a Socratic rather than a Neoplatonic view of human independence, a Socratic autarchy at odds with the Timaean subordination of humankind within a cosmic hierarchy beneath the star-gods and the spiritual beings who serve them, those starry demons who, as the *Statesman* had declared, watch over us as shepherds.

The moral and practical meaning of human nature is Pico della Mirandola's theme in the opening pages of his most renowned work—indeed, the most renowned work, since Jacob Burckhardt, Walter Pater, and Ernst Cassirer singled it out, of Renaissance philosophy—the *Oration*, written (but never delivered) to introduce his nine hundred *Conclusions* and in some later versions subtitled *On the Dignity of Man*. Pico della Mirandola's exordium makes mankind—or at least the prelapsarian Adam—free to choose a place on the cosmic ladder and thus to move up or down from the middle rung traditionally assigned to humanity. Ficino had called man the "knot and the bond of the world." Pico della Mirandola does not disagree, but he imagines that God created Adam of "indeterminate essence," thus endowing him with the duty to elect from among the manifold determinations of all that had been created before him: to be himself the artificer of God's final artifact, to be whatsoever he chose, to elect to ascend or to descend. This suggests not so much the Pythagorean-Platonic notion that humanity is the microcosm, the mean, the measure of all things as it does the questing Socratic intelligence, the far-ranging mind whose predicament and whose destiny is ethical rather than metaphysical. Pico della Mirandola rarely mentions Socrates, but his position recalls Socrates the defender at his own trial rather than the Neoplatonic magus attending to the planetary demons. Pico della Mirandola's youthful optimistic anthropology is starkly at odds with the jeremiads of Savonarola, to whose influence he later succumbed, though their weighing of human misery over human dignity has been the subject of debate among Christians for centuries.

In the genre of technical philosophy as distinct from the philosophical manifesto, Pico della Mirandola's highest achievements were two short works, both of them coherent and relatively straightforward statements, unlike the rhetorical exhortations of the *Oration* or the spacious but rambling and esoteric program of the nine hundred *Conclusions*. *On Being and the One* is a brief position paper examining whether the

One is prior to being, as the Neoplatonists had taught, or coincident with it, as Aristotle had argued. Pico della Mirandola takes the Aristotelian side, utilizing a number of subtle distinctions from Aquinas concerning essence and existence and presenting a basically Thomist position. In the process, he dismissed the *Parmenides* as a dialectical game and the *Sophist* with it, thereby rejecting two texts especially revered by Proclus and Ficino, who was annoyed at what he called the count's "temerity" in dismissing their ontology. In the *Heptaplus*, however, Pico della Mirandola moved from metaphysics to theology, offering an intricate analysis of the Mosaic story of the six days of creation in the tradition of medieval hexaemeral literature. But he explains many biblical terms and images by way of Neoplatonic metaphysics, again showing his wide learning and remarkable powers of synthesis. The *Heptaplus* also nods briefly and perhaps rashly in the direction of the Kabbalah while emphasizing some central Christological themes.

Pico della Mirandola was a dazzling, courageous thinker equipped with precocious learning and a prehensile memory, an eclectic polemicist who roamed across whole continents of philosophy and theology. The new Platonism was just part of his intellectual world, which included the Aristotelian and Peripatetic canons, kabbalist speculations that he first turned to Christian use, a wide range of Scholastics whom Ficino seldom mentions, and the pre-Platonic sages whom Ficino also honored—all this in the space of a decade that ended with Pico della Mirandola's entry into the circle of Savonarola's ascetic devotees. Despite the considerable differences between them, Pico della Mirandola probably would have relished being known as Ficino's brother Platonist or *conplatonicus*. Both were philosopher-sages, and both lived in the conviction that a soul could rise by contemplation back toward the intelligible divine and freely elect or refuse the demonic life of the mind. However, Pico della Mirandola's preoccupation with the theme of freedom speaks to an anthropology more narrow and yet more liberated than Ficino's, one less bound to the ancient and medieval world of magical sympathies, less constrained by the intricate dance of the star gods and their demon attendants circling forever above us and within us. Pico della Mirandola's personal story hastens forward like a tragedy that Christopher Marlowe or William Shakespeare might have written, while Ficino's longer, more tranquil life came to abide in the maturity and deliberation of his judgments, his visionary completeness, his serene musicality.

Other thinkers were variously indebted to the Renaissance Platonists, though much more to Ficino than to Pico della Mirandola or Nicholas of Cusa. Some such as Francesco da Diacceto (1466–1522), Ficino's successor in Florence, or the Spaniard Sebastian Fox Morcillo (1526/1528–1560) followed Ficino rather faithfully, while others such as the imaginative Francesco Giorgi (1460/1466–1540) or the adventurous Francesco Patrizi built braver speculations on ground that Ficino had already prepared. The Vatican librarian, Agostino Steuco (1497/1498–1548), founded a universal scheme of concordist cultural history on the irenic attitude to non-Christian beliefs encouraged by Ficino and Pico della Mirandola. Leone Ebreo (ca. 1460–after 1523) and Pietro Bembo (1470–1547) repeated the arguments from Ficino's groundbreaking work *On Love,* initiating a derivative but influential literature on love and beauty. Others, among them Paracelsus, Telesio, and most powerfully Giordano Bruno, were drawn to Ficino's cosmological and magical speculations concerning the world's harmonies and sympathies in such works as his *Timaeus* commentary and his *Three Books on Life*. These two lines of Ficino's influence converged easily because Plato and Plotinus had both exalted love as the motive force in nature, the visible beauty of the world being a reflection of divine beauty. In short, the intricate complementarity of the *Symposium,* the *Phaedrus,* and the *Timaeus* as Ficino understood them was a rich source of inspiration for many Renaissance philosophers.

Perhaps the most striking outcome of the new Platonism was a revived interest in classical demonology and Platonic astrology. This led on the one hand to daring speculations about a new human paradigm—the magus—and on the other to a heightened fascination with discerning the ratios, harmonies, and proportions—arithmetic, geometric, musical—that link the macrocosm and the microcosm. While the medieval ideal of the *doctor subtilissimus* (most subtle doctor) lived on—ironically finding a perfect avatar in Pico della Mirandola—it yielded gradually to a different view of humankind as possessing plenary powers over nature and over itself. Meanwhile, again ironically, Platonism was to make a much deeper mark on religion, poetry, music, and the visual arts than on the emerging natural sciences or on the new philosophy that arose with them in the seventeenth century, though here Johannes Kepler's story and even Galileo's assuredly remind us how wide and lasting the effects of Platonism were.

As for philosophy itself, the course later charted by Descartes and followed by his successors turned so far from the paths explored by Ficino, Nicholas of Cusa, and Pico della Mirandola that their championing of philosophy's Platonic renaissance soon became more a poppy of oblivion than an enduring memory. Marin Mersenne and other contemporaries of the young Descartes worried about Bruno, and Pierre Gassendi respected Patrizi's attack on Aristotle, but Bruno soon became an unfashionable martyr while Patrizi's original system (and later Tommaso Campanella's) went the way of many other capacious constructions. The Platonic revival at Cambridge after mid-century was local and short-lived, save for its effects on Isaac Newton's theology. That Platonism became the imaginative domain of painters and poets, that its contemplative magus became the modern artist but not the modern scientist or the analytic philosopher would have been inconceivable to Ficino and Pico della Mirandola. Both would have hastened rather toward the cosmos revealed by Newton, rejoicing to be his conplatonici in the fervent conviction that he had succeeded in probing deeper still into the mathematico-musical and intelligible nature of Plato's and Pythagoras's reality.

Bibliography

Allen, M. J. B. *Icastes: Marsilio Ficino's Interpretation of Plato's Sophist*. Berkeley and Los Angeles: University of California Press, 1989.

———. *Marsilio Ficino and the Phaedran Charioteer*. Berkeley and Los Angeles: University of California Press, 1981.
———. *The Platonism of Marsilio Ficino: A Study of His Phaedrus Commentary, Its Sources and Genesis*. Berkeley and Los Angeles: University of California Press, 1984.
———. *Plato's Third Eye: Studies in Marsilio Ficino's Metaphysics and Its Sources*. Aldershot, Hampshire: Variorum, 1995.
Field, A. *The Origins of the Platonic Academy of Florence*. Princeton: Princeton University Press, 1989.
Garin, E. *Giovanni Pico della Mirandola: Vita e dottrina*. Florence: F. Le Monnier, 1937.
Gentile, S., et al. *Marsilio Ficino e il ritorno di Platone: Mostra di manoscritti, stampe e documenti, 17 maggio–16 giugno 1984*. Florence: Le Lettere, 1984.
Hankins, J. *Plato in the Italian Renaissance*. 2 vols. Leiden: E. J. Brill, 1991.
Kristeller, P. O. *The Philosophy of Marsilio Ficino*. Gloucester, Mass.: Peter Smith, 1964 [1943].
Walker, D. P. *The Ancient Theology: Studies in Christian Platonism from the Fifteenth to the Eighteenth Century*. London: Duckworth, 1972.
Watts, P. M. *Nicolaus Cusanus: A Fifteenth-Century Vision of Man*. Leiden: E. J. Brill, 1982.

2

CULTURA HOMINIS: GIOVANNI PICO, MARSILIO FICINO AND THE IDEA OF MAN *

"Who does not wonder at this chameleon we are?" Man as a chameleon is a familiar Renaissance conceit with a rich antiquity behind it. But it is just one of several leading conceits studding the famous opening paragraphs of Pico's *Oratio*, later subtitled *De dignitate hominis*, where man is declared to be "a great wonder", a "messenger (*internuntius*) between creatures", "the interpreter of nature", "what is in between (*interstitius*) eternity's steadfastness and the flux of time", "the bond, as the Persians say, that knots the world together, indeed the nuptial bond" *(mundi copula, immo hymenaeum)*, "the animal that is most happy".[1] Because "our nature changes and transforms itself" (*versipellis huius et se ipsam transformantis naturae*), according to Asclepius, man is the Proteus as he appears "in the secret rites" (*in mysteriis*); and he is a godlike son of the Most High, according to Asaph the prophet in

---

* I wish to thank the city of Mirandola along with the advisory comittee and organizers of the splendid 1994 Convegno for honouring me with an invitation to speak and for their truly princely hospitality.

[1] Giovanni Pico della Mirandola, *Oratio de hominis dignitate*, ed. and tr. E. Garin, Pordenone, Edizioni Studio Tesi, 1994, pp. 1ff. This edition reproduces the text published in Garin's 1942 *De hominis dignitate, Heptaplus, De ente et uno e scritti vari*, Florence, Vallecchi, pp. 101-165, a text which follows that of the Bologna 1496 *editio princeps* prepared from the manuscript by Pico's distinguished nephew, Gian Francesco. In this 1994 edition «sono state comunque introdotte alcune correzioni al testo e alla traduzione e qualche aggiunta nelle indicazioni delle fonti» (p. xlii).

For details concerning the two redactions and the editions of the *Oratio*, see G. Di Napoli, *Giovanni Pico della Mirandola e la problematica dottrinale del suo tempo*, Rome, Desclée, 1965, pp. 271, 521-523; and specifically for the first redaction, which Pico probably wrote in Fratta in the October and November of 1486, see E. Garin, *La cultura filosofica del Rinascimento italiano: ricerche e documenti*, Florence, Sansoni, 1979², pp. 231-240. As scholars have often pointed out, the subtitle *de hominis dignitate* was not apparently Pico's own, first appearing in the Strassburg edition of Pico's *Opera omnia* of 1504 (edited by J. Wimpfeling) and subsequently (and thereafter invariably) in the Basel edition of the *Opera omnia* published by Heinrich Petri in 1557.

Psalm 81 [82]:6. Perhaps the most famous passage in all of Renaissance philosophy since it was singled out by Burckhardt, it rises to its climactic asseveration, "O great and wonderful happiness of man! to whom it is given to have that which he chooses and to be that which he wills".[2] It would seem indeed to be a high point for the voluntarists' emphasis on the preeminence of the faculty of the will. For it is the will which governs our choice of what to be, what sphere to take as our own, what colour to become in our chameleonic lives.

Chameleonic man is established as the "midpoint" between the four determinate worlds of the organic or vegetative, the animal, the celestial (the realm of the planets and the stars), and the intellectual or angelic. But he himself is a work of indeterminate form (*indiscretae opus imaginis*), with "no fixed seat" (*nec certam sedem*), "no distinguishable semblance" (*nec propriam faciem*), no "gift" peculiarly his (*nec munus ullum peculiare*). Accordingly, goes the well-known argument, whereas the "natures" of other created things – plants, animals, celestial souls, and angelic intellects – are "confined" within the limits God has composed for them, Adamic man is not so confined: he can choose his own bounds.[3] From his central position he can gaze upon the world, and then set about sculpting himself into whatever shape or determination he elects, whether brutish or divine. As the undetermined one, he will

---

2 «O summam Dei patris liberalitatem, summam et admirandam hominis felicitatem! cui datum id habere quod optat, id esse quod velit» (ed. Garin, p. 8).

We should recall that neither Proteus nor the chameleon came to Pico with consistently positive connotations; Vergil, for instance, refers in the fourth *Georgic* 406-9 to the «changing shapes and forms of beasts» to which Proteus has recourse. Ficino compares the imagination, defined as «what feigns (*effingit*) the actions of reason under the condition of sensible things,» to Proteus or a chameleon in the *explanatio* he provided for chapter 2 of the second part of his own translation of Priscianus Lydus' *Metaphrasis in Theophrastum*, the part he entitled *De phantasia et intellectu* (*Opera omnia*, Basel, Heinrich Petri, 1576, p. 1825.2). And Pico himself speaks derogatively of the chameleon's «inconstancy» in his *Disputationes VI* (ed. E. Garin, 2 vols., Florence, Vallecchi, 1946-1952, II, p. 583).

3 «Definita ceteris natura intra praescriptas a nobis leges coercetur. Tu, nullis angustiis coercitus, pro tuo arbitrio, in cuius manu te posui, tibi illam praefinies» (ed. Garin, p. 6). As Di Napoli, *La problematica dottrinale* cit., pp. 377-379, and H. De Lubac, *Pic de la Mirandole: études et discussions*, Paris, Aubier Montaigne, 1974, p. 76, in particular have observed, the *Heptaplus* has a number of refs. to the «nature» of man even though he has the «natures» of all which are separate and distinct in the created world. We cannot suppose that Pico thought of man as having no nature. See too W. G. Craven, *Giovanni Pico della Mirandola, symbol of his age: modern interpretations of a Renaissance philosopher*, Geneva, Droz, 1981, pp. 32-34. This, incidentally, is a brilliant but combative study that attacks everyone who has written authoritatively on Pico. While scoring a number of bull's eyes, it is unattuned to Pico's Neoplatonic learning; and I take as rash its assertion on p. 45 that «the first part of the *Oratio* tells us very little about the content of his [Pico's] philosophy. It certainly proposes no ideas which were to serve as a matrix for his thought».

determine his own limit: from being of indeterminate form, he will adopt a form, the "molder and maker (*plastes et fictor*) of himself". This whole argumentation occurs in the context of a supposed exhortation by God the Father, "the master-builder" (*architectus*), to Adam; and one of its sources, as Pico himself indicates, was the notable apostrophe in the Hermetic *Asclepius* 6,[4] an apostrophe which Pico would cite again just two and a half years later, though with different resonances, in a parallel passage in the *Heptaplus* 5.6.[5]

As a creation myth focussing on God and the primal man, the passage is also clearly reminiscent of Plato's myth in the *Protagoras* and especially of 321B ff. where Epimetheus, a dull witted Titan, is described as having exhausted his gifts on the brute creation so that he had nothing left to bestow on man, who issued accordingly forth "naked, unshod, unbedded and unarmed". It was left to Prometheus, his sagacious brother, to steal fire from Hephaestus, and to steal the arts, particularly the skills involved in harnessing fire and the loom, from Hephaestus and Athena in order to give them to us as our unique gifts. We were thus able to survive. Indeed, "since we shared in the portion of the gods" and were kin to the divine, we believed in the gods and erected altars to them; we developed speech, and attributed names to things; and we lived in scattered groups. Nevertheless, we were still prey to the beasts, since we needed something that only Zeus could give us: the art of politics, of knowing how to dwell together in well governed cities and states.[6] Pico is not interested in

---

[4] *Corpus Hermeticum*, ed. A. D. Nock and A.-J. Festugière, Paris, Belles Lettres, 1945, II, pp. 301-302, cf. p. 361, n. 45. Ficino had already cited the passage in his *Theologia Platonica* 3.2 and 14.3 (ed. and tr. R. Marcel, 3 vols., Paris, Belles Lettres, 1964-1970, I, p. 141; II, p. 257), as has been pointed out, for instance, by P. O. Kristeller, *The dignity of man*, now in *Renaissance thought and its sources*, ed. M. Mooney, New York, Columbia University Press, 1979, pp. 169-181: 174. Pico requested this huge work, finished by 1474 but not published until November 1482, in a letter to Ficino just when it was about to appear (*Opera*, p. 373; see Garin, *La cultura* cit., p. 255).

We should bear in mind that the *Asclepius*, and therefore the passage, had long been known in the Latin West; see Nock and Festugière's list of testimonia (*ed. cit.* II, pp. 264-275) beginning with Augustine, and notably the *City of God* 10.12. Pico was in fact referring to a commonplace as Frances Yates neglected to bear in mind in *Giovanni Pico della Mirandola and magic*, in *L'Opera e il pensiero di Giovanni Pico della Mirandola nella storia dell'umanesimo*, Convegno internazionale (Mirandola: 15-18 Settembre 1963), 2 vols. Florence, Istituto nazionale di studi sul Rinascimento, 1965, I, pp. 159-196.

[5] Ed. E. Garin in his 1942 volume *De hominis dignitate*, p. 304 – see note 1 above. All future references to the *Heptaplus* in either the text or the notes will include references in parentheses to the pagination of this edition. Di Napoli, *La problematica dottrinale* cit., pp. 375-379, draws attention to the differing resonances of the same quotation in the two works.

[6] Cf. Ficino's epitome, *Opera*, pp. 1296-1300.

these political dimensions of the fable, however, but rather in its opening section, and above all in the notion of the providential gift of fire, which the ancient Neoplatonists had long ago interpreted figuratively to mean the fire of dialectic, the art of intellectual ascent to the contemplation of the Ideas.[7]

The *Asclepius* and the *Protagoras* are just two of the obvious sources for the passage in the *Oratio*, and scholars have adduced others, ancient, patristic and medieval, in praise of man's dignity.[8] At this *convegno*, however, I wish to raise the question of Pico's various debts to, if not dependence on, passages in several major later Platonic dialogues as they were interpreted by the Neoplatonists and as he probably encountered them in the voluminous scholarly commentaries of Marsilio Ficino, the very dialogues he would adduce, incidentally, in presenting an anti-Ficinian thesis in the *De Ente et Uno*.[9]

The value of these later texts for an understanding of the Neoplatonic context of the *Oratio* – and it is not the only context of course – has not been sufficiently investigated or appreciated. This is surprising, given the continuing vitality in the work of such scho-

---

[7] See Ficino's *In Philebum* 1.26 (ed. M. J. B. ALLEN, Berkeley, University of California Press, 1975, p. 245).

[8] See, for example, E. GARIN, *La 'Dignitas Hominis' e la letteratura patristica*, «La Rinascita», I, 1938, pp. 102-146; A. AUER, *G. Manetti und Pico della Mirandola «De hominis dignitate»*, in *Vitae et veritati, Festgabe für Karl Adam*, Düsseldorf, Patmos, 1956, pp. 83-102; P. O. KRISTELLER, *Giovanni Pico della Mirandola and his sources*, in *L'Opera e il pensiero* cit., pp. 35-133 at 52-53, 55-56 (this has now been reprinted in his *Studies in Renaissance thought and letters: volume III*, Rome, Edizioni di storia e di letteratura, 1993, pp. 227-304); A. BUCK, *Die Rangstellung des Menschen in der Renaissance: dignitas et miseria hominis*, «Archiv für Kulturgeschichte», XLII, 1960, pp. 61-75; E. MONNERJAHN, *Giovanni Pico della Mirandola: ein Beitrag zur philosophischen Theologie des italienischen Humanismus*, Wiesbaden, Steiner, 1960, pp. 185-190; C. TRINKAUS, *In our image and likeness: humanity and divinity in Italian humanist thought*, 2 vols. London, Constable, 1970, I, pp. 171-321 (on Pico's humanist predecessors), II, pp. 505-526 (on Pico); DE LUBAC, *Pic de la Mirandole* cit., pp. 160-169, 224-226; and E. P. MAHONEY, *Giovanni Pico della Mirandola and Origen on humans, choice and hierarchy*, «Vivens Homo», V, 1994, pp. 359-376. The obvious Renaissance analogues, besides Manetti's *De excellentia et praestantia hominis*, are Bracciolini's *De nobilitate*, Platina's *De vera nobilitate*, and Landino's *De nobilitate animae*.

[9] Pico scholars have failed to understand the subtlety of Ficino analyses of the *Parmenides* and *Sophist* and therefore his role in the generation of and reaction to the *De ente et uno*. See my *The second Ficino-Pico controversy: Parmenidean poetry, eristic, and the One*, in *Marsilio Ficino e il ritorno di Platone: studi e documenti*, ed. G. C. GARFAGNINI, Florence, Olschki, 1986, pp. 417-455 at 421-431, 454-455; and *Icastes: Marsilio Ficino's interpretation of Plato's «Sophist»*, Berkeley, University of California Press, 1991, pp. 35-48. For Pico specifically, see G. MARTANO, *Il «Parmenide» e il «Sofista» in una interpretazione teologica di Pico della Mirandola*, «Atti e memorie: deputazione di storia patria per le antiche provincie modenesi», s. IX, IV-V, 1964-1965, pp. 349-355.

lars as Anagnine, Cordier, and Kristeller of the older if now minority view that Pico was a Neoplatonist,[10] as against what has become, since Garin's seminal 1937 study, the majority view: namely, that Pico was an eclectic preeminently committed to the Scholastics – notwithstanding his engagement with the Cabala – and by way of them to Aristotle and to Aristotle's Greek and Arab commentators, especially Averroes.[11]

* * *

Let us begin with the term *indiscretus*, which comes from *in* plus the past participle of the verb *discerno*. Pico is portraying Adam at that primal and originary moment as lacking distinguishing features, lacking determination and a face. Now the notion of indetermination has a number of problematic, at times even negative, connotations. Inspired, scholars have suggested, perhaps by Anaximander and certainly by the Pythagoreans to whom Aristotle attributes the notion, Plato had introduced in the *Philebus* 23C ff. the theory that all things are the result of the indeterminate or infinite (*to apeiron*) being

---

10 E. ANAGNINE, *G. Pico della Mirandola: sincretismo religioso-filosofico 1463-1494*, Bari, Laterza, 1937; and, to a lesser degree, P.-M. CORDIER, *Jean Pic de la Mirandole, ou «la plus pure figure de l'humanisme chrétien»*, Paris, Debresse, 1957. But see Craven's objections to both studies, *Giovanni Pico della Mirandola* cit., pp. 9-10, 108. Kristeller, having accepted Pico's debt to the Scholastics, and having referred in general to his «pervasive» use of Platonist sources and to «a basic affinity» between Pico and Ficino, writes that he «is inclined to attribute a special significance to the Platonic and Neoplatonic element in Pico's work» (*Pico and his sources* cit., pp. 64-69). In related articles, *Entre raison et foi: le néoplatonisme de Pic de la Mirandole*, «Recherches de théologie ancienne et médiévale», LIV, 1987, pp. 186-237; *Humanisme et scolastique: le «conflit des deux cultures» chez Jean Pic de la Mirandole*, *ibid.*, LVI, 1989, pp. 164-199; and *Giovanni Pico della Mirandole e il ritorno ad Aristotele*, this volume, pp. 327-349, L. Valcke presents three variations on the view that Pico developed in the course of his brief career, postulating a youthful scholastic Aristotelianism followed by a full fledged engagement with Orphism, Plotinus, rhetoric, and the poetry of analogy, and then finally, beginning with the *De ente et uno* of 1491, a return to Aristotle and the Scholastics. In two other articles, Valcke underscores what he sees as the deep reservations Pico had towards Neoplatonism, *Jean Pic de la Mirandole et le chant néoplatonicien*, «Laval théologique et philosophique», XLIX, 1993, pp. 487-504, and *Pic de la Mirandole, Duns Scot et la question de la Toute-puissance divine*, «Vivens Homo», V, 1994, pp. 377-399.

11 E. GARIN, *Giovanni Pico della Mirandola: vita e dottrina*, Florence, Le Monnier, 1937, pp. 217-223. For Pico's scholasticism, see in particular A. DULLES, *Princeps Concordiae, Pico della Mirandola and the scholastic tradition*, Cambridge, Mass., Harvard University Press, 1941; DE LUBAC, *Pic de la Mirandole* cit.; F. ROULIER, *Jean Pic de la Mirandole (1463-1494), humaniste, philosophe et théologien*, Geneva, Slatkine, 1989; and H. REINHARDT, *Freiheit zu Gott: Der Grundgedanke des Systematikers Giovanni Pico della Mirandola (1463-1494)*, Darmstadt, Weinheim, 1989; ID., *De illis Pico vestigiis quae in regno theologiae ac praesertim in provincia huius saeculi vicesimi supersunt*, «Vivens Homo», V, 1994, pp. 269-298.

bounded by the determinate or finite (*to peras*).[12] When a Christian argues that God is infinite and endures no limit, he is postulating infinity in a different sense from that intended by *to apeiron* here, which signifies the chaos of infinite matter, formlessness awaiting the imposition of form, or what Ficino at some length in his *Philebus* Commentary 2.1,[13] and Pico briefly in his *Commento* 1.9,[14] both argue on Aristotelian grounds is the potentiality for the determination which is act (*actus*). Moreover, in the Neoplatonic interpretation which had the Pythagorean table of opposites in mind, the *Sophist* had divided up what it postulated as the primary ontological categories into two contrasting sets: under the finite placing existence, identity, and rest, and under the indeterminate, essence, difference, and motion (motion signifying every kind of change and not merely locomotion).[15] This in turn pointed to an ethical and consequently aesthetic polarity between the finite which was good (and beautiful) and the indeterminate which was bad (and misshapen).

At all events, for Pico to call man a work *indiscretae imaginis* is harking back to the *to apeiron* of the *Philebus* and thus to the notion of infinity as potentiality; and it begs a number of interesting questions with their roots in traditional Neoplatonic analysis of *to apeiron*. How can one have a "work" of this kind, when the notion of an opus (in the sense of a work of art or fabrication) implies the imposition of something more than an *imago* let alone an *indiscreta imago* on undetermined matter? How indeed can matter receive such an image without becoming moulded, shaped and therefore formed? Moreover, how can man in this strangely formless or semi-formed condition then set about choosing one of the determinations that will lead him to ascend the ladder of creatures or to descend to its bottom rung? In the myth of Er in the last book of the *Republic*, Plato playfully tells of souls choosing their lots before descending into this terrestrial life and of the demons that will accompany them when

---

12 Cf. Aristotle, *Physics* 3.4.203a4 ff., *Metaphysics* 1.5.987a13 ff., 8.990a8, etc. K. M. SAYRE, *Plato's late ontology: a riddle resolved*, Princeton, Princeton University Press, 1983, pp. 133-155.

13 Ed. M. J. B. ALLEN, pp. 384-403 – Ficino carefully distinguishes between the «infinity» of God and the «infinity» of potentiality.

14 Ed. GARIN in his 1942 volume *De hominis dignitate* cit., p. 472 – see note 1 above. All future references to the *Commento* in either the text or the notes will include references in parentheses to the pagination of this edition.

15 See my *Icastes*, pp. 59-61. The Sophist postulates five categories (*genera*) of being but Ficino transformed them into six by dividing «being» into essence and existence following the Scholastics; see his *In Philebum* 2.2 (ed. ALLEN, pp. 404-407).

they abandon the realm of the Ideas and enter into becoming; but nowhere does he speak of them choosing to show either an *indiscreta* or a *discreta imago* to the world. However, from the perspective of the *Philebus* and its two primal categories, Adam is man in his infinite potentiality awaiting the determination that will bring him into act, into full being, a determination that God is allowing him, uniquely, to choose for himself.

Nevertheless, in the end he cannot but elect the determination, *to peras*, that will bring him into his full and authentic actuality. If he chooses the wrong, in the sense of a partial, determination, he will be postponing his assumption of that actuality and miring himself in partial being, in the partial chaos of a half and therefore ill-formed infinity; and he will remain a quasi man, a slave still struggling to emerge from chaotic bestiality, from vegetable life, from earth and stone into the cosmos, the order, of complete humanness. To one versed in the Plato texts, these *Philebus* resonances are unmistakeable, however deeply indebted the language of God's address may also be to Christian sources, and notably, as Di Napoli has emphasized, to St. John, St. Paul, St. Augustine and the Areopagite.[16] At the very least they should be explored.

* * *

One of the most vexed questions in the history of Platonism has always been the status of the Ideas, the most penetrating attacks on the theory being that by Plato himself in the first part of the *Parmenides* and that by Aristotle in the *Metaphysics*.[17] In addition to focussing on the ontological problems Plato everywhere raises concerning whether and in what way such Ideas may or may not exist – indeed may possess primary and truly authentic being – commentators in the past have also noted the specific lemmata at 130C5-D2 and speculated on what has an Idea and what does not. The *Dida-*

[16] *La problematica dottrinale* cit., p. 501. These *Philebus* echoes were ignored, incidentally, by R. Lazzarini, *Significato dell'uomo come «Indiscretae opus imaginis»*, «Atti e Memorie della Deputazione di storia patria per le antiche provincie modenesi», 4-5, 1964-1965, pp. 339-347. For the possible debt to Origen, see Mahoney, *Pico and Origen* cit., pp. 373-376. Incidentally, to dismiss the speech as some have done because it is, *inter alia*, a rhetorical exercise is naive when one considers the central role of rhetoric in Renaissance intellectual life.

[17] See, for example, F. M. Cornford, *Plato and Parmenides*, London, Routledge & Kegan Paul, 1939; W. G. Runciman, *Plato's later epistemology*, Cambridge, Cambridge University Press, 1962; and Sayre, *Plato's late ontology* cit., pp. 18-37. For Aristotle, see the classic study by H. F. Cherniss, *Aristotle's criticism of Plato and the Academy*, Baltimore 1944.

skalikos of Albinus (though attributed during the Renaissance to Alcinous),[18] provides in its ninth chapter just one of several lists from antiquity that tell us what, according to "most Platonists", do not have Ideas, but are caused instead by *logoi*, reason principles in nature. The most extensive treatment of the much discussed theme is to be found, as we might have anticipated, in the third book of Proclus's *Parmenides* Commentary.[19] Here Proclus demonstrates why there cannot be Ideas of the Intellect (the Plotinian hypostasis of *nous*); of artifacts like a shield and even of the lower, artisanal arts and skills; of unnatural conditions such as sickness; of relational concepts like greater and less; of trivial or disgusting objects like chaff, hair or dung; of the parts of whole animals, such as fingers and eyes; of accidental qualities such as whiteness; and of evils or the opposites of moral or aesthetic qualities. Most controversially, at 824.13-825.35 Proclus denies there are Ideas of individuals, arguing that the causes of individuals are not intelligible powers outside the cosmos but include regional, seasonal and other causes within the cosmos. Plotinus, to the contrary, had recognized Ideas of individual men – an Idea of Socrates, an Idea of Plato – if not of other living creatures.[20]

Ficino was fully apprised of the issues and difficulties. In a letter to his friend Francesco da Diacceto dated 11 July 1493, seventeen months incidentally before Pico's death, he observed circumspectly, "The Ideas of individuals are not distinguished from each other in the Divine Mind in any absolute way but only relatively (*sed quadam relatione*)" – thus subscribing (despite his assertion to the contrary) neither to the views of Plotinus nor to those of Proclus. He concludes with a reference to the famous extended conceit in Plato's *Timaeus* 27D ff. where sublunar individuals are described as being assembled in the workshop of "the elder gods and daemons" following the mandate of "the architect",

---

18 F. Invernizzi, *Il «Didaskalikos» di Albino e il medioplatonismo*, 2 vols., Rome, Abate, 1976; J. M. Dillon, *The middle Platonists 80 B.C. to A.D. 220*, Ithaca, Cornell University Press, 1977, pp. 267-306 at 281. Ficino had translated Alcinous's treatise – it appears in his *Opera*, pp. 1946-1962 – before 1464; see P. O. Kristeller, *Supplementum Ficinianum*, 2 vols., Florence, Olschki, 1937, I, cxxxv-cxxxvi.

19 Ed. V. Cousin, *Procli philosophi Platonici opera inedita*, Paris 1864, repr. Frankfurt am Main, Minerva, 1962, cols. 617-1258 at 815.14-833.23. See the English translation by G. L. Morrow-J. M. Dillon, *Proclus's commentary on Plato's «Parmenides»*, Princeton, Princeton University Press, 1987, pp. 179-192; also Ficino's lengthy analysis, only partially following Proclus's, in his *In Parmenidem* 6-14 (*Opera*, pp. 1140-41).

20 *Enneads*, 4.3.5, 5.7, 5.9.12, 6.4.4,34-46, 6.7.12, etc. See H. J. Blumenthal, *Plotinus' psychology: his doctrines of the embodied soul*, The Hague, Nijhoff, 1971, chap. 9.

namely the Demiurge, who remains contemplating "the ideal and eternal model".[21]

The *Timaeus* and its creation myth had long been an attractive text for both Christians and pagans. For hundreds of years it was the only Platonic dialogue known to the Latin West, albeit in a truncated form (up to 53C) and embedded in Calcidius's extensive commentary, the *In Timaeum*. Despite, perhaps because of, the arresting parallels with Genesis, medieval commentators beginning with the School of Chartres found it enmeshed in difficulties just as the ancient, middle and new Platonists had found it before them, if sometimes for different reasons. Interpretation of the nature and role of the Demiurge was probably the most intricate of these difficulties, given on the one hand the Demiurge's obvious role as a creator and his designation at 28C3 and elsewhere as the "father" and "maker" of the universe, and on the other, his subordination to the paradigms which he gazes up at as a humble craftsman looking to his model. Ficino's engagement with the dialogue and preeminently with its Demiurge myth spanned many years from his youth until just three or so years before his death in 1499 when he completed the final version of the *Timaeus* Commentary for his 1496 volume *Commentaria in Platonem*.[22] Pico's engagement with the *Timaeus* was likewise sustained, if confined to the eight years of his meteoric career: it is second only to the *Phaedrus* in supplying him with Platonic material for his *Conclusiones DCCCC* and it is the palimpsest of the *Heptaplus* and occasionally of the *Disputationes*, inevitably surely, given his cosmological concerns and the availability of Calcidius' Latin exposition.

---

[21] *Opera*, p. 952: «Non putas proprias singulorum ideas in mente prima inter se absolute quidem sed quadam relatione distingui. Neque id quidem a Plotino iam tuo arbitror alienum... Negat & in Parmenide Proclus ideas proprias singulorum videlicet absolute distinctas. Id proculdubio Platoni maxime consonat in Timaeo dicenti ideale exemplar aeternum esse, quodve ad ipsum exprimetur atque per ipsum sempiternum fore significanti. Unde colligitur naturalium species illinc penitus exprimi tanquam videlicet sempiternas, singula vero non aeque, sed sequentibus deinceps causis ad extremum inter se discerni. Quae tamen distinctio intellectum primum non lateat, universi ordinis conditorem. Hinc in Timaeo seniores dii daemonesque, architecto mandante atque disponente, singulorum sub Luna fabricam prosequuntur.»

In his *In Parmenidem* 4-5 (*Opera*, pp. 1139-40), which he was composing at the same time, Ficino distinguishes between *communissimae* Ideas such as the *megista gene* of the *Sophist* (i.e., being, identity, difference, rest and motion), *specialissimae* Ideas such as Man and Horse, and *mediae* Ideas such as the Beautiful, Just, Great, Small, Like and Unlike (cap. 4), observing that the youthful Socrates had wanted to convey too many things by using the one word «idea».

[22] See my *Marsilio Ficino's interpretation of Plato's «Timaeus» and its myth of the demiurge*, in *Supplementum festivum: studies in honor of Paul Oskar Kristeller*, ed. J. Hankins, J. Monfasani, and F. Purnell, Jr., Binghamton, Center for Medieval and Early Renaissance Studies, 1987, pp. 399-439 at 402-403.

What both Ficino and Pico saw at the heart of the *Timaeus* was the daunting notion of the universal paradigm, of what 27D6 had called "that which always is and has no becoming", 29A6-7, "that which is apprehended by reason and mind and is unchangeable or self-identical (*kata tauta echon*)", and 28D6, the "pattern" (*paradeigma*) of the "unchangeable" (29A1) and "eternal" (29A5). Neoplatonically interpreted, this "pattern" is the Idea of the Cosmos, which in turn "embraces" the Ideas of other created entities such as the Idea of Man, though only in a Christian framework would it also embrace such sublime ethical Ideas as Justice and Truth.[23] In the dialogue named after him, Parmenides asks, "And is there a form (*eidos*) of man, apart from ourselves and all other men like us – a form of man as something by itself? Or a form of fire or of water?" (130C1-2).

Socrates admits to being puzzled whether there are such forms, though it became generally accepted by the Neoplatonists that Plato was arguing here for a Form or Idea of Man. Proclus takes up this lemma in the section we have already had occasion to refer to in his *Parmenides* Commentary, and proceeds to set out a chain (*seira*) of different types of men descending from the Idea of Man down through each sphere in the physical cosmos, the links being a celestial (skyey) man, a fiery man, an airy man, and a watery man in descending order above the earthy man. He argues that "all this series, that comes to be as the Form proceeds through successive downward steps, is dependent upon the intelligible henad we have called Man Himself" (812.10-16).[24] This chain, furthermore, is not peculiar to Man; for he adds that parallel *seirai* do indeed exist for Horse and Lion and in general for each species of animal and plant (812.16-18).

Proclus's logic, predictably, is to provide a series of mediations, a procession, between the intelligible and intellectual realms of immaterial being and "the multitude of senseless enmattered individuals whose character is ever changing" (812.5-6). But at the very apex of the hu-

[23] As has been often remarked, Plato toys with two kinds of Ideas: those of created species such as Man or Horse, and those of abstractions such as Justice or Truth. For the Idea or model of the World, see Proclus's *In Timaeum* I:319.26-339.2, 416.9-458.11 (ed. E. DIEHL, 3 vols., Leipzig 1903-06, repr. Amsterdam 1965).

[24] Tr. MORROW-DILLON, p. 176. Ficino refers to the Idea of Man as both *idea hominis* and *homo idealis* and later as *ipsa humanitatis idea* in his *In Parmenidem* cap. 5, 21 (*Opera*, pp. 1139-40, 1144.2; cf. the letters to Tommaso Minerbetti and to Matteo da Forlì, *Opera*, pp. 635, 861). And Pico himself, in his *Commento* 1.6 (p. 468), refers to the «Idea of men» as being in Mind. For the notion of the «heavenly» or «celestial» man; cf. *I Corinthians* 15:42-5, and Augustine, *City of God* 18.23.

man chain is the Idea of Man which Proclus sees as an independent unity, a henad, affirming that "The whole number of men in this world, descending through many processions and ranks, depends upon that intellectual henad that we have called Man Himself, since that henad is the primary cause and source of the series of men" (812.38-813.3). Even so, he believes that it is "a more particular monad" (813.6-9) than the general or universal Forms such as those of Beauty or the Just; and that it is "dangerous" (*episphales*) to inquire too deeply into the nature of its specificity (813.11-12). He is referring, that is, to the vexed question of establishing a hierarchy for the Ideas and the grounds for subordinating some of them to others without detracting from their unique status as Ideas.

The Proclan henads are problematic in a number of ways, but were not unfamiliar or unaccommodatable to the Renaissance Platonists.[25] Ficino renders them as *unitates ideales* in his commentary on the *Parmenides* chapter 4, where he is obviously writing with a sharp eye on Proclus's *Parmenides* commentary, having worked through its many leaves with assiduity and remarkable insight.[26] In glossing the lemmata at 130C ff., he argues that just as the natural forms, for all their diversity, are in one matter, so these ideal unities, for all their diversity, are also in one something and this is Mind, the second hypostasis, which is both uniform and multiform.[27] Pico, in the *Commento* 1.4,5, duly equates the "son" of the Good with this Mind and argues that "the highest father", namely the One, has established "this universal world" in Mind, the first intellect.[28] The "son" that is Mind is therefore what

---

25 Proclus's doctrine of the henads became accessible to the Renaissance in his *Theologia Platonica* 3.1-6 (ed. H. D. Saffrey and L. G. Westerink, 5 vols. so far, Paris, Belles Lettres, III, pp. 5-28), in his *Elements of theology* 113-165 (ed. E. R. Dodds, 2d ed. Oxford, Clarendon, 1963², pp. 100-145), and later in book VI of his *In Parmenidem*, cols. 1043.4-1051.33 (ed. Cousin).

26 *Opera*, p. 1139. Later, in cap. 51 (misnumbered 52), he defines them thus: «Si Proclum sequimur, dicemus omne principium alicuius multitudinis supereminens & maxime unum procreare prius multitudinem sibi similem, id est unitates quasdam eminentes sibique similiores, quam multitudinem longe distantem & uniones singulorum in multitudine proprias» (*Opera*, p. 1166.2).

27 Cf. Pico, *Commento* 1.13, 2.10, 2.12, 2.13 (ed. E. Garin, pp. 480-481, 498, 500, 501 ff.).

28 Ed. E. Garin, pp. 466-467: «Secondo e' Platonici da Dio immediatamente non proviene altra creatura che questa prima mente... Questa prima creatura, da' Platonici e da antiqui filosofi Mercurio Tri[s]megisto e Zoroastre e chiamato ora figliuolo di Dio, ora sapienzia, ora mente, ora ragione divina, il che alcuni interpretono ancora Verbo. Ed abbi ciascuno diligente avvertenzia di non intendere che questo sia quello che da' nostri Teologi e detto figliuolo di Dio, perchè noi intendiamo per il figliuolo una medesima essenzia col padre... ma debbesi comparare quello che e' Platonici chiamano figliuolo di Dio al primo e più nobile angelo da Dio creato»; cf. *Commento* 1.3 (ed. Garin, pp. 464-465). See Di Napoli, *La problematica dottrinale* cit., pp. 349, 356, 432, 447, 506; Craven, *Giovanni Pico della Mirandola* cit., p. 99; and A. Raspanti, *Filosofia, teologia, religione: l'unità della visione in Giovanni Pico della Mirandola*, Palermo, Edi Oftes, 1991, p. 226.

the *Commento* 1.6 will call, using a familiar formula derived from the *Timaeus* 30C7 ff., "the intelligible world" of the Ideas. Both Ficino and Pico were acutely aware that "son" used in this sense by the ancient Platonists could not be equated with the notion of the Son of God.[29] But even so we have arrived in Pico's *Oratio*, given the Genesis setting, at something that closely approximates the orthodox Pauline notion that Man is in the Son who is the universal Logos; and that the Son is also Man, is indeed, as Ficino declares in his epitome of Plato's *Second Epistle*, "the one idea of good men", or what Proclus had designated the henad Man.[30]

In his *Timaeus* Commentary summa 29, Ficino, like Pico in the *Oratio*, turns to contemplate the marvellous nature of man, compounded as he is from the immortal and the mortal, "For it behooves him to be the animal which would worship those above (*superos*), being the mean between the animals on high (*suprema*) which are immortal in body as in soul, and the animals whose soul and body have fallen. That is, man is mortal through the body but immortal through the soul. The soul descends to earth not only for these reasons but so that, in addition to its pristine contemplation, it might also imitate divine providence. Man finally is the whole world. By way of his intellect he has some proportion with the firmament; by way of his speculative reason with Saturn; by way of his practical reason with Jove; by way each is articulated with Mercury; by way of his sense and imagination with the Sun; by way of his irascible [faculty] with Mars; by way of his concupiscible faculty with Venus; by way of his vegetable [power] with the Moon; by way of his soul's vehicle [i.e. the *spiritus*] with the sky; by way of his tractable

---

29 See, for example, Ficino's letter to Cavalcanti and his *In Parmenidem* cap. 94 (*Opera*, pp. 629-630, 1169). Valcke's view, *Pic, Scot et la question de la Toute-puissance divine* cit., pp. 388-389 – namely that Pico's references to the «better Platonists» in the *Commento* 1.4,5 are also directed against Ficino – sidesteps the evidence of 1.4, which explicitly sets Ficino apart from these Platonists on the issue of God's direct creation of human souls, and ignores the numerous occasions on which Ficino carefully distinguishes between the Neoplatonic hypostases and the Christian Trinity, for which see my *Marsilio Ficino on Plato, the Neoplatonists and the Christian doctrine of the Trinity*, «Renaissance Quarterly», XXXVII, 1984, pp. 555-584. Accounting in Christian terms for the «sons» of the «father» referred to in the *Timaeus* 28C3 and elsewhere in Plato was beset by similar difficulties with which both Ficino and Pico were likewise familiar.

30 «Ordo denique idearum in mentem ab immenso et simplici divini boni splendore descendit, siquidem una hominum idea bonorum, id est ipse Deus, alias aliorum bonorum menti angelicae ideas infundit» (*Opera*, p. 1531).

31 «Homo animal admirandum ex immortali mortalique constitutum. Oportuit enim hic esse animal, quod superos coleret, medium inter animalia illa suprema tam corpore quam animo immortalia atque inferiora utrinque caduca: ipsum scilicet per corpus quidem mortale, immortale vero per animam quae non his solum de causis descendit in terram sed etiam ut hic, ultra con-

body with the region of the elements".[31] Thus man is the universe by virtue of the hierarchy of his parts: his structure parallels and reflects the world's structure, and unlike any animal or angel, he is not only the world's *copula* or *medium*, but the world's copy, the microcosm.[32] His descent in part at least is due to his having been given the opportunity to "imitate" the downward regarding, caring concerns of providence. He can travel up and down the ladder that passes like a radius through the concentric spheres of his powers and faculties, and can provide for his own martian, lunar, or watery realms, and so on. In this he becomes a micro-providence, a caring for each of the ontological levels, that imitates and mirrors the all-embracing powers of the universal providence.

Obviously, Ficino is governed here by his text; and the *Timaeus*'s creation myth establishes a very different set of criteria for analysing the nature and role of man from the dualistic criteria articulated, say, in the *Phaedo*. Even so, he is focussing on the cosmic hierarchy in its totality and on the question of man's place, or places, in it.

* * *

Let us briefly compare Ficino's and Pico's positions here since they have customarily been contrasted. Ficino speculates that we are or mirror all things, not because of what we will, but in that we share in the variety and order of, and within, the cosmic spheres because we are compounded from intellectual and physical parts which are similarly ordered. Pico likewise is partially concerned with man's role as the animate bond and copula linking the levels of intelligible and corporeal

templationem pristinam, providentiam quoque divinam imitaretur. Homo denique totus est mundus, per intellectum quidem refert proportione aliqua firmamentum, per rationem speculativam Saturnum, per practicam Iovem, per utriusque expressionem Mercurium, per sensum imaginationemque Solem, per irascibilem Martem, per concupiscentiam Venerem, per vegetalem Lunam, per vehiculum coelum, per corpus tractabile regionem elementalem» (*Opera*, p. 1472.2). One can parallel this passage to others in the *Platonic Theology* that are better known, particularly to those in 3.2 and 13.2 (for an analysis of which see C. TRINKAUS, *Cosmos and Man: Marsilio Ficino and Giovanni Pico on the Structure of the Universe and the Freedom of Man*, «Vivens Homo», V, 1994, pp. 335-357 at 336-339). But it seems important at this point to retain the *Timaeus* in the forefront of our minds.

32 See in general, with several important distinctions and a wealth of refs, R. ALLERS, *Microcosmus: from Anaximandros to Paracelsus*, «Traditio», II, 1944, pp. 319-407; and E. CASSIRER, *The individual and the cosmos in Renaissance philosophy*, trans. M. DOMANDI, New York 1964, chap. 3: «Freedom and necessity» (this famous study was originally published in German in 1927).

With CRAVEN, *Giovanni Pico della Mirandola* cit., pp. 29-30, and TRINKAUS, *Cosmos and Man* cit., p. 350, I cannot accept Garin's view, *Vita e dottrina* cit., p. 200, that Pico rejected the idea of the microcosm (though I dissent from Craven's attack on Garin on other issues).

being together in order to complete and perfect the unfolded or emanated structure of the world, and to ensure its unity and its union in diversity. Witness the opening paragraph of the *Oratio*, and, with reference to the *Timaeus* 41D, the important passage in the *Commento* 1.12 (p. 478) which declares that human nature, being "so to speak the knot and bond of the world, has been placed in the mid point of the universe" and is customarily called the microcosm, since it has "communion" with and "agreement (*convenienzia*) with all the universe's parts". Nevertheless his stress seems to be on man's autonomy: Adam is given the freedom to be what he chooses (*optare*) or prefers (*malle*), to will what his *voluntas*, his *votum*, his *arbitrium*, his *libera optio*, his *animi sententia* wills.[33] We are faced with an apparent contrast, that is, between the Boddhisattva and the Buddha ideals, both of which are articulated, often memorably, in Platonism.

While acknowledging there are different emphases, I would question the principal contention, however, of such distinguished scholars as Cassirer, Garin, Kristeller, Trinkaus, and Buck: namely, that Pico is propounding a notably different view of man.[34] Professor Kristeller, to cite perhaps the most cautious of these exponents on this issue, argues that whereas for Ficino man has a central place, "for Pico, man has no determined nature and no fixed place in the hierarchy of beings, but he is somehow placed outside this hierarchy" with "unlimited freedom". Consequently, he says, Pico is taking "one of the first steps in dissolving the notion of the great chain of being that had dominated Western thought for so many centuries".[35] Let me adduce two not unrelated lines of argument to counter, or at least modify, this claim, not

---

[33] All these are terms, presented apparently as equivalents, in God's speech to the protoplasmic Adam in the *Oratio* (ed. GARIN, pp. 6, 8).

[34] E. CASSIRER, *Giovanni Pico della Mirandola: a study in the history of Renaissance ideas*, «Journal of the History of Ideas», III, 1942, pp. 123-144, 319-346; repr. in *Renaissance essays*, ed. P. O. KRISTELLER and P. P. WIENER, New York, Harper & Row, 1968, pp. 11-59; GARIN, *Vita e dottrina* cit., pp. 55-72; P. O. KRISTELLER, *The philosophy of Marsilio Ficino*, New York, Columbia University Press, 1943 (Reprint Gloucester, Mass. Peter Smith, 1964), pp. 407-410; ID., *Dignity of man* cit., pp. 173-178; ID., *Pico and his sources* cit., p. 67; TRINKAUS, *Image and likeness* cit., II, pp. 461-526; and A. BUCK, *G. Pico della Mirandola e l'antropologia dell'umanesimo italiano*, this volume, pp. 1-12.

[35] *Dignity of man* cit., p. 175. With his customary deliberation he does however argue that, even if Pico modified Ficino's doctrine of man «in a number of significant points» (173), he nevertheless followed it in other respects, for instance with regard to man's universal nature and gifts. Kristeller has certain passages from the *Platonic Theology* in mind, a work, we should recall, that Pico requested from Ficino. See Craven's critique, *Giovanni Pico della Mirandola* cit., pp. 27-28. Trinkaus is also circumspect, even arguing in *Cosmos and Man* cit., pp. 355-356, that Ficino more than Pico «stresses the power and importance of will».

as Dulles, De Lubac, Di Napoli and others have argued on the grounds of a shared familiarity with medieval and/or humanist topoi, but specifically on Platonic grounds.

First, I believe the governing context for both positions is the Plotinian metaphysical system and therefore, necessarily, the existence of the intelligible realm of the Ideas including the Idea of Man, and possibly even the controversial question of whether there can be Ideas of individuals. In Pico's great passage the architect-creator is addressing the prelapsarian Adam, the first man but also a work, as Evantes the Persian or Chaldaean had written, of "indistinct" or rather "of many extraneous and fortuitous features" (*non esse homini suam ullam et nativam imaginem, extrarias multas et adventitias*).[36] Adam can, in theory, occupy any rung on the world's ladder but at the beginning God places him on the middle rung so that he "may look around more easily and see whatsoever is in the world" (*ut circumspiceres inde commodius quicquid est in mundo*). From this midpoint he can select a "form" that he can "fashion" as the "moulder" and "shaper" of himself (*ut tui ipsius quasi arbitrarius honorariusque plastes et fictor in quam malueris tute formam effingas*).[37] There is no real question, it seems to me, of being "outside" the universal hierarchy, but rather of "moving" within it: there is freedom, but not "unlimited freedom". This is entirely in accord with Neoplatonism's traditional concern with the procession and return of all things to the One, with the innate love, and therefore motion in longing, of emanated being itself, and accordingly of all entities, for their source in the first hypostasis. This concern, as we shall see, runs *pari passu* with Neoplatonism's other central concern, namely with articulating a comprehensive ontology, with Soul (and thus with souls) at its centre.[38]

Neither Pico nor Ficino formulate the following questions, but they suggest themselves as the logical consequences of the theses they are engaging. Is Adam the celestial or the fiery man of Proclus's analysis of the lemma in the *Parmenides* (or we might add of Augustine's

---

36 Ed. GARIN, pp. 10-12. The grammar of this is odd: one would have expected an adversative somewhere after *imaginem*.

37 Ed. GARIN, p. 6.

38 The problem of the relationship between Soul as a hypostasis, the World-Soul and subsequent rational souls was of long-standing in the Neoplatonic tradition, as was the problem of the relationship between soul and intellect (*nous*), telescoping of the hypostases being most prominent in the thought of Porphyry. See A. C. LLOYD in *The Cambridge history of later Greek and early medieval philosophy*, ed. A. H. ARMSTRONG, Cambridge, Cambridge University Press, 1970, pp. 287-293; and R. T. WALLIS, *Neoplatonism*, London, Duckworth, 1972, pp. 69-73, 81-82, 110-113, 119-120, 152-153, etc. Cf. Pico's own *Commento* 1.3 (ed. GARIN, pp. 464-465).

City of God 18.23)? Or is he merely the first, the progenitor of earthy men? And given that Adam has been fashioned, according to Genesis, in God's image and likeness, is Adam, potentially at least, an image of the Creator creating, or an image of the world the Creator has created? Is he therefore an image of the Idea or paradigm of the World? And how in Pico's case can we reconcile the notion that Adam is the ideal created entity with his apparent formlessness, with his potentiality to become any other kind of created thing? For in the *Commento* 2.14 (p. 504), Pico, like Ficino in the *De Amore* 1.3, thinks of such a state of potentiality as constituting a "chaos" awaiting transition into a cosmos, as the Penia even of the *Symposium* 203B longing for union with Plenty.[39] Furthermore, is there an Idea of Adam risen and thus of Humanity redeemed, and if so, how does such an Idea mingle or participate with the Ideas of individuals, Adam's offspring and descendants? And what, as we shall see, of the second Adam of the Scriptures?

Ficino and Pico were both intrigued by man's special status and drawn for philosophical reasons to the theme of human dignity. But they both formulated their views in terms of a basically Neoplatonic ontology and thus in terms of man's ascent to the intelligible realm of the Ideas, including the Idea of Man. Significantly, the *Oratio* is concerned not with the subtle but particular issue (stemming from the Pythagorean doctrine of metempsychosis) of what happens to man's essence if he chooses to become a particular non-human entity, a fly, a pig, even an angel;[40] but rather with the broader question regarding his choice of a fundamental ontological level. Adam can elect to dwell in the sensual or the animate realms, or, gathered into the centre of his own unity, he can enter the intellectual realm of the pure angelic intellects, or even wing his way into the "solitary darkness of the Father".[41] The issue then is what hypostatic realm, what generic

[39] The notion of such a chaos derives from Plotinus's references on the one hand, in Aristotelian language, to «intelligible matter» (*Enneads* II.4.5), and on the other, in Pythagorean terms, to the «indefinite dyad» (V.1.5). See ARMSTRONG in *The Cambridge history* cit., pp. 241-242.

[40] Both Pico and Ficino rejected metempsychosis. To believe that the rational soul could pass into irrational animals was the sublime Plotinus's one great error, rejected by his successors in the pagan as well as the Christian traditions. See WALLIS, *Neoplatonism* cit., pp. 72, 92, 113, 120; and, for Pico, DE LUBAC, *Pic de la Mirandole* cit., pp. 82, 187.

[41] «et si nulla creaturarum sorte contentus in unitatis centrum suae se receperit, unus cum Deo spiritus factus, in solitaria Patris caligine qui est super omnia constitutus omnibus antestabit» (ed. E. GARIN, p. 8); cf. Pico's *Commento* 1.12 (ed. GARIN, p. 479). For the Neoplatonic doctrine of the *unitas*, see W. BEIERWALTES, *Der Begriff des 'unum in nobis' bei Proklos*, «Miscellanea

kind of being, not what particular entity, should he and can he properly will for himself? Should he elect to be a soul or aspire to an angelic nature or to a mystical oneness with the divine darkness? Again we come up against the twin aspects of Plotinian metaphysics: on the one hand, the recognition of multiple and not merely dualistic divisions of being in the world and correspondingly in man (made even more complex by the scholastic distinctions of Plotinus's successors and notably of Proclus); and on the other hand, the monistic yearning of all things to be enfolded as one in the One, the flight, in the *Enneads*' closing words, "of the alone to the alone".

* * *

Behind the injunction in the *Oratio* to choose to be what we will exists another metaphysical tension intrinsic to Neoplatonism. As both an individual and a species man is potentially all things (we should recall that *homoios* in Greek means both "similar to" and "the same as" in either an absolute or a partial sense, with the resulting fallacies and logical puzzles). His soul can climb up and down the rungs of the cosmic ladder in the process of ratiocination, thus entering discursively into the species and genera of the entire creation. Not only is he the little world, the creation in minature, the perfect image of the macrocosm in the time-honoured conceit (the meaning, as Craven has correctly observed, of Pico's phrase "tritum in scholis verbum"); he is also a soul which is "in some senses" all things precisely because it understands all things, as Aristotle had suggestively argued in the *De Anima* and Aquinas had reiterated. Pico adduces several related propositions to this effect in other works. Number LXII, for example, of his *Conclusiones paradoxae numero LXXI secundum opinionem propriam* states, "The soul always understands itself, and, in understanding itself, it understands in a way (*quodammodo*) all that exists (*omnia entia*)";[42] while

Medievalia», II, Cologne, 1963, pp. 255-266, and J. M. Rist, *Mysticism and transcendence in later Neoplatonism*, «Hermes», XCII, 1964, pp. 213-225, with further refs. For the «unity» in Ficino, see Kristeller, *Philosophy of Ficino* cit., pp. 250-251, 368-369.

[42] *Opera*, p. 92. We should align this with the thirteenth of the theses–No. 60 of the same *Conclusiones paradoxae* that the commission set up by Innocent VIII found objectionable in various ways: «Nihil intelligit actu et distincte anima nisi seipsam» (*Opera*, p. 92). Pico defended this in his *Apologia* by way of substituting two more propositions (*Opera*, pp. 235, 240 – nos. 45 and 46), though his chief opponent, Pedro Garsias, traced both of them back to Averroes. See Dulles, *Princeps Concordiae* cit., pp. 138-143 (with the claim that the defence of this proposition is the «weakest section of the *Apologia*»); and Di Napoli, *La problematica dottrinale* cit., pp. 174-175 (on the proposition), 184-185 (on Garsias's objections).

the *Commento* 2.6 (p. 492) argues that "our soul is all things because it can understand all things".[43] As a rational soul, man had joined before his descent into the flesh – and will join again upon his liberation from it – with all other rational souls in the universal cavalcade under what the *Phaedrus* calls "great" Jove (interpreted by the Neoplatonists as the World Soul), a cavalcade which ascends to the rim of the intellectual or angelic heaven thence to gaze from afar at the intelligible beauty of the Ideas.[44] These include the *Timaeus*'s pattern of the universe, the ideal beauty of the cosmos, that the Demiurge, Plotinus's Intellect, had contemplated when he set about the fabrication of the world.[45] Man had joined, that is, in the cavalcade of all the souls to gaze upon the All, having then been all and entirely soul, the radiant image and likeness of God's face.[46]

What appears then in God's speech to Adam to be an injunction to choose a "form" of being, and even by implication to choose once and

---

[43] As I see it, the Aristotelian ref. here collates statements in the *De Anima* III at 5.430a14-15, a20, 7.431a1, b16-17, and above all 8.431b20-21; with the key phrase being *pos apanta* («all things in a certain way»). Cf. Proclus, *Elements of Theology*, prop. 195 (ed. DODDS, pp. 170-171 [text], 299-300 [commentary]), which concludes «Thus every soul is all that is» in so far as it participates in what is prior and serves as an exemplary cause of what is posterior. Cf. too Aquinas, *In III de anima* 1.13, and *Summa theologica* I, q.84, a.2, ad 2m, who again refers to the soul being all things «in a way» (*quodammodo*), a qualification, interestingly, that Pico omits.

We cannot enter here into the complexities of Pico's epistemology: suffice it to say that for him the innate *species* (Ficino's *formulae idearum*) are the means of knowledge and he explicitly rejects the materialistic view propounded by Aristotle in the *Physics* that such *species* have been «a phantasmatibus abstractas».

[44] See my *The Platonism of Marsilio Ficino*, Berkeley, University of California Press, 1984, pp. 126-128, 144-152.

[45] T. GREGORY has observed that the attempt to accommodate this Platonic creator with the Creator of the Judeo-Christian tradition was enthusiastically pursued by some and strenuously opposed by others in Christian antiquity and again, beginning with the School of Chartres, in the Middle Ages, *Anima mundi: la filosofia di Guglielmo di Conches e la scuola di Chartres*, Florence, Sansoni, 1955, pp. 115-121, and chaps. 3 and 4 passim; ID., *Platonismo medievale: studi e ricerche*, Rome, Istituto storico italiano per il medio evo, 1958, pp. 53-150. The bibliography on this issue is predictably enormous.

[46] Note the famous syllogistic passage in the *Phaedrus* 245C-246A, beginning «All (or every) soul is immortal, for what is always in motion is immortal» a passage known since antiquity, incidentally, in three Latin versions: in Cicero's *Tusculanae* 1.23.53-54 and *De republica* 6.25.27-26.28, and in Calcidius's *In Timaeum* 57 (ed. J. H. WASZINK, pp. 104-105). Interestingly, Pico restricts the meaning of «all soul» in this immortality syllogism to «every celestial soul» (*de coelesti qualibet anima*) in No. 36 of his *Conclusiones secundum propriam opinionem numero LXII in doctrinam Platonis* (*Opera*, p. 98); see DI NAPOLI, *La problematica dottrinale* cit., p. 375. In the *Commento* 3.4 (ed. GARIN, p. 529), however, he interprets the related all soul syllogism at 246B6-7 «All soul cares for all that is inanimate and traverses the whole universe, though in ever-changing forms», to mean «every soul which has been constituted rational in its nature cares for the whole corporeal universe»; while in No. 50 of the section of the *Conclusiones* just cited he declares that «all soul» here refers to «whatever is truly soul» (*de quacunque vere anima*) (*Opera*, p. 99).

definitively an individual form, is in reality an injunction to acknowledge our authentic status as soul, and with it to embrace the *totus mundus*, the created realm which is animated by the World Soul, the Soul which some of the early Scholastics had identified with Nature and others even with the Holy Spirit.[47] This may not be at first glance for the providential reasons that Ficino had in the forefront of his mind; but it is articulating a will to entirety, to universal *sympatheia*, to ontological fullness, that is entirely consonant with a Neoplatonic, and specifically with a Ficinian, insistence on our providential as well as our contemplative roles: it speaks to an injunction to each and every soul to be all soul, and thus "in a way" – and this is of course the crucial qualifying phrase – to be the Soul of the All, one with the Soul of the world.[48]

This was not just an epistemological accommodation, moreover, arrived at on the Aristotelian grounds that the soul is "in a way" all things because it knows them. It was also the logical consequence of the more complex proposition which had first been mooted by Plato in the *Theaetetus* 204A-205D and the *Timaeus* 30C4 ff., then developed by Plotinus in the *Enneads* 4.2, 5.8.4, etc., and finally schematized by Proclus in the *Elements of Theology*, props. 67-69, etc.: namely, that "the all (whole) is in the part" (*totus in qualibet parte*),[49] a proposition contrary at first glance to the commonsensical axiom that the whole is greater than the part or than the sum of the parts. Since the Neoplatonists thought of this "all is in the part" as a universally valid proposition, they could adduce it in any relationship, though it had a particular relevance to a consideration of the problem of the individual soul's union with, even identification with, the World Soul, and with the hypostasis Soul; in other words,

---

47 ALLERS, *Microcosmus* cit., pp. 352-362. Allers reminds us that Abelard, for one, equated the World Soul with the Holy Spirit and had his opinion condemned at the Council of Soissons in 1121 and again at the Council of Sens in 1140. But Abelard was not alone: William of Conches seems to have entertained the identification also in his glosses on Boethius and in the first, but not the final, version of his glosses on the *Timaeus*. See GREGORY, *Anima mundi* cit., pp. 17, 37, 133-151.

48 DULLES, *Princeps Concordiae* cit., p. 141, is incorrect in claiming *tout court* that the Florentine Platonists «vociferously repudiated all suggestions of the Commentator's [Averroes'] monopsychism». For monopsychism was part of the challenging legacy of the *Phaedrus*'s syllogisms and had to be carefully accommodated in a Christian scheme that promised an individual salvation. For antiquity, see P. MERLAN, *Monopsychism, mysticism, metaconsciousness: problems of the soul in the neo-Aristotelian and Neoplatonic tradition*, The Hague, Nijhoff, 1963, 2d ed. 1969.

49 Ed. DODDS, pp. 64-67 (text), 236-238 (commentary). The notion of participation (*methexis*) also involves the *totus in qualibet parte* argument as Iamblichus was to clearly demonstrate; see A. C. LLOYD in *The Cambridge history* cit., pp. 298-301, and WALLIS, *Neoplatonism* cit., pp. 126-127. For the problem in Ficino, see KRISTELLER, *Philosophy of Ficino* cit., pp. 126-130.

relevance to a consideration of the soul's status as a part of the all in the all, and therefore, mysteriously, as the all.[50] In focussing on this partitive or part-whole relationship of soul to Soul, Pico is thus indebted to both Neoplatonic and Aristotelian propositions. At one time the soul descends with its discursive reason, tearing Soul into many as a Set dismembering Osiris – to use the *Oratio*'s own imagery; at another time it ascends, gathering the many into Soul as an Isis reassembling the limbs of the god. And thus it exercises both titanic and apollonian powers. This may be merely a figurative way of saying that Adam, the universal man – and potentially Adam in everyone of his descendants – is the master of a universe within, but it certainly suggests the more radical Neoplatonic notion stemming from the *Phaedrus* that our soul is one with the World Soul, *homo totus est mundus*, and accordingly with whatever a Christian interpreter chooses to identify as the World Soul.

Thus the *Oratio*'s vision of man (whether directly dependent or not on Ficino's "orthodox" account of man as the "face" of all, as the "bond" and "knot" of the universe) is indebted, I am suggesting, not only to the notions of the limit and the indeterminate in the *Philebus* and correlatively to the ontology of the *Sophist*, but more particularly to the great myths of the *Timaeus* and *Phaedrus*, and to the notions of the universal paradigm, the intelligible world, and the Idea of Man in the *Timaeus* and *Parmenides*; in other words, to Platonic anthropology and cosmology and to their accompanying epistemology.

* * *

Furthermore, these Platonic debts in the *Oratio* were more than passing ones; for Pico almost immediately elaborated and reworked his anthropocentric rhetoric of 1486 when, just two years later in the second half of 1488, he started on the *Heptaplus*,[51] though this may

---

[50] For Christians the proposition bore even more importantly both on Christ's relationship with the individual soul and with the collective soul of the Church, and on the problem of the soul's presence in the body. Augustine's definition in the *De Trinitate* 6.6, that the soul «in unoquoque corpore et in toto tota est et in qualibet parte eius tota est» was endlessly repeated and often attributed, erroneously, to Aristotle. Cf. Aquinas, *Summa theologica* 1.76.8, and *Summa contra gentiles* 2.72. Note the related Neoplatonic proposition, «all is in all but appropriately» (*panta en pasin all'oikeios*); Cf. Proclus, *Elemente of Theology*, prop. 103.

See Allers, *Microcosmus*, pp. 358-359. For Pico see Di Napoli, *La problematica dottrinale* cit., pp. 386-393, «il circolo dell'anima è innanzitutto da sé a sé, è proprio perché è da sé a sé, esso è pure da sé a Dio, da sé al mondo, dal mondo al mondo, dal mondo a Dio» (p. 387). For Ficino, see Kristeller, *Philosophy of Ficino* cit., pp. 114-120.

[51] Cf. Di Napoli, *La problematica dottrinale* cit., pp. 375-379.

not have been his primary intention when he undertook the sevenfold analysis on cabalastic lines of the opening verses of Genesis. A few pointers are in order.

In the second general proem, man is called the fourth world after the angelic, the celestial and the sublunar worlds. In 5.6 (p. 300), however, Pico qualifies this notion by arguing that man is not so much a fourth world as the "link" (*complexus*) or "bond" (*colligatio*) of the other three (cf. 5.7, p. 304); or, as he puts it in 3.7 (pp. 264, 266), man can serve as the terminus of the angelic world and as the beginning of corruptible nature. In 5.6 (pp. 300, 302) he resorts to the architectural notion that man resembles a statue of his Maker erected in the centre of a great city, at the same time asserting that the substance of man "embraces the substances of all natures in himself and in truth the plenitude of the whole universe",[52] and again quoting the famous apostrophe to the *magnum miraculum* in the *Asclepius* 6. The final *expositio* (p. 380), moreover, introduces a variation on the notion that man is a microcosm. Perhaps with Philo Judaeus,[53] and surely with the cabalistic notion of *Adam kadmon* in mind,[54] Pico observes that the world is by the same token "a great man" (*utique mundus est homo magnus*), thereby mysteriously inverting the authority, and accordingly the origin, of the correspondence between the two cosmoses and, by implication, between the Idea of the World and the Idea of Man. In sum, the *Heptaplus* reenacts even as it refines or redefines some of the basic arguments of the *Oratio*.

As scholars have noted, however, several familiar Christological, and explicitly Johannine and Pauline, themes appear that are absent in the earlier work.[55] Christ is the new Adam (4.7, p. 286), the perfection (*consummatio*) of all men (1.7, p. 220), the firstborn

---

52 «hominis substantia... omnium in se naturarum substantias et totius universitatis plenitudinem re ipsa complectitur».

53 ALLERS, *Microcosmus* cit., p. 355, citing Philo Judaeus, *De migr. Abrah.* 220, *De opific.* 146, and *De aetern.* 80. But cf. Macrobius, *Somn.* 2.12.11: «Mundum magnum hominem».

54 See GARIN, *Vita e dottrina* cit., pp. 93-94, 197-198; and, more pertinently, C. WIRSZUBSKI, *Pico della Mirandola's encounter with Jewish mysticism*, Cambridge, Mass., Harvard University Press, 1989.

55 S. PIGNAGNOLI, *Lineamenti cristologici nel pensiero di Pico della Mirandola*, «Atti e Memorie della Deputazione di storia patria per le antiche provincie modenesi», 4-5, 1964-1965, pp. 379-398; and more importantly R. B. WADDINGTON, *The sun at the center: structure as meaning in Pico della Mirandola's Heptaplus*, «Journal of Medieval and Renaissance Studies», III, 1973, 69-86; and in general MONNERJAHN, *Pico: Beitrag zur philosophischen Theologie* cit. But see Craven's objections, *Giovanni Pico della Mirandola* cit., pp. 15-16 (to Monnerjahn), 31-32 (to Waddington).

of all creation (5.7, p. 308), the universal mean (6.7, p. 324), and the power (*virtus*) and wisdom (*sapientia*) of God (proem to 7, p. 338). Pico declares we are perfected in Christ since he is the first in the genus of man (1.7, p. 220), having already accommodated in the *Commento* 1.6 (pp. 467-468) the scholastic notion of the *primum in aliquo genere* to the Platonic theory of Ideas.[56] And he asserts in 3.7 (p. 266) both that man is lower than the angels (predictably referring to Psalm 8:5[6], "Minuisti eum paulominus ab angelis"; cf. *Oratio*, p. 1); and yet that, when perfected in Christ, man is raised either above them (citing Hebrews 1:4, "Tanto melior angelis effectus") or at least to a fellowship with them (as 4.2, p. 274, argues, mis-citing I John 1:3, "et societas nostra cum angelis est"). Indeed, in so far as we enter into Christ the perfect man, into Man Himself, we assume his cosmic perfection. Instead of the "great man" being the world as he will suggest in the final *expositio*, the great man, he says in 2.7 (p. 244), is the Man who is the Son of God, the Power and Wisdom of God, the beginning and principle (*principium*) of the cosmos wherein Adam is the final, the perfect work (*opus*). In sum, what had commenced as a pointedly Hermetic moment in the *Oratio* concludes by becoming in the *Heptaplus* an aspect of an orthodox Christology or rather Christological cosmology (though informed, it has been argued, by the Cabala).[57]

Now it is easier to define the perfect first in a genus than to analyse the defective succedents. However, while Plato's metaphysical notion of participation in the Ideas was fraught from the onset with conceptual difficulties, St. Paul's psychological notion of becoming one with Christ had repeatedly been attested to by the faithful; was indeed the ultimate goal, the defining event in the Christian experience, and thus at the core of the theology of belief. Pico's image of man ascending and descending the universal ladder and becoming all things may be too bold a cosmological abstraction for a Christian to accept unhesitatingly or at all; but not when it is recast into the Pauline notion of becoming one with Christ who is all things. Platonically, however, the perfect Man, the Idea of Man, is Christ, the very God of earth and heaven, the paradigm of the world and of man. Christ as the ultimate Idea, the Logos beyond all *logoi*, is the *maximum miraculum*, a *miraculum* dimly foreseen by

---

[56] For a full introduction to this notion, see KRISTELLER, *Philosophy of Ficino* cit., chap. 9.

[57] RASPANTI, *Filosofia, teologia, religione* cit., pp. 101-104.

Hermes as prophet, and only then if we bring other hermetic texts to bear on the *Asclepius* passage.[58]

* * *

The dual orientation, Neo-Platonic and anthropocentric, of Pico's views necessarily draws attention to the Idea of Man, almost exclusively so. Herein, surely, lies the most significant difference between himself and Ficino.[59]

Whereas Ficino was unremittingly concerned throughout his life with systematically exploring Neoplatonic metaphysics in its many aspects, including of course the theory of Ideas, Pico's debts were more specific, and in the event more immediately dramatic. To focus on man and thus in a Platonic context on one preeminent Idea, the Idea of Man, inevitably brought into sharp relief the philosophical difficulties, and for a Christian the theological mysteries, uniquely accompanying this Idea, and correlatively accompanying the general theory of Ideas.[60] If we must continue to think of Pico as the bolder and more confrontational of the two great Florentines with regard to the theme of human dignity, however, it is precisely because of these signal Christocentric concerns in the *Heptaplus*. For a Christocentric system necessarily anthropomorphizes any variation on the Platonic scheme: Man – not Truth, Justice, Beauty, Temperance, and so forth, not even the world paradigm – becomes the prime Idea, the one to which the others are entailed or subordinate. This in turn underscores the metaphysical conviction that the Idea of Man is neither Protagoras's universal measure with the Promethean gift of fire, nor Aristotle's rational being who knows all things, but rather Plato's and Plotinus's Idea of the intelligible universe, and thus, according to 5.7 (p. 308), "Him through whom all nature was established". Christ, the Idea of Man, is the perfection, in sum, of the Platonic theory of Ideas, its sublime fulfilment, cause and end.[61]

---

[58] Notably, of course, passages from the fourteen treatises known to Ficino and Pico of the *Corpus Hermeticum* and referred to collectively by Ficino in his 1463 Latin translation as the *Pimander*.

[59] RASPANTI, *Filosofia, teologia, religione* cit., pp. 116-118, emphasizes, rather, the difference between Platonic and Christian anthropology, arguing that Pico expounds the former in the *Commento* and the latter in the *Oratio* and in the commentary on Psalm 47.

[60] Pico had declared in his *Commento* 1.13 (ed. GARIN, p. 480) that he would take up this issue in his «council» and in his *Symposium* Commentary.

[61] For a Christian apologist, the roots of this argument lie of course in the pro and anti Platonic polemics of the Church Fathers, notably of Augustine. The transference by Christian Platonists of attributes associated with the three Plotinian hypostases of Soul, Mind and the One

If Pico's debts to Platonism, and notably to the later dialogues, led him in the *Heptaplus* to adumbrate a Platonized Christology, nevertheless this Christology is already implicit I am suggesting in the famous apostrophe in the *Oratio* where Adam is created in the image of the Platonic Idea of Man, an Idea which is at the head of the macrocosm as the paradigm of all things and of all things as they are contained in the microcosm. Its first Adam is thus paradoxically an image of Him who will come as the second Adam. In enjoining the old Adam to shape himself, the Creator is enjoining him to assume his role as the universal being made in imitation of, and therefore in the Platonic sense made a participant in, the new Adam, the Son who is perpetually one with the Father and yet the *paradeigma* of the world, and who will descend into time, in the words of the future creed, to be incarnate by the Holy Ghost, of the Virgin Mary and made man. At least, I would argue, an awareness of the doctrine of the Ideas as it appears in the *Timaeus* and in the first part of the *Parmenides*, and of the arresting problems associated in the Neoplatonic tradition with the introduction in the *Parmenides* of the Idea of Man, lends a new dimension to our appreciation both of the sources of Pico's coruscating *Oratio de hominis dignitate* and of the role of the "fourth world" in his *Heptaplus*.

---

variously to God, to the Trinity, to the persons of the Trinity, and to the angels was beset with difficulties and these became most acute, predictably, in formulating a Platonic account of the Son of Man. For the situation in Ficino, see KRISTELLER, *Philosophy of Ficino* cit., pp. 167-169, 240.

Another related issue was the Averroistic account of the Active Intellect, though the view that Pico himself was, or was at one time, an Averroist has not been generally accepted.

3

Renaissance Neoplatonism [and Literary Criticism]

Renaissance Neoplatonism was the creation of the fifteenth-century Florentines Marsilio Ficino and Giovanni Pico della Mirandola and had a profound and far-reaching impact on the cultural as well as the intellectual and religious life of Europe for well over two centuries. It contributed a *forma mentis* that transcended disciplinary and national boundaries without necessarily coming into direct conflict with other contemporary mind-sets, those we associate with Aristotelianism, Protestantism, Ramism, neo-scholasticism, Hermeticism, Copernicanism, Tridentism, and so forth. Literature and its interpretation only played an ancillary role in what was at heart a philosophico-theological movement anchored in the concerns of medieval Catholicism but inspired by the attractive example of Plato's newly discovered dialogues on the one hand and by the dauntingly technical commentaries of the Neoplatonists on the other. But it did mean that the Platonic dialogue, with its dramatic shifts from interrogation to exposition to myth to fable to quotation to dialectical division in various sequences and combinations, was set up not so much as the literary but as the hermeneutical model; and that Plato's style, with its lucidity, suppleness, and figurative and ironic variety, became acknowledged as a way of doing philosophy that was in marked contrast to the wrangling of the schools and to the analytic systematizing of Aristotle. Plato became not only the great alternative to the Stagirite as a philosopher but a more profound and compelling alternative to Cicero as a model rhetorician.

One of the obvious issues the Platonic dialogue poses is that of genre. Ancient doxologists, such as Diogenes Laertius in his *Lives of the philosophers* 3.49–51, 58–61, had divided up the dialogues rather crudely under such heads as 'political', 'ethical', 'logical', 'physical', and 'obstetrical'; but this could not satisfy those who were impressed by the dramatic unity of many of Plato's masterpieces and by the complexity and variety that subsisted in that unity. The Florentine Neoplatonists accordingly turned to their predecessors among the ancient Neoplatonists for authority in establishing a view of the Platonic dialogue as unified by an overriding theme, a *skopos*, but at the same time as accommodating a variety of concerns. The monistic orientation of their metaphysics conditioned this holistic approach to the forms and structures of Plato's writings, yet it sprang too from a deeply held conviction that Plato the rhetorician had understood the human psyche, its addiction to pleasure and its search for transcendence; that he was a magus who could enchant with his spells, a poet who had been inspired by the nine Muses and their leader Apollo (etymologized as the Not-of-Many) to inspire others.

The theme of inspiration was necessarily primary, given Socrates's account in the *Phaedrus* 244A–245C of the four divine madnesses of poetry, prophecy, priesthood, and love, and given the serious challenge the *Ion* presented to a Neoplatonist. Ficino analysed both texts at various times – the myth of the charioteer in the *Phaedrus*, for example, with its score or so of memorable images is constantly invoked throughout his and Pico's works and supplies them with a number of standard terms and phrases. But he used them to generate not a poetics so much as an 'ecstatics', a theory of inspiration that is not peculiarly literary but which nonetheless stems from the rhapsodic experience of Ion as a reciter of Homer's poetry. Even if we do not accede to Socrates's line of argument in the *Ion*, we tend to see this little colloquy nowadays as an essentially comic portrait of a naïve rhapsode, an actor with no real grasp of what he is doing. In his introduction to the dialogue for his great 1484 Latin translation of the collected works of Plato, Ficino saw it otherwise: as a major statement on the descent of divine madness into a human being who becomes a medium for a god's voice, a trumpet for the divine. In the process he addresses, not the epistemological question Socrates keeps asking – What does Ion know as he recites and afterwards? – but rather the psychological question – What does it feel like to be a medium of poetry? Is it an experience of total possession and loss of self or does one discover another and higher self which becomes creatively involved in, or changed by, the poem and its rendering? Should we examine the post-rhapsodic Ion Socratically on what he knows about the technicalities of Homer's acquaintance with the skills of chariot-driving, concocting posset remedies, or fishing with leads (537A–538D), three of Homer's themes? Or should we give him the coveted gold crown for his narrative evocation of Achilles springing upon Hector, for his empathic weeping at the sorrows of Andromache, Hecuba, or Priam (535B), for the 'force' of his acting?

Plato had introduced the image of the magnet to us somewhat ironically, but it was Ficino who teased out the logical consequences: that the god or gods inspired the poet with a divine madness which he in turn transmitted to the rhapsode reciting his poetry, who then transmitted it to his auditors. The result was a 'chain' of inspiration that descended from the divine but was all of a piece, enabling the ordinary listener to come into touch with the originary god. In this concatenation, the poem is merely one of the links, a carrier of the magnetic force which flows through it and on to the rhapsode and then to his audience, uniting it both with the

Muses, the source of all poetic activity, and with Apollo as the unitary god beyond them. The characteristics of the poem, and certainly the features that prompt a formalistic analysis, are irrelevant to the principal issue: that to hear the poem is merely to step on the first rung on the long ladder of inner ascent. Certainly, the kinds of questions that Aristotle's *Poetics* invites are not germane. Ficino is generating rather an audience response theory that assumes that all auditors will ultimately respond in the same way to contact with the power of the divine; and it is a theory – initially at least – of passivity: the more passive the rhapsode, the better he may serve as a medium. This is to look at it perhaps too negatively, for Ficino's assumptions are predicated on the authority that Christianity has traditionally accorded virginity, humility, foolishness for Christ's sake, submission to the divine Will, patience even unto death. The paradoxes with which its otherworldliness invests the pleasures of this world necessarily transform the Socratic Ion into a holy fool, a patient expounder of the epics, even as they enmesh Socrates himself in an intricate web of ironies not of his own making.

However, neither the *Iliad* nor the *Odyssey* is the kind of poem that Ficino has in mind in adumbrating his theory of Platonic ecstatics, even though Plato, like any cultured Greek, had frequently quoted from them. The proper medium of divine inspiration is the divine hymn that Plato had lauded in his *Republic* and *Laws*, and one of which the *Phaedo* 60D declares Socrates had himself composed in prison in honour of Apollo. It was best exemplified for Ficino, however, in the collection of Orphic hymns which the Renaissance supposed of immense antiquity, but which we now view as a compilation of the third or fourth century AD. Plato had quoted from various *Orphica* known to him and the later Neoplatonists from the collection of hymns; and this in itself invested the Orphic poem with Platonic authority. Moreover, Ficino and Pico had inherited from Proclus and others a conception of a line of six ancient theologians, the *prisci theologi*, stemming from the poet-priest Zoroaster and the Egyptian magus Hermes Trismegistus and culminating in Plato. Third in the succession was Orpheus who had charmed the beasts and descended into the underworld, but more importantly had sung hymns to all the gods to the accompaniment of ritual fumigations of incense, myrrh, saffron, and other odoriferous substances.

The hymns consist almost exclusively of ritual invocations of a deity's names and attributes, of a list of *aretai*, the good deeds associated with its power, and of an exultatory recognition of the extent of this power in the cosmos and of man's indebtedness to its gifts. Given Orpheus's traditional association with a lyre – the subject of considerable debate among Renaissance lutanists and musicologists as to its stringing and tuning – Ficino supposed that the hymns were sung or chanted in a perfect wedding of words and chords, of the quantities that words have in Greek and Latin and of the notes and intervals of the lost musical scales of antiquity. Moreover, Ficino possessed what he called an Orphic lyre, with a picture of Orpheus enchanting the beasts painted on it; and his rapturous performances of Orphic-Platonic hymns to that lyre became musical events in Florentine patrician circles, and notably with the Medici.

That the Orphic hymns could possess such authority in a Christian community, however secular and enlightened, was due almost entirely to the fact that, although they were thoroughly polytheistic in sentiment and Ficino himself had not publicized his translations for fear that they would promote a new demonolatry (as he writes in a letter to a close friend), they were prefaced by a famous monotheistic palinode. This served, not to invalidate the eighty-six subsequent hymns, but to characterize them as veils of images and attributes investing the unimaginable divine. Orpheus became the gentiles' counterpart to David, his hymns their psalms, his Thracian lyre the harp of the Lord. In striking Orphic chords and intoning Platonic hymns, Ficino was therefore recalling in part at least the biblical singer, extending the canon of the psalter and reaffirming the ideal wedding of poetry and music in the act of worship. The impact of this revived Ficinian Orphism or 'Ionism' on Renaissance lyric and particularly on Ronsard and the Pléiade should not be underemphasized. It would be interesting to explore its impact both on Renaissance psalmody, given that rendering the psalms into verse became a penitential exercise for Protestants, and on the attempts by poets such as Sidney and Campion to revive the classical metres and to wed them to music.

Renaissance poets and critics became preoccupied, however, not by the ideal of the divine hymn – even Sir Philip Sidney sets it aside in his *Apology for poetry* in order to discuss 'right' poetry instead – but by the interpretative challenges of the classical, and particularly the Roman, epic and its imitations. In Italy this preoccupation was complicated, moreover, by the presence of the *Divine comedy*. Nurtured on both Virgil and Dante, the Italian Platonists generated a hermeneutic that was indebted alike to medieval allegoresis, religious and secular, and to the ancient allegorizing of Homer and Virgil. In this they were not striving to be original – the adventures of Landino's Aeneas for instance are predictably those of a soul on the Platonic quest – but the authority of these two great poems and the universal acceptance of their high seriousness did force them to confront Plato's expulsion of the poets from his ideal republic. While Sidney and others, enamoured of Plato's own powers as a poetic writer, might later explain this expulsion away, Ficino in particular felt compelled to explore the arguments behind Plato's attack on poetry and to confront its repudiation of Homer and Hesiod. Here, obviously, the model of Ion did not pertain.

The two great originary Greek poets had erred in two major respects: they had both attributed human passions and failings to the immortal gods, anthropomorphizing them in our own frail image as creatures of anger, jealousy, fear, and desire; and they had articulated a false theogony that had the primal gods emerging from chaos and then copulating together in the manner of humans to produce subsequent generations. In the second error they thus aligned themselves with those natural philosophers (physicists and cosmologists) who denied the sovereignty of providence and the primacy of beauty and order in the generation of the world. Ironically, in the Neoplatonic reading of the *Symposium* Plato had discussed the 'chaos' of longing that is the condition of each hypostasis in the ontological hierarchy before it is actualized by the One and the Good, thus incorporating the Hesiodic notion into his metaphysics. Still, it was not the same as positing Chaos as the primal state, a move that effectively linked the poets with the atheists and Epicureans of later polemics. On this foundation of false metaphysics and theology, it was almost inevitable that the poets should build an edifice of false ethics, re-creating as the primal psychological condition the chaos of passion from which the ordering virtues of temperance, justice, courage, and prudence could never emerge. In short, the poets had promoted an upside-down view of the world which, since it lacked the fundamental insights of true philosophy, lacked too the grounds of an authentic piety.

Nevertheless, the philosopher could listen to their siren songs with impunity and even ultimately with profit, because he could interpret all for the best by reference to the One and the Good, and not to Chaos, as the beginning and end of all things. The rightmindedness, the virtue, and the subtlety of the interpreter (and not now of a rhapsode like Ion) became the new key to the validity of poetry in the Platonic republic. We must banish the popular poets from the city, writes Ficino, but not from the state. Far from the callow throng of the city's susceptible and suggestible youths, the poets can do no harm. To the contrary, they can be safely and profitably heard as it were in exile by the philosophers, since they can reinterpret their mysteries *more Platonico*, and turn their stories [*mythoi*] to the cause of the Good. Thus the intention of the interpreter not that of the poet determines what is good or bad poetry in the sense of what can and cannot serve virtue. Not only can the interpreter pierce through the veils of allegory and imagery to gaze on the eternal truths, he can validate the poets' errors by reinterpreting their figures in the light of Plotinian metaphysics. Hermes, not Apollo or the Muses, becomes the presiding deity of poetry because he is the deity of its reception. The chain of magnetic force that linked Ion to the bard has been replaced by the caducean staff that dispels in the intelligent and pious auditor the clouds, however golden, of misconceit.

Even so, the 'ancient enmity', the 'old quarrel' between philosophy and poetry, as the *Republic* 10.607BC puts it, remained a bitter one, more particularly in that the comic poets had played a role in the condemnation of Socrates on the grounds, hypocritically given their own irreligiousness, of impiety: blood was on their hands. Obviously, this was not true of the dead poets: Socrates had himself declared that from boyhood he had been possessed by 'a certain love and reverence for Homer' (*Republic* 10.595B) and that he would willingly die ten times to meet 'Orpheus and Musaeus, Hesiod and Homer' (*Apology* 41A); and throughout his life, as with any educated Athenian, Homer had been constantly on his lips as the creative genius of Greek, the generator of its ornaments and flowers. We thus have a profoundly fissured sense of poetry and poets in the Neoplatonic tradition that derived heterogeneously from Socrates's personal reverence for Homer and yet the role of the comic poets in his trial and condemnation; and from Plato's moral and political strictures and yet the witness of his myths of divine frenzy and of his own soaring flights.

A controversy simmered too between the poets and the philosophers over the nature of the Platonic Forms and our apprehension of them. If artists' pictorial imitations of physical objects had been condemned in the *Republic* 10.596A ff. as being at three removes from reality, the verbal imitations of poets were less easily dismissed. Plotinus had spoken to the beauty and truth of pure colours and abstract shapes and promoted the theory that the artist was imitating the ideal Forms of objects rather than confining himself to a necessarily faulty reproduction of what was already a faulty artefact or object in nature. In this regard he appears to be the first Platonist to provide on Platonic grounds, and despite Plato himself, a non-mimetic defence of art. But an epic poet imitates not so much static objects like the shield of Achilles as the deeds of men, the unfolding in time of the virtues of Odysseus, Cyrus, or Aeneas. Plato's metaphysics is essentialist and timeless and regards all temporal phenomena at best as participating in essence, at worst as illusory. But the Neoplatonists, in focusing on Soul as the third hypostasis and basing themselves on the argument on self-motion in the *Phaedrus* 245C–246A, underscored the necessarily temporal nature of all that exists in and through movement, corporeal or rational (that is, of discursive reasoning). If the angelic intelligence [*mens*] is the faculty in traditional psychology of intuitive perception, by contrast the human reason [*ratio*] must wheel from premises to conclusions, must circle in the *circus maximus* of ratiocination round the analysis of an Idea that only the *mens* can contemplate directly. Even so, this circling, beginning as the gradatory movement of logic or analysis, approaches in ever tighter and tighter circles to the angelic stasis of intuition. For the end of thought is the enforming power of an Idea.

In so far as the great poets are able to speak to the shaping power of Ideas, they re-enact the circling with which we approach the Ideas ever more closely in the process of reasoning. Hence their poems can serve our soul-chariots, the vehicles by which we ascend to the outermost convex rim of the intellectual heaven thence to contemplate afar what the *Phaedrus* 247A calls the 'blessed spectacles' of intelligible reality. Again we are closer to the divine hymns of Orpheus and David than to the complex surface of an epic narrative however hermetically allegorized. Indeed, it would be fair to say that Neoplatonism, for all the encouragement it accorded in antiquity and the Renaissance to the bolder displacements of allegoresis, was nonetheless anchored in the world of the divine lyric, of the incantation and the laud; and thus to the state of rapture that song induced in the singer and listener alike, each bound to the other and to the god, enthusiasts in the original meaning of the word. That enthusiasm, *furor* or *mania* defines Neoplatonism's engagement with poetry, and thus with the poet not the poem, accounts for the centrality of passages from the *Ion* and the *Phaedrus* rather than those from the *Republic* and *Laws* in the Renaissance's re-engagement with Neoplatonism. They not only define the nature of the new Platonic poetics, they also redefine Plato's banishment of the poets, amongst whom were two of the most venerable mentors of the Greeks, the source of their *paideia*.

In the Cinquecento Aristotelian poetics was revived by Italian academicians, as Bernard Weinberg has amply documented,[1] and occasioned a major shift of perspective: from the state of the poet to the shape and genre of the poem; from the nature of inspiration to the labour of the file; from the unveiling of metaphysical truths to the establishing of proper canons for plotting, characterization, and style; from the elusive music of inward ascent to the determination of matters of diction and metre. The confusion that ensued even in the most gifted minds in choosing between these two competing, if not diametrically opposite poetics, is evident in the case of Sidney's *Apology*, but must have been general. However, while a new generation turned with curiosity to Aristotle's ideas on the poem as an object of study and analysis, still it remained fascinated by the Platonic emphasis on the poet as god-possessed subject. These twin foci, indeed, continued to determine the nature of critical debate through the Enlightenment until the situation was transformed by the Romantics and their revolutionary theory concerning the 'esemplastic' powers of what had always been a subordinate and easily deluded faculty, the imagination.

[1] B. Weinberg, *A history of literary criticism in the Italian Renaissance*, 2 vols. (Chicago: University of Chicago Press, 1961).

* * *

Structures of thought: Renaissance Neoplatonism

Primary sources and texts

Ficino, Marsilio, *Opera omnia*; 1576; reprint Turin: Bottega d'Erasmo, 1959, 1962, 1983, ed. P. O. Kristeller and M. Sancipriano, 2 vols.
Landino, Cristoforo, *Scritti critici e teorici*, ed. R. Cardini, Rome: Bulzoni, 1974.
Pico della Mirandola, Giovanni, *Opera omnia*; 1572; reprint Turin: Bottega d'Erasmo, 1971, ed. E. Garin, 2 vols.

Secondary sources

Allen, Michael J. B. *The Platonism of Marsilio Ficino*, Berkeley: University of California Press, 1984.
Plato's third eye: studies in Marsilio Ficino's metaphysics and its sources, Aldershot, Hampshire: Variorum, 1995.
Synoptic art: Marsilio Ficino on the history of Platonic interpretation, Florence: Olschki, 1998.
Cardini, Roberto, *La critica del Landino*, Florence: Sansoni, 1973.
Chastel, André, *Art et humanisme à Florence au temps de Laurent le Magnifique*, Paris: Presses Universitaires de France, 1961.
Marsile Ficin et l'art (1954). Geneva: Droz. 1975.

Coulter, James A. *The literary microcosm: theories of interpretation of the later Neoplatonists*, Leiden: Brill, 1976.

Field, Arthur, *The origins of the Platonic Academy of Florence*, Princeton: Princeton University Press, 1988.

Gombrich, Ernst H. 'Icones symbolicae: philosophies of symbolism and their bearing on art', in *Symbolic images: studies in the art of the Renaissance*, London: Phaidon, 1972, pp. 123–95.

Hankins, James, *Plato in the Italian Renaissance*, Leiden and New York: Brill, 1990, 2 vols.

Kallendorf, Craig, *In praise of Aeneas: Virgil and epideictic rhetoric in the early Italian Renaissance*; 1943; reprint Gloucester, MA: Peter Smith, 1964.

Kristeller, Paul Oskar, *The philosophy of Marsilio Ficino*, New York: Columbia University Press, 1943.

Lamberton, Robert, *Homer the theologian: Neoplatonist allegorical reading and the growth of the epic tradition*, Berkeley: University of California Press, 1986.

Sheppard, Anne D. R. *Studies in the 5th and 6th essays of Proclus' Commentary on the Republic*, Hypomnemata 61, Göttingen: Vandenhoeck and Ruprecht, 1980.

Tigerstedt, E. N. *Plato's idea of poetical inspiration*, Commentationes humanarum litterarum: societas scientiarum Fennica, 44, 2, Helsinki: no pub., 1969.

'The poet as creator: origins of a metaphor', *Comparative literature studies* 5, 4 (1968), 455–88.

Tomlinson, Gary, *Music in Renaissance magic: towards a historiography of others*, Chicago: University of Chicago Press, 1993.

Trimpi, Wesley, *Muses of one mind: the literary analysis of experience and its continuity*, Princeton: Princeton University Press, 1983.

Walker, D. P. *The ancient theology: studies in Christian Platonism from the fifteenth to the eighteenth century*, Ithaca: Cornell University Press, 1972.

Warden, John (ed.), *Orpheus: the metamorphoses of a myth*, Toronto: University of Toronto Press, 1982.

Weinberg, Bernard, *A history of literary criticism in the Italian Renaissance*, Chicago: University of Chicago Press, 1961, 2 vols.

Wind, Edgar, *Pagan mysteries in the Renaissance*, rev. edn, New York: Norton, 1968.

4

Marsilio Ficino: Daemonic Mathematics and the Hypotenuse of the Spirit

One of the enduring questions in medieval and Renaissance philosophy concerns the relationship between nature and art (in Greek *technē*), given that nature herself is full of Plinian art, given too that man's nature is defined by his art, his skills, and his ingeniousness, and given that the daemons and angels are by nature ingenious and intellectual beings. "In brief all things," wrote Sir Thomas Browne in the *Religio Medici* 16, "are artificial." One of the interesting thinkers in this regard is the Florentine Platonist Marsilio Ficino (1433–1499), who produced some of the age's most arresting analyses of the artfulness, and thus of the structure, of both human and daemonic nature and by implication of their capacities to be moved and to be acted on.

Of particular interest is material in the commentary, subtitled *De numero fatali,* that he compiled in the last decade of his life on Plato's notoriously enigmatic passage on the fatal number in book 8 of the *Republic.* But in order to understand Ficino's psychology—both of human beings and of daemons—and his speculative ideas concerning the soul's various faculties, we should first briefly consider some of the mathematical issues confronting him in Plato. For our story has an extraordinary ending and concerns the manner in which the triangular "powers" of the human spirit and habit can be the object of what we would now think of as scientific, and specifically as mathematical, manipulation.

While some interpreters have argued that Plato's metaphysics is fundamentally dualistic in that it postulates an intelligible real world and an illusory material world, Aristotle claimed in his *Metaphysics* 1.6 that Plato had divided all reality into three spheres: ideas or intelligibles, mathematicals, and sensibles. His source for this trichotomy may have been Plato's "Lecture on the Good," as Philip Merlan and others have suggested,[1] or it may have been some later development in Plato's thought. However, as early as the *Phaedo* 101B9–C9 Plato had postulated Forms of numbers, Ideal Numbers, at the same time implying that individual numbers participate in such Numbers while being inferior to them.[2] But Speusippus, Plato's nephew and his successor as head of the Academy from 347 to 339 B.C.E., had apparently dismissed the Ideal Numbers along with the other Forms, and derived the mathematical numbers directly from the One or from the One and the Indefinite Dyad, arguing, according to Aristotle, that such mathematicals were then followed by Soul. Xenocrates, who succeeded Speusippus, is said to have identified Forms with the mathematicals.[3] In the *Enneads* 5.4.2, Plotinus had also derived numbers and the Ideas from the two metaphysical principles of the One and the Indefinite Dyad, as Ficino well knew.[4]

What Speusippus' view does underscore, however, is the problem, given Plato's account in the *Timaeus,* of the role played by the mathematicals, and specifically by ratios, in the creation of Soul and souls. For the Demiurge creates the World-Soul as a kind of mathematical entity, or at least with an arithmetico-geometrical structure. Plutarch's *De animae procreatione* 2.1012D, which Ficino had worked through carefully, asserts indeed that Crantor had interpreted the psychogony in the *Timaeus* as an arithmogony, as the emergence of numbers as the first and principal sphere of reality. Speusippus and Xenocrates also had maintained that the World-Soul was a mathematical entity.[5] According to Iamblichus, Speusippus had described the soul (the World-Soul?) "as the form (*idea*) of what extends in all directions, this form being constituted according to mathematical ratios"; for his part, Xenocrates had defined the soul as "a self-changing number."[6] However, as Plutarch remarked in his *De animae procreatione* 1013CD, to say the soul is constructed with numerical proportions is not the same as saying it is itself a number, and Plato never called the soul a number.

Furthermore, a strange if isolated observation in the *Laws* 10.894A seems to argue that sensibles derive from mathematicals: "things are created when the first principle receives increase and attains to the second dimension, and from this arrives at the one which is neighbor to this, and after reaching the third becomes perceptible to sense."[7] Plato appears to be postulating two "creations": the first of that which is created in "the second dimension," the second of the sensibles in the "third" dimension. The *Timaeus* too is concerned not only with the ratios of the World-Soul but with the mathematics of sensibles. In a famous passage at 53C ff., Timaeus addresses the question concerning the basic constituent of the physical world, arguing that "every rectilinear surface is composed of triangles," meaning presumably that it can be divided up into triangles and that the triangle is the surface created or contained by the least number of straight lines. "Originally," he says, these triangles were only of two kinds, being made up of "one right and two acute angles." The archetypal triangle in the *Timaeus* (and thus, in Ficino's eyes, for Plato) is accordingly a right triangle: subordinate to it are all the obtuse and acute triangles, including the equilateral triangle as well as all non-right scalenes.

The first kind of right triangle is the isosceles with 45 degree angles subtending the right angle, that is, the half-square, and this exists obviously in only one form or nature (*mian physin,* 54A2). The second kind is the right scalene, which exists in a "countless" (*aperantous*) number of forms. But, Timaeus continues, of these countless right scalene forms we must select "the fairest" (*to kalliston,* 54A3); and the fairest triangle is that having "the square of the longer side equal to three times the square of the lesser side" (54B4–5).[8] What Plato must have in mind therefore—since Timaeus had already said at 54A7 that a pair of such triangles would form an equilateral triangle and now says that the squares, not the square roots, have the ratio—is a half-equilateral triangle, one with angles of 90, 60, and 30 degrees and a base of 1 (the lesser side), a perpendicular of $\sqrt{3}$ (the greater or longer side), and a hypotenuse of 2. This at least is the traditional view (espoused, for instance, by Albinus in his *Didaskalikos* 13, which Ficino translated, though he like others attributed it to Alcinous); and it is the one carefully propounded by Ficino himself in chapter 41 of his appendix for the final version of his *Timaeus* commentary.[9] It means, of course, that the perpendicular is not a whole number, the first instance of a triangle with all three sides as whole numbers being the famous 5–4–3 triangle beloved of the Pythagoreans. But Ficino recognized that this 5–4–3 triangle cannot itself be "the fairest" of scalenes, since the square of its "lesser" side is not a third that of the square of either of the two longer sides. In short, Timaeus must mean by the "fairest" the *hemitrigon,* the half-equilateral, of 1, $\sqrt{3}$, and 2.

Timaeus goes on to assert that both the isosceles and the half-equilateral triangles are the "original constituents" or "principles" (*archai*) of the four material elements at the heart of nature because they are the constituents of four of the five regular solids. The half-equilateral, with its $\sqrt{3}$ perpendicular, is the base principle of three of them, since 24 such scalenes constitute the tetrahedron or pyramid that makes up the molecules, as it were, of fire; 48 of them, the octahedron that makes up the molecules of air; and 120 of them, the icosahedron that makes up the molecules of water (each of the tetrahedron's 4, the octahedron's 8, and the icosahedron's 20 equilateral faces having 6 constituent half-equilaterals—6 being in traditional Platonic arithmology the perfect, the Jovian number).[10] The salient implication is that the Pythagorean theorem is the first mathematical tool needed by a natural philosopher in order to understand both the three superior elements and the fiery, airy, and watery bodies they compose, those animated by the souls of the daemons. The cube, however, which is the regular solid that makes up the molecules of earth, is constituted from 24 isosceles right triangles: that is, from 24 half-squares.[11] The fifth regular solid, the dodecahedron with 12 pentagonal faces, is assigned by the *Timaeus* 55C to "the whole" that is decorated with designs, namely with the 12 heavenly constellations (though the *Epinomis* 981C assigns the dodecahedron to the aether). It cannot, however, be constructed from the right triangles, although ancient commentators including Albinus and Ficino himself thought it consisted of 360 such triangles (again 12 x 5 x 6), the number of the degrees of the zodiacal circle.[12] The physical sublunar world consists of the perpetual dissolution and accretion of the triangles constituting four of these five regular solids, which at 54D6 are said to be like the "syllables" in nature's book, the elementary triangles being the letters of those syllables.[13] Fire, air, and water can be transformed into each other, since they all consist of half-equilaterals, while earth can be broken up only into its isosceles triangles.

Given the figural nature of early arithmetic in the Pythagorean tradition that Ficino revived and adhered to, and given the primacy it accorded to the monad and therefore to the odd numbers, it follows that the series of odd numbers, 1 + 3 + 5 + 7 + 9 . . . , figuring as it does a gnomon of increasing size in what Ficino calls the equilateral sequence summing 4, 9, 16, 25, . . . , privileges the isosceles right triangle. The scalene, by contrast, figures the summing of even numbers in the unequilateral series of 6, 12, 20, 30, . . . , and the equilateral triangle, the summing of odd and even numbers in the regular trigon series of 3, 6, 10, 15, ... But since two equal isosceles triangles constitute a square and their shared hypotenuse the diagonal of that square, the hypotenuse can never be rational in the sense of being a whole number. Thus we get a series of irrational hypotenuses on the model of $\sqrt{2}$ for a side of 1, of $\sqrt{8}$ for a side of 2, of $\sqrt{18}$ for a side of 3, and then of $\sqrt{32}$, $\sqrt{50}$, $\sqrt{72}$, and so on.

However, Ficino supposed that Plato was already familiar with a formula that could determine what he and his contemporaries thought of as the rational value of the diagonals of a particular series of these $\sqrt{2}$ squares, and therefore of the hypotenuses of their constituent isosceles triangles; namely, those having sides of 1, 2, 5, 12, 29, 70, and so on. This formula, which Ficino encountered in Theon of Smyrna's *Expositio* 1.31, demonstrates that if we subtract and add 1 in alternation to the sum of the squares of the two equal sides, then we end up with 2 – 1, 8 + 1, 50 – 1, 288 + 1, and so on; that is, with square powers for which rational square roots exist. Put algebraically, the formula of subtracting or adding one provides a series of positive, integral solutions for the equation $y^2 = 2z^2 + /- 1$ or $y^2 + /- 1 = 2z^2$, where y is the diagonal and z is the side. Accordingly, Ficino thought of the hypotenuses of such a series of isosceles triangles (or the squares they constitute) as having both rational and irrational square roots, the rational roots being primary: for example, 50 has the irrational root of 7.0710678 . . . but the rational root of 7. Since the +1/–1 alternation providing us with rational roots for what would otherwise possess only irrational roots is regular (if the sides are odd, 1 has to be subtracted from the sum of their squares; if even, then added to it), the powers of the diagonals in the series can be viewed in the long run as maintaining a ratio of 2:1 to the powers of the side. To arrive at the sequence of such rational diagonals, we must add the value of the diagonal to the side, while adding twice the value of the side to the diagonal. The sequence of diagonals then runs 3, 7, 17, 41, 99, and that of the sides 1, 2, 5, 12, 29, 70, and so on.[14]

Ficino thought of these diagonal numbers as being "of the 5" because the first instance in the series, leaving aside the isosceles with a side of 1, is the isosceles with a side of 2 and a rational diagonal of 3, and 2 + 3 = 5. Aristides Quintilianus, incidentally, had declared in the case of another kind of perfect triangle—the Pythagoreans' right scalene of 5–4–3—that the sides at the right angle are in the relationship of epitritus (4:3), and that "it is the root of epitritus [meaning 7 (4 + 3)] added to 5 [the root of the 3:2 ratio] that Plato was referring to in the *Republic* [8.546A ff.]."[15] This "perfect" scalene provided Ficino with the keys to solving the great mystery of the Fatal Number, for the value of its sides sum to 12, which when cubed produces 1,728—the value, for him, of the Number. But if its "root" of 7 is added to 5, which is the "root" of the first isosceles, the sum is also 12. Ficino sees these roots as 4:3 and 3:2 ratios, and as being invested with musical connotations as the "consonances" of diatesseron, the perfect fourth, and of diapente, the perfect fifth.[16]

Hence for the two kinds of right triangle, Ficino knew of two ways to determine the value of the hypotenuse as an integer: first for the Pythagoreans' "perfect" scalenes with sides of 3 and 4, 9 and 12, 27 and 36, and so on, by way of the Pythagorean theorem; and second for those isosceles triangles (half-squares) with sides of 2, 5, 12, 29, and so on, by way of the same theorem after the application of Theon's plus or minus one rule.[17] He knew of no way, however, to determine rational perpendiculars for the half-equilateral triangles, Plato's "fairest" scalenes.

If the triangle dominates the subelemental world of planes and surfaces (the "second dimension" of the *Laws* 10 passage) and the solids they constitute, then man too must be subject to the triangle, at least insofar as he is subject in this life to time and space, his nature to Nature.[18] However, his nature is defined for Ficino by his possession of a *habitus,* from which indeed we and the monks get the word "habit," and which is etymologically linked to the verb *habere,* "to have." *Habitus* can be rendered in English as "character" and "condition," though it cannot be used to signify the interdependent notions of skill, talent, wit, and ingenuity for which Ficino deploys the term *ingenium.* The *habitus* can refer, his *Platonic Theology* maintains, to the natural optimum condition of the body—the goal, if you will, of medicine[19]—and as such it can be said "to pass into" or "to take over" our nature, or to become as it were a second nature that moves us while remaining immobile itself.[20] It can also "play the part of" or "do duty for" our "natural form."[21] The soul itself, even when separated from the body, has a *habitus* by which it is moved. Ficino believes of course that the soul only (re)acquires its true *habitus* when it has returned to its "head," that is, to its "intelligence" *(mens).*[22]

Indeed, the acquisition of such a *habitus* becomes man's primary goal, since it contains the soul's *formulae idearum,* which, when led forth into act, enable the soul to rise from the sensible to the intelligible, and to be joined with the Ideas.[23] For the true *habitus* contains the species or Ideas as they are present in us, the species indeed that correspond to all things that exist in the world in act.[24] What makes for the acquisition of a perfect *habitus,* whether of the body, the soul, the human mind, or the angelic mind, is both *praeparatio* and *affectio.*[25] The *habitus* is thus tied conceptually both to the notion of form—the *habitus* being the condition of ourselves or of some part of ourselves that most nearly approximates to the perfection of our form—and to the notion of power, the power that we have been born with but have nurtured by *praeparatio* and by *disciplina.* We can even think of it as the potentiality in our soul for becoming pure mind in the actuality of its perfect circular motion, the motion-in-rest of contemplation. Immobile itself, it nevertheless provides the soul with the "proclivity" for the absolute motion that is blessed, eternal life.

In arguing Platonically in his *De numero fatali* 16 that our "composed body" is a "discordant concord," Ficino turns predictably to two analogies, a musical one and a mathematical one, for what endows it with concord—namely an even *habitus.* Even *habitus* are like the harmonies of different voices in a choir, uniting in the diapason; and they also resemble the sums that are generated from the odd numbers in the equilateral addition series of 1 + 3 + 5 + 7, and so on. Odd *habitus,* by contrast, are generated from even numbers, meaning from the even numbers in the unequilateral addition series of 2 + 4 + 6 + 8, and so on. Thus an even-tempered *habitus* is like any equilateral sum—4, 9, 16. As a sum it is the child of the odd numbers, but as a product it is the result of equality and balance, of a number having multiplied itself, that is, having raised itself to the second power, squaring or square-rooting being the meaning of *dynamis* in Greek in a mathematical context, as both Plato's and Euclid's usage bears witness.[26]

If the *habitus,* our nature, is a kind of mathematical and specifically a geometrical power, squaring, then must we think of it as functioning like such a power, at least in particular contexts? In other words, does the *habitus* or nature of the soul (and of its spirit and its body) work like the square power of the hypotenuse of an isosceles right-angled triangle (or of the diagonal of a square constituted from two such triangles, which is the same thing); and is it therefore equal to double the square of either side (i.e., to the sum of the squares of both sides)? If so, we must entertain the possibility that the Pythagorean theorem has come to haunt the face of Ficino's faculty psychology. But what is the evidence that this is anything more than just an arresting image or a mere turn of phrase?

The traditional schema of the point progressing to the line to the plane (surface) to the solid goes back at least to the Pythagoreans and is repeated throughout antiquity and the Middle Ages.[27] Ficino turns to it on occasion to help define the serial subordination of the four hypostases in the Plotinian metaphysical system, the One, Mind, Soul, and Body;[28] and in doing so he often identifies the point with the One and the solid with Body—examples abound throughout his work. But he also identifies the line (and certainly the circular line) with Mind, and the plane with Soul.[29] While, to my knowledge, he nowhere advances all the elements of this series of analogies in one formal argument, he does introduce them here and there, and the schema obviously serves as one of his paradigms for metaphysical progression and hierarchical subordination. The implications for our understanding of the soul's internal structure and of its position on the Platonic scale of being in Ficino are, I believe, as bizarre as they are unexpected.

Ficino's governing text here is again the *Timaeus* 53C ff., duly bracketed by Timaeus himself as presenting views that are only "probable." Having introduced the two kinds of right-angled triangles, Timaeus had proceeded at 69C ff. to describe the creation by the Demiurge's sons of the irrational soul and at 73B ff. their taking up the triangles (i.e., before their combination into the regular solids) to mix them in "due proportions" in order to make the marrow, which will serve as a "universal seed" and a vehicle for the soul. Ficino clearly rejoiced in some at least of the figural extensions (with the puns this term implies) of the Pythagorean mathematics that Timaeus is propounding here. For his own *Timaeus* commentary explores the implications and arrives at an interpretation that identified the soul itself as the exemplary triangle, its triple powers corresponding to the three angles and the three sides of the archetypal geometrical figure. At the end of chapter 28, having observed that "mathematicals accord with the soul, for we judge both of them to be midway between divine and natural things," he writes:

> We use not only numbers to describe the soul but also <geometrical> figures so that we can think of the soul by way of numbers as incorporeal but by way of figures as naturally declining toward the corporeal. The triangle accords with the soul; for just as the triangle from one angle extends to two more, so the soul, which flows out from an indivisible and divine substance, sinks into the entirely divisible nature of the body. If we compare the soul as it were to things divine, then it seems divided. For what they achieve through one unchanging power and in an instant, the soul achieves through many changing powers and actions and over intervals of time. But if we compare the soul to things natural, then we judge it to be indivisible. For it has no sundry parts as they have, separated here and there in place, but it is whole even in any one part of the whole; nor, as they do, does it pursue everything in motion and in time, but it attains something in a moment and possesses it eternally. In this we can compare the soul, moreover, to the triangle, because the triangle is the first figure of those figures which consist of many lines and are led forth into extension or in a right angle (*in rectum*). Similarly, the soul is the first of all to be divided up into many powers—powers that are subjected in it to the understanding—and it seems to be led forth into extension when it sinks from divinity down into nature. In this descent it flows out from the highest understanding down into three lower powers, that is, into discursive reasoning, into sense, and into the power of quickening, just as the triangle too, having been led forth from the point (*signum*),[30] is drawn out into three angles. But I say the soul is the first in the genus of all to be mingled from many powers in a way, and to fall, so to speak, into extension or into a right angle (*in rectum*). For above the soul the angelic mind requires no inferior powers within itself at all and is pure and whole and sufficient.[31]

Given this fully worked out analogy of the soul with the triangle, preeminently the right-angled triangle, and given that the triangle is the premier figure of the planar realm of surfaces, Ficino clearly thinks of soul, or at least of soul in its fallen triplicity, as planar.[32] Indeed, given the variety of geometrical and arithmetical structures that govern our notion of a two-dimensional realm, the plane and its subdivisions are ideally suited to modeling the complex and ambivalent status of soul and its various faculties as intermediary between the three-dimensional body and the paradoxically linear or circular realm of pure mind—linear because it is both one and many, and circular because it is "one and equal" like the line that returns upon itself to constitute the figure that is not a figure but rather the principle and end of figures. Furthermore, the secret of the planar realm of the triangle for Ficino is the notion of power, *dynamis,* again meaning squaring or square-rooting.[33] For it is this alone that enables us to comprehend the complex, invisible proportionality and comparability of hypotenuse to side, to comprehend the geometrical ratios that govern reality.

If the *habitus* is, or functions like, a planar number, and specifically a square number or the root of such a number, it would serve in unexpected ways to validate the efficacy of, and to enlarge the scope of, a purely mathematical magic; in so doing it would privilege the beings preeminently gifted in Ficino's view for the subtleties of mathematics, namely the daemons. We might imagine a special mathematical dimension for the lower daemons on the one hand in supervising the diet, regimen, and exercise that ensures an even *habitus* in the body; and for the higher daemons on the other in disciplining the soul—over and beyond, that is, instructing it in ordinary mathematical procedures—so that it too attains an even *habitus.* But nowhere would their role be more arresting than in the case of the *habitus* of the *spiritus,* since the *spiritus* is for Ficino the object of manipulation by magicians using the resources of natural and of astral magic (and perhaps using, however unconsciously, the mathematical structures and powers that underlie such magics).[34] The *habitus* of the spirit, the hypotenuse if you will of the spirit, would be subject a fortiori to expressly mathematical manipulation—especially to the manipulation of human and daemonic geometers, those skilled above all others in the understanding of planes and surfaces. It would lend a dramatic but also a scientific dimension to the monitory exhortation in the vestibule to the Platonic Academy, "Let no one enter here who is not an adept in geometry," and to Plutarch's declaration, in a phrase he attributes to Plato, that "God is always working as a geometer" (*Aei theos geōmetrei*).[35]

Ficino had an abiding fascination with the branch of applied geometry having a singular role in daemonic magic, namely the science of optics.[36] Ficino seems to have thought of the magician using his own *spiritus* as a mirror to catch, focus, and reflect the streams or rays of *idola* or images that flow ceaselessly out from animate and inanimate objects.[37] The *idola,* and the *spiritus* that focuses the *idola,* are the means whereby he can work with and work upon anything, living as well as inert, from a distance. Aspects of his skill may be irrational or sophistical, and may be controlled in large part by his phantasy; but a particular magician, one skilled in mathematics, Ficino imagines as being able to draw on numbers, I believe, and notably on figured numbers, to effect a rational magic by way of his *spiritus* upon the *idola.* Such a magician might even consciously program his *spiritus* like a radar dish, tilting and rotating its planes according to geometrical formulae encoding and controlling particular magical operations; those formulae, in other words, best suited to affecting the dimensions, the angles, the powers that govern a physical world constituted from triangles and from the four (or for Ficino obviously the five) regular solids to which they give rise. After all, such a geometer-magus would be exercising his sovereignty over the powers governing the optical triangles formed by the objects and the *idola* he wished to perceive or manipulate, the reflecting surface of his *spiritus,* and the line of his intelligence. Clearly such triangles would themselves consist of laterals and diagonals and have rational and irrational powers; and double the sum of the degrees of their varying angles would equal the 360 degrees of the perfect circle, the zodiac, of the understanding.

In exercising these geometrical powers, the geometer-magus would be drawing on the computational and manipulative skills that Ficino and the later Platonic tradition he inherited had already assigned to the daemons. For daemons not only are the masters of mathematics, they also preside over the world of light and its optical effects and illusions, and consequently over the singular role that mirrors and prisms, reflections and refractions, play in our understanding of, and in our manipulation of, light. Moreover, they are the denizens preeminently of the world of surfaces, planes, and powers, and only the basest of them choose regularly to inhabit the three-dimensional cubicity of the physical world. In this they resemble other higher souls; for all souls are properly inhabitants, in Ficino's Platonic imagination, of the realm of planes and surfaces (preeminently rectilinear ones), though they may be imprisoned for a time in solids. In that they aspire to return to the intellectual realm, however, to become pure intellects and to contemplate the mathematicals and the Ideas of numbers, they aspire, mathematically speaking, to the "one and equal" line, the circling line of Nous; ultimately they wish to return to the unity at the apex of intelligible reality, to the One in its transcendence. Specifically, given the unique role of the triangle in Platonic mathematics and psychology (and of the Pythagorean theorem in computing the relationship of the power of the hypotenuse to the powers of the sides), we must think of the highest rational souls—those of the daemons, or at least of the higher ones who dwell far above the terraqueous orb—as the lords of triangularity and of the "comparability" that governs it, triangularity being the essence of the planar realm. We might even speculate about the devious ways the daemons practice on our mathematical sanity with irrational hypotenuses and surds or torment us with Theon's plus or minus one theorem!

The planar world occurs in Nature herself in the mirrors of lakes and pools and of other water and ice surfaces; one can also think of snow, salt, white sand, and even various rock surfaces, as well as of certain mist and cloud phenomena, that have planar qualities and whose surfaces reflect or refract light. Preeminently of course the planar world occurs in the natural faceting of precious stones, gems, and crystals. It is in the play of light on such surfaces that the presence of daemonic geometry and its science of powers can best be glimpsed by the geometer-magus. On occasions he is able even to use his own *spiritus* as a mirror-plane to capture and affect the *idola,* immaterial and material alike, that stream off objects, refiguring them by way of recourse to the laws of figured numbers. For physical light is the intermediary between the sensible and the purely intelligible realms, and in this regard it is spiritual: it resembles and therefore—given the ancient formula that like affects like[38]—can be influenced by the *spiritus,* the substance that mediates between the body and the soul and serves as the link, as light itself does, between the otherwise divided realms of the pure forms and of informed matter.

It was this eccentric nexus of concerns that, I believe, slowly emerged in Ficino's mind and led him to posit a problematic set of interdependent connections between magic, geometry, figural arithmetic, the daemons, and light in its various manifestations. Underlying the nexus is the notion of a mathematical power and the mysterious hold it exercises over our understanding of both planes and solids. And with this understanding, predictably, comes actual power to affect and change. In all this we can glimpse the profound impact on Ficino of Plato's Pythagorean mathematics, and specifically of the Pythagorean theorem, together with Theon's discussion of diagonal powers, on the one hand, and Plato's fanciful but influential presentation in the *Timaeus* of a triangle-based physics on the other.

The relationship in Ficino's mind between optics, and notably daemonic optics, and music—that is, between light wave theory and sound wave theory and the "harmonic" proportions that govern them—has yet to be explored.[39] What we must now realize, however, is that for him the planar numbers and especially the square numbers occupy a mysterious but all-powerful position between the prime numbers and the cubes;[40] and the mathematical functions of squaring and of square-rooting are envisaged as the powers that govern these planar numbers and therefore govern two-dimensional, and particularly triangular, space. This is the space that constitutes preeminently the realm of the daemons, or at least of the airy daemons and the daemons inferior to them, whose spiritual "bodies" or airy "envelopes" we might think of as themselves functioning like two-dimensional surfaces, governed by their *habitus,* by *dynameis,* by squares, and by square roots. Hence the manipulative power the daemons exercise over all two-dimensional surfaces, including each other's, and hence their innate attraction to such surfaces and especially to crystals, to faceted stones and gems, and to mirrors. But this entire planar world is, from a Platonic viewpoint, presided over by the Pythagorean geometry of hypotenuses and thus of triangles, half-squares and half-equilaterals, themselves vestiges of the greatest triangle of all, the Trinity. From the geometry of the triangle we ascend to the still more mysterious geometry of the circle and thence of the point, the unextended monad that is the image of the One.

In short, apart from the psychological and theological dimensions, four related scientific fields are affected by this Platonic triangularism: optics, music (specifically harmonics), astronomy-astrology with its star and therefore time triangles, and finally what we might call scientific daemonology. For Ficino's assumptions about the planar realm and its triangularity make the summoning of daemons a kind of science, however strained or paradoxical this claim might first appear. Communication or traffic with them has for him a mathematical, and specifically a geometrical, foundation. The notion of roots and powers—that is, of self-division and self-multiplication—suggests that daemonic agency is ever present in the realm of mathematics. But it suggests too that daemonic depths and angelic heights in ourselves are at heart mathematical conditions, *habitus* subject to mathematical laws, and that our ideas and the absolute Ideas can even be numbers with their powers and roots, as Xenocrates had originally supposed.

One of the curiosities of Platonism in the Renaissance is its impact on areas we would not immediately associate with it: daemonology, astrology, optics, and musical theory. But in many respects Ficino was simply recovering the enthusiasms and interests of the mathematical Platonism that had also interested Plotinus. It had emerged from the accounts in Aristotle and in the notices he and others had provided of the views of such early Platonists as Speusippus, Xenocrates, and Crantor, whose mathematical interests were later channeled into the works of Theon, Nicomachus, Aristoxenus, and Aristides. These were the thinkers who, in Ficino's view, had truly understood the *Timaeus* and were thus in a position to interpret the various enigmatic mathematical references elsewhere in Plato: in the *Laws,* in the *Epinomis,* and in book 8 of the *Republic.* An awareness of this mathematical Platonism (dominated by geometrical ratios) is surely called for if we are ever to establish with confidence the valencies governing early modern science, its artful exploration of Browne's "things artificial." Certainly, though awaiting further exploration, it will constitute an important chapter in the history of that science.

NOTES

1. Philip Merlan, "Greek Philosophy from Plato to Plotinus," *Cambridge History of Later Greek and Early Medieval Philosophy,* ed. A. H. Armstrong, repr. with corrections (Cambridge: Cambridge University Press, 1970), p. 16. For the "Lecture" see, for example, Ingemar Düring, *Aristotle in the Ancient Biographical Tradition* (Göteborg; [distr. Stockholm: Almqvist and Wiksell,] 1957), pp. 357–361; Konrad Gaiser, *Platons ungeschriebene Lehre* (Stuttgart: Klett, 1963), pp. 452–453; and Gilbert Ryle, *Plato's Progress* (Cambridge: Cambridge University Press, 1966), pp. 251–256.

2. W. K. C. Guthrie, *A History of Greek Philosophy* (Cambridge: Cambridge University Press, 1962–1981), 4:523.

3. Thomas L. Heath, *Mathematics in Aristotle* (Oxford: Clarendon, 1949), p. 220; Merlan, "Greek Philosophy," p. 31; Guthrie, *History,* 5:459–460, 473.

4. Merlan, "Greek Philosophy," p. 21n.

5. Ibid., p. 18.

6. Speusippus fr. 40 in *De Speusippi Academici scriptis,* ed. P. Lang (Bonn, 1911; reprinted Frankfurt: Minerva, 1964); Xenocrates fr. 60 in *Xenokrates: Darstellung der Lehre und Sammlung der Fragmente,* ed. R. Heinze (Leipzig: Teubner, 1892). Cf. Diogenes Laertius, *Lives of the Philosophers* 3.67. Merlan concludes that "the *Timaeus* and the doctrines of Speusippus and Xenocrates seem to point to some kind of equation between the mathematicals and the soul, whether we take soul to mean cosmic or individual soul" ("Greek Philosophy," p. 18). We might note, incidentally, that in his *De defectu oraculorum* 13 (*Moralia* 416CD), Plutarch says that Xenocrates assimilated the equilateral triangle (where all parts are equal) to the divine class, the scalene (where all parts are unequal) to the mortal, and the isosceles (where they are mixed) to the daemonic. See Richard Heinze in *Xenokrates . . . Fragmente,* pp. 166–167, fr. 24; D. H. Fowler, *The Mathematics of Plato's Academy: A New Reconstruction* (Oxford: Clarendon; New York: Oxford University Press, 1987), p. 299; and Guthrie, *History,* 5:467, 479.

7. Merlan, "Greek Philosophy," pp. 19–20; see also Francis M. Cornford, *Plato and Parmenides* (London: K. Paul, Trench, Trübner, 1939), pp. 14 ff., 198.

8. *Timaeus,* in *The Dialogues of Plato,* trans. Benjamin Jowett, 4th ed. (Oxford: Clarendon, 1953), 3:741.

9. See Ficino's *Opera Omnia* (Basel, 1576; reprinted, Turin: Bottega d'Erasmo, 1983), p. 1475.1: "Cum in triangulo aequilatero per divisionem a summo scalenum designaveris, scito latus huius scaleni longius, id est, erectum super angulum rectum esse, secundum potentiam triplo maiorem latere minore iacente eundemque rectum angulum continente. Nam si ex illo latere quadratum aequilaterum constitueris seorsumque ex hoc latere alterum, illud ad hoc erit triplum. Linea hypotinusa, id est subducta vel subtendens [*Op.* subtendus], est quae quasi e transverso ab hoc latere ad illud producitur opposita angulo recto ipsa, angulos utrinque acutos efficiens. Nam [*Op.* Nec] longitudine latus minus duplo superat. Haec enim totum aequilateri primi latus adaequat. Hoc vero dimidium lateris

illius existit. Si autem ex linea subducta aequilaterum fiat quadratum, aequale erit duobus quadratis, hinc quidem ex maiore latere, inde vero ex minore confectis. Pythagorae hoc inventum." In general, see A. E. Taylor, *A Commentary on Plato's Timaeus* (Oxford: Clarendon, 1928), p. 372. For Ficino's rendering of Albinus' *Didaskalikos,* see his *Opera,* p. 1953.1.

10. Cf. Albinus, *Didaskalikos* 13. For six's perfection, see my *Nuptial Arithmetic: Marsilio Ficino's Commentary on the Fatal Number in Book VIII of Plato's "Republic"* (Berkeley: University of California Press, 1994), pp. 50–53, 67–68, 129–132. Francis M. Cornford, *Plato's Cosmology: The Timaeus of Plato Translated with a Running Commentary* (London: K. Paul, Trench, Trübner; New York: Harcourt, Brace, 1937), p. 213, notes that the equilateral triangle, despite its being non-right, is present in the faces of the polyhedra constituting the first three solids.

11. Cf. Albinus, *Didaskalikos* 13; Ficino, *In Timaeum* 44 (misnumbered XLI) (*Opera,* pp. 1953.1, 1464v.1). Incidentally, Ficino thought Plato had used the cube for the Fatal Number in part because it presides over time, and thus over the twenty-four-hour cycle. Karl Popper, *Conjectures and Refutations,* 3rd ed. (London: Routledge and Kegan Paul, 1969), pp. 75–93, has argued that Plato chose the isosceles and the half-equilateral triangles because they pose the problem of $\sqrt{2}$ and $\sqrt{3}$ and therefore of the rational existence of irrational numbers. See also Stephen Toulmin and June Goodfield, *The Architecture of Matter* (London: Pelican Books, 1965), pp. 75–82.

12. Again see Albinus, *Didaskalikos* 13; Ficino, *In Timaeum* 44 (*Opera,* pp. 1953.1, 1464v.1). See also Cornford, *Plato's Cosmology,* p. 218.

13. Taylor, *Commentary on Timaeus,* p. 373.

14. For Plato and this Pythagorean mathematics, see, for example, Thomas L. Heath, *A History of Greek Mathematics,* 2 vols. (Oxford, 1921; reprinted, New York: Dover, 1981); Charles Mugler, *Platon et la recherche mathématique de son époque* (Strasbourg, 1948; reprinted, Naarden: A. W. van Bekhoven, 1969); Paul Henri Michel, *De Pythagore à Euclide: Contribution à l'histoire des mathématiques préeuclidiennes* (Paris: Les Belles Lettres, 1950); idem, *Les nombres figurés dans l'arithmétique pythagoricienne* (Paris: [En vente à la librairie du Palais de la decouverte], 1958).

15. Aristides Quintilianus, *De musica* 3.23, ed. R. P. Winnington-Ingram (Leipzig: Teubner, 1963), p. 124.25–26.

16. See my *Nuptial Arithmetic,* pp. 28–30, 74–80.

17. Ibid., pp. 56–57.

18. The following section is adapted from my *Nuptial Arithmetic,* pp. 89–99.

19. Marsilio Ficino, *Platonic Theology* 11.5 (ed. Raymond Marcel [Paris: Les Belles Lettres, 1964–1970], 2:129): "Complexio quoque plantarum et animalium quam mirabili medicinae artis solertia utitur in conservando habitu naturali aut recuperando" (Marcel renders *habitu* here as "équilibre").

20. Ibid. 15.18 (ed. Marcel, 3:98): "habitus, qui transit in subiecti naturam, immo subiecti naturam usurpat ipse sibi, certam praestat proclivitatem et subiectum movet immobilis."

21. Ibid. 15.19 (ed. Marcel, 3:103): "habitus non imaginarium quiddam est, sed naturalis formae gerit vicem."

22. Ibid. 18.8 (ed. Marcel, 3:200): "Ita enim animus habitu movetur et agit, sicut natura formis. . . . Remanere vero in anima separata habitus tum morum tum disciplinarum tam bonos quam malos . . . dicitur habitum ita in naturam converti"; 16.7 (ed. Marcel, 3:134–135): "motus et habitus animae, quatenus intellectualis rationalisque est, circuitus esse debeat . . . cum primum animus in caput suum, id est mentem, erectus, in habitum suum prorsus restituetur."

23. Ibid. 12.1 (ed. Marcel, 2:154): "Igitur mens per formulam suam ex habitu eductam in actum ideae divinae quadam praeparatione subnectitur."

24. Ibid. 15.16 (ed. Marcel, 3:83–84): "habitum reformandi, . . . respondebimus vim mentis eandem, quae et contrahit et servat habitum in eius naturam iam pene conversum, contrahere in intima sua speciem atque servare. Siquidem habitus fundatur in speciebus, species in habitu concluduntur. Proinde si habitus fit a mente, specie atque actu, ab aliquo istorum stabilitatem suam nanciscitur. . . . A specie igitur"; 13.2 (ed. Marcel, 2:210): "Mens autem . . . habitu quodam et, ut vult Plotinus [2.9.1; 3.9.1(?)], actu simul continet omnia."

25. Ibid. 14.6 (ed. Marcel, 2:268): "Nam praeparatio sive affectio formam habitumque respicit, atque certa quaedam affectio certum habitum"; and again 15.19 (ed. Marcel, 3:102), "praeparationes, quantum ad certos habitus conferunt atque cum illis proportione aliqua congruunt, tantum habitus diversos impediunt."

26. Cf. Plato's *Republic* 9.587D9 (square) with the *Theaetetus* 147D3 ff. (square root); and Euclid, *Elements* 10. See Heath, *History of Greek Mathematics,* 1:155; Taylor, *Commentary on Timaeus,* p. 372.

27. Ficino was probably introduced to the schema in Aristotle: see, for example, *Topics* 4, 141b5–22, and *Metaphysics* 3.5, 1001b26–1002b11.

28. On Ficino's variations on this system, see Paul O. Kristeller, *The Philosophy of Marsilio Ficino* (New York, 1943; reprinted, Gloucester, Mass.: P. Smith, 1964), pp. 106–108, 167–169, 266, 370, 384, 400–401; and my "Ficino's Theory of the Five Substances and the Neoplatonists' *Parmenides,*" *Journal of Medieval and Renaissance Studies* 12 (1982): 19–44, with further references. See also Tamara Albertini, *Marsilio Ficino: Das Problem der Vermittlung von Denken und Welt in einer Metaphysik der Einfachheit* (Munich: Wilhelm Fink Verlag, 1997), part 2.

29. See, for instance, Ficino's letter to Lotterio Neroni, the penultimate letter in the third book of his *Epistulae* (*Opera*, p. 750.3). Here he speaks of being either in "the undivided and motionless center" as in the one God, or in "the divided and mobile circumference" as in heaven and the elements, or in the "individual lines" that mediate between them, beginning at the center as undivided and motionless but gradually becoming divided and

"mutable" as they approach the circumference. In these lines are the souls and minds. Cf. Pico della Mirandola, *Conclusiones DCCCC, Conclusiones secundum mathematicam Pythagorae,* nos. 13 ("Quilibet numerus planus aequilaterus animam symbolizat") and 14 ("Quilibet numerus linearis symbolizat deos"), in his *Opera Omnia* (Basel, 1572), p. 79.

30. Cf. Ficino's *Timaeus* commentary 22 (*Opera,* p. 1449.3): "Quattuor apud mathematicum: signum, linea, planum atque profundum."

31. *Platonis Opera Omnia,* 2nd ed. (Venice, 1491), trans. M. Ficino, fol. 246v (sig. G[6]v) (i.e., *Opera,* pp. 1452–1453 [misnumbered 1450 and 1417]): "Congruunt animae mathematica, utraque enim inter divina et naturalia media iudicantur. Congruunt musici numeri animae plurimum, mobiles enim sunt; proptereaque animam quae est principium motionis rite significant. Non solum vero per numeros sed etiam per figuras describitur anima ut per numeros quidem incorporea cogitetur, per figuras autem cognoscatur ad corpora naturaliter declinare. Convenit triangulus animae. Quia sicut triangulus ab uno angulo in duos protenditur, sic anima ab individua divinaque substantia profluens in naturam corporis labitur penitus divisibilem. Ac si cum divinis conferatur, divisa videtur; quae enim illa per unam et stabilem virtutem agunt atque subito, haec per plures mutabilesque vires actionesque peragit ac temporis intervallis. Sin autem conferatur cum naturalibus, indivisa censetur; non enim alibi habet partes alias loco disiunctas ut illa [*Op.* alia], sed etiam [*Op.* est] in qualibet totius parte tota; neque omnia mobiliter temporeque persequitur sicut illa, sed nonnihil etiam subito [*Op.* subiecto] consequitur aeterneque possidet. Licet in hoc insuper animam cum triangulo comparare, quod triangulus prima figura est earum quae pluribus constantes lineis producuntur in rectum; anima similiter prima omnium in plures distribuitur vires quae in ipsa intelligentiae subiguntur, ac produci videtur in rectum dum a divinitate labitur in naturam. In quo quidem descensu ab intelligentia summa in tres profluit vires inferiores, id est, in discursum quendam rationalem, in sensum, in vegetandi virtutem, quemadmodum et triangulus a signo productus in tres deducitur angulos. Dico autem animam ex omnium genere primam et ex pluribus quodammodo viribus commisceri et in rectum, ut ita dixerim, cadere. Mens enim angelica super [*Plat. Op.* semper] animam inferioribus intra se nullis indiget viribus, sed pura [*Op.* plura] mens est totaque mens atque sufficiens."

Chapter 28 is titled "De compositione animae et quod per quinarium in ea componenda opportune proceditur."

32. In his *Timaeus* commentary 34 (*Opera,* p. 1460), having discussed the lambda numbers, Ficino goes on to describe a metaphysical triangle governed by the double, sesquialteral, and sesquitertial properties: its apex is essence and its two sides consist of the infinite, difference, and motion, and of the limit, identity, and rest—the fundamental ontological categories explored in the *Sophist* and *Philebus;* see my *Icastes: Marsilio Ficino's Interpretation of Plato's Sophist* (Berkeley: University of California Press, 1989), chap. 2. He concludes by postulating a corresponding triangle for the soul: its unity is its essence, its will the infinite, its understanding the limit, its imagination difference, its reason identity, its power to procreate (*generandi vis*) motion, its power to join (*connectendi virtus*) rest. The whole topic awaits investigation.

33. For Ficino, either rational and irrational square roots or the squares of these roots can be deemed "powers."

34. In the *De amore* 7.4 (ed. Raymond Marcel [Paris: Les Belles Lettres, 1956], p. 247), Ficino had defined *spiritus* as "a vapor of the blood." For the various senses of *spiritus* in Ficino, see my *Platonism of Marsilio Ficino: A Study of His Phaedrus Commentary. Its Sources, and Genesis* (Berkeley: University of California Press, 1984), pp. 102–103n. The study by Ioan Petru Coulianu [Culianu], *Eros et magie à la Renaissance (1484)* (Paris: Flammarion, 1984; translated into English by Margaret Cook as *Eros and Magic in the Renaissance* [Chicago: University of Chicago Press, 1987]), has many speculative things to say about spirit and the raylike *idola*, but it should be used with great caution since it rides roughshod over Ficino's careful distinctions; this is a pity, since *spiritus*, spiritual magic, and Ficino form the nub of its concerns. In general, see the papers in the collection *Spiritus: IV° Colloquio Internazionale del Lessico Intellettuale Europeo (Roma, 7–9 gennaio 1983)*, ed. Marta Fattori and Massimo Bianchi (Rome: Edizioni dell' Ateneo, 1984).

35. Plutarch, *Quaestiones Convivales* 8.2 (*Moralia* 718B–720C, specifically 718BC). Ficino gives a Latin rendering of the inscription on the Academy's entrance in his *Vita Platonis* (under *Discipuli Platonis praecipui; Opera*, p. 766.1) and glosses it thus: "Understand that Plato was intending this to apply not only to the proper measurement of lines but also of [our] passions (*affectuum*)."

36. See S. Otto, "Geometrie und Optik in der Philosophie des Marsilio Ficino," *Philosophisches Jahrbuch* 98 (1991): 290–313; Albertini, *Marsilio Ficino*, pp. 76–85.

37. Allen, *Icastes*, chap. 5.

38. Cf. Plato's *Gorgias* 510B; *Lysis* 214B; *Republic* 1.329A, 4.425C; etc.

39. But see D. P. Walker's *Spiritual and Demonic Magic: From Ficino to Campanella* (London, 1958; reprinted, Notre Dame, Ind.: University of Notre Dame Press, 1975), chap. 1; idem, *Music, Spirit and Language in the Renaissance*, ed. Penelope Gouk (London: Variorum Reprints, 1984); Gary Tomlinson, *Music in Renaissance Magic: Toward a Historiography of Others* (Chicago: University of Chicago Press, 1993), chaps. 3, 4; and my *Platonism of Marsilio Ficino*, pp. 51–58.

40. Cf. the *Timaeus* 31C–32B on the planar numbers as means.

5

In principio: Marsilio Ficino on the Life of Text

Several scholars, beginning with Allison Coudert[1], and including Brian Vickers[2] and most recently James Bono[3], have argued that the Renaissance Neoplatonist Ficino espoused a magical view of language, identifying the powers of names with their referents and in general adopting the position that Socrates and his respondent Hermogenes attribute to Cratylus in his eponymous Platonic dialogue[4]. All three have used as their starting point the arresting passages in the *Philebus* Commentary 1.11,12 which speak to the power of divine names[5]. In this essay I am not going to address the onomastic issue directly, but rather point to some of the complex metaphysical and theological issues that should give us pause, whether we distinguish, in the Hermogenean, Aristotelian and modern scientific manner, between an object and its name, holding the latter to be the result of convention, or whether we expound, as Socrates himself does for a while, what S. J. Tambiah perhaps too glibly designated the "more primitive" notion that a real connection exists between the two[6].

1 "Some Theories of a Natural Language from the Renaissance to the Seventeenth Century", in *Magia Naturalis und die Entstehung der modernen Naturwissenschaften: Studia Leibnitiana*, Sonderheft 7 (Wiesbaden, 1978), pp. 56 – 114 at 65.

2 "Analogy versus Identity: The Rejection of Occult Symbolism, 1580 – 1680", in *Occult and Scientific Mentalities in the Renaissance*, ed. B. Vickers (Cambridge, 1984), pp. 95 – 163 at 117 – 123. On the Perils of Analogy, cf. Plato's *Theaetetus* 231A.

3 *The Word of God and the Languages of Man: Vol. 1: Ficino to Descartes* (Madison, 1995), chap. 2, p. 31.

4 383A ff. and 390D ff. Diogenes Laertius, *Lives* 3.6, says Hermogenes was a pupil of Parmenides and a teacher of Plato; see Ficino's *Vita Platonis* and his *Cratylus* epitome (*Opera*, pp. 764.1, 1310).

5 Ed. and trans. M. J. B. Allen (Berkeley & Los Angeles, 1975), pp. 138 – 145.

6 "The Magical Power of Words", *Man*, n. s. 3 (1968), 175 – 208, as cited in Vickers, pp. 96 – 97. Vickers, pp. 97 – 100, appropriately warns us against identifying Plato or for that matter Socrates with the essentialist view. The *Cratylus* is a complex study of language. In general see, Marie-Luce Demonet's brilliant book *Les voix du signe. Nature et origine du langage à la Renaissance (1480 – 1580)* (Paris, 1992); also M. M. Slaughter, *Universal Language and Scientific Taxonomy in the Seventeenth Century* (Cambridge, 1982); Michel Foucault, *The Order of Things: An Ar-*

For a Platonist, we should recall, the intelligible Ideas are the *res verae*. The *res/verba* problem is the problem, therefore, of how to talk about what is, though intelligible, humanly ineffable and hence how to deploy the *via analogica* and the *via negativa*: the consideration both of negative propositions and of symbols, metaphors, figures, the modalities of likeness. Can we have symbols or figures indeed that function as negative propositions, and if so what are their defining characteristics? Conversely, can negative propositions be analogues, predicating figures? And in a Platonic-Plotinian context what would these alternatives look like? Obviously myths of violence or disorder – Uranus' castration, Saturn's devouring of his children, Zeus's rape of various women, the theomachies, the dismemberment of Dionysus, the Titans' rebellion, the flaying of Marsyas, the various incestuous unions among the gods – occur throughout Greek and Roman mythology. The Platonic tradition, influenced doubtless by the ancient allegorizing of Homer's epics, interpreted such myths theologically as figurative presentations of being's origin in the One, its emanation into the many, its conversion and return to the One. As Edgar Wind[7], Robert Lamberton[8] and others have justly remarked, the violence or immorality of these myths – antithetical it would seem to the figuring forth of what is truly divine and at first glance impious and blasphemous – functions apotropaically to repel those uninitiated in the mysteries and in their correct interpretation. The more profound or fundamental the mystery, the more apposite or appropriate the violence of the story: the more precious the fruit, the uglier, the more repellent the rind. But violent or unruly myths are not per se myths about negation. Rather, the myths and figures of concealment, of silence, of night, of chaos are those that point to the paradoxes investing the notion of the One as being beyond being and non-being: as being not being and as not being

chaeology of the Human Sciences (London & New York: Vintage books, 1973); Richard Waswo, *Language and Meaning in the Renaissance*, Princeton: Princeton University Press, 1987; Martin Elsky, *Authorizing Words: Speech, Writing, and Print in the English Renaissance* (Ithaca, N.Y.: Cornell University Press, 1989); and Judith H. Anderson, *Words that Matter: Linguistic Perception in Renaissance English* (Stanford, Calif.: Stanford University Press, 1996).

7 *Pagan Mysteries in the Renaissance*, rev. ed. (New York, 1968), pp. 133 – 138.

8 *Homer the Theologian: Neoplatonist Allegorical Reading and the Growth of the Epic Tradition* (Berkeley & Los Angeles, 1986), pp. 207 – 208, 245, citing Pseudo-Areopagite, *Celestial Hierarchy* 2.3; and Wind, *Pagan Mysteries*, pp. 12 – 13, citing the same Areopagitian text but 2.5.

being. For the Neoplatonic One transcends our every notion of a *res*, though the origin, cause and end of all *res*.

In considering the problematics of Plato's intelligible *res* and thus of his theory of the Ideas, several thorny issues confront us. The *Sophist* postulates six super Ideas, pairs of which are binary and therefore defined by opposition: Identity v. Difference, Rest v. Motion, and more contentiously Essence v. Existence[9]. In what sense can these be Platonic *Res*, since they are above or more fundamental than the other Ideas? Moreover, can there be an Idea of an individual or for that matter of individuals, a *Res* of a *res* or of many *res*?[10] Can there be a *Res* of Cosmos and correspondingly of Chaos? Does the language of *res* with which we define chaos and cosmos "participate in" truth, just as the species of sensible things participate in their intelligible Ideas? Is there an Idea or *Res* of language corresponding to the Idea of Truth? Can one *Reify* Truth in this special Platonic sense?

From the onset Platonism has been a dualistic philosophy and has always had a dual sense of language. The philosopher's words serve as midwives to the birth of truth, while the sophist's words deceive and confuse; and poetic texts are not sacred or profane in themselves so much as open to sacred or profane readings, to allegorical and anagogic interpretations. The instability in the sense of the polysemy or plurisignification of words is of course an ancient philosophical and rhetorical topos, but it is central both to the Platonic tradition and to the Pythagorean tradition from which it grew. Moreover, the notion of words has always been potentially what the Schoolmen called a universal; that is, a paradigm that can configure or reticulate reality in the manner that Panurge's notion of debt or the Elizabethan poet John Davies' notion of the dance configure the entire ordering and functioning of natural, human and social life, of the cosmos itself. Medieval and Renaissance thinkers could toy with the interrelated notions of the

9 *Sophist* 248A – 256D. For Ficino's analysis, see my *Icastes: Marsilio Ficino's Interpretation of Plato's "Sophist"* (Berkeley & Los Angeles, 1989), pp. 49 – 82.

10 While Plotinus recognised Ideas of individual men in his *Enneads* 5.7 (cf. 4.3.5, 4.5.7, 5.9.12, 6.4.4.34 – 46, 6.7.12), though whether he consistently held to the doctrine is unclear, Proclus denied there were Ideas of individuals in his *In Parmenidem* 824.13 – 825.35 (ed. V. Cousin in *Procli philosophi Platonici opera inedita*, Paris, 1864, repr. Frankfurt, 1962, cols. 617 – 1258). In a letter to Francesco da Diacceto of 11 July 1493 (*Opera*, p. 952.1), Ficino writes that "the Ideas of individuals are not mutually distinguished in the prime Mind absolutely, but relatively", and that this reconciles Plotinus's views with Proclus's.

night sky as words, nature as words, death as words, man or his body or his soul as texts, nations or institutions or communities as texts, almost anything complex as text. In part this was a game, albeit a serious one; in part it was the consequence of the conviction that analogy and correspondence govern the relationships between the disparate spheres and orders of being; in part it was an acknowledgement of the Hebraic emphasis on the authority of the Bible as the word which God has given to man as a guide for his salvation; and in part, as we shall see, it spoke to the Greek and Judeo-Christian fascination with the idea of the Divine Logos, the Divine Word, creating and ordering the world as text.

Interestingly, and despite the primacy in the Hebreo-Christian tradition both of a sacred text and of a logos theology and cosmogony, our word "text" began as an image of something quite different. In the majority of the European languages, it is etymologically derived from the Latin verb *texere* meaning to weave or plait, a *textus* being literally something that is woven, a product of the goddess of weaving, Athene[11]. In the *Statesman* 274C ff. Plato refers to the various gifts mankind received in the beginning from the gods, chief among them being the art of forging metals from Hephaestus (preeminently a male activity), and the arts of weaving and sewing from Athene (preeminently a female one)[12]. Without these two master sets of skills, mankind could not have survived, given its lack of horns, claws, wings and other animal attributes. Whereas Hephaestus remained the god of metallurgy and a mythological sport as Aphrodite's cuckolded husband who had netted his wife in the arms of Ares to his own public humiliation, Athene was the virgin goddess of wisdom, born parthenogenetically from the head of her divine father, Zeus. Her attributes were the little owl that sees in darkness, the aegis with the boss of Medusa's Gorgonizing head, the spear of truth, and the helmet of invincibility.

11 See John Scheid & Jesper Svenbro, *The Craft of Zeus: Myths of Weaving and Fabric*, trans. Carol Volk (Cambridge, Mass.: Harvard University Press, 1996); original title *Le métier de Zeus*. Starting with Ernst Robert Curtius' chapter, "The Book as Symbol" in his *European Literature in the Latin Middle Ages*, tr. Willard R. Trask (Princeton, 1953), pp. 302 – 347, the notion of the human heart as text, codex, or book has a rich scholarly history; see, for example, Jesse M. Gellrich, *The Idea of the Book in the Middle Ages: Language Theory, Mythology and Fiction* (Ithaca, N.Y., 1985); Mary J. Carruthers, *The Book of Memory: A Study of Memory in Medieval Culture* (Cambridge, 1990); and Eric Jager, *The Book of the Heart* (Chicago, 2000).

12 Cf. *Protagoras* 320D ff.

In other words, whereas Hephaestus's gift enabled man to dig and wound the earth, and thus to forsake the fabled, irenic ages of gold and silver for the bellicose ages of bronze and iron, metals being used for money and for weapons, Athene's gifts first protected us from the cold without and then supplied garments for the inner self, provided a *textus* for the soul. Every fifth year of the Panathenaea, the annual festival to celebrate the union of Attica under Theseus, a *peplos*, an outer robe or shawl worn by the women of Athens, was woven for the statue of Athene. It was then carried in the triumphal procession to her sanctuary on the Acropolis, commentary as it were, the warp and woof of her intellectual and spiritual life, brought in tribute to the originary deity of Athens, to the virgin of the city's sacred text, to the armed virgin who could vanquish Ares, accoutred though he was in armour forged by Hephaestus.

Later in the *Statesman* 279B – 283B, Plato took up the notion of weaving a fabric, a *textus*, in order to use it as an example of the kind of correct divisions and subdivisions which dialectic as the "capstone of the sciences"[13] must learn to deploy if she is ever to attain an understanding equally of the relationship of genus to subgenus to species and subspecies, and of the role of the Ideas in structuring – in reifying – the world. This image was not selected at random. For the *Statesman* 308D ff. goes on to speak of the "royal science" – the knowledge of the ruler – as being analogous to the art of weaving. Ruling must expertly weave together the citizens of the commonwealth, republic or *polis* as though they were various strands and threads, just as the dialectician must weave our concepts into a web of philosophical arguments, and just as "the central element of the soul itself" must be bound "with a divine cord to which it is akin" (309C1 – 3).

Weaving thus constitutes one of the images which in the Latin tradition informs and even at times controls, at least in part, our notion of verbal communication, orally and in writing: we weave semantic threads. Interpretation is thus the careful unravelling and reweaving of the weft, a procedure open to the tangles, the sophistry, of misinterpretation, and therefore, *ante rem*, deconstruction. But presiding over the text as woven fabric is the goddess to whom Paris should have awarded the golden apple on the slopes of Mt. Ida, the goddess to whom Socrates and after him all the philosophers in the occidental tra-

13 This famous phrase occurs in the *Republic* 7.534E; cf. 6.498A.

dition have been devoted. Athene in effect valorizes the notion of text as she does the notion of weaving, being the *arche*, the origin and cause, of both.

Socrates, however, who entered death with the pious certainty of crossing the threshold into another and immortal life, was deemed impious in his mortal life for creating uncertainty; for urging the youths he loved to question their assumptions about loving, and to become steadfast in their doubting of what unquestioning men upheld too steadfastly. Moreover, Socrates had deliberately distinguished between the oral and the written media, and in particular had eschewed writing and rejected the notion of handing down his wisdom in a written text, however dexterously woven by the skills of Athene. This refusal of writing, ironically, links him with Pythagoras, though in terms of metaphysics it was Plato, one of the sublime creators of text, who was the more deeply and obviously indebted to the Pythagoreans[14]. For Pythagoras reputedly had refused to let his disciples record his *verba*, though in later antiquity his school had compiled a series of cryptic *aurea dicta* which they attributed to him[15]. But in the beginning, and for many subsequent centuries, it was said of the Pythagoreans that they would attribute their wisdom only to what the master had said, using a formula that is still famous as theirs, *autos epha*, in Latin *ipse dixit*. Here the enemy is not the sophist with his sleights of logical hand, but the notion itself of writing down, of weaving a signifying warp and woof of *textus*, even of a tributary *peplos*.

Plato's *Phaedrus* 274C – 275B refers to the story of the Egyptian deity Thoth or Theuth, the god of ingenuity and interpretation. Associated with him, Plato writes, following Egyptian lore, are such clever

14 Plato's debts to Pythagoras and the Pythagoreans were recognized as early as Aristotle's *Metaphysics* A. 6.987a29 ff., but are everywhere in the Platonic tradition, e.g. Diogenes Laertius, *Lives* 3.6 ff; Porphyry, *Vita Pythagorae* 53; Iamblichus, *De vita Pythagorica* 27.131, 30.167, 31.199; Proclus, *Theologia Platonica* 1.5; idem, *In Timaeum* 1.1.11 – 25, 1.2.29 ff., 1.7.19 – 25; idem, *In Alcibiadem* 317.11 ff., 18 ff. In particular, see Cornelia J. De Vogel, *Pythagoras and Early Pythagoreanism* (Assen, 1966); and for Ficino, Christopher S. Celenza, "Pythagoras in the Renaissance: The Case of Marsilio Ficino," *Renaissance Quarterly* 52.3 (1999), 667 – 711; also my *Icastes*, pp. 73 – 81, and *Synoptic Art*, pp. 43 – 47.

15 Ficino's translation of these and the Pythagorean *Symbola* conclude his *Opera omnia*, pp. 1978 – 79; see Paul O. Kristeller, *Supplementum Ficinianum* I, pp. cxxxviii – cxxxix; II, pp. 98 – 103. Pico, in his *Heptaplus*, proem 1, claimed on the other hand that Philolaus not Pythagoras was the author of the dicta.

beasts as the sacred ibis (and Ficino adds hunting dogs and apes), along with such taxing games of skill as draughts and dice. He was the inventor, more importantly, of the intellectual "disciplines" of arithmetic, geometry and astronomy and above all of writing which he introduced as an aid to wisdom and a prop to the memory. In Plato's tale, Theuth journeyed from his own city of Naucratis (Hermopolis) to the Upper Egyptian city of Thebes, where Jupiter was worshipped as Ammon, and revealed his inventions to the king of Thebes, Thamus. the king then questioned whether the arts should be passed on to the Egyptian people in general, and proceeded "to condemn what he thought were the bad points and to praise what he thought were the good", marshalling for each art "a number of views for and against". But when it came to writing, Thamus distinguished between the skill necessary to invent an art and the judgement needed to determine the measure of profit or harm it would bring to those exercising it. He then rejected writing on two counts: first, that it would implant forgetfulness in men's souls so that they would cease to rely on, and thus to exercise, their memory; and second, that in the process of telling men about many things without truly educating them, Theuth would enable them to seem to know much, while for the most part they knew little or nothing. As sophists filled, not with wisdom, but with the conceit of wisdom, they would become a burden to their fellows (275AB); or, in Ficino's gloss, "writing would make them careless about finding things out (*ad inventionem negligentiores*), inasmuch as they would rely on the acuity (*ingenium*) of their superiors and not on their own"[16]. These twin reservations, note, are keyed to writing alone, and thus to the perceived disjunction between words and things, and not apparently to Theuth's inventions of the three mathematical skills. Presumably mathematics is not subject to the same kind of callow, self-deceiving appropriation.

In interpreting this passage, Ficino clearly thinks of Plato as having ethical or theological truths in mind. For he notes in his *In Phaedrum* 3.3 that "In the manner of the Pythagoreans, Socrates affirms that the contemplation and transmission of truth occurs in souls rather than in books"; and then in summa 50 that Socrates prefers "living discourse which has been impressed by the teacher on the pupil's soul and not

16 *In Philebum* 1.29.273 (ed. Allen); cf. Ficino's *In Phaedrum*, s. 49 (ed. Allen as *Marsilio Ficino and the Phaedran Charioteer*, Berkeley & Los Angeles, 1981, p. 211).

merely written down in texts (*scriptis*)"[17], the implication being that *scripta* in themselves are dead or at least moribund discourses. Picturesquely, in summa 49, Ficino had borrowed a gloss from the ancient *Phaedrus* commentator, Hermias, in referring to the appropriateness of the ibis as Mercury's bird: "it advances with uniform steps and gives birth to eggs from its throat, just as Mercury too produces his offspring from the mouth"[18]. However, in the *Phaedrus* 275DE, Plato has Socrates compare writing to painting on the grounds that both merely seem to be alive; and yet,

> "if you question them, they maintain a most majestic silence ...; written words seem to talk to you as if they were intelligent, but if you ask them anything about what they say, from a desire to be instructed, they go on telling you just the same thing for ever. And once a thing is put in writing, the composition, whatever it may be, drifts all over the place, getting into the hands not only of those who understand it, but equally of those who have no business with it; it doesn't know how to address the right people, and not address the wrong. And when it is ill-treated and unfairly abused it always needs its parent to come to its help."

Writing here is inanimate or, at the most, is suspended animation.

Although it might contribute to, or enhance, the lethal effects of Lethe, the river that souls sipped upon their entry into the world and that made them dead to their former lives, Plato's story does not say that Thamus absolutely commanded Theuth to forego his invention. "Socrates does not forbid us to write", Ficino notes circumspectly, "but he does condemn our putting any confidence in writing"[19], our assuming that "instruction (*disciplina*) will be clear and secure (*perspicua tutaque*) in writing"[20]. After all, in Ficino's Neoplatonic interpretation, Theuth had been inspired to discover the *disciplinae* by the high god Ammon, that is by Jupiter himself. Socrates is advocating in effect a compromise. To entrust doctrine to writing is to cultivate "a garden of Adonis", that is, a garden cultivated for the sake of flowers not fruit or produce[21]. Cultivating such a garden may be "the most

---

17 See fn. 16, pp. 81, 83, 211. Jacques Derrida has an influential reading of this text in "Plato's Pharmacy, I," in his *Dissemination*, tr. Barbara Johnson (Chicago, 1981), pp. 65 – 119.

18 See fn. 16, p. 211; cf. Hermias, *In Phaedrum*, p. 254 (ed. Couvreur).

19 *In Phaedrum*, s. 50 (see fn. 16, p. 211).

20 Ibid., s. 52 (see fn. 16, p. 213).

21 Ibid., s. 51 (see fn. 16, p. 213). Anna de Pace writes, "Durante le Adonie, feste in onore di Adone, il primo giorno le donne esponevano vasi con piante che presto germogliano e sfioriscono (appunto i "giardini di Adone"), i quali nell'ultimo

beautiful of all pastimes or games" – an act of remembering and of memorializing the dead Adonis in the flower named after him, with "flowers" being the favored trope for the ornaments of rhetoric. Nevertheless, he who entrusts the various disciplines, "the lawful offspring of understanding", to the minds of people worthy to receive them, "to souls worthy of the mystery", is practising "a better agriculture, one that is serious and worthy of the highest study". Interestingly, Ficino refuses to take up Socrates' analogies between written words and first a painting and then a helpless child constantly in need of protective parents.

Ficino's interpretation of Theuthian writing involves, I would argue, a radical departure from Socrates' little story. For he was drawn to identifying Theuth variously, even simultaneously with the Greek god Mercury, with one of his principal daimon followers, and with the sage Hermes Trismegistus, the founder of Egyptian religion and cult and one of the first, if not the first, of the *prisci theologi* culminating in Plato[22]. Hence his invention of Egyptian writing, writes Ficino in his *In Philebum* 1.29, was the invention of hieroglyphs (we recall we are in the era of Horapollo not of Champollion). Here the shapes (*figurae*) of animals and plants were used as the principal characters, the object of such sacred writing being to keep the mysteries contained therein concealed from the vulgar gaze[23]. Thus Theuth's invention was a clever one. Rather than inventing something "for the Egyptians in general", as Plato's myth had implied, Theuth had invented something for the elite, or more properly for those few *purgati* worthy of initiation into the secrets of the ancient theology.

---

giorno venivano buttati giù dai tetti. Il rito fa riferimento al giovinetto morto nel fiore dell'età, e l'espressione "giardini di Adone" è assunta a significare "ciò che è effimero" (private communication). See Marcel Detienne, *The Gardens of Adonis: Spices in Greek Mythology*, tr. from the French by Janet Lloyd, with an introd. by J.-P. Vernant (repr. Princeton, 1989), with all the relevant literary and iconographical sources.

22 For Hermes as the second in the line of six ancient theologians, see my *Synoptic Art* (Florence, 1998), pp. 24 – 31, with further refs.; also Eugenio Garin, *Il ritorno dei filosofi antichi* (Naples, 1983), pp. 67 – 77. In his *In Phaedrum*, s. 49, however, Ficino allegorizes Theuth as both a human being and as a demon, and Thamus as both an actual king and as the planetary god Mercury or even as the Intellect Mercury in the realm of pure Mind; see my *Platonism of Ficino* (Berkeley, 1984), pp. 36 – 38.

23 See fn. 16, p. 271. For the separate problem of Zoroaster's priority as THE inventor of writing using the stars and constellations as the "letters", see my *Synoptic Art*, pp. 35 – 36.

Plato's myth and its Renaissance interpretation point to an ambivalence, an anxiety even, about the authority and role of words separated from the mind of the teacher, taken as it were out of his mouth. Truth for the many resides in words only when they are orally transmitted from teacher to disciple and are part of an ethical and axiological exchange, the transmission of knowledge in the context of ultimate values, a living discourse of the heart. As Ficino notes in his commentary on Romans 1.1 – 2 and 2.14, Christ had never written his teachings down in any tablet or book, but only in the hearts and souls of those who believed in him[24]. For ambivalence about mankind's encounter with writing and thus with text is associated not only with the loss of innocence, the departure from the golden age of the pastoral, and the taking up of the survival gifts of Hephaestus and Athene; but also, more provocatively, with the onset of transcription, with the entombing of sacred mysteries in the living grave of astromorphological and zoomorphological hieroglyphs. There, moribund, they await the coming of the theologian-interpreter who will resurrect and revivify them, lead them out of the mouth of their long silence.

Ostensibly a myth cautioning against the dangers of inventing writing at all, the Theuth story became for Ficino the story of the beginning specifically of sacred writing, of the protective veiling, the warping and woofing, the textualization of truths, and thus of words requiring not only meditation by the righteous but careful interpretation and transmission by a line of hermeneut-masters. Writing was now, in the time-worn simile, like a winter seed, apparently dead and buried in the earth, but awaiting a vernal, blossoming life when watered and tended by a learned gardener and illumined by the Sun of Truth. Although Thamus had warned against the giving of writing to the people, yet Jupiter Ammon, writes Ficino, had been the inspiration behind Theuth's invention; and Plato seems in fact to be identifying Thamus with Ammon or identifying him with an attribute of Ammon, witness the reference at 275C to "Ammon's utterance"[25].

---

24 *In epistolas divi Pauli* 1, 15 (*Opera*, pp. 428, 450).

25 Indeed, the text is often emended here to identify Thamus with Ammon. Ficino, however, retained the reading *theon* while acknowledging that Socrates's words seem "to include Thamus and Ammon under the same person", even though "reason in its precision" should continue to distinguish between Jupiter in himself and the mercurial qualities in Jupiter which we can refer to as Thamus. Again see the subtle Proclus-inspired analysis in his *In Phaedrum*, s. 49 (see fn. 16, p. 209).

In any event we have a typically sacred paradox wherein the deity both attracts and repels, excites and forbids, gives and takes away his *verba* and his *res*. The originary written text, like the *peplos* woven with the art given us by Athene, emerges as a malediction and a blessing. From the old Pythagorean viewpoint it is words in a grave, but from the Ficinian it is a secluded garden memorializing the untimely rape of Aphrodite's untimely consort, a virgin's floral defloration, a March's transformation into cruellest April. Here the written text must be viewed *sub mysterio mortis*, as possessing a complementary if another kind of life than the life of *oratio*, of living speech. No longer seen as a shroud however beautiful, however cunningly woven (testifying to the loss of true converse between soul and soul, and thus to a sacrificial love), it has become a seminary, a hortulan source of metamorphosis and the new life.

Hence, instead of recalling the Pythagorean and Socratic tradition with its distrust of all but living instruction, it recalls the Bible as the *scriptum sacrum*, the book with supreme sovereignty over the *verba sacra* of the individual prophets in the post Mosaic line of prophets. For the Scriptures are the living word testifying to the Living Word made flesh, the incarnate Christ. He is the master text of creation, the alpha and omega of God's scheme for man's redemption, the eternal *Verbum* who entered once and forever into flesh and time, into the *res* and *verba* of man's post-lapsarian worlds and alphabets. The three Abrahamic religions attribute a unique authority to certain words as the instrument of God and as the way to eternal life. If man's words by analogy are participating commentary, his life for a Christian is a participation in the text of the Lord and the Redeemer, is the life of that living text, that *oratio eterna*.

In Plotinian metaphysics also "life" has a special status. Given the famous passage in the *Sophist* on the need for life to be present in the realm of intelligible being[26], Plotinus emphasizes the presence of "life" among the intelligibles in the well known triad of being-life-intellect[27], and upholds the notion that as souls we participate in the "life" of

26 *Sophist* 248E – 249D; for Ficino's analysis, see my *Icastes*, pp. 56 – 59.

27 See R. T. Wallis, *Neoplatonism* (London, 1972), pp. 67, 106, 124 – 25, 130, 132 – 33, 149 – 51; the important article by P. Hadot, "Etre, vie, pensée chez Plotin et avant Plotin," in *Entretiens Hardt V: Les sources de Plotin* (Vandoeuvres-Geneva, 1960), pp. 107 – 157; and A. H. Armstrong, "Eternity, Life and Movement in Plotinus' Accounts of *Nous*," in *Le Néoplatonisme* (Paris, 1971), pp. 67 – 76.

Truth and therefore in absolute Life, in the Idea of Life, the middle term in the definition of absolute Being. Indeed, for a Neoplatonist, the distinction between *res* and *verbum* slips out of focus when we cross the conceptual threshold signalled by life. For it is "life" that haunts the metaphysics of the Platonists not the Aristotelians; and it is "life" that also preoccupies Christian theology, given Christ's central exhortation that we search for a more full, a more perfect life, a life of the spirit liberated from the death of the sensible world, of the shadowy earthly *res* which are alien to the luminous *verbum* of heaven. For man and his thoughts participate, however variously, in eternal Life; and by virtue of that participation are endowed with the eternal being of the Word. This Johannine-Pauline theology, fraught as it is with paradoxes, and grafted onto the transcendental, idealist metaphysics of Platonism, inevitably problematizes the traditional schemata of logical analysis by contraries, including, as we have seen, analysis by way of any *res/verba* distinction, which is anchored in a materialist metaphysics, and specifically in Aristotelian form-matter theory. At first glance it might even appear to elevate *verba* over *res*. But Platonism is a philosophy that seeks to recover and to validate as the supreme realities the *res exemplares* as the *verba exemplares*: to point to their union in the transcendental realm as the ideal objects, the Ideas, and to recover an understanding of their unitary relationship. At the core of Plotinian epistemology and semiotics is the mystery of how either *res* or *verbum* can signify at all in the realm of what is "here" in the illusory non-signifying world, when "there" *res* is *verbum*, and to participate in *res* there is to participate in *verbum*. It is one of Ficino's contributions that he explored not only, or not particularly, the essentialist notions of language, and preeminently of names, advanced for a while in the *Cratylus*, but these broader notions of signification and participation: what we might call the existentialist dimensions of language as the product of *actus*, and of *verba* consequently as the actuation, the unfolding life of enfolded thoughts.

Insofar as both *verba* and *res* "here" participate in the Ideas "there", both are *umbrae* here[28]. For inferior or impaired participation – itself a problematic notion – results in false, umbratile opinions and not in the

28 The fundamental passage is of course the *Republic*'s allegory of the cave in books 6 and 7; and the most famous shadow image is the twenty-third Psalm's "the valley of the shadow of death". Renaissance shadow lore, skiagraphy and skialogy, is a science, but not merely a science, since it has far reaching imaginative and religious associations.

truth or in the true opinions that result from full, from luminous participation, however defined. Correspondingly, the more impaired the participation and the more material the condition of the *res*, the darker they are as *umbrae*. Does this mean that our perception of such *umbrae* must always depend on vagrant opinions; or can we know the constant truth about the inconstant shadows? And what then about the sophists, the jugglers with their adumbrations, the conjurors of shadow play and manipulation, the protean shape-changers in the murk of opinions? Must we suppose their words brazen when compared to the golden words of a Pythagoras? And do love (*eros*) and strife (*eris*) contend in the oceanic realm of *verba* as they do perpetually in the realm of *res*? Can we effect a compromise between a Heraclitian and a Democritean view of *verba*? Can we imagine ourselves in our own linguistic *Aeneid*: on a journey, that is, which leads us away from the Troy of *verba voluptuosa* to the Carthage of *verba activa* and thence to the Italy of *verba contemplativa*; from the *verba mortua mundi* – for Virgil's Christian allegorists like Landino – to the *verba viva Dei vivi*?[29] And does this correspond to a journey from non *res* to *res* to *Res*, from nothingness, matter and penumbral illusion to the sunlight of the Ideas? And finally in this run of speculative questions, what is a non *verbum* and what could be the relationship between a non *res* and a non *verbum*? Any answer must turn to consider the antithesis of life, the death which lurks in the valley of shadows, in the sophist's opinions. For dead words and dead things, *verba mortua atque res mortuae*, are scattered like Ezekiel's dry bones in the world as a dead text, a dead *verbum*, a dead *res* awaiting resurrection and rebirth as a living word inseminated and animated by the living Word. Indeed, no correspondence can truly exist between the dead *res* and the dead *verbum*, since death is itself defined by non-correspondence, by the death of the love that binds *verbum* to *res*, like to like. All becomes *eris* instead of *eros*, eristic instead of truth.

By contrast, the paradigmatic life, Life itself, consists in the union of *res* and *verbum* in the words of the seven Sacraments, above all in the words of the eucharistic transubstantiation of the wafer and the wine

29 See Cristoforo Landino's *Disputationes Camaldulenses* (c. 1472), books 3 and 4, where one of the principal characters, Alberti, interprets the *Aeneid* 1 – 6 Platonically: that is, as the story of the hero's arrival at contemplative perfection (Italy), having conquered the vices and passions of the *vita voluptuosa* (Troy) and the *vita activa* (Carthage). See too Landino's commentary on the *Aeneid*.

into salvific body and blood in Christianity's central act of hylomorphic magic. It is here clearly that the *res/verba* problem becomes a sacred mystery, given the analogy of the body with the word (Eph 4:4, 5:30 etc.) – of Christ the perfect *res* with the Son who is the perfect *verbum* – and the theological extensions of the Platonic notion of participation in an Idea. For we participate in Christ and therefore in the Word that Simeon in St. Luke's Gospel cradled in his arms in the temple as he acknowledged that at last the promise, the prophetic word had been fulfilled. He had lived to see the coming of the light to lighten the Gentiles, the child "set for the fall and the rising again of many in Israel; and for a sign which shall be spoken against" (2:34)[30], the Messiah that was and is the Idea of Man[31].

Prophecy, however, raises complex issues. For the *verba* of an authentic prophet forewarn us of coming events and in certain permitted instances enable us to avoid the dangers attending them, to avoid *res adversae*, or rather to fashion for ourselves a new set of *res prosperae et secundae*. The *verba* determine, in a propitious context (*pro re*), their own *res* to our advantage (*nostra re*) and can be said to have priority and therefore control over them[32].

In the opening remarks of a letter written to Giovanni Cavalcanti late in his career – it is dated 12 Dec. 1494 – Ficino attempts to justify the existence of evil as ultimately serving the cause of good: "Divine providence wished our souls while on earth to be troubled by hosts of violent perturbations"[33]. He cites Plato's *De scientia* (i. e. the famous passage in the *Theaetetus* 176A) to the effect that it is impossible to root out evils entirely, "for evil is necessary always for someone as a

30 See Ficino's sermon on Simeon's "Nunc dimittis", *Opera*, pp. 491.2 – 492.

31 The question as to whether Plato had postulated an Idea of Man is complicated. Parmenides asks, in his eponymous dialogue, "And is there a form (*eidos*) of man, apart from ourselves and all other men like us – a form of man as something by itself?" (130C). Socrates admits to being puzzled about this. Proclus takes up this passage in his commentary and establishes a chain of different levels of man descending from the Idea of Man (812.10 – 16). Thus Ficino accepts the Idea of Man as *idea hominis*, as *homo idealis*, and as *ipsa humanitatis idea* in his own *In Parmenidem* 5, 21 (*Opera*, pp. 1139 – 40, 1144.2), while Pico too refers to the "Idea of men" as being in the hypostasis Mind in his *Commento* 1.6. There are obvious Christological implications.

32 It is difficult not to pun on the many idioms in Latin employing *res* and thus to *res*tore their weft!

33 *Opera*, pp. 961.2 – 963.

contrary to the good". The disease makes us appreciate the doctor more, the storm whipped seas make the sailors admire the prudence of the pilot. At this point Ficino introduces an opportunistic variation on this ethical Stoicism, arguing that "sometimes" God allows us by way of prophecy to avoid imminent evils; witness, he says, the following notices in Plato. In the *Symposium* [201D] "the priestess" Diotima warned the Athenians about a pending plague ten years before it actually struck, and thus enabled them to sacrifice to the gods in order to delay its onset. Likewise in the *Phaedrus* [244A – E] Plato refers to the sibyl and others endowed with prophecy: "the ancients testify that prophecy is the result of a divine fury and is much more eminent than human conjecture and human prudence ... the divine fury comes to certain among the gentiles from elsewhere, enabling them to predict future events". When they then turn to prayers and divine worship, to expiations and propitiations, they are rendered safe and whole. In the *Laws* 1 [642DE], Epimenides of Crete, inspired by an oracle of God, warned the Athenians ten years before the outbreak of the Persian war that the Persians would not come for ten more years and that they would depart with their goal unaccomplished. Such prophecies are frequently greeted with incredulity, continues Ficino recalling the *Phaedrus* 244A – D, inasmuch as the authentic prophet, "who has rightly used divine meditations and always is imbued with the perfect mysteries", is thought a fool by the many who suppose him a man beside himself (*extra se positus*). For even though he is inspired by God and clings to the divine (*divino inhaerens*), he is cut off from ordinary human studies and enthusiasms, from ordinary *res*. Prophecy so far exceeds human wisdom that we must account the prophetic mind a mind on fire with divine love, as rapt in amatory ecstasy. A fury and an alienation, prophecy excels not only human wisdom but all other divine gifts: hence St. Paul's words "but greater than these is charity" (I. Cor. 13:13). For the words of the prophet ultimately proceed from love, from the heat and the light of the Holy Spirit.

Prophets are sent by God, Ficino advises Cavalcanti, as the instruments of His pity (*misericordia*); for we are fated to encounter adversities because of the sin of our first parents. However, as Plato too had declared [in the *Phaedrus* 244E], "God, moved as it were with pity, often inspires the prophets to predict coming afflictions, so that warned by the prophets we might seek refuge in prayers and sacred expiations. When we perform these as we should, often we escape the scourges unharmed". Interestingly, Ficino instances Savonarola as having been "elected divinely" to perform this monitory task, a view of the Dominican he was to abandon a few years later when he vehemently turned against the friar after his execution. God's pity for mankind thus validates the prophet's words if they excite the hearer to prayer, to repentance and to acts of propitiatory devotion, expiation and purification. This is a special instance of the divinizing of *verba* and it follows naturally on the notion of the creative divine Word – "And God said, 'let there be light'" (Genesis 1.3). But in this theological context it does point to the verbalizing of *res* and to the reifying of *verba*, that is, to the interweaving of the Logos in the unfolding of the things of nature, the *res creatae* that depend for their very existence on the divine utterance. This is more than the magic of names or spells. It looks to a logology, that is, to an understanding, however partial or contingent, of an eternal creating and sustaining *verbum* that gives life to all *res*, and lends its authority to the lesser *verba* of the divinely inspired prophet in his amatory ecstasy – *verba* which sustain our lives of action and contemplation alike, inspire us to more fervent devotion, and shield us providentially from the blows of an inimical Fate and from the endless vicissitudes of Fortune.

A theological vision of this kind blurs to the point of nullifying the distinctions we customarily draw between *res* and *verba*. For it is predicated on a radically different conceptual set, which at first glance seems to invert the values with which we normally invest the two terms, but which is ultimately transvaluative. In Ficino's exalted conception, the philosopher is a lover of the divine Word which is the word of the Father consubstantial with the Word, His Son, and whose Holy Spirit in its procession breathes the Word into the hearts and souls of all who truly worship and believe in Him, endowing them with the fullness of life. Man in this salvation context is thus a newly living text, a living *verbum*, a prayerful *oratio*. But since a living word is by definition prophetic, anticipating the world to come, anticipating the *dies novissima* and the *res publica nova* of the heavenly Jerusalem, the paradigmatic man is the prophet prophesying the heavenly life to come. Such a man shares in the primacy of the word over things, being created in the likeness and image of the Logos, the Word that was with God and was God in the *in principio* that opens both Genesis and the Gospel of St. John.

But the theology of *verba* and of non *verba* is itself trinitarian. In commenting on a section in the memorable opening chapter of the Areopagite's *De mystica theologia* (*De Trinitate*), Ficino writes:

> It seems the mind uses three steps to approach God. Firstly it uses as many words as possible, secondly as few as possible, thirdly none. It uses as many as possible when the mind affirms and denies equally – using the same words but in a different sense – whatever men may adduce concerning God. It uses as few words as possible when it refers to [just the causal] relationships, that is, refers things to God as to [their] principle, end, and mean, and as their conserving, converting, and perfecting [cause]. But the mind uses no words at all, when it neither refers things to God or the reverse by way of analogy, nor denies anything [of Him], nor restores to Him by way as it were of affirmation anything that depends on Him. But when it is about to affirm something of God Himself, the mind breaks off inner speech and falls immediately silent, lest by setting a limit to God by affirming this something, it might insolently predicate the finite of Him instead of the infinite. Therefore, if speech is remitted to the degree that the love of the Good is intensified, immediately (as we said) in this blazing fire in the presence of the Good the light of the Good blazes forth; and it exhales the Good.[34]

Here Ficino defines three ways of approaching God, three deployments of *verba*, though the third is their suspension, the abandonment of all discourse, whether affirmative, negative or analogical. As the love of God intensifies and the soul enters the presence of the Good, the Harpocratean act of falling silent sets a term to the first breaking into words which signalled both The Creation and our creation by the Divine Word. Here the sense of an ending, the sense of having allowed discourse to run its course, of allowing speech to return to silence, signals the return of the many to the One, of the radiating lines back to the centre's point, of the emanated splendour back to its luminous source. It also signals the perfection of *verba* and of *res* equally, or rather a perfection that transcends the distinction. The Bible has been opened, read, and closed, returned to the beginning, ended in its genesis: its sacred Word falls silent in the fullness, in the fulfilment of

34 *Opera*, p. 1018.3: "Mens circa Deum tres (ut videtur) gradus agit. In primo verbis quam plurimis utitur; in secundo paucis; in tertio nullis. Quam plurimis, inquam, ubi quotcunque occurrunt de Deo affirmat pariter atque negat, paribus quidem verbis, sed ratione diversa. Paucis autem ubi relationibus utitur, referendo videlicet res ad Deum tanquam ad principium, finem, medium, conservantem, convertentem, perficientem. Nullis [*Op.* Nullus] autem quando nec ulterius res ad Deum refert neque vicissim, neque negat quicquam, neque dependens a Deo aliquid Deo quodammodo reddit affirmans. Sed ipsum Deum mox affirmatura, sermonem rumpit intimum siletque protinus, ne affirmando finiens insolenter reportet pro infinito finitum. Tunc igitur si quatenus sermo remittitur eatenus intenditur amor boni, statim (ut diximus) in hoc ipso incendio penes bonum effulget boni lumen spiratque bonum."

meaning, all *res* perfected both in its opening "beryshit" and in its final "Amen", in the alpha and omega, the aleph and tav of the divine alphabet.

Correspondingly, we too are the three conditions of utterance. We are subject to the manifold fullness of predication, negation, and analogy. We are stark simplicity. We are silence. We are the many *res* and *verba* rejoicing in the mystery of the Holy Spirit. We are the single *res* and *verbum* gathered into the mystery of the Son. We are eventually the non *res* and the non *verba* annihilated in the mystery of the Father. In such paradoxical formulations the quotidian alternatives of *res* and *verbum*, non *res* and non *verbum*, quasi *res* and quasi *verbum*, fall away as we approach the Janus guarded gateway into the supramundane realm. We pass through to the time before the semantic fall and the expulsion from meaning, before the curse of Babel's many tongues with their *verba*'s diverse significations of many *res*. And we pass beyond Eden with its naming to the pre-Adamic, genesis moment when darkness was upon the face of the deep and the earth was without form and void. For then even the language of God was "in the beginning", in the sublime obscurity of the divine night from which proceeded the creation command "fiat lux". In this deep but dazzling darkness – to quote Henry Vaughan's most famous poem – temporal man was not yet a lucid, an enlightened text, neither an affirmation nor a negation, not a figure, not a thread, neither a living word nor a dead thing, even as the Idea of Man had already been begotten eternally of the Father full of grace and truth.

6

THE FICINIAN *TIMAEUS* AND RENAISSANCE SCIENCE

Along with the biblical Genesis, Plato's *Timaeus* is the great cosmological and therefore theological text in the Western tradition, long admired for its creation myth, the work of a divine Demiurge, and for the tantalizing nature of both the parallels and the differences between it and the creation account(s) of Moses' first book. Briefly I wish to focus here, however, on the reading of the *Timaeus* as a scientific text by the important and immensely influential Florentine Neoplatonist, Marsilio Ficino (1433 – 99), even though it was for him also preeminently a theological and metaphysical revelation, the culminating witness to what he supposed, following the Neoplatonist tradition, were Plato's Pythagorean debts to Philolaus and to Timaeus Locrus.[1]

Ficino's most important speculations on the science of the *Timaeus* appear in his bulky commentary on the dialogue (which he was the first to translate into Latin in its entirety).[2] As we might expect, however, he also treats in other commentaries what he thought of as the scientific, and therefore the Timaean, material in such dialogues as the *Republic* and the *Epinomis* (which he accepted as canonical), and I shall later deal with his interpretation of some of that material in the *Republic,* notably in book 8.

Medieval philosophers, notably those associated with the School of Chartres, had variously attempted to reconcile the *Timaeus* — for them accessible only in Calcidius' Latin and thus only up to 53C — with their own conceptions of nature and also, predictably, with a theology of the Holy Ghost and of God's indwelling love for his creation. Even so, their accommodations had bordered at times on the heterodox or, in the case of Abelard, on the heretical.[3] Ficino may be indebted to them, but his understanding of Plato's text far exceeds theirs. This is necessarily so, given that he was the first scholar since Antiquity (besides perhaps his older Byzantine-born contemporary Cardinal Bessarion) who was accomplished enough to master the entire text in the original Greek and also to bring to bear the important material in Proclus' immense and difficult *Timaeus* commentary. He was thus able to advance beyond Calcidius' essentially Middle-Platonist interpretation of the dialogue (about which scholars still disagree).[4] Moreover, as the only Quattrocento humanist to confront fully the challenges of Plato's most influential and at the same time most Pythagorean text, he became the leading theoretician of the vitalistic or animistic metaphysics it propounds and hence of the physics, astronomy, and cosmology contingent on and corresponding to it.[5] In sum, the Renaissance's *Timaeus* is Ficino's Neoplatonist one, and its science provides the matrix for his account of the physical world as it had for the ancient Neoplatonists. His physical world, however, was already undergoing radical, if pre-Copernican, reconceptualization.

At *Timaeus* 28Aff. the eponymous spokesman for what is "probable" outlines a myth of the world's creation by a divine Demiurge, a craftsman or artificer whom he refers to at 28C as a "father" and "maker" who "is past finding out" and who looks up at the "eternal" and "unchangeable" Idea, pattern, or paradigm of the changeable cosmos he is about to fashion, a pattern which is "beautiful" and "perfect." Plato's Greek emphasizes the notion of gazing up toward, though Ficino, like earlier Middle-Platonist and Neoplatonist interpreters, was drawn to the different notion of looking within, because he could not conceive of the Demiurge as being other than Mind, the second hypostasis in Neoplatonist metaphysics, and thus as containing or embracing the realm of the Platonic Ideas in its entirety.[6] As a Christian commentator he was committed, moreover, to identifying the Demiurge with God the Creator, and thus to God's looking within to the Ideas in his own mind. In any event, prior to the imperfect becoming of the cosmos, the cosmos existed as a perfect Idea (though "existed" in an absolute sense), and Timaeus declares that the cosmos can be called "heaven" or "world."[7] Given that the cosmos "became," it had a cause that is prior to becoming; and this is the "best of causes" because the cosmos is the "fairest of creations" (28B–C). The best of causes is the Idea of the cosmos, and hence of what is ordered, beautiful and good, unchaotic. In his important letter to Braccio Martelli, entitled "Concordia Mosis & Platonis," Ficino writes that "Timaeus shows that the world was created by God for the sake of (*gratia*) His goodness; that God created the heavens and the earth from the beginning, and then poured the airy spirit out over the waters; that all these things will endure as long as it pleases the Divine Will; and that God made man to be so like Him that He set him up as the unique worshipper on earth of God, and as the lord of earthly things."[8] Plato's text was interpreted by the ancient commentators to imply that, although the world became, it had nevertheless existed from, and would exist for, eternity. Christian commentators, along with Plutarch and a few other dissenting voices, had long argued to the contrary that Plato intended us to understand that the world had a beginning in time.[9] Ficino was able to convince himself, moreover, on the basis of myths in such dialogues as the *Statesman* and the *Republic,* that Plato believed that the world would endure "as long as it pleased the Divine Will," as the letter declares, whereas Plato almost certainly discounted the notion of a divine will and believed instead in the world's eternity and in a cyclical notion of time.

The Demiurge is described as benevolent, free of jealousy, and desirous that all things should be as like himself as possible. He therefore framed the universe in such a way that he put intelligence in soul and soul in body "that he might be the creator of a work which was by nature fairest and best" (30B); in other words, Plato declares, "We may say that the world came into being — a living creature truly endowed with soul and intelligence by the providence of God." Here is the root of the antimechanical notion of the physical universe as a living creature, as ensouled, as endowed with its own motion, and by implication therefore as best approached by way of biology and psychology rather than the physics of inanimate matter.

To Ficino, however, Plato had also introduced some subtle mathematical elaborations that go beyond a simple vitalistic account of the universe as "one visible animal comprehending within itself all other animals of a kindred nature" (30D; cf. 33B). For Timaeus proceeds to describe the two means that always govern a solid body compounded of the four elements and that have the same proportion: as fire is to air, so air is to water, and as air is to water, so water is to earth. Thus the world was "harmonized by proportion" and has "the spirit of friendship," being "reconciled to itself." First, it was made spherical and, without outward parts or senses, to move in the same manner and on the same spot, having a rounded surface in every direction equidistant from the center; it was ensouled and its soul was diffused in its every part and it was "a blessed god" (34B). But more importantly, Timaeus describes the creation and therefore the structure of the World Soul as the result of blending together "the same and the different," according to the twin geometric harmonies that consist of 1–2–4–8 and 1–3–9–27, each step of which is itself bridged by two kinds of means:

$$1-[\tfrac{4}{3}-\tfrac{3}{2}]-2-[\tfrac{8}{3}-3]-4-[\tfrac{16}{3}-6]-8$$

$$1-[\tfrac{3}{2}-2]-3-[\tfrac{9}{2}-6]-9-[\tfrac{27}{2}-18]-27$$

This World Soul therefore "partakes of reason and harmony" (37A), being divided up and united "in due proportion" and "returning upon herself" in her revolutions. Thus the notion of mathematical proportion — which Plato links to the notion of musical harmonies — is the key to an understanding of the World Soul, its goodness and perfection.[10] By implication it is also the key to an understanding of individual souls and, interestingly, for Ficino, of entities or institutions that can be said by analogy to have a soul: a state, a city, a church, an episcopate, a reign, and so forth. Thus creation of Soul is an arithmogony, a flowing forth of numbers in harmonic ratios and proportions, musical proportions.

Accordingly, Timaeus postulates a harmonic set of relationships between the seven planets and their distances and a perfect number of time "when all the eight revolutions . . . are accomplished together and attain their completion at the same time" (39D). This Platonic Great Year was variously calculated, though the majority of the Neoplatonists thought of it as amounting to thirty-six thousand solar years (which runs counter to the traditional Hebreo-Christian notion that the world began in 5199 B.C., according to the Vulgate).[11] Significantly too, Plato sets up the planetary order as Moon, Sun with Mercury and Venus moving in equally swift orbits but "endowed with an opposite force." Presumably, Mars, Jupiter, and Saturn follow. In any event, this is an un-Ptolemaic order and Ficino's revival of it (and of the Porphyrian variant that transposes Venus and Mercury) may have helped weaken the general learned commitment to the Ptolemaic (or what was often known also as the Chaldaean) order.[12] This is particularly the case in light of the attribution in Neoplatonist metaphysics generally of a central role to the Sun as the eye of heaven, and the image there of the divine Mind even as it is the source of light and of life on earth.[13] Though not the World Soul, the Sun is in a way the supreme soul of the heavens, and Ficino views it as the intermediary almost between the World Soul and all other souls.[14]

This raises a question that has occasioned much debate this century since Ernst Cassirer and E. A. Burtt first proposed that the Renaissance Platonists were heralds of the Copernican revolution in two respects.[15] First, they brought Plato's emphasis on mathematics (and therefore by implication on quantity) to bear on the traditional Aristotelian and its alleged antimathematical concern with qualities, and thus ushered in a new commitment to mathematics, or at least to measuring, the tool *par excellence* of the revolution. Second, they drew attention to Plato's solarian imagery, obviously in the allegory of the cave in the *Republic* 6.508, where the Sun is compared to the Idea of the Good, but also in *Timaeus* 38Cff.; *Theaetetus* 153D; *Laws* 7.821Bff.; 10.898Dff.; etc., and dovetailed it with the solar theology found in some of the hermetic writings, in Macrobius, and in Julian the Apostate's memorable *Hymn to Helios.* They thus imaginatively, if unwittingly, prepared the ground for a heliocentric theory. These twin claims have both been attacked, reasserted, and modified, perhaps the boldest proponents being Frances Yates and Eugenio Garin, two outstanding historians of the Renaissance *mentalité* but neither one a scientist or historian of science, and the severest critic being E. W. Strong, a scholar with only a partial understanding of Renaissance Hermetism and Neoplatonism.[16] The question remains an interesting but contested one, particularly with regard to Galileo and Kepler.[17]

Among the various mathematical passages in the *Timaeus,* Ficino was drawn to Plato's complicated presentation at 53Cff. of the elements as being compounded of four of the five regular solids — pyramid, octahedron, icosahedron, and cube — their faces themselves consisting of two basic kinds of right triangle. The faces of the cubes composing the element of earth consist of half-square or isosceles triangles (24 in the traditional interpretation). But the 20 faces of the icosahedra composing water are each made up of 6 half-equilateral scalenes (120 in all); the 8 faces of the octahedra composing air are each made up again of 6 such scalenes (48 in all); and the 4 faces of the pyramids composing fire similarly (24 scalenes in all). The first such half-equilateral scalene has a side of 1, a hypotenuse of 2, and a perpendicular of root 3. With the help of the Pythagorean theorem and of other theorems he derived from Theon of Smyrna's *Expositio Rerum Mathematicarum ad Legendum Platonem Utilium* and from Nicomachus of Gerasa's two-book *Introductio Mathematica,*[18] Ficino was able, by adding or subtracting one, to establish, in addition to their obvious irrational square roots, what he calls rational square roots (because they are whole numbers) for a particular sequence of isosceles triangles.[19] Thus armed he eventually felt confident enough to set about explicating Plato's impenetrable reference in the *Republic* 8.546A–D to a fatal or nuptial number that determines the life cycle of even an ideally constituted republic, and thus the effectiveness of state-planned population control, seasonal matings, and eugenics.[20] This represents one of the signal instances in ancient philosophy of bringing mathematical and musical theories of harmony to bear on sociological and historical prediction, and specifically to chart not only such obviously periodic phenomena as fevers and plagues, but institutional "lives" and other phenomena we now assign to the purview of the social sciences. Statistical analysis and the problem of determining significant correlations have, in short, a Platonic genealogy, however odd this may first appear.

Interestingly, the fifth regular solid, the dodecahedron with its twelve pentagonal faces, Timaeus assigns at 55C to "the whole" decorated with its animal designs. Traditionally this has been taken to mean decorated with the twelve constellations of the zodiac, though Plato may have intended the ether defined at 58D as "the brightest part of air" (the *Epinomis* 984BC defines it rather as the most fiery form of air, intermediate between the pure air and the pure fire, the two identifications being not easily reconciled). Similarly, Plato's *Phaedo* 110Bff. compares the earth to a ball made by sewing twelve pentagonal bits of parti-colored leather together. This dodecahedron cannot in reality be constructed from right triangles,[21] though ancient commentators such as Albinus thought that it consisted of 360 such triangles (the 12 pentagons being divided into 5 triangles subdivided in turn into 6 right scalenes). This would of course correspond to the 360 degrees of the heavenly circle and was compelling for that reason, as well as for the numerological implications of 5, 6, and 12. The important postulation, however, is that the sublunar and the celestial realms are linked in that both consist ultimately of one of the two forms of right triangle. Ficino's championship of this triangle-based physics,[22] opposing as it does the Aristotelian claim that the translunar realms consist of a fifth element essentially different from the other four, highlights the role of Euclidean, and more particularly of Pythagorean, geometry as the tool for what we now think of as chemical and physical analysis. It was not only Galileo's subsequent gazing at the moon that altered men's perceptions of the nature of the difference between the translunar and the sublunar orbs, but the newly revived Platonic geometry of right triangles, their hypotenuses, and the insistent problem they posed of finding rational roots for square powers. For such a mathematics sought to account for the fiery heavens, the air, and the terraqueous orb alike.

For Ficino there were also important psychological implications. From the Scholastics and from Aristotle he inherited the notion of our "habitus,"[23] meaning our natural condition or character, what governs or moves our nature and the nature of any soul; and he believes that the soul reacquires its true habitus when it turns back toward its own intelligence, for the habitus contains the formulas of the Ideas in us, which mirror the absolute Ideas and enable us accordingly to participate in the intelligible realm. The habitus is tied, on the one hand, to the notion of form and, on the other, to the notion of power or potency: we can even think of it apparently as the potentiality in our soul for becoming pure mind. The reacquisition of our habitus is the attainment of a kind of musical concord (the recurrent analogy) and thus of a kind of arithmetical evenness. But not an evenness associated with the even numbers as such; for in the Pythagorean-Platonic mathematical tradition, even numbers, because they take their origin from the two, the dyad, are inferior to the odd numbers which take their origin from the one, the monad.[24] Because the tradition thinks of the succession of odd numbers geometrically as forming ever-increasing squares, the summing of such numbers is the key to the succession of arithmetic squares — $1 + 3 = 4$ (2^2); $1 + 3 + 5 = 9$ (3^2); $1 + 3 + 5 + 7 = 16$ (4^2); and so on — and is known as the equilateral series, because it produces the two equal sides we predicate of a geometric square.[25] By contrast, the summing of even numbers results in numbers for which there are no rational (integral) square roots — $2 + 4 = 6$; $2 + 4 + 6 = 12$; $2 + 4 + 6 + 8 = 20$; and so on — which summing is known as the unequilateral series.[26] Our true habitus is made analogous to the equilateral sums because it is even, balanced, equal to itself: as a sum it is the child of odd numbers, but as a product it has a whole number root. Unstable and dangerous habitus are by contrast the result of unequilateral summing, and as products they result not from the squaring of one number but from the multiplication of two different numbers (2×3; 3×4 or 2×6; 4×5 or 2×10). And here we must note that "power" (δύναμις) in Greek signifies in any mathematical context either the square or the square root of a number.[27]

If our perfected habitus is this kind of geometric power, then we must think of it as a square or a square root; think of it, in other words, as resembling the rational power or the rational square root of the hypotenuse of a right triangle and particularly, because its sides are equal, of an isosceles right triangle (the key triangle we recall in Timaeus' presentation of the cube forming the fundamental constituent of earth), in which case the Pythagorean theorem is one of the keys to psychology. Ficino does in fact think of our soul, and even of the hypostasis Soul, as analogous to a surface or plane formed by a triangle's three sides (to which correspond the soul's three powers of understanding, wrath, and desire). Planar Soul stands, therefore, in contrast, on the one hand, to Body that is like a three-dimensional solid and, on the other, to pure Mind that is like the line. Beyond all extension is the One that resembles not so much the point as the unextended monad. Thus the soul can be treated as if it were a right triangle, and its habitus as the power, so to speak, of its hypotenuse. This has a number of medical, psychiatric, musical, astrological, and magical implications; and we stand on the brink if not of a bio-mathematics, then of an iatro-mathematics, however primitive and bizarre. At the very least it is implicit, as Ficino discovered, in the triangle-based physics of the *Timaeus.*

Demonological issues also emerge at this point along with an attendant science.[28] In Renaissance Neoplatonism, given the allegiance to the twin principles of God's having made the world as full as possible and of his having made it continuous, the demons had to exist to fill what would otherwise have been a huge gap of air, divided into three zones of misty, pure, and fiery, between the teeming life of the terraqueous Earth and the realm of the celestial gods (often identified with the lower angels). This last is in the realm of the pure fire that begins with the Moon and stretches out to the sphere of Saturn, on to the sphere of the fixed stars and the *primum mobile,* and beyond to the angelic orders surrounding God himself. Birds were not thought to fill the sublunar space of air and were located rather in the watery and earthy spheres. Thus some kind of being had to live between us and the fiery gods, and such had to be the airy spirits, the Greeks' *daimones,* who were thought to crowd the three zones of the air. For a Platonist, such airy demons were both a cosmological necessity and essentially beautiful and good; and even for a Christian Platonist they stood as a necessary witness to creation's plenitude and continuity and not merely as an ornament of nature. Ficino was accordingly reluctant to accept the orthodox equation of the demons with the fallen satanic host, though he had to acknowledge that some demons were bad for us (as a trained exorcist he apparently expelled two saturnian poltergeists from some shabby quarters in Florence in October 1493 and December 1494).[29] Predictably, for any Neoplatonist interpreter the *loci classici* on the topic are Socrates' references in a number of dialogues to his warning voice, his τὸ δαιμόνιον.[30]

Demonology was therefore a legitimate area of Platonic, Plotinian, and, in a way, scientific and cosmological speculation. But given the *Timaeus'* triangles and the standard Neoplatonist definition of a demon as a higher rational soul intermediate between the human and the celestial, between men and the star gods, mathematics was also a way of understanding and, Ficino averred, of controlling the planar structure of the demons' souls, their habitus, and other triangulated powers. Nowhere would this be more apposite than in that branch of applied geometry with extraordinary implications for the practice of demonic magic, the science of optics.[31] Ficino visualized the Platonic magician as someone who uses his spirit-habitus to catch, focus, and reflect the streams of images that flow from objects, to establish as it were a planar control over the solid elemental world. But the Platonic demons have the same magical capacities, to a higher degree than even the most accomplished magus. Ficino seems to have thought of them, presiding as they do over the planar realm, as the lords of the world's triangles and of the Pythagorean comparabilities that govern their sides and their various powers.

Nature is full of planes — water and ice, sand and rock surfaces, mist and cloud phenomena — that reflect or refract light rays, light being the intermediary between the sensible and the intelligible realms. But we encounter planes most obviously in the natural faceting of gems and crystals. The play of light on such planar surfaces is what the magus and the demon alike can manipulate with the habitus of their spirit, the faculty that resembles light in that it too is an intermediary between the sensible and intelligible. Furthermore, given the ancient formula that "like affects like," the demons can act upon and influence light, being the preeminent powers in the realm of light. This is in part because they are traditionally the beings most skilled in mathematics, and especially in geometry, without which, so the vestibule had warned aspirants, none should enter the Academy, God himself being a geometer. The demons are adept in geometry — and in the applied geometries of optics, music, and astronomy — in part because their spiritual bodies or airy envelopes function like two-dimensional surfaces governed by their habitus, and thus by powers that resemble squaring and square-rooting; and in part because the souls of the higher demons at least are governed by geometric ratios, though governed too by astrological considerations, given that they are variously assigned to the seven planets as mediums of different planetary qualities. Hovering as beings with two-dimensional, planar powers above our solid bodies, they can perform mathematical marvels and serve as intermediaries between our elemental solidity and the fiery realm of the celestial gods.

Moreover, as geometers the demons are especially drawn to the planar optics we associate with mirrors, prisms, and faceting. Indeed, we are most likely to glimpse the higher demons, who love to dwell in and to play with light and with its reflections and refractions, in the presence of gems and mirrors. By a familiar metaphorical extension or retrojection, this suggests that, when we enter or reacquire our demonic state — pass like Alice into our light-filled mirror or gemlike selves after what Plato's *Phaedrus* 249A hazards as three thousand years as a philosopher — we become not only consummate mathematicians but essentially mathematical beings, numbers even in the old Pythagorean sense that Aristotle had deprecated. Correspondingly, we will then contemplate the Platonic Ideas either as Numbers or as being like numbers, just as several disciples of Plato — Speusippus and Xenocrates in particular — had argued.[32] In short, Ficino became fascinated by what is a highly problematic set of scientific or quasiscientific problems and methodologies involving geometry (especially the geometry of right triangles), figural arithmetic, optics, the demons, the philosophy of forms, astrology, and magic theory — a set derived ultimately from Plato's Pythagorean natural philosophy, but governed by some fundamental notions he encountered in ancient number theory. Most notably, communication with the demons has for Ficino a mathematical, and specifically a geometric, foundation and involves therefore a kind of scientific procedure, however subject to further astrological considerations.

Ficino's emphasis on Soul, moreover, and thus on the World Soul, directs our attention away from the notion of particular entities and species toward the general concepts of life, potentiality, being, and specifically of being part of a greater whole, while reflecting the whole in the part that is ourselves.[33] Whereas the anthropocentric focus on the Genesis myths of his younger contemporary Giovanni Pico della Mirandola would serve to underscore the uniqueness of man and the sciences that focus on his nature and institutions, Ficino's vision is more unitary, more panentheistic. His metaphysics is attuned to his abiding fascination with harmony, with the antiphonal and responsive play of voices in the choir of creation, with the counterturns of the cosmic dance; and he looked, as we still do, to mathematics, and particularly to the key notions of ratio and proportion, as the initiatory discipline for our entry into this choir, this starry dance. This originally musical concern is arguably his most arresting imaginative legacy, and it makes him in a way a harbinger of modern cosmology and of our commitment to the discovery of fundamental and mutually corroborative and interacting laws that is now the preoccupation of particle physics and astrophysics alike.

To conclude, Ficino's Neoplatonist interpretation of the *Timaeus* played a complicated role, I believe, in the birth of modern science. It made interesting, if ephemeral, contributions to what later became the physical sciences of astronomy, cosmology, and physics and to the life sciences of medicine, including psychology and psychiatry. It also contributed both to the defense of, and to the attack on, astrology, later denominated a pseudoscience, while eschewing for the most part that other important pseudoscience, alchemy. It dabbled too, by cross-referring to Plato's *Republic,* in the study of such social-science problems as population-control theory, eugenics, and the theory of cycles in states and polities; and it presented demonology as a science. Above all, it foregrounded Plato's great cosmogonic myth of the Demiurge, on the one hand, and the sections on the right triangles and on the elements of Pythagorean ratio and harmony theory, on the other. With the possible exception of his psychiatric speculations, none of these was a lasting contribution, not surprisingly so because Ficino's revival of the *Timaeus* preceded the discovery of the New World, the harnessing of the telescope and microscope, Copernicus, Vesalius, Brahe's new star tables, Galileo, Gilbert's work on the magnet, and Harvey's on the circulatory system. But the mindset of Ficino was nonetheless attuned to science; and in reviving Plato's *Timaeus* he inevitably engaged some of the central questions still engaging modern scientists. Assuredly, he would have given precedence to Kepler and Newton as "brother Platonists" over and against others drawn to the dialogue for literary or even theological reasons.

Finally, we must recognize, as in the case of any profoundly original philosophical system, that the level of abstraction and generalization in Ficino's Timaean Platonism ensures for many of its key ideas a continuing imaginative life and even an intellectual validity—on occasions certainly a suggestive bearing and appropriateness—*mutatis mutandis,* providing one adjusts them to the question under discussion. By the same token we must remain constantly alert to the dangers of analogy. For all his theoretical and interpretative sophistication, Ficino was not in the final analysis one of the founders, the necessary causes, of modern science; and its epochal discoveries occurred independently of him and the *Timaeus* he translated and expounded. Whether he and/or it acted in any way as a contributory cause remains, however, an open and a fascinating question.

Notes

1. For a critical edition of the text which the ancient Neoplatonists, Ficino, and others all attributed to the pre-Platonic "Timaeus Locrus," but which is in fact a later (probably first century A.D.) summary of Plato's dialogue, see W. Marg, *Timaeus Locrus: "De Natura Mundi et Animae,"* Philosophia Antiqua 24 (Leiden: Brill, 1972). This includes a description of the many Renaissance manuscripts.

2. The first version was originally published in 1484 in Ficino's great *Platonis Opera Omnia* translation. The final version appeared in his 1496 *Commentaria In Platonem,* and this was then republished in the various editions of Ficino's own *Opera Omnia* of 1561, 1576, and 1641, the Basel 1576 edition (repr. Turin: Bottega d'Erasmo, 1983) now being the standard one. For the various details, see my "Marsilio Ficino's Interpretation of Plato's *Timaeus* and Its Myth of the Demiurge," in *Supplementum Festivum: Studies in Honor of Paul Oskar Kristeller,* ed. J. Hankins, J. Monfasani, and F. Purnell Jr. (Binghamton, N.Y.: MRTS, 1987), 399–439, at 402–4.

3. Tullio Gregory, *"Anima Mundi": La filosofia di Guglielmo di Conches e la scuola di Chartres* (Florence: Sansoni, 1955), 17, 37, 133–51; idem, *Platonismo medievale: studi e ricerche* (Rome: Istituto storico italiano per il Medio Evo, 1958), chap. 4 ("Il *Timeo* e i problemi del platonismo medievale"); M.-D. Chenu, *La théologie au douzième siècle* (Paris: Vrin, 1957), 118–28; and Eugenio Garin, *Studi sul platonismo medievale* (Florence: Le Monnier, 1958), chap. 1, esp. 82–84.

4. The case for Calcidius' debt to Neoplatonism, and particularly to Porphyry's *In Timaeum,* was argued by J.H. Waszink in the introduction to his great edition, *Calcidius: In Timaeum,* Corpus Platonicum Medii Aevi 4 (2d ed.; London: Warburg Institute, 1975), xvii–cvi; see also his *Studien zum "Timaioskommentar" des Calcidius,*

vol. 1: *Die erste Hälfte des Kommentars (mit Ausnahme der Kapitel über die Weltseele)*, Philosophia Antiqua 12 (Leiden: Brill, 1964). The case against was succinctly put by John Dillon in *The Middle Platonists, 80 B.C. to A.D. 220* (Ithaca, N.Y.: Cornell University Press, 1977), 401–8. For a survey of the *Timaeus'* fortune in Antiquity, see M. Baltes, *Die Weltentstehung des platonischen "Timaios" nach den antiken Interpreten*, 2 vols., Philosophia Antiqua 30 and 35 (Leiden: Brill, 1976–78); and for the views of Plotinus in particular, see J.-M. Charrue, *Plotin: Lecteur de Platon* (Paris: Belles Lettres, 1978), 117–55.

5. For other Renaissance responses to the *Timaeus*, see James Hankins, "The Study of the *Timaeus* in Early Renaissance Italy," in *Natural Particulars: Nature and the Disciplines in Renaissance Europe*, ed. A. Grafton and N.G. Siraisi (Cambridge: MIT Press, 1999), 77–119. For the medieval situation, see Gregory, *"Anima Mundi"*; idem, *Platonismo medievale;* Chenu, *La théologie au douzième siècle;* Garin, *Studi sul platonismo medievale;* and P.E. Dutton, "Material Remains of the Study of the *Timaeus* in the Later Middle Ages," in *L'enseignement de la philosophie au XIIIe siècle: Autour du "Guide de l'étudiant" du MS. Ripoll 109*, ed. C. Lafleur and J. Carrier, Studia Artistarum: Études sur la Faculté des arts dans les Universités médiévales 5 (Turnhout: Brepols, 1997), 203–30.

6. P.O. Kristeller, *The Philosophy of Marsilio Ficino* (New York: Columbia University Press, 1943; repr. Gloucester, Mass.: Peter Smith, 1964), 168ff., 252; Allen, "Marsilio Ficino's Interpretation," 410–17; Jörg Lauster, *Die Erlösungslehre Marsilio Ficinos: Theologiegeschichtliche Aspekte des Renaissanceplatonismus* (Berlin: de Gruyter, 1998), 133, 162.

7. See Ficino's *In Phaedrum* 11, ed. Allen (Berkeley, 1981), 120ff., 126ff., for a Neoplatonist analysis of this particular use of "heaven."

8. *Opera Omnia* 866.3–867: "Timaeus ostendens mundum a Deo suae bonitatis gratia fuisse creatum, Deumque a principio coelum terramque creavisse, deinde aereum spiritum super aquas circumfudisse, atque haec omnia tamdiu permansura [*Opera* reads permansuram] quamdiu divinae placuerit voluntati. Deum fecisse hominem adeo sibi similem ut unicum Dei in terris cultorem terrenorumque dominum collocaverit."

9. See L. Bianchi, *L'errore di Aristotele: la polemica contro l'eternità del mondo nel XIII secolo* (Florence: La Nuova Italia, 1984) for the backdrop.

10. For a fascinating study, see Stephen Gersh, *Concord in Discourse: Harmonics and Semiotics in Late Classical and Early Medieval Platonism* (Berlin/New York: Mouton de Gruyter, 1996).

11. Bishop Ussher's famous date of 23 Oct. 4004 B.C. for the world's birthday is just one of a number of speculative options promoted since Antiquity.

12. In his *In Timaeum* 35 (*Opera Omnia* 1461), Ficino argues that "Geber" (Abu Musa Jabir ibn Hayyan) had proved Plato correct. For the planetary order in Plato, see A.E. Taylor's venerable *Commentary on Plato's "Timaeus"* (Oxford: Clarendon, 1928), 192–93; and for the controversy in the Renaissance, see S.K. Heninger Jr., *The Cosmographical Glass: Renaissance Diagrams of the Universe* (San Marino, Calif.: Huntington Library, 1977), 58–59, 66–79; and in general the recent magisterial study by E. Grant, *Planets, Stars and Orbs: The Medieval Cosmos, 1200–1687* (Cambridge: Cambridge University Press, 1994).

13. See especially Ficino's two later tracts, the *De Sole* and the *De Lumine* (of 1492–93), now in his *Opera Omnia* 965–67, 976–86. There is an English translation of the former by Graeme Tobyn and others in *Sphinx* 6 (1994): 124–48.

14. Of central importance were the Emperor Julian's *Hymn to Helios* and the eighth Orphic hymn, the *Hymn to Helios* (8 – 9 Quandt). See the various essays collected in *Le Soleil à la Renaissance, sciences et mythes* (Brussels: Presses universitaires de Bruxelles, 1965).

15. Ernst Cassirer, *The Individual and the Cosmos in Renaissance Philosophy,* trans. Mario Domandi (1927; Oxford: Blackwell, 1963); idem, "Mathematische Mystik und Mathematische Naturwissenschaft: Betrachtungen zur Entstehungsgeschichte der exacten Wissenschaft," *Lychnos* 5 (1940): 248 – 65 (trans. E.W. Strong in *Galileo: Man of Science,* ed. E. McMullin [New York: Basic Books, 1967], 338 – 51); idem, "Galileo's Platonism," in *Studies and Essays in the History of Science and Learning,* ed. M.F. Ashley Montagu (New York: Schuman, 1946), 277 – 97; E.A. Burtt, *The Metaphysical Foundations of Modern Physical Science: A Historical and Critical Essay* (New York: Harcourt Brace, 1924; rev. ed. 1932).

16. Frances Yates, *Giordano Bruno and the Hermetic Tradition* (Chicago: University of Chicago Press, 1964); idem, "The Hermetic Tradition in Renaissance Science," in *Art, Science, and History in the Renaissance,* ed. C.S. Singleton (Baltimore: Johns Hopkins University Press, 1967), 255 – 74. Of many cautionary assessments, the best is Robert Westman's "Magical Reform and Astronomical Reform: The Yates Thesis Reconsidered," in *Hermeticism and the Scientific Revolution,* ed. R. Westman and J.E. McGuire (Los Angeles: Clark Library, 1977), 1 – 91. For Eugenio Garin, see *Scienza e vita civile nel Rinascimento italiano* (Rome/Bari: Laterza, 1965); trans. Peter Munz as *Science and Civic Life in the Italian Renaissance* (Garden City, N.Y.: Anchor, 1969), esp. chaps. 5 – 6; idem, "La rivoluzione copernicana e il mito solare," in Garin's *Rinascite e rivoluzioni: Movimenti culturale dal XIV al XVIII secolo* (Rome: Laterza, 1975), 255 – 95. For E.W. Strong, see *Procedures and Metaphysics: A Study in the Philosophy of Mathematical-Physical Science in the Sixteenth and Seventeenth Centuries* (Berkeley: University of California Press, 1936; repr. Hildesheim: Olms, 1966).

17. The literature is enormous, but particularly helpful are Stillman Drake, "Galileo's Platonic Cosmogony and Kepler's *Prodromos,*" *Journal of the History of Astronomy* 4.3 (1973): 174 – 91; A. Koyré, "Galileo and Plato," *Journal of the History of Ideas* 4 (1943): 400 – 428; T.P. McTighe, "Galileo's Platonism: A Reconsideration," in *Galileo: Man of Science,* ed. E. McMullin (New York: Basic Books, 1967), 365 – 87; T.R. Girill, "Galileo and Platonistic Methodology," *Journal of the History of Ideas* 31 (1970): 501 – 20; and James Hankins, "Galileo, Ficino, and Renaissance Platonism," in *Humanism and Early Modern Philosophy,* ed. J. Kraye and M.W.F. Stone (London: Routledge, 2000), 209 – 37.

18. See Sebastiano Gentile, "Sulle prime traduzioni dal greco di Marsilio Ficino," *Rinascimento,* 2d ser. 30 (1990): 74 – 76; and my *Nuptial Arithmetic: Marsilio Ficino's Commentary on the Fatal Number in Book VIII of Plato's "Republic"* (Berkeley: University of California Press, 1994), 31 – 34.

19. Allen, *Nuptial Arithmetic,* 56 – 58.

20. Ibid., chaps. 2 – 3.

21. As noted by Francis M. Cornford, *Plato's Cosmology,* International Library of Psychology, Philosophy and Scientific Method (New York: Harcourt, Brace/London: Kegan Paul, 1937), 213, 218.

22. Allen, *Nuptial Arithmetic,* 93 – 100; see also my "Marsilio Ficino: Daemonic Mathematics and the Hypotenuse of the Spirit," in *Natural Particulars: Nature and the*

Disciplines in Renaissance Europe, ed. A. Grafton and N.G. Siraisi (Cambridge: Harvard University Press, 1999), 121–37, where several of the themes treated below are developed at greater length.

23. Allen, "Marsilio Ficino: Daemonic Mathematics," 125–30.

24. Hence the Neoplatonist popularity of line 75 from Vergil's eighth eclogue, "Numero deus impare gaudet."

25. Allen, *Nuptial Arithmetic,* 54.

26. Ibid., 55.

27. Taylor, *Commentary on Plato's "Timaeus,"* 372; and Thomas L. Heath, *A History of Greek Mathematics* (Oxford: Clarendon, 1921; repr. New York, 1981), 1.155. The key texts are Plato's *Republic* 9.587D9 (square) and *Theaetetus* 147D3ff. (square root) and Euclid's *Elements* 10.

28. Allen, *Nuptial Arithmetic,* 98–100.

29. *In Timaeum,* summa 24 (*Opera Omnia* 1469–70); Paul Oskar Kristeller, *Supplementum Ficinianum* (Florence: Olschki, 1937), 1.cxxi. See also Ficino's letter on ensnaring demons, to his great friend Giovanni Cavalcanti on 12 Dec. 1494 (*Opera Omnia* 961.2).

30. See my *Synoptic Art: Marsilio Ficino on the History of Platonic Interpretation* (Florence: Olschki, 1998), chap. 4 ("Socrates and the Daemonic Voice of Conscience").

31. Tamara Albertini, *Marsilio Ficino: Das Problem der Vermittlung von Denken und Welt in einer Metaphysik der Einfachheit* (Munich: Fink, 1997), 76–85.

32. Thomas L. Heath, *Mathematics in Aristotle* (Oxford: Clarendon, 1949), 220; W.K.C. Guthrie, *A History of Greek Philosophy* (Cambridge: Cambridge University Press, 1962–81), 5.459–60, 473.

33. For Ficino's intricate grasp of the problems associated with part/whole arguments, see his *Platonic Theology* 4.4.2–4, ed. and trans. Michael J. B. Allen and J. Hankins (Cambridge: Harvard University Press, 2001), 1.296–301.

7

PAUL OSKAR KRISTELLER AND MARSILIO FICINO: *E TENEBRIS REVOCAVERUNT*

I WAS NEVER one of Kristeller's graduate students at Columbia, though I sometimes wish now, given my subsequent close encounters with several in that golden *brigata*, that I had had the opportunity. I first came to Kristeller's scholarship by way of a copy of *The Philosophy of Marsilio Ficino* that I read in Ann Arbor in January of 1969,[1] the year of Cambodia, of the Chicago Seven, of the Moon walk, and of Nixon's tape-recorded attempt to join the Second Sophistic. I found the 1964 reprint in a bookshop on the campus perimeter, having been pushed into its doorway by someone, possibly official, racing after what turned out to be a streaker with a coonskin hat. Thus this Lupercalian Anthony and POK, if I might be permitted this one use of the acronym by which Kristeller's friends commonly referred to him, are jointly responsible for my family's long hedonistic career in southern California. However, it was not until after my doctoral work on the *Philebus Commentary* that I summoned up enough courage to write to Kristeller with my fardel of queries. He answered almost by return of mail with a host of valuable suggestions and invited me to lunch with him and to a postprandial stroll under the stoas of a still turbulent Columbia. He was thereafter immensely and characteristically generous to me as a scholar, even as my understanding of Ficino began gradually to diverge from, and sometimes to challenge, his own.

■

In the preface to his book, several chapters of which had already appeared as articles,[2] Kristeller reviewed the state of Ficino studies and Ficino's reputation

1. Trans. Virginia Conant (New York: Columbia University Press, 1943; reprint Gloucester, MA: P. Smith, 1964). Hereafter *Philosophy of Marsilio Ficino*.

2. See Kristeller's preface for details.

I

in 1937, the year he completed (in German) the original version of a study which he had planned as early as 1931 and for which he had laid the ground work, by his own testimony, two years later.[3] Because of his own troubled career in the anti-semitic years leading up to the Second World War and his flight from Germany to Italy and thence to the United States, his work first appeared in the English version of 1943, then in the Italian version of 1953 (though this had been ready since 1938),[4] and finally in the German of 1972.[5] In it he underscored the contributions particularly of Marian Heitzman, a Polish scholar who sometimes wrote in Italian and who had explored in some depth the arcane topic of Ficino's epistemological debts to Avicenna and to the Avicennizing Augustinianism of the Middle Ages along with the equally challenging topic of Ficino's views on liberty and fate.[6] But he also paid tribute to Ernst Cassirer and Giovanni Gentile, and to one of their prickly disciples, Guiseppe Saitta, whose 1923 book on Ficino was the best and substantially the only one to precede his own (in the second and third editions of 1943 and 1954, however, Saitta took only partial account of Kristeller's fundamental scholarly contribution).[7] Cassirer, Gentile, and Saitta represented the neo-Kantian and neo-Hegelian idealists that W. G. Craven, in a revisionary and bellicose 1981 study of Giovanni Pico della Mirandola, attacked on every ground possible as tendentious "misreaders" of Pico, and by implication of Ficino too.[8]

In 1940 — and therefore presumably in the midst of raging anti-Axis sentiments — Avery Dulles, who went on to become a Jesuit, a distinguished theologian, and recently a cardinal, wrote an amazingly accomplished

3. See his *A Life of Learning.* Charles Homer Haskins Lecture, American Council of Learned Societies, New York, NY. April 26, 1990. ACLS Occasional Paper 12, p. 7.

4. *Il pensiero filosofico di Marsilio Ficino* (Florence: Sansoni, 1953; Le Lettere 1988). Kristeller always regarded this as the superior version since it contained two important indices (of authors cited in Ficino's works and of passages cited in the study itself), along with citations from Ficino in their original Latin.

5. *Die Philosophie des Marsilio Ficino* (Frankfurt-am-Main: Kostermann, 1972). I shall be using the English version here.

6. Marian Heitzman, "L'agostinismo avicennizzante e il punto di partenza della filosofia di Marsilio Ficino," *Giornale critico della filosofia italiana* 16 (1935): 295–322, 460–80; and 17 (1936), 1–11; idem, "La libertà e il fato nella filosofia di Marsilio Ficino," *Rivista di filosofia neo-scolastica* 28 (1936): 350–71; and 29 (1937): 59–82.

7. *La filosofia di Marsilio Ficino* (Messina: G. Principato, 1923); 2nd ed., with a new title, *Marsilio Ficino e la filosofia dell'umanesimo* (Florence: F. Le Monnier, 1943); 3rd ed. (Bologna: Fiammenghi & Nanni, 1954).

8. *Giovanni Pico della Mirandola, Symbol of His Age: Modern Interpretations of a Renaissance Philosopher* (Geneva: Librairie Droz, 1981).

Harvard Phi Beta Kappa prize essay entitled *Princeps Concordiae: Pico della Mirandola and the Scholastic Tradition.*[9] In a little appendix, "Italian Historiography and the Problem of Pico," he declared magisterially, at the ripe old age of twenty-one, that "In general, the standard Italian works on Renaissance philosophy, and especially on Pico, must be read with extreme caution. In recent years almost every scholar who has entered the field has written for the sake of demonstrating some preconceived theory. Impartial scholarship is scarcely to be found."[10] He singled out Croce and Gentile, and then Saitta and Semprini, and, by idealist association, Cassirer, as mere immanentists committed to expounding the theme of man's autonomy. But he went on to note, "Another German, Kristeller, merits our attention ...because most of his works have appeared in Italian and because he was formerly associated with Gentile. Kristeller, however, is not to be classed among the idealists.... Unlike [them], Kristeller is apparently unbiased in his approach, and deals in ideas rather than in empty words. Unfortunately for our purposes, he has done far less research on Pico than on Ficino."[11] Kristeller subsequently, if unintentionally, obliged Dulles by writing for the Mirandola commemorative conference of 1963 what is to this day the most comprehensive essay on Pico's multiple sources.[12]

The idealists' appropriation of Ficino for an Italian national intellectual and historiographical agenda accorded Ficino a central position in the emergence of an anthropocentric metaphysics trumpeted as Italy's signal contribution to the history of Western philosophy. This distorted if eye-catching perspective was in many ways the least of Kristeller's problems in the Ficinian world of 1931. First he had to contend with the still nascent state of Ficinian scholarship. Apart from some brief but seminal analyses by Cassirer, especially in his *Individuum und Kosmos in der Philosophie der Renaissance* of 1927,[13] along with the massive if misleading work on Ficino's Platonic Academy by Arnaldo della Torre,[14] and Saitta's important

9. Cambridge, MA: Harvard University Press, 1941.

10. Ibid., 170.

11. Ibid., 170–71.

12. "Giovanni Pico della Mirandola and His Sources," in *L'opera e il pensiero di Giovanni Pico della Mirandola nella storia dell'umanesimo, Convegno internazionale (Mirandola 15-18 Settembre 1963)*, 2 vols (Florence: Istituto nazionale di studi sul Rinascimento, 1965), 35–133, and reprinted in his *Studies in Renaissance Thought and Letters*, 4 vols. (Rome: Edizioni di storia e letteratura, 1956–96), 3:227–304.

13. Leipzig and Berlin: B.G. Teubner, 1927.

14. *Storia dell'Accademia Platonica di Firenze* (Florence: Carnesecchi, 1902). Its assumptions, though accepted, at least initially, by Kristeller, have been radically called into question by

but tendentious book, he could turn to just a few preliminary general expositions of Ficino's views, many of them inaccurate or at best summaries of one or two texts, or to various specialized studies: Ferdinando Gabotto on Ficino's pleasure theory in the *De Voluptate*,[15] Walter Dress's Protestant exploration of Ficino's incomplete Commentary on Romans,[16] and so on.[17] But he also had to confront the old Enlightenment (effectively Anglo-Saxon and anti-idealist) argument that Ficino, like many of the other influential thinkers of the pre-Cartesian Renaissance, was just a mystery-mongering philosophaster. This detraction was still being voiced — surprisingly, given the distinction of his work in the history of science and magic — by Lynn Thorndike,[18] and it is occasionally heard from historians who have not read Kristeller's collected works or those of his long-time friend and compeer Eugenio Garin, the two greatest modern scholars in the entire field of Renaissance philosophy and humanism.[19]

James Hankins, Kristeller's last dissertation student, and now himself the leading expert on Italian Platonism. In a series of articles he has advanced the notion that Ficino's Platonic Academy was largely the product of sixteenth-century Medici propaganda. See especially his "Cosimo de' Medici and the Platonic Academy," *Journal of the Warburg and Courtauld Institutes* 53 (1990): 144–62; "The Myth of the Platonic Academy in Florence," *Renaissance Quarterly* 44 (1991): 429–75; "Lorenzo de' Medici as a Patron of Philosophy," *Rinascimento*, 2nd ser. 34 (1994): 15–53; and "The Invention of the Platonic Academy of Florence," *Rinascimento*, 2nd ser. 41 (2001): 3–38. His views have in turn been contested by Arthur Field in "The Platonic Academy of Florence," in *Marsilio Ficino: His Theology, His Philosophy, His Legacy*, ed. Michael J.B. Allen and Valery Rees with Martin Davies (Leiden: E.J. Brill, 2002), 359–76.

15. "L'Epicureismo di Marsilio Ficino," *Rivista di filosofia scientifica* 10 (1891): 428–42.

16. *Die Mystik des Marsilio Ficino* (Berlin-Leipzig: W. de Gruyter, 1929).

17. See Kristeller's preface, p. ix, for a survey.

18. *A History of Magic and Experimental Science*, 8 vols. (New York: Macmillan, 1923–58). For the title of his chapter on Ficino, Thorndike borrowed the derogatory "philosophaster' from the Spanish humanist and philosopher, Juan Luís Vives (1492–1540). For the many critics of Ficino in the later fifteenth and sixteenth centuries, see Jill Kraye, "Ficino in the Firing Line: A Renaissance Neoplatonist and His Critics," in Allen and Rees, *Marsilio Ficino*, 377–97.

19. See James Hankins, "Two Twentieth-century Interpreters of Renaissance Humanism: Eugenio Garin and Paul Oskar Kristeller," *Comparative Criticism* 23 (2001): 3–19; and Christopher S. Celenza, *The Lost Italian Renaissance: Humanists, Historians, and Latin's Legacy* (Baltimore: The Johns Hopkins University Press, 2004). Though Garin focused on thinkers other than Ficino, his many works continually and suggestively refer to Ficino; and he has written articles on Ficino's debt to Augustine and to medieval astrology. See especially his *Lo zodiaco della vita: La polemica sull'astrologia dal Trecento al Cinquecento* (Rome-Bari: Laterza, 1976); "Immagini e simboli in Marsilio

Thus Kristeller was faced with both a daunting interpretative and a scholarly challenge: he had to establish Ficino's philosophical principles from some 2,000 folio pages of Latin, many of which no one had elucidated for centuries, and also from a cornucopia of material not in the *Opera Omnia* but still in manuscript collections throughout Europe, not all of them catalogued or catalogued correctly. At the same time he had to accept the possibility that in the end he might discover that he had labored to untangle the work of a prolific and accomplished but nonetheless derivative scholar who had nothing original to say, at least in terms of what the history of proper, or professional, philosophy, *Geistesgeschichte*, considered original in the Europe of the mid-twentieth century.

■

Having completed his doctoral work on Plotinus,[20] Kristeller turned to the legion of problems connected with Ficino: some of the manuscripts were troublesome to decipher and all three of the printed editions of the *Opera* were corrupt; there were knotty issues involved in distinguishing *canonica, spuria* and *dubia*; Ficino's bulky correspondence posed its own difficulties, not least of chronology and dating; many of the facts of Ficino's ecclesiastical career, his debts to patrons, and his intellectual development were awaiting discovery or authentication; and the horizon of the many, often recondite sources — sources frequently mediated via other sources — shimmered with a mirage of possibilities. If Kristeller immediately recognized the extent to which Ficino was acquainted with the works of Plato, Aristotle, Plotinus, the Areopagite, Augustine, Aquinas, and Dante, to name the seven most obvious pillars of his wisdom, I am not so sure he suspected the extent of Ficino's sustained indebtedness to the convoluted works of Proclus, and beyond Proclus indeed to a range of other daunting figures: Cicero, Apuleius, Theon of Smyrna, Nicomachus of Gerasa, Calcidius, Origen, Eusebius, Clement of Alexandria, Macrobius, Porphyry, Iamblichus, Synesius, Boethius, Psellus, Avicenna, Henry of Ghent, *et alii.*

He was aware too of the methodological and rhetorical issues posed by a repetitive thinker like Ficino whose most arresting ideas are often buried in

---

Ficino" now in his *Medioevo e Rinascimento: Studi e Ricerche* (Bari: Laterza, 1954, 2nd ed. 1961), 288–310; and various other essays in that collection and in his *La cultura filosofica del Rinascimento italiano* (Florence: Sansoni, 1961).

20. His doctoral thesis on Plotinus was "Der Begriff der Seele in der Ethik des Plotin," *Heidelberger Abhandlungen zur Philosophie und ihrer Geschichte* 19 (Tübingen: J.C.B. Mohr, 1929).

the veins of Platonic or Plotinian commentary. More than ascertaining his solution to, or his views on, this or that philosophical question, Kristeller insisted that we arrive at an understanding of Ficino's *forma mentis*, at what he called his "complex conception of the universe."[21] In a superficial sense all Platonists are alike, as ancient Epicureans or Californian academics are generically alike. But, as he repeatedly reminded us, there are extraordinary differences of texture separating the works say of Eriugena from those of Plotinus or of Iamblichus. And a great gulf separates Christian from non-Christian Platonists, Renaissance ones from ancient ones, a gulf as wide as that dividing the Pazzi chapel from the Pantheon, despite their shared architectural motifs. Interestingly, for all his close attention to the technical aspects of Ficino's philosophy — the theories of causality, of the *idolum*, of passive potentiality, of intention, of being the first in any genus *(primum in aliquo genere)*, and so on — Kristeller nonetheless emphasized a visionary Ficino, a man dominated by interiority, by the need to live the inner life,[22] and someone who pursued philosophy for essentially religious goals: to see the truth in the divine and to rise to the divine in the contemplation of truth, goals that from the sixteenth through to the early twentieth centuries prompted both attacks on and defenses of the integrity and orthodoxy of Ficino's Catholicism.[23]

Many of us have been drawn to some of the less systematic, more imaginative aspects of Ficino's thought and learning, aspects explored by Garin,[24] André Chastel,[25] Frances Yates,[26] D.P. Walker,[27] Ernst

21. *Philosophy of Marsilio Ficino*, 7.

22. See his *Philosophy of Marsilio Ficino*, Chapter 11, entitled "Internal Experience."

23. Kristeller especially notes Giuseppe Anichini, *L'Umanesimo e il problema della salvezza in Marsilio Ficino* (Milan: Società Editrice "Vita e Pensiero," 1937). But for earlier attacks on Ficino's Catholicism, see Kraye, "Ficino in the Firing Line."

24. See n. 9 above.

25. *Art et humanisme à Florence au temps de Laurent le Magnifique: Études sur la Renaissance et l'humanisme platonicien* (Paris: Presses universitaires de France, 1959; 2nd ed., 1961); idem, *Marsile Ficin et l'art* (Geneva-Lille: Droz, 1954; reprint Geneva: Droz, 1975).

26. *Giordano Bruno and the Hermetic Tradition* (London: Routledge & Kegan Paul, 1964; reprint New York: Random House, 1969; Chicago: University of Chicago Press, 1979), esp. Chapters 1 to 4.

27. *The Ancient Theology: Studies in Christian Platonism from the Fifteenth to the Eighteenth Century* (London: Duckworth, 1972); idem, *Music, Spirit, and Language in the Renaissance*, ed. P. Gouk (London: Variorum Reprints, 1985); idem, *Spiritual and Demonic Magic: From Ficino to Campanella* (London: Warburg Institute, 1958; reprint Notre Dame: University of Notre Dame Press, 1975).

Gombrich,[28] Edgar Wind.[29] These are the scholarly Corybantes who speak of Marsilio and the universal harmonies, of pantheism and panentheism, of cult and demonic magic and Orphic prayer and song; and it is they who have presented Ficino as a seeker after the ancient, but perennial wisdom, as a hermeticist, an astrologer, an occultist, as one of the first, perhaps the first, in the long line of Renaissance sages and mages whose magical and animistic world view was about to be eclipsed by the founding fathers of the philosophy of the mechanistic universe. Legatees in some fascinating ways of the Italian idealists, these scholars have found interwoven pagan and Christian mysteries in Ficino and in particular in the psycho-therapeutic masterpiece, the *De Vita* of 1489 (now finely edited and translated by Carol Kaske and John Clark[30] who generously thank Kristeller for his encouragement and advice). As someone who has also become entangled in unravelling the coils of poetic and numerological theology — of how the unity of Venus is divided into the trinity of the Graces, the unity of Fate into that of the Parcae, the unity of Saturn into that of Jupiter, Neptune and Pluto — I too have followed (like Attis?) in their priestly footsteps.

Kristeller, however, was temperamentally and intellectually averse to many of these enchanting, if not necessarily unorthodox, aspects of Ficino's thought. While acknowledging them in passing and dutifully explaining the concepts of the *spiritus* and the *idolum*, he never undertook a full inquiry into the background of Ficino's theosophy of the soul's ascent, and into his complex and potentially heretical notion of the World-Soul, and the cognate concept of a World-Spirit, mediating between the World-Soul and the World-Body or World-Machine, and binding the one to the other. These concepts are of crucial importance, however, for an understanding of the *De Vita* and its complex doctrine of Nature and its proportions and harmonies, and especially of the medical and magic theories presented in its third book; and they have unexpected psychological and musical implications that have recently been explored by such scholars as Brian Copenhaver,[31]

28. *Symbolic Images* (Oxford: Phaidon, 1972; 2nd ed., 1978).

29. *Pagan Mysteries in the Renaissance*, rev. ed. (New York: W.W. Norton, 1968).

30. Marsilio Ficino, *Three Books on Life* (Binghamton: Medieval & Renaissance Texts & Studies, 1989).

31. "Hermes Trismegistus, Proclus, and the Question of a Philosophy of Magic in the Renaissance," in *Hermeticism and the Renaissance: Intellectual History and the Occult in Early Modern Europe*, ed. I. Merkel and A.G. Debus (London: Associated University Presses; Washington, DC: Folger Shakespeare Library, 1988), 79–110; idem, "Hermes Theologus: The Sienese Mercury and Ficino's Hermetic Demons," in *Humanity and Divinity in Renaissance and Reformation: Essays in Honor of Charles Trinkaus*, ed. J.W. O'Malley, T.M. Izbicki, and G. Christianson (Leiden: E.J. Brill, 1993), 149–82; idem,

Gary Tomlinson,[32] Tamara Albertini,[33] William R. Bowen,[34] and Grantley Mcdonald.[35]

To the contrary, Kristeller was committed to what we might call the scholastic Ficino of the eighteen book *magnum opus* published in 1482, the *Platonic Theology*. By "scholastic" I do not mean Ficino's specific debts to the School Men, important and under-researched though they still are,[36] but rather his position as a bona fide medieval philosopher in his methodology, and, to a large extent, in his arguments and goals. Furthermore, by choosing to immerse himself in the *Platonic Theology* rather than the *De Vita*, or the Plato or Plotinus commentaries, and by digging down to the fundamental

---

"Iamblichus, Synesius and the Chaldaean Oracles in Marsilio Ficino's *De Vita Libri Tres:* Hermetic Magic or Neoplatonic Magic?" in *Supplementum Festivum: Studies in Honor of Paul Oskar Kristeller*, ed. James Hankins, John Monfasani, and Frederick Purnell, Jr. (Binghamton: Medieval & Renaissance Texts & Studies, 1987), 44–55; idem, "Lorenzo de' Medici, Marsilio Ficino and the Domesticated Hermes," in *Lorenzo il Magnifico e il suo mondo: Convegno internazionale di studi, Firenze 9–13 giugno 1992*, ed. Gian Carlo Garfagnini, (Florence: L.S. Olschki, 1994), 225–57; idem, "Renaissance Magic and Neoplatonic Philosophy: *Ennead* 4.3–5 in Ficino's *De Vita Coelitus Comparanda,*" in *Marsilio Ficino e il ritorno di Platone: Studi e documenti*, ed. G.C. Garfagnini, 2 vols. (Florence: L.S. Olschki, 1986), 351–69; idem, "Scholastic Philosophy and Renaissance Magic in the *De Vita* of Marsilio Ficino," *Renaissance Quarterly* 37 (1984): 523–54.

32. *Music in Renaissance Magic: Toward a Historiography of Others* (Chicago: University of Chicago Press, 1993).

33. *Marsilio Ficino: Das Problem der Vermittlung von Denken und Welt in einer Metaphysik der Einfachheit* (Munich: W. Fink, 1997).

34. "Ficino's Analysis of Musical Harmonia," in *Ficino and Renaissance Neoplatonism*, ed. Konrad Eisenbichler and Olga Pugliese (Ottawa: Dovehouse Editions, 1986), 17–27.

35. "Orpheus Germanicus: Metrical Music and the Reception of Marsilio Ficino's Poetics and Music Theory in Renaissance Germany," dissertation, University of Melbourne (Melbourne, 2002).

36. But see Kristeller's own "The Scholastic Background of Marsilio Ficino: With an Edition of Unpublished Texts," *Traditio* 2 (1944): 257–318, now in his *Studies*, 1:35–97; "Florentine Platonism and Its Relations with Humanism and Scholasticism," *Church History* 8 (1939): 201–11, now in his *Studies*, 3:39–48; and most importantly *Le Thomisme et la pensée italienne de la Renaissance* (Montreal: Institut d'études médievales, 1967), now in his *Medieval Aspects of Renaissance Learning: Three Essays*, trans. and ed. Edward P. Mahoney (Durham, NC: Duke University Press, 1974; rev. ed. New York: Columbia University Press, 1992). See also James Hankins, "Marsilio Ficino as a Critic of Scholasticism," *Vivens Homo* 5 (1994): 325–33; and Ardis B. Collins, *The Secular is Sacred: Platonism and Thomism in Marsilio Ficino's Platonic Theology* (The Hague: Nijhoff, 1974).

categories of Ficino's systematic thinking in that formidable summa, Kristeller developed an extraordinarily accurate conceptual "feel" for Ficino both as a late scholastic philosopher with a tilt towards Franciscan theological positions and as an early Renaissance Neoplatonist; so much so that he was able to anticipate Ficino's position on a given issue, even when the texts he was treating were silent or lacked the requisite formulations.

■

Let me turn, briefly, to an example of how *The Philosophy of Marsilio Ficino* continues to demonstrate its authority in this regard, an example that addresses the haunting metaphysical theme of not being there. It shows us how Kristeller was able to predict the top quarks that I subsequently found in the *Sophist* and *Parmenides Commentaries*,[37] texts that he had (he later confessed to me) merely skimmed through at the time. For in his important eighth chapter on causality, we can see him arriving at an intuitive understanding of what Ficino would and should have thought about the philosophy of not-being.

In the *Sophist Commentary* Ficino devotes chapters 35 through 38 to an analysis of difference. Unlike rest and motion that are "absolutes" and cannot easily be mixed together, "either formally or denominatively," identity and difference (or the same and the other) are "relative" and thus, though opposites, can be easily mingled (261.5–9).[38] But "the power of otherness," having been mingled from the beginning in the ideal forms, "makes negation" and "mixes not-being with being" (261.12–13). This is to assert that we can in a way equate not-being with otherness, and see the "communion" that pertains between identity and difference in that each shares in the characteristic of not being the other. This characteristic of not being something else marks the mutual relationships pertaining between the five classes and also those pertaining among different aspects of the same Idea. It means that even at this highest of ontological levels we must

37. Icastes: *Marsilio Ficino's Interpretation of Plato's* Sophist (Berkeley–Los Angeles: University of California Press, 1991), Chapters 1 and 2; also "Ficino's Theory of the Five Substances and the Neoplatonists' Parmenides," *Journal of Medieval and Renaissance Studies* 12 (1982): 19–44, and reprinted in *Plato's Third Eye: Studies in Marsilio Ficino's Metaphysics and its Sources* (Aldershot: Variorum, 1995); "The Second Ficino–Pico Controversy: Parmenidean Poetry, Eristic and the One," in *Marsilio Ficino e il ritorno*, 417–55, and reprinted in *Plato's Third Eye*; and my *Synoptic Art: Marsilio Ficino on the History of Platonic Interpretation* (Florence: L.S. Olschki, 1998), 78–79, 165–93.

38. All references are to the right-hand page and line-numbering in my edition (and translation) of the *In Sophistam* in *Icastes*, Part 2, 220–78; Chapters 35 to 38 are on 258–65.

predicate the communion of being with not-being, a communion that is present from the very origins of intelligible reality and not simply confined to the sensible realm. The first principles of ontology are necessarily those too of meontology.

How can we reconcile the hallowed Plotinian definition of matter as absolute not-being with what would seem to be both the *Sophist's* argument and the logic of Plotinian ontology? If being and not-being are mutually dependent — or what we would now think of as self-predicating — and if being extends through the realms of Mind, Soul, Forms-in-Body, and even Body but not to the One or to matter, then surely not-being, dependent as it is on being, will also extend through those realms, but not to the One or to matter: it cannot therefore be predicated of matter. One of the solutions to this dilemma is to predicate univocal and equivocal senses of not-being itself. Thus Ficino hastens to reject the idea that the realms of Mind, Soul, Forms-in-Body (sometimes equated with Quality), and Body (matter in extension) constitute a simple ontological pyramid, where absolute being gradually decreases into equivocal being, thence into equivocal not-being, and thence into absolute not-being. For this would have amounted, for all its schematic tidiness, to a refusal again to confront the chief interpretative challenge, or what Ficino would call the mystery, at the heart of the *Sophist,* where Plato's argument clearly envisages the copresence (if not coexistence exactly) of being and of not-being, not at the extremes of an ontological hierarchy but within each of its existents.

In Chapter 37 Ficino argues that "otherness" in the *Sophist* seems to signify "divisibility" and thus "deservedly it is also called not-being"; it can even be referred to as "the essence or nature or power or origin of not-being," though the notion of the "essence" of not-being has a paradoxical cast to it. This essence, furthermore, has been "sown in all beings": everything that is also is not (263.2–11). But the issue of equivocation inevitably arises. Surely difference, and therefore not-being, cannot be the same (if we may accept this paradoxical formulation) with regard to the realms of being on the one hand and to matter on the other? Ficino observes: "Otherness in the intelligible world is as it were a kind of matter; it is the cause there of any defect and difference, just as the matter in the sensible world, along simultaneously with dimension, is the cause of defect and disagreement everywhere and of distance" (263.11–14). But, whereas the otherness in the intelligible realm is the cause only of relative not-being, the otherness that is the foundation, the substrate of the sensible world, matter in other words, is the "beginning" *(initium),* not only, Ficino writes, of relative not-being, "the not-being of this or that" aspect or attribute or individual entity in the sensible realm, but also of absolute not-being (263.14–16). Difference, therefore, is univocal with regard to the realms of being — in that they and their constituent individual beings differ relatively from each other — but equivocal with regard to their relationship to matter — in that they differ from it absolutely. Thus Ficino is led to think of difference in the intelligible world analogously as a kind of matter, since it is matter's cause. Presumably, this quasi-matter which is difference is the same as Plotinus's intelligible matter as set forth in the *Enneads* 2:4.1–5, where it is associated with the procession *(proodos)* from the One (as elsewhere with the "indefinite dyad"), and where two of the *megista genê*, motion and difference, are associated with the descent into plurality that accompanies that procession.[39]

Now on page 135 of *The Philosophy of Marsilio Ficino* Kristeller had written, "Nonbeing is the opposite of Being [and]...does not participate in Being, and Being does not participate in Nonbeing. Consequently, if created things partipate in Being in different degrees, and if they are placed in a continual series between Nothing and the first Being, or God, it would be easy to assert that all things are composed of Being and Nonbeing and that their share in existence, which they receive from God, depends on their previous share in Nonbeing. Though Ficino does not formulate such a solution, it seems to result from his previous conceptions and to correspond perfectly to the theological dogma of creation out of nothing." Kristeller continued by arguing that this conception cannot be upheld "because of the dialectical character of Nonbeing." We must bear in mind that Kristeller did not have the *Sophist* in mind, let alone the *Sophist Commentary* which he had not studied in any detail, and that he was discussing the apologetic *Platonic Theology*, a work that was explicitly aimed at arguing for the immortality of the soul using various Platonic arguments but that was not intended as an exposition of Platonism per se, let alone of Plato's theory of being. And let me add that we should perhaps distinguish more carefully than we have in the past between what Ficino expounded as a Christian philosopher and what he presented by way of interpreting Plato and Plotinus correctly. Nonetheless, Kristeller had in fact intuited Ficino's analysis of the *Sophist*'s position, namely that "all things are composed of Being and Nonbeing" even though Being itself does not "participate" in Nonbeing.

Moreover, he had observed in an illuminating aside that this situation seems "to correspond perfectly to the theological dogma of creation out of nothing."[40] For in the *Sophist*'s terminology this is tantamount to saying that God created the world out of "difference" which is dialectically linked to one of the other primary ontological classes, namely, "sameness." In the *Timaeus* similarly, the Demiurge is described as mixing the creation in his bowl, his krater, out of sameness and difference,[41] a pair which seems to correspond to

39. Ibid., Chapter 2, esp., 69–73.

40. *Philosophy of Marsilio Ficino*, 135.

41. 35A, 37A, 41D ff.

the "limit" and the "indefinite" of *Philebus* 23C ff. and, with adjustments, to Aristotle's "form" and "matter." It points to the subtle problem of determining where Ficino stood on the contentious question of whether God created out of "relative" not-being — this being formless matter or Aristotle's not-being *per accidens* (as Clement of Alexandria had argued in his *Stromateis* 5:89.92); or out of "absolute" not-being, not-being per se, or total privation (as Origen had argued in the *De principiis* 2:1.4 without identifying matter with that privation). It is a controversial question whether, for a Christian, privation itself preexists the world's creation and, if so, in what sense one can think of its relationship to God. Clearly in a Proclian system God's oneness extends to sensible matter which Plotinus had equated with privation in the *Enneads* 2:4.14–16: and by this equation privation is in a sense one, or in Aristotelian terms the potentiality to be one. If it were not one, it would be many, the potentiality already becoming actuality.[42]

Most importantly, Kristeller alerts us to the complications introduced by transferring a number of the attributes the Platonists associated with *Nous*, the primary existent, to the Christian God, making God not only the equivalent of the Plotinian One but also, in part at least, of *Nous*, or of the One and *Nous* together. For Ficino himself always thought of God as more than the One, and was accustomed to transferring or reapportioning attributes, as Kristeller has well demonstrated.[43] Since God is being (however preeminently), God is also not-being (hence the validity of apophatic theology and its formulations), though Kristeller added the caveat that the attributes which might belong perhaps to Nothing "in its ontological function" "can find no hold in it because of its complete nullity" and "are therefore necessarily included in the all-comprehensive concept of God. This may explain," he concludes, "why the Christian metaphysicians do not oppose matter to God as did the ancient philosophers. Instead they oppose to Him impotent Nothing."[44] This suggests to me the arresting notion that God for Ficino can be defined as omnipotent Nothing.

Kristeller's insights here are the more impressive in that they were incidental; for in all of the four hundred odd pages of the book he never focuses on the problems of meontology. In accommodating Plotinian metaphysics, Ficino had to make a number of radical adjustments. From our viewpoint this got him into consistency problems; but from his viewpoint, it was the recurring challenge of adapting the ancient Arian theology, with its clearcut subordinationism, to Christian trinitarianism, where the Son is consubstantial with the Father

42. For the classic medieval discussion of *creatio ex nihilo*, see Thomas Aquinas, *Contra Gentiles*, 2, cc. 6–38; and *Summa Theologiae*, 1, qq. 44–46.

43. *Philosophy of Marsilio Ficino*, 167–69.

44. Ibid., 135–36.

and the Holy Spirit.[45] In essence, this became a duel in his mind between the metaphysics of Unity and the metaphysics of Being, where the goal was reconciliation on Platonic, not Aristotelian, grounds.

■

This takes us to what, in my view, are two problematic contentions Kristeller advanced in the monograph and never thereafter modified or retracted. The first is his claim that Ficino was original in devising an ontological scheme of five hypostases — the One, Mind, Soul, Quality, and Body — in order to highlight the central position of Soul, and by extension of the human soul.[46] My own research indicates that Ficino found this scheme clearly set forth in the two major works of Proclus he studied most carefully and which had an enormous impact on him, the *Theologia Platonica* and the *In Parmenidem*, works that are both centered on Plato's *Parmenides* and its interpretation and indeed on the history of that interpretation.[47] This history, fully grasped by Ficino in a remarkable feat of scholarly enquiry, has only recently been unravelled by Dodds, Saffrey, Westerink, Rist, Dillon, Trouillard, and others,[48] and Kristeller had not studied this tradition, though he did take Ficino's knowledge of Proclus' *Elements of Theology* into due account. Kristeller's claim for Ficino's originality in selecting a pentad thus becomes highly questionable, though the issue is complicated and someone might still be able to demonstrate a degree of originality in

45. See my "Marsilio Ficino on Plato, the Neoplatonists and the Christian Doctrine of the Trinity," *Renaissance Quarterly* 37 (1984): 555–84, and reprinted in *Plato's Third Eye*.

46. *Philosophy of Marsilio Ficino*, 106–8, 167–70, 266, 370, 384, 400–401. Kristeller continued to maintain that this was a Ficinian innovation in various later studies, e.g., in his "Ficino and Pomponazzi on the Place of Man in the Universe," in *Renaissance Thought II* (New York: Harper & Row, 1965), 102–10, at 109; and "Renaissance Concepts of Man. The Arensberg Lectures. 1. The Dignity of Man," in his *Renaissance Concepts of Man* (New York: Harper & Row, 1972), 1–21, at 10, reprinted in his *Renaissance Thought and Its Sources*, ed. Michael Mooney (New York: Columbia University Press, 1979), 161–81, at 173.

47. "Ficino's Theory of the Five Substances"; and *Icastes*, Chapter 2, passim. See also Anna De Pace, "Ficino e Plutarco: Storia di un equivoco," *Rivista di storia della filosofia* 1 (1996): 113–35; also her fascinating new book, *La scepsi, il sapere e l'anima: Dissonanze nella cerchia laurenziana* (Milan: LED, 2002), especially Chapter 1, sec. 2, 66–111: "La lezione di Proclo."

48. See especially H.D. Saffrey and L.G. Westerink's edition of Proclus' *Platonic Theology*, 6 vols. (Paris: Société d'Études "Les Belles Lettres," 1968–97), 1:lxxv-lxxxix, and my "Ficino's Five Substances," 26–29, for further references.

Ficino's presentation of each of the individual hypostases, and notably of Quality. What is incontestable is that the centrality of Soul in a scheme of five hypostases is something Ficino inherited from the Neoplatonists but did not engineer for himself, however brilliantly, extensively, and, we might note, continually he elaborated on the implications.

However, this remains a secondary problem, since it does not undermine — in fact, it reinforces — Kristeller's pivotal contention that Ficino's Christian Platonism was necessarily focused upon Soul as the mediating hypostasis of the cosmos. This focus on Soul does indeed render Ficino's Neoplatonism in many subtle ways different from Plotinus's own Platonism with its emphasis on the second hypostasis, *Nous*, and on the *nous* in us. For this noetic emphasis has the effect of making Plotinus's system more intellectualistic and less voluntaristic than Ficino's, with a host of ramifications that are not always found in, or derivable from, Proclus's analyses. Nevertheless, his decision, ultimately, to settle on the pentadic scheme, having toyed earlier with both a tetradic and an hexadic scheme as well, further underscores Ficino's continuing debt to Proclus (a debt that was also the Middle Age's). I suspect that Kristeller only came to appreciate the full extent of this debt in his later scholarly career, perhaps as a result of his becoming aware of the renewed interest, on the part of historians of ancient philosophy, in Proclian metaphysics; but he never had time to pursue it comprehensively, though he did compose an important over-view article.[49] The very title, however, of Ficino's *magnum opus*, identical as it is with the title of Proclus' own masterwork, suggests that the debt was a huge and indeed explicit one; and it continues to engage scholars as recent contributions by Werner Beierwaltes himself,[50] and by Christopher Celenza,[51] Alexandre Etienne,[52] Dilwyn Knox[53] and others testify.

49. "Proclus as a Reader of Plato and Plotinus, and his Influence in the Middle Ages and the Renaissance," in *Proclus: Lecteur et interprète des anciens; Actes du colloque international du Centre National de la Recherche Scientifique, Paris 2–4 Octobre 1985*, ed. J. Pépin and H.D. Saffrey (Paris: Éditions du Centre national de la recherche scientifique, 1987), 191–211, and reprinted in his *Studies*, 4:115–37.

50. See especially his Marsilio Ficinos Theorie des Schönen im Kontext des Platonismus, *Sitzungsberichte der Heidelberger Akademie der Wissenschaften, Philosophisch-historische Klasse*, 1980, 11. Abhandlung (Heidelberg, 1980).

51. Christopher S. Celenza, "Late Antiquity and Florentine Platonism: The 'Post-Plotinian' Ficino," in Allen and Rees, *Marsilio Ficino*, 71–97.

52. "Visages d'un interprète: Marsile Ficin et le *Timée*: De la découverte à la réception de la "physique" platonicienne," 2 vols. (Dissertation, University of Lausanne, 1998).

53. In a detailed forthcoming study of Ficino's *De Amore*.

The second and more important problem with *The Philosophy of Marsilio Ficino* is Kristeller's omission of any real consideration of Ficino's understanding of, and engagement with, classical and medieval dialectic and more particularly with Platonic and Neoplatonic dialectic. Indeed, he went so far as to declare that "there is almost nothing left in Ficino of Plato's conceptual dialectic."[54] Again, my own researches indicate to the contrary that Ficino has a sophisticated understanding of the Neoplatonic dialectical tradition, its origins and development, not surprisingly given his lifetime's engagement with the very dialogues that constitute its foundations — the *Sophist, Philebus, Statesman, Republic,* and above all the *Parmenides,* the pivotal text in Neoplatonic logic and dialectic as it was in Neoplatonic metaphysics. We cannot embark on a study of the problem here; and I must egotistically refer the reader to the last chapter in my own *Synoptic Art,* which is devoted to the topic of "Promethean Dialectic."[55] Suffice it to say that Ficino was fascinated by two dimensions of dialectical discourse. One is its links to love theory and the theories of reciprocation, amatory transformation, and magic. The other is its role in the development of the *via negativa,* the apophaticism which Ficino believed began with the *Parmenides* and reached its apogee with the works of the Areopagite, for him the authentic Athenian disciple of St. Paul and the crown *(culmen)* of Christian Platonism. Since both love theory and the *via negativa* are fundamental to Ficino's theory of the soul's ascent to union with the divine, Platonic dialectic, centered as it is on disuniting and uniting, *diairesis* and *synagôgê,* is unquestionably the capstone of Ficino's epistemology and psychology, and the key to an understanding of his intellectual mysticism. Again, we must bear in mind that in the 1930s Kristeller was writing before the major breakthroughs in our modern understanding of Proclus and the later Neoplatonic tradition, and notably in our understanding of the central, all-encompassing role played by the *Parmenides* in Proclus' thought, and therefore in the thought of the late fifth century [Pseudo-]Areopagite who was in fact his disciple.

■

The springs that sustain decades of scholarly energy are often hidden. Kristeller never abandoned Ficino after his magisterial monograph and the comprehensive achievement of the two volumes of his *Supplementum Ficinianum* that he published in 1937.[56] These volumes are still the authoritative

54. *Philosophy of Marsilio Ficino,* 240.

55. Pp. 149–93.

56. Florence: L.S. Olschki, 1937; reprinted 1973.

sorting out of the canon and its texts and of a host of other issues; and they include the first publication of most of the authentic writings that do not appear for various reasons in Ficino's *Opera Omnia.* They also provide biographies of Ficino's many correspondents, many of them difficult to track down. That they are in Latin, however, means that only the tattered remnant of the Latinate can toil in their vineyards; and this is a pity given Kristeller's lifelong concern with educating a broader public and his constant reaching out to younger scholars lacking his own elite humanistic and philological training. Just a few years ago, for the quincentennial celebration in Naples, Florence, and Figline of the 1484 *Platonis Opera Omnia,* he produced a supplementary volume to the *Supplementum* in English, *Marsilio Ficino and His Work After Five Hundred Years.*[57] This constitutes the definitive bibliographical guide to work on Ficino in every European language up to 1986,[58] and is a compendium of his own recent discoveries besides. It provides new letters and documents; lists of additions and corrections to the list of printed editions of Ficino's works and to the catalogue of his writings; new light on documents concerning Ficino and his family; an account of the biographies of Ficino and of the portraits of him; and lists of corrections and additions to the collection of testimonia. It also includes a census of manuscripts containing original works and letters of Ficino or of those copied, annotated or owned by him; an alphabetical list of authors that Ficino used, owned, copied or annotated; and finally a list of translations of his works. Nonetheless, it serves to supplement, not to replace, the *Supplementum* volumes.

■

Despite his encyclopedic learning, his probing curiosity about every aspect of both medieval and Renaissance humanism, and his range of philosophical interests, deeply influenced as they were by his abiding interest in Immanuel Kant, Marsilio Ficino remained central to Kristeller's own scholarly mission and vision, as many of his pellucid papers testify. Craven may have dragged up a number of ballistae for hurling Australian fire against the walls of Pico's twentieth-century reputation — making enemies right and left among Piconians, beginning with Garin. But he would have had a much tougher time breaching Kristeller's *Ficino.* For Kristeller never trumpeted a superficial originality for Ficino as other scholars have often been led to do

57. Florence: L.S. Olschki, 1987. An earlier version appeared in *Marsilio Ficino e il ritorno,* 15–196.

58. But see also *Marsilio Ficino e il ritorno di Platone: Mostra di manoscritti, stampe e documenti (17 maggio – 16 giugno 1984),* ed. Sebastiano Gentile, Sandra Niccoli, and Paolo Viti (Florence: Le Lettere, 1984). Updated bibliographies by Teodoro Katinis appear regularly in the journal of the Société Marsile Ficin, *Accademia.*

for Pico as a result of focusing too exclusively on the celebrated rhetorical (and hermetic) excursus on man as the great miracle in the *Oration*. He devoted himself rather to the daunting labor of establishing and interpreting the texts, and of arriving at a full understanding of Ficino's philosophy in the deep conviction, modestly but pointedly phrased, that Ficino was "a thinker of wide interests and of remarkable speculative force."[59] It is the "force" — what perhaps Sir Philip Sidney would have called *enargeia* — that surely sustained Kristeller's own interest in the Florentine over a long and splendidly productive lifetime.

Moreover, given his engagement with the entire field of Ficino's contemporaries, he was able to underscore Ficino's centrality to his age, his voicing of some of its deepest aspirations and convictions. Signally, while he did not himself share these convictions per se, or at least share them in their totality, he was obviously moved by the faith and the erudition that originally sustained them. With other great interpreters of Plato and the Platonic tradition — Dodds, Saffrey, Armstrong, Beierwaltes, Dillon, Gersh and so on — he was concerned to champion Platonism's and not just Plato's enduring importance. Indeed, for all his Aristotelian accomplishments as palaeographer, codicologist, textual critic, editor, annotator, archivalist, historian, biographer, and bibliographer, Kristeller remained what he signed himself at the end of one of his very first scholarly articles, *Platonicus*.[60] Ficinians above all others will continue to be grateful to him: generally for his passionate interest in the Platonic tradition, and especially in its Renaissance revival(s), and specifically for his synthetic accomplishment in *The Philosophy of Marsilio Ficino* with its deliberation, clarity, sympathy, and comprehensiveness.

Even so, we have become increasingly aware over the last sixty years that Ficino is a more complex, less easily definable figure, even as a scholastic philosopher, than Kristeller had presented him in 1937, and, I believe, a good deal less orthodox. First there are the theosophical, demonological, prophetic, medical, and magical themes, indeed dimensions, that Kristeller chose not to address, or to address fully, in his book — even though they are central, most would now argue, to our understanding of the mentality and the values of the Quattrocento. I suspect his grounds for omitting or downplaying these hinged on the fact that they were not part, as I intimated earlier, of what most philosophers (or theologians), at least in the formative years of his career, were prepared to accept as legitimate areas of philosophical (or theological) enquiry. Moreover, even the indisputably

59. *Philosophy of Marsilio Ficino*, 16.

60. *Platonicus* [Paul O. Kristeller], "Per la biografia di Marsilio Ficino," *Civiltà Moderna* 10 (1938): 277–98, and reprinted in his *Studies*, 1:191–211.

philosophical and theological ideas in Ficino diverge, to a far greater degree than Kristeller was able to, or chose to, educe in his essentially rationalist study, both from those of what we now think of as fundamental to any account of Platonism per se, and from those continually debated by Aquinas and the Scholastics in their *quaestiones disputatae.* That Kristeller in his later years was happy to acknowledge this to me and to others bears witness both to his scholarly openness and integrity and to his generosity of spirit. Unquestionably, even as his remarkable intellectual curiosity and energy, his love of learning, bore him in so many other fruitful directions, enabling him to make such monumental contributions to the vast field of late medieval and Renaissance studies, the Florentine philosopher continued to exercise a benign but powerful influence over him.

In brief, a full assessment of Kristeller's life and work, and certainly of his magisterial contributions to the history of Renaissance thought, should probably end where it effectively began: with Plotinus and with the revival and reinterpretation of his luminous philosophy, his *disciplina,* by the gifted son of one of Cosimo de' Medici's physicians.

■ ■ ■

8

Marsilio Ficino, Levitation, and the Ascent to Capricorn

In the post Burckhardtian succession of historical re-appraisals, we have now come to assume that the Renaissance was still profoundly Christian, and that it was deeply tied to the intellectual and certainly the theological worlds of scholasticism. If it witnessed a rebirth of learning and the visual arts, it remained in essence medieval in its spirituality, until at least the coming of Luther and the Reformers in the early sixteenth century (and even that is problematic given the Reformers' obsession with Augustine). In this brief paper, however, I wish to dwell upon a disturbingly innovative theologian, the Florentine Neoplatonist, Marsilio Ficino (1433-99), whose ideas regarding death, and the attendant notion of rebirth, were shaped not only by the medieval theological vision of a holy dying, and by Plato's compelling portrait of Socrates' death, but even more interestingly by Plato's myths and intimations of the immortal soul's antenatal existence and its afterlife, and even of its cyclical return, as they were interpreted by a variety of later Neoplatonic analyses, particularly those of Plotinus and Proclus. These problematic themes along with various unorthodox, even heretical, notions of reincarnation and transmigration were of abiding interest to him and not just, I suspect, as a Platonic commentator.

In ancient Neoplatonism Cancer was the constellation from which souls descend to be corporeally born *here* in this world, and therefore to enter a kind of death, even as they depart from their authentic existence as souls *there* in the intelligible beyond. In a 1490 letter to Lorenzo now in his tenth book of *Letters*, Marsilio Ficino writes, in a passage obviously indebted to Macrobius, that « souls cross over [from heaven] into the realm of lower things by way of Cancer, the house of the Moon—or so was the opinion of the ancient theologians. When the souls reach the region subject to generation and are themselves desirous of generation, the theologians properly supposed that they traverse the Moon's region that favors generation. Wherefore the ancients called Cancer 'the gateway of mortals.' But Capricorn who is opposed to Cancer they called 'the gateway of the gods.' Through it, they imagined, the purged souls finally fly back to heaven, their native home »[1]. Cancer and Capricorn are therefore the twin portals of heaven, the one presided over by the nearest of the Ptolemaic planets, the Moon, the other by the furthest, Saturn. « For in Capricorn », Ficino declares in the letter, « Saturn traverses that most beautiful of ways », the Milky Way, which the astronomers have named « the celestial way ».

The Moon is important here precisely because it is the presiding planet of generation and therefore of our submission to the yoke of mortality and of mutability. But generation is also a kind of sublunar reflection, even as reflection of another kind is a key to understanding the translunar condition from which we departed and the immortal nature of our souls. Hence the poets' notion that begetting children is governed, albeit in the sublunar realm, by the hope for a kind of generative immortality : « From fairest creatures we desire increase », writes Shakespeare in his opening sonnet, « That thereby beauty's rose might never die », since we may be immortalized through our progeny.

Let us look closely at one of Ficino's meditations on the central notion of reflection in the ninth book of his eighteen-book magnum opus, the *Platonic Theology : On the Immortality of Souls* first published in 1482. It is important to do so, because it enables us to see how death must be philosophically paradoxical to any Platonist. Ficino's

---

1 *Opera Omnia* (Basel : Heinrich Petri, 1576), p. 917.1 ; cf. Ficino's *Platonic Theology* 18.5.2, ed and tr. Michael J. B. Allen and James Hankins, 6 vols., I Tatti Renaissance Library (Cambridge, Mass. : Harvard University Press, 2000-2006). See my « Homo ad zodiacum : Marsilio Ficino and the Boethian Hercules, » now in *Plato's Third Eye : Studies in Marsilio Ficino's Metaphysics and its Sources* (Aldershot : Variorum, 1995) as no. XIII, p. 215-216.

Augustine-influenced argument is that the soul reflects upon itself in four ways : through the intellect it reflects upon its own nature when it seeks, finds, and considers itself ; through the will, upon this same nature when it desires and loves itself ; through the intellect, upon the very act of understanding when it understands an object and understands it is understanding ; and through the will, upon the act of the will when it wills something and wills itself to will[2]. Plato's famous « mythical hymn » in the *Phaedrus* 246Aff., 257A imagines these as the wheels of the soul's chariot. Ficino numbers them as four, partly, as he says himself, in order to make them correspond to « the fourfold fountain of perpetual nature » granted by Jupiter to the souls of men adduced in one of the Pythagorean golden sayings[3]. If no divided thing ever reflects upon itself, then our rational four-horse chariot, which « turns upon itself by way of its four wheels », must be completely indivisible, as is our fourfold fountain within, whose streams issue from, and return to, their source. Reflection of this kind, however, is not the sublunar generative conversion of body to body, but of soul to soul itself ; and the soul is indivisible precisely because it reflects upon itself, and reflects upon its own act of reflection. So self-reflection must be free of the body, Ficino's argument proceeds, since it neither begins from nor returns to the body ; and the soul's substance must be even freer, if its reflection, which is its natural motion, is free of the body. Hence the rational soul, in being as in moving and doing, does not depend on the body ; and it can never die except to the world of death[4].

Now if each thing's conversion is linked to its progression and the reverse, then the self-reflecting soul exists from and of itself principally in three ways : in terms of its form, because it is not being formed via another form (otherwise it would return not to itself but to that form) ; in terms of its foundation, because it is not being sustained by another (for this form which rests on itself does not rest on another form) ; and finally

2 *Platonic Theology* 9.1.3.

3 *Carmina aurea* 47–48 (ed. Thom), tr. Ficino : « per eum qui animo nostro quadriplicem fontem perpetuo fluentis naturae tradidit » (*Opera*, p. 1979). Any mention of four in a Pythagorean context should be referred to the tetraktys, the sacred quaternary of 4, 3, 2 and 1 summing to 10 ; cf. Porphyry, *Vita Pythagorae* 20, Iamblichus, *De vita pythagorica* 28.150, and Macrobius, *In somnium Scipionis* 1.6.41. See my *Nuptial Arithmetic : Marsilio Ficino's Commentary on the Fatal Number in Book VIII of Plato's* Republic (Berkeley & Los Angeles : University of California Press, 1994), p. 29, 66.

4 *Platonic Theology* 9.1.3.

in terms of its simplicity, because it is not compounded from parts (for how can a form be unfolding across a surface of parts when it is folding back upon its own center ?). What comes from itself in this way exists forever, since, when something stops existing, it does so because it is either being abandoned by its forming cause, or losing its foundation, or being dissolved into parts. But what reflects upon itself, being undivided, is not dissolved. As the form of itself, it is not abandoned by the forming cause ; and remaining in itself, it is never without its foundation.[5]

Orchestrating these intricate notions of reflection, conversion, and death is the fundamental image of the circle, and of the cyclical turning of spirituality, the circle and soul being both indissoluble and, in a non-pejorative sense, self-centred, free, and therefore never subject to death. Our will declares it is truly free « when it reaches the point of willing to be alone under its own control »[6]. For then « it liberates itself in a way from the rest of creatures and is content just with itself ». This also happens : a) « when it bends itself in a circle round on its own act — for a spiritual circuit is not subject to an external end » ; b) « when it not only wills in response to one inference and not another, but also wills the fact that it can equally will and not will - in this event it seems to be indifferent equally to willing and not willing and totally bound to neither » ; and c) « when it chooses the total emptying of every desire - for then it releases itself from the attraction of every special object. » But motion is only free, Ficino declares, when it is the first motion, because what is first is so of and through itself[7]. Since the first motion is in the soul, Plato calls the soul self-moved[8]. Hence the rotating or circling soul is essentially free : it acts and lives freely, being free « from the violent impulse of any particular thing whether good or bad. » Since it is not shaken by violence, it can never be destroyed : it is indeed emancipated by the death of the body, and in its own self-motion it remains unmoved by the body's motion.

---

5 Ibid. 9.1.4.
6 Ibid. 9.4.18.
7 Ibid. 9.4.19.
8 *Laws* 10.893B-899D—the most obvious of Ficino's several sources.

This familiar but nonetheless intricate set of proofs leads us to the crux of the zodiacal experience in the ancient theology that never ceased to haunt the Florentine. We were drawn down through Cancer towards the elemental body by the desire to nurture it - drawn down, that is, through the planetary spheres in such a way that, like a falling star, our pure aetherial or fiery body was coarsened or thickened or veiled by gradual accretions of air and water, and finally of earth. Concomitantly, our original sphericity was gradually distorted into the angular human shape we now wrongly assume is peculiarly and permanently ours ; and one can see how this would seem to clash with the Genesis declarations that we were made in the likeness and image of God, unless God is deemed (heretically) to be a sphere. Our descent is in a way imitative of the divine insofar as we yearn to be instruments of God's Providence, and to provide for our corporeal world as God provides for the corporeal world. But in descending into the body, we are compelled to drink of Lethe and to become subject for a while to the body, ministering to its desires. However, as the body ages, we are more and more drawn to escaping what has become our prison and a tomb ; and we yearn to be converted, or rather, to convert ourselves, to return to our pristine (spherical) form as we pass through Capricorn as the « portal of the gods. » In dying physically, we return to our Author and Creator in an act that reverses our being born from the womb into the corporeal world : in converting ourselves, we convert death itself[9].

Ficino focuses upon the central paradoxes of these conversion metaphors by focusing on the twin notions of dying to a former life and of falling to sleep ; and in the context of refuting the epicurean notion that when the body dies the soul must die. « Since Lucretius did not believe in immortality on the grounds that, with the approach of death, the rational soul's powers seem to fail, » we must note, » he says, « that the life of the body consists of a tempering of moisture and of heat, and that the body dies when either the heat disperses the moisture, or the moisture extinguishes the heat »[10]. At that time, since the soul is less pre-occupied than usual with governing the body, « it gathers itself into its

[9] See my « Life as a Dead Platonist » in *Marsilio Ficino : His Theology, His Philosophy, His Legacy*, edd. Allen and Valery Rees (Leiden : Brill, 2002), p. 159-178.

[10] *Platonic Theology* 9.5.26.

own mind and perceives mysteries and foretells future events. » Hence the soul waxes stronger as the body weakens. « Since union is the opposite of dissolution, the soul must therefore be considered most distant from dissolution at the very time it most gathers itself into itself, and, having cast off its animal nature, ascends into its own mind »[11]. This is clearly what happens in the death that occurs « because of release » in the moments of what Ficino, in commenting on Plato's *Phaedrus*, calls *alienatio*, moments which are experienced by prophets, priests, poets, and those in love[12], and also, strangely, by rhapsodes like Ion who are « out of their right minds »[13]. In the thirteenth book of his *Platonic Theology* Ficino links this *alienatio* to what he calls *vacatio*, the « emptying or release » which occurs in seven kinds of emptiness : in sleep, in swoon, in the depths of melancholy, in the enjoyment of a perfect tempering of the complexion, in solitude, in wonder and awe, and in chastity[14]. But in the death that occurs « because of extinction, » *i.e.* in the normal process of dying, the soul's life-giving power is « momentarily intent on curing the humours and their commotions ». For a while, therefore, reason does not do its duty : it only resumes its office « after the din and tumult », the *strepitus* of death, just as it customarily awakens, says Ficino, after our dreams are over[15].

Perhaps the most convincing proof for Ficino that the soul at death does not lose its powers and mental gifts is that many people who have been restored to life from the brink of death by the effort of doctors never recover their body's former powers, or do so only after a long period of recuperation. But they do recover the powers of their souls just as soon as they have purged way « the humoural excess that causes death ». Whereas the body's powers are almost extinguished in this near death experience, the light of the rational soul is merely hidden away, like embers under the ashes. Hence the body returns to life « with difficulty and tardily », but the soul returns « easily and at once ». For at that moment the soul has lost nothing of itself, since it brings back its

---

11 Ibid.

12 *Phaedrus* 244D-245A.

13 *Ion* 533E-535D. See Ficino's *Ion Commentary* (*Opera*, pp. 1281-84) ; and my « The Soul as Rhapsode : Marsilio Ficino's Interpretation of Plato's *Ion*, » now in *Plato's Third Eye* as no. XV.

14 *Platonic Theology* 13.2.24-38 : « septem vacationis genera. »

15 *Platonic Theology* 9.5.26.

talents, natural and acquired, immediately to the light of day. It has made itself ready, writes Ficino mixing metaphors, like a snake, to slough its skin and to emerge from its prison-house into the light, as it first emerged from its mother's womb. « But the wise man, when he leaves his body, supposes, not that he is losing part of himself, but rather that he is being liberated from a heavy burden »[16]. He sees death as an unburdening, a reacquiring of lightness, of the levity that will enable him, like a flame, to rise towards his original fiery, aetherial home. We might note that there is no mention here of virtually any of the cardinal assumptions of Christianity about dying : about repentance and the hope of atonement, about the need for grace, about faith in a redemption, about a saviour. We are closer instead to the ancient Gnostic notion that we are sparks of fallen fire yearning to rise to our proper, our empyrean sphere, beyond the fixed stars, beyond even the portal of the gods, yearning to reacquire our original flame-like purity.

Ficino then turns to another proof that seems a description almost of the death of a scholar in the midst of profound study. « The senses get tired when they work for a long time, but never the mind. Whereas the longer you look at something, the less distinctly you see it, the longer you study something with your intellect, the more clearly you understand it. All the work of the body and the senses becomes exhausted with use, but the mind's work by contrast is strengthened »[17]. Nevertheless, the head usually becomes heavy with prolonged thinking and the eye is dimmed precisely because movements in the phantasy « often accompany mental exercise », and « vibration of the spirit » accompanies these phantasmic movements, and injury of the actual brain or eye results in turn from the vibration. « But the cutting edge of the mind itself becomes quicker and sharper ; and it would certainly continue uninterruptedly to direct its thoughts upward if it did not, out of pity, interrupt its proper task for the sake of reviving the body entrusted to it ». This obviously occurs with people who, when they contemplate something particularly intently,

[16] Ibid. 9.5.27.
[17] Ibid. 9.5.28.

become annoyed that their bodies are tiring. « In them the mind is unwilling in a way to halt its work, though the body and the senses are eager to stop. It is as if the mind itself were never exhausted by working. But, Ficino triumphantly concludes, « what is never exhausted must be also immortal »[18].

It is precisely at this final moment of vigilant weariness, of waking sleep, of thinking while dying that prophecy occurs. Prophecy indeed becomes for Ficino one of the prime witnesses to a Platonic death. « Since the soul's most outstanding parts are the intellect and the will, when we are pre-occupied with corporeals, the intellect either perceives nothing at all or does not discern truly, being deceived by the senses and by the phantasy ; and the will is afflicted as long as it is vexed by many bodily cares. Contrariwise, when the soul despises corporeals and the senses have been allayed and the clouds of phantasmata dissipated, and when it perceives something on its own, then the intellect discerns truly and is at its brightest »[19]. We see this in the case of those who prophesy during the quiet of sleep or when they are otherwise alienated from the body. Hence, as Plato declares in the *Crito* and *Apology*[20], many as they approach death predict future events. At that moment they foresee, as it were, « the events written beforehand in the higher spirits to which the rational soul is naturally joined, provided it is not impeded by the body ». Ficino's chief example is Socrates : having been brought to judgment by false accusers, « first he predicted to the judges their future penitence, to his accusers, their downfall, and to the state, future sedition ; and then in prison he announced beforehand that the day of his death had been revealed to him by a spirit while he was resting (*per quietem*) ».

Ficino also adduces from Cicero's *Tusculanae* the example of Theramenes : when he had been cast into prison and was drinking the poison, he predicted to his adversary Critias that his death was imminent (it happened just a short time later)[21]. From Cicero's *De*

---

[18] Ibid.

[19] Ibid., 9.2.2. Note that this and parts of the following argument are repeated, with variations, in Ficino's sermon *De vita animae immortali* (*Opera*, p. 476.1).

[20] *Crito* 44AB, *Apology* 39CD (Socrates predicting his own death).

[21] Cicero, *Tusculan Disputations* 1.40.96-97. Theramenes was an Athenian statesman of moderate views who was executed in 404 BC by the thirty tyrants under Critias. Critias died in battle the following year.

divinatione he takes both Posidonius' account of a dying citizen of Rhodes who called out the names of six contemporaries and declared who among them would die first, who second, and so on[22] ; and Aristotle's account of Eudemus of Cyprus, who, when he had arrived at the city of Phaerae in Thessaly, fell gravely ill and saw in his sleep a youth of surpassing beauty who triply declared that he would shortly recover ; that Alexander, the tyrant of that city, would die in a few days ; and that Eudemus himself would return home five years later. All three prophecies came to pass, though the last ironically so in that Eudemus only returned home in the figurative sense when he died five years later, and his soul was free therefore to return to its native soil[23] !

Underlying these labyrinthine arguments and examples (and there are more) are many sources and tropes. But I would like to underscore, in the light of our concern here with *renovatio*, the importance of the image from the *Phaedrus* of the chariot bearing the soul forward even as its wheels turn back upon themselves in the mystery of self-moved reflection and conversion. Since God is the prime mover of all things, He is in a sense the paradigm of self-motion ; and human souls, made in His image and likeness, are therefore, by virtue of their creation and definition, self-movers. But unlike God who remains at rest in His eternal motion, turning upon Himself in eternal conversion and reflection[24], the soul, even as it turns within, also advances in its chariot—its mysterious reflection of God's self-motion producing motion around itself but also motion towards Him. All this follows predictably on the image of the wheel, the symbol so often of Boethian fortune, but here presented as an Ezekielian symbol of spiritual life, of the turning that is God's turning and returning in us.

For Ficino, however, the climactic act of reflection, and thus of miraculous transformation is not Cancer's but Capricorn's. This

[22] Cicero, *De divinatione* 1.30.64. When Cicero attended his lectures in Rhodes, Posidonius (c.135-51 BC) was already an important eclectic Stoic and an authority on divination.
[23] Ibid.,1.25.53.
[24] See Stephen E. Gersh's fine study, *Kinêsis akinêtos : A Study of Spiritual Motion in the Philosophy of Proclus* (Leiden : Brill 1973).

transformation was long ago described by the Chaldaean Magi as the goal of the magic taught them by their founder, Zoroaster, the first magus and their « prince »[25], and the putative author of the wisdom embodied in the *Chaldaean Oracles*[26]. For the Magi thought that the soul's supreme miracle results from its ability to surround its own body with light gathered together from scattered rays, and to lift its body on high with the levity intrinsic to rays, a feat that some of them attributed to Zoroaster himself[27]. This is significant given that one of the oracles declares, « You must ascend to the light itself and to the rays of the father, the source from which soul, enveloped in the ample light of the mind, flowed into you »[28]. Zoroaster had, incidentally, also experienced the fifth of the « emptyings », the emptying that came with twenty years of solitude and that enabled him to intuit what the divinities presiding over the stars and planets were contemplating enacting ; and also to create an alphabetical, or rather hieroglyphical, system that used astrological-astronomical symbols as the basis of writing[29].

Ficino speculates that this levitation miracle is possible for the following reason. « The first light is in God and it is such that it surpasses the intellect, and thus cannot even be called the intelligible light »[30]. But this divine light whenever it is poured forth into the angel at once becomes an intellectual light and can be understood intuitively. When it is then poured into the soul it becomes a rational light and can be understood intuitively and also thought about discursively. Thence it passes down to the soul's *idolum*, which is the « soul's foot » or reason's image and which inheres in the aetherial vehicle as its life containing as it does the phantasy, sense, and vital force[31] ; here the light becomes sensitive but not yet corporeal. Then it flows down into the *idolum's*

[25] In his *Opera*, p. 844.2, Ficino defines magic as « the Zoroastrian art. » See my *Synoptic Art*, pp. 35-41.

[26] For the status and history *Chaldaean Oracles* for Ficino and his contemporaries, see Karl H. Dannenfeldt, « The Pseudo-Zoroastrian Oracles in the Renaissance, » *Studies in the Renaissance* 4 (1957), 7-30 ; also his « Hermetica Philosophica » and « Oracula Chaldaica » in *Catalogus Translationum et Commentariorum*, vol. 1, ed. Paul Oskar Kristeller (Washington, D.C. : Catholic University of America Press, 1960), p. 137-151, 157-164.

[27] *Platonic Theology* 13.4.15.

[28] *Chaldaean Oracle* 115 (ed. Des Places) ; it is cited by Ficino in his *Platonic Theology* 10.8.4.

[29] *Platonic Theology* 13.2.35.

[30] Ibid. 13.4.15.

[31] *Platonic Theology* 13.2.15-20. See Paul Oskar Kristeller, *The Philosophy of Marsilio Ficino* (New York : Columbia University Press, 1943), p. 371-375.

aetherial vehicle where it does become corporeal but not yet manifestly visible. Finally it crosses over into the elemental body, whether into the simpler airy body or into the composite body, which are the vessels as it were of the aetherial body ; and in this elemental body it becomes visible at last. Ficino equates it with the golden chain in Homer's *Iliad* 8.15-28 stretching from heaven to the earth ; and he declares that men who have seized hold of it can raise themselves to the heavens.

Moreover, « celestial souls abound with so much light from heaven that the overflowing plenty of that light spills over into their bodies as in the case of the stars. And whenever a human soul focuses its gaze on God and is filled and possessed by the divine light to the point that it becomes equally coruscating, then that soul pours the copious rays out into its aetherial vehicle ; and thence, via that vehicle and via its airy body, out into the ordinary visible body. Filled to the brim with the copiousness of the rays, this ordinary body is at last set ablaze, rarefied, lifted up », transformed it seems into both an aetherial and an airy body, « like tow wafted through the flame »[32]. In such a fiery chariot, so the Magi and the Platonists would have declared, Elijah[33] and Paul[34] were swept up into the vault of heaven ; and eventually, after the Last Judgment, the body that the Christian theologians call the « glorified body » will be similarly enraptured.

Ficino is haunted here by a verse from the *Chaldaean Oracles* in which Zoroaster declares : « Because the soul becomes a resplendent fire through the power of the Father, may the immortal profundity of the soul dominate you and raise all eyes as one on high, and then even the material body you will not abandon to the precipice »[35]. By the phrase « becoming a resplendent fire, » Ficino interprets Zoroaster to be referring to the soul, having been converted « through the power of the Father back to the Father, » as overflowing with the divine light that overflows in God Himself[36]. Since God is absolute unity above mind and 'the centre of essences above essence », the soul is united to Him,

---

[32] Ibid. 13.4.16. Is this image recalled from Lucretius' *De rerum natura* 6.879-880 : « There is also a fountain of such a nature that, when tow is suspended over it, it often catches fire immediately and bursts into flame » ?

[33] II Kings 2 :11-12.

[34] II Corinthians 12 :2-4.

[35] *Platonic Theology* 13.4.16 assembles the four lines of this *dictum* from three fragments 96 (the first line), 112 (both lines), and 158 (the one line) (ed. Des Places).

[36] Cf. *Platonic Theology* 13.5.1 (last line) : « for the soul is divine light (*lumen*). »

properly speaking, not through its mind but through its unity, which is the mind's head and the soul's centre. Thus Zoroaster exhorts us, « Let the immortal profundity of the soul be your leader », meaning let the soul's unity be the faculty that unites us with God, since God impressed this unity on the soul from the very beginning as a print of the unity divine. On it all the other powers of the soul depend and to it they return, as the lines of a circle proceed from and revert to its centre. In telling us to raise « all eyes as one on high », Ficino interprets Zoroaster to mean that all the soul's powers concerned with knowing, must be first gathered together into mind and then into its unity. He sees the twenty-fourth psalm as trumpeting the same exhortation : « Lift up your gates, o ye princes ; and be ye lifted up, ye everlasting doors »[37]. Finally, when Zoroaster asserts that the « material body » - meaning not just the aetherial body or the airy one as we might have anticipated, but the earthly body too - « is not to be abandoned to the precipice » at the time of death, he is affirming the doctrine of the resurrection of the body. For the body too will be raised along with the soul and not abandoned in the world's lowest place, what the Magi call the « precipice »[38]. Ficino adds that Mercurius Trismegistus also describes the power and effect of this resurrection-levitation miracle when he discusses regeneration with his son Tat[39].

In the *Platonic Theology* 18.9.15, Ficino again confronts the issue of a (or of the) resurrection, and specifically a resurrection of the body. In the end, he says, it is God's measureless power that is the efficient cause of this. For it is most appropriate that « the infinity of life that raises the dead » be the same infinity that preserves the dead free from death for eternity. For the only proper counterpart to such a stupendous miracle as restoring to life is the bestowing of future everlasting life. For this supreme miracle, God in His omnipotence makes bodies submit to the sway of their souls « to such a degree that the everlasting life of the soul flows over everlastingly also into the body ». This situation calls for the imposition of the most outstanding form possible (as against the matter subjected to it), though it is thoroughly in keeping with the order

[37] Psalm 24 :7,9 (the Roman psalter).
[38] *Platonic Theology* 13.4.16.
[39] *Corpus Hermeticum* (*Pimander*) 10.13, 16-18, 21.

of actual nature[40]. But, as the theologians tell us, Ficino continues, it also « greatly accords with the order of merits that bodies be totally joined, not only with respect to life to all men's souls (souls being particular lives), but also, with respect to their qualities and actions, to souls that are pure, just as these very souls are joined to God. » So the intellect is filled to overflowing with divine light, and the will is filled with gladness, and « with incomparable power together they transfuse their wonderful splendour and capacity for motion entirely into the body The result is that, just as souls are elevated to the clarity and power of celestial minds, so are bodies elevated to the clarity and power of celestial bodies. « Nor should it seem surprising », he says, that the human body, « which by nature and on account of its temperance is not dissimilar to the heavens, when it is clothed again in a kind of celestial form as a gift, is suddenly raised on high to the celestial region, having as its leader the soul borne up by the infinite power of God ». At present even on earth and disjoined from God, the soul unites, sustains, and lifts the body contrary to the nature of its elements. So it is not surprising that later, « conjoined with God above the heavens, the soul is able to raise the body with itself to the sublime region of the aether », as the author in effect of its own resurrection. In penetrating the aetherial region, the glorified body of the resurrection neither damages the aether nor is itself damaged, having itself been rendered aetherial already in power and quality[41].

This whole series of arguments is interesting on three counts. It establishes levitation by way of concentrated and abundant light as a foretaste of, and a witness to, the final resurrection of the soul and body on the Day of Judgment. For on that day all the souls of the redeemed will levitate in an overflowing of light divine ; and human beings will become like shooting stars again or blazing tow wafted upwards by the wind to Capricorn and beyond. Secondly, quite apart from the implications for light metaphysics, this levitatory vision also has the effect of valorising *levitas* as the ultimate physical and mystical force,

[40] Cf. Aquinas, *Summa contra Gentiles* 4.85.5. For two recent, very different perspectives on the notion bodily resurrection, see Caroline Bynn, *The ressurection of the Body in western christianity*, 200-1336 (New-York ; Columbia University Press, 1995) ; and F. Vidal, « Brains, Bodies, Selves, and Science : Anthropologies of identity and the resurrection of the Body », *Critical Inquiry* 28 (2002), 930-74

[41] *Platonic Theology* 18.9.15 ; cf. Aquinas, *Summa contra Gentiles* 4.86.

interestingly so since it is going to be the countervailing force of gravity that will dominate the scientific world view for the ensuing four centuries[42]. And thirdly, Ficino sees Zoroaster, the most ancient of the ancient theologians, as not only prophesying the final resurrection of body and soul in an intense blaze of light as we understand it in a Christian context, but as himself bearing witness to it experientially. This has a direct bearing on our understanding of the value Renaissance thinkers accorded the *Chaldaean Oracles*. For Ficino is in effect interpreting the collection of oracles as a whole *sub specie levitatis*, that is, in terms of the supreme religious and psychological experience of levitation by way of incandescent light. This is their gravamen for him. In turn, there are obvious and arresting implications for our understanding of the contexts, in the many Quattrocento depictions of the Epiphany, of the journey of the Magi following the star to Bethlehem.

This is not the occasion to explore the absolutely fundamental role of light, both outer and inner, in Ficino's thought, but it behooves us finally to look at a remarkable visionary passage, again in the ninth book of the *Platonic Theology*. For it presents us with a sort of Diotima's ladder in that it leads us, not from corporeal love to the idea of love, but from ordinary visible light to the idea of divine light and to the absolute source of that light, which Ficino links to the mystical Biblical notion of the « glory » with which God appears to men. In the Old Testament God appears in glory on Mt. Sinai in a cloud or devouring fire[43] and in the visions of Ezekiel[44] ; and in the New Testament it is Christ himself who is or who will be invested in glory. The term is most familiar to us perhaps in the memorable phrasing at the end of the *logos* opening of St. John's Gospel, « and we beheld his glory, the glory as of the only

[42] Cf. Ficino's *Platonic Theology* 18.8.11 which speaks of the souls of the blessed as having a habit that is like « a natural levity » that bears them upwards towards the angels, whereas a « natural weight » casts the souls of the reprobate down among the demons.

[43] Exodus 16 :10, 24 :16-17 ; cf. Numbers 16 :19, 42. It is also associated with the Temple and Tabernacle ; see Exodus 40 :34, Numbers 20 :6, Psalms 24 :7-10, 78 :60-61.

[44] Ezekiel 10 :4, 28 :22, 43 :2-5 ; cf. Isaiah 4 :5, 60 :1-2, 66 :5. The Hebrew Shekinah as the « presence » of God is a related concept.

begotten of the Father (1.14) »[45]. It is a glory, furthermore, in which we hope to participate, as Paul declares in Romans 5 :2, and as we have seen in the case of the glorified body of the Resurrection. For at the Second Coming, in the words of Matthew 25 :31, « the Son of man shall come in his glory, and all the holy angels with him, » and the saved will partake of the Son's glory. But in Platonic terms, how do we set about approaching this luminous « glory » ?

« Do you want to gaze upon the face of God again ? », Ficino begins in 9.3.4, « Look at the universal world full of the light of the sun. Look at the light in the world's matter full of all the universal forms and forever changing. Subtract, I beg you, matter from the light and put the rest aside : suddenly you have soul, that is, incorporeal light, replete with all the forms, but changeable. Again subtract change from this soul-light. Now you have arrived at angelic intellect, at incorporeal light filled with all the forms but [now] unchanging. Subtract from this the diversity by means of which each form is different from the light and brought into the light from elsewhere, with the result that the essence of the light and of each form is now the same ; and the light forms itself and through its forms forms all. This light shines out infinitely, since it is naturally radiant, and it is neither sullied nor constrained by the admixture of anything else. Because it dwells in no one thing, it is poured through all things. It dwells in no one thing in order that it may blaze in its fullness through all things. It lives from itself and it gives life to all, since its shadow, like the sun's light, is alone what gives rise to life in bodies. It senses all and gives sense to all, if its shadow awakens all the senses in all things. Finally, it loves individual things if they are pre-eminently its own. So what is the sun's light ? The shadow of God. So what is God ? God is the Sun of the sun. The sun's light is God in the body of the world ; [but] God is the Sun above the angelic intellects. O soul, here, here is your God ! The phantasy shows you only His shadow - though the shadow of God is such that it is the most beautiful of sensible things. What do you think the light of God is like ? If the shadow of God shines so dazzlingly, how much more intensely does the light of God shine ? You love the sun's light everywhere over and above all other things, or rather you love it alone. Love God alone, His light

[45] It is a Johannine theme. Cf. John 12 :23, 13 :31, 17 :1,5, 22 ; and Matthew 24 :30, 25 :31, Mark 8 :38, Luke 21 :27.

alone, o soul. Love infinitely the infinite light of God in His beneficence. You will then be radiant and experience infinite joy »[46].

This powerful, hymn-like passage may be questionably orthodox, but it is certainly profoundly Platonic both in its meditative progression up from the cavernous world of shadows into the world of light, and in its commitment to abstracting what is extraneous until it arrives at the notion of pure and absolute light as if this were the ultimate Platonic Idea. This abstracting takes place in one of the divine frenzies ; in the occasional emptying of the spirit out of the body ; in the moments when a prophet or seer can alienate all that is not light. But more importantly it also occurs for the righteous soul at the approach of death itself. Preceded often by the sudden ability to prophesy, it occurs in the climactic act of self-motion, in the levitation of the soul in the triumphant chariot ride of the Platonic philosopher-seer, in the final departing moment of conversion, of self-turning. Interestingly, however, it is not the compelling figure of the charioteer himself, the traditional symbol of human mastery and the central image in the greatest of all Plato's visionary myths, that defines the notion of our escape from mortal limitations. Rather it is the image of the soul as a spark of light returning whence it came, like a fragment of incandescent tow wafted upwards, which defines for Ficino the very nature and origin of spirituality as both the light and the lightness of being.

I would like to close with two observations that are not perhaps unconnected. To begin with, I am urging us to re-examine the whole notion of Platonic dying for Ficino, along with the notion of the deathbed conversion. For it was influenced and indeed configured as we have seen, not just by Plato's dramatic retelling of Socrates' last days, but by three other considerations too. First, by Plato's various self-motion arguments, and especially those in the *Phaedrus*, however mediated by Neoplatonic and subsequently by scholastic elaborations ; second, by the cognate notions in Neoplatonism of reflection, conversion, and

[46] *Dei faciem rursus intueri...oblectaberis infinite* : repeated, with variations, in Ficino's *Dialogus inter Deum et animam theologicus* sent as a letter to Mercati and now in Ficino's *Letters* 1.4.80-103 (ed. Gentile, p. 15 = *Opera*, p. 610-611).

eventually of levitation ; and third by a light metaphysics which Ficino derived from both pagan and Biblical notions of an intense and sacred light, a « glory » that surrounds us and in which we ourselves are glorified[47]. The ascent through the portal of the gods is the ascent to such a glory for the soul and, more importantly perhaps, for its aetherial body (with the implication, from a Platonic perspective at least, that this resurrected glorious body will be spherical and star-like).

Finally, the heavens for Ficino are not the heavens of the ordinary astrologer, although he himself was a knowledgeable if circumspect theorist of astrology and familiar with many of its procedures (he never went entirely along with Pico's attack, preserved for us now in the posthumous *Disputationes adversus astrologiam divinatricem* of 1496, on its key assumptions). That is, they are not the heavens primarily of the planets in their conjunctions and oppositions, and they are not even the heavens, the firmament, of traditional Christian belief that, in the words of Psalm 19 : 1, « declare the glory of God » and « sheweth His handywork. » Rather, they are the heavens of the twin Macrobian portals of our own descent and ascent, the gates of Cancer and of Capricorn[48] : for our aetherial bodies, our spirit-chariots, come hither from the one and return thither to the other. And suspended for a brief mortal life between them is Platonic man, the philosopher *puer-senex*, the *magnum miraculum*, the « lapsed angelic mind », the « mortal god » of the ancient theology and of those Renaissance thinkers, like Ficino, who sought to harness that theology anew. From the onset this harnessing was always, we should recall, in the interests, not just of ecclesiastical or even more generally of religious reform, but of inner transformation, of the return, whether in Christian prayer or philosophical contemplation, to the divine light and thus to luminous transfiguration. Indeed, it is my contention that Christ's Transfiguration on Mt. Tabor - when his face and raiment shone exceeding white as snow, the evangelists declare, and when Moses and Elijah, two figures linked with dazzling fire, appeared

[47] This is not just a halo or aureole, but rather the full-body aura, mandorla, or vesica familiar to us from the pictorial and iconographic traditions of both the medieval Latin West and of the Byzantine East.

[48] Perhaps we should look more carefully at the depictions of these two zodiacal signs in the artistic, and generally in the iconographic programmes of the Renaissance, given the implications of the arguments examined here.

to him.[49] - not his Nativity in Bethlehem, his Ministry with its miracles, or his Crucifixion on Golgotha, that is at the very centre of Ficino's mystical Christianized Neoplatonism. For it would seem that the re-ascent and fiery levitation of the light-filled soul - ablaze in Elijah's incandescent « glory », in the blinding whiteness of the transfigured, glorified Christ - is wonderfully synonymous for him, or virtually so, with the philosopher's *alienatio*, his Plotinian flight of the alone to the alone.

[49] Mathew 17 : 1-8, Mark 9 :2-8, Luke 9 : 28-36, 2 Peter 1 :16-18.

9

MARSILIO FICINO AND THE LANGUAGE OF THE PAST

1492 was the year when Columbus sailed the wine-dark Atlantic and discovered the Caribbean. But it was also the year of Lorenzo the Magnificent's death and of the magnificent publication of the first complete Latin translation of Plotinus' *Enneads* by the great Florentine Platonist, Marsilio Ficino (1433-99). Several humanists from the German speaking lands, including such important figures as Johannes Reuchlin and Johannes Streler of Ulm, were in correspondence with Ficino, and a study of them would certainly cast an interesting light both on his impact on German humanism and on the formation and dissemination of his own thought. But four 1492 letters to three German figures – Paul of Middelburg, Martin Prenninger, and his employer, Eberhard VI, first Count of Württemberg and then Duke when the county became a duchy in 1495 – are of more than passing interest. For they bear upon a number of related themes central to our understanding of Ficino's thought and hermeneutics, in particular, to his notion of a global or universal language and its status with regard to other languages in a Platonically inspired system where language itself is a «rind» (*cortex*) or «veil» (*integumentum*), or at best an allegorical envelope that enwraps rather than reveals the truth. They also bear on the notion of linguistic hegemonies and notably, for the moment, of English.

Let us toy initially with a duality: in European politics and culture Latin and its daughters are the languages of the south (and Latin eventually of the ancient past) and German and the other Germanic languages are those of the north (and English eventually of the global present). As with all dualities, it is all too easy to be beguiled by the notion of opposition: German thought versus Latin thought, Latin thought versus German interpretation; or mesmerized by paradox and the coincidence of opposites: German thought in Latin, Latinity in German or Latin-German, thought as interpretation. In either case we are confronted with the perpetually intriguing problems associated with relationship and therefore at the most fundamental level with parent and child and sibling relationships.

Interestingly, intrinsic to the Latin sense of Germany, German, and being a German is the notion of being or having a full brother or sister. But it is a brother or sister that leaps like Minerva out of the splitting headache of a pun: *germanus* or *germana* means of course being germed or born in the same place, from the Latin verb *gero/gerere*: budded on the same tree, having the same germen and womb for parents, the same *germanitas*, being perhaps separable or even inseparable twins. This pun is absent in the German word *deutsch* or *teutonisch* or the Italian *tedesco*, and one wonders whether Tacitus would have named a daughter Germana, honouring the cognomen of Nero Claudius Drusus and his son. It was a pun among many, however, that Ficino did not hesitate to deploy.

In a letter of 29 April 1491,[1] at the beginning of his eleventh book of *Letters*, he thanks George Herivart for the gift of a silver cup and benevolently declares: «From my earliest years, dear George, I have had a natural liking for Germans, the good result of causes hidden to me (*benevolentia causis occultis conciliata*)»; and he goes on to praise the families of Pico and of Cavalcanti as German in origin. «Therefore, if all my German companions (*Germani comites*) are my brothers (*germani*), what shall I say about the men and the friends well known to you? About Martinus Uranius my uranian friend? And about you my excellent George? For whosoever is most germane to me (*mihi plusquam germanus*) is undoubtedly my alter ego». Ficino wittily concludes that Martin and George are therefore himself, German and germane, martini and gin. It is a familiar trope of friendship and letter writing but one given point and force both by Ficino's Platonic cult of *eros*, and by his conviction that puns, particularly those that prompted etymologizing, often pointed to *causae occultae*, to a genuine if concealed relationship: to the brotherhood, the *germanitas*, that governed languages and language itself.

In turning to three of Ficino's German correspondents and focusing on four of his 1492 letters to them, I hope to unravel some of the problems that attend the notion of *causae occultae*, the relationships not so much

[1] FICINI *Opera omnia*, Basileae 1576, p. 924.3. It has been photographically reproduced several times, most recently in Paris, 2000.

between words and their meanings – an ancient littered battleground, where Socrates for one strode like a pelican and *optima spolia semantica* are still to be found by academic scavengers – as between languages themselves when they are seen as having different kinds of authority, different planetary spheres if you will of meaning. The notion of a hierarchy of language structures is very politically incorrect, unless you relegate English to the very bottom of the pile, as Hamlet might put it, a very drab. But it is, nonetheless, an ancient and venerable notion tied to the nostalgia and reverence either for a 'classical' language per se, Sanskrit, Greek, Hebrew, or more importantly perhaps for a 'classical' state of a language as embodied in the canonical texts of that language, usually a sacred text such as the *Koran* or the *Diamond Sutra*, or a great poem, the *Iliad*, the *Aeneid*, the *Commedia*. This classical state can be variously defined: philologically in terms of its morphology and syntax; or more expansively or poetically in terms of its sonority, metaphorical richness, oratorical suppleness, and so on. The absence of such a 'classical' text is often tied either in radical instances to the subjugation or even death of a language, or to its metamorphosis into a variety of dialectal or regional forms, as is the case, to a certain extent, with the many varieties of non-Mandarin Chinese.

However, the notion of the 'classical' stage of a language or of a classical language per se is frequently, some would argue invariably, tied to a certain degree of nostalgia, of a past oriented sense of loss, even as it is usually the nostalgia of an elite user, or rather of a speaker who has a special mastery of the language and a cultural and social investment in the authority of the texts which he or she understands as few others do. Nostalgia is thus tied to a sense of self worth juxtaposed with a sense of self-exclusiveness. The love of a classical language or language state is frequently, in fact, deeply neurotic: it looks back longingly, like Claude Lorraine's gold enfolding canvasses or Jacopo Sannazaro's poetry, into the idyll and the pastoral, the structures of that other time and place when men and women spoke the language of the gods, themselves godlike and god accompanied. At this juncture we confront a paradox: the union of the sophistication even erudition that marks the mature mastery of a language – and every language is a difficult one to master – with the longing for a distant home, for a recollected past, for the parental language both of instruction and of love; in short for the, or for a, linguistic golden age, for the *aurea dicta aetatis aureae*, the golden talk of the golden-tongued heroes and their fathers. For the golden age is not just a time when men meant what they said, when meaning and word were one without what Hamlet was to call «seeming», but a time when words were more than they are now, had a more central, more profound role to play in the life of the mind because invested with a metaphysical, even cosmological status that made them «living words». At this point obviously we are bordering on theology, and notably Johannine theology, life itself as the Word.

In a famous letter of 13 September 1492 to the first of our three German correspondents, Paul of Middelburg, «distinguished natural philosopher (*physicus*) and astronomer (astrologer?)», Ficino praises his own century as a golden age created by its «golden wits» (*ab ingeniis aureis*), what we would now call, too loosely perhaps, its men of genius.[2] Behind the affirmation lie first the poets' four ages, though interestingly they are reversed to begin with the age of lead and to end with the age of gold, and then Plato's appropriation in the *Republic* Book 4 of these four ages to describe men's wits as being either «naturally» and «innately» leaden or iron or silvery or golden. Certainly, Ficino is impressed by the *inventa* of his time and notably the «leading back into the light» of seven liberal disciplines (though not the trivium and quadrivium subjects per se) that had almost died out: grammar, poesy, oratory, painting, sculpture, architecture, music, and «the ancient singing of songs to the Orphic lyre», «and all this in Florence». More importantly, however, he invokes the revival of something venerated by the ancients but «now almost destroyed»: namely the union of different skills and disciplines; and he specifically adduces the union of eloquence with wisdom, of martial prowess and prudence, in Federico Duke of Urbino (and in his son and brother, the heirs of his 'virtue'). The union was the chief marker of Pallas Athene, the warrior goddess of peace and wisdom, of the aegis and the loom, the virgin and motherless protectress of Athens, *terque quaterque beata*. But her twinning of the roles of philosopher and of ruler was a haunting motif that Plato had addressed in the *Republic* and *Epinomis*, the *Second Letter*, and elsewhere, and that Ficino time and again addressed in his letters to such *signori* as Lorenzo de' Medici, Federico, and indeed Eberhard VI.[3] For one of the central Pla-

[2] FICINI *Opera omnia*, cit., p. 944.3 – it concludes the eleventh book of Ficino's *Letters*.

[3] See V. REES, *Ficino's Advice to Princes*, in *Marsilio Ficino: His Theology, His Philosophy, His Legacy*, ed. by M. J. B. ALLEN-V. REES, with M. DAVIES, Leiden 2002, pp. 339-357. Ficino was influenced, as Rees aptly points out, by Plato's *Letters*, and especially the *Seventh Letter*.

tonic dogmas concerned the necessity of uniting wisdom with power and thus restoring an age of gold, including linguistic gold, when Jupiter, the ruler of gods and men, lived at peace with his father Saturn, the contemplator of disembodied ideas. Indeed, Ficino thinks of Germany itself in Dantean terms as the natural seat of the Holy Roman Emperor, the ultimate *signore*, who will in an age of gold rule conjunctively with the (Italian) Pope, the ultimate philosopher priest in a kind of Platonic-Christian bi-consulship.[4] The union of the secular and spiritual powers emerges indeed as a central Platonic and Ficinian aspiration as Ficino's rarely studied but important little commentary on the *Second Letter* demonstrates,[5] but it had for Ficino a specific embodiment in the ideal relationship of papacy and empire, the twin shepherds ideally of the European flock.

The age had perfected astronomy in Paul himself, even as it had recalled the 'Platonic discipline' from the darkness into the light. Here Ficino links astronomy-astrology with Platonism merely by juxtaposition. Elsewhere, however, he publicly champions the importance of linking the two, and it is probable that the publication of his great Plato edition was delayed until 1484 in order to sally forth at the most auspicious stellar moment, in a year when Jupiter and Saturn were again in conjunction and expectations of something imminent and momentous were everywhere proclaimed.[6] We should recall that the philosopher guardians of Plato's *Epinomis*, which the age accepted as not only authentic but as the thirteenth book or epilogue of the *Laws*, are also astronomer-astrologers, and that the nocturnal council is nocturnal precisely because they are then able to consult the stars, as Ficino makes clear in his epitome.[7]

For Ficino the Germans were famous as astrologers. Indeed, two final *inventa* that he adduces as twin signs of his own age of gold is the recent discovery in Germany of the printing press, but more importantly still of «tables wherein the entire face of the sky over the course of a century is opened up in a single hour as it were», tables that eclipsed in his mind the machine he had seen in Florence that reproduced the daily motions of the

---

[4] Ficino had of course translated Dante's *De Monarchia*, the textbook of imperial apology; see P. O. Kristeller, *Supplementum Ficinianum*, 2 voll., Firenze 1937, I, pp. clxi-clxii; P. Shaw, *La versione ficiniana della* Monarchia, «Studi danteschi», LI, 1978, pp. 289-408.

[5] Ficini *Opera omnia*, cit., pp. 1530-1532.

[6] J. Hankins, *Plato in the Italian Renaissance*, 2 vols., Leiden 1990, I, pp. 302-304.

[7] Ficini *Opera omnia*, cit., pp. 1525-1530.

celestial spheres, presumably an Archimedean clock.[8] These «German tables» had been sent to and dedicated to Paul's employer, the Duke of Württemberg (the founder we should recall in 1477 of the University of Tübingen), «a celestial gift worthy a celestial prince and worthy of the approval of Paul, a contemplator of celestial things». And Ficino is amazed that the German printing press had been able to master the motions of the heavens, to capture a century's unfolding in an hour, to unite wisdom and power. The Germans became in this admiring portrait not merely contributors to Florence's age of gold, to the new Platonic age of his own aspirations, but in a way the perfecters of it in that they have reproduced the evermoving language, the classical language, of a century of stars in a book, writing down, as it were, the spheres. And 'reproduced' should more properly be 'recaptured' because the first symbolic system for writing down a language was Zoroaster's decision to use the stars and constellations as his signs,[9] and the Germans have thus recaptured the first, hieratic, celestial language of the ancient theology. Moreover, the implication is that such tables enable men not only to know but to change or adjust their activities and choices, to make their lives 'conform' to the celestial influences, to align their words with the words of Nature. And Zoroaster, as his name suggests, was thought to be the founder of astrology, or at least to share that distinction with Abraham.[10] At all events, the new astronomy, not yet of Copernicus but of the German star tables, had revived the notion of the language of the stars.

This star-language theme attends the second of our *teutonici complatonici* Eberhard himself, whom Ficino praises in an epistolary proem accompanying a copy of his *De Sole*, which he is sending him via Johannes Streler, as the Sun among all the princes of Germany.[11] He is therefore the

---

[8] Cfr. CICERO, *Tusculanae*, I, XXV, 63; FICINO, *Platonic Theology*, ed. by M. J. B. ALLEN-J. HANKINS, 3 vols., Cambridge, Mass. 2001, IV, 1, pp. 278-279. The tables were probably those of Johannes Regiomontanus' *Ephemerides*, Venice 1474. On Ficino and clocks, see S. TOUSSAINT, *Ficino, Archimedes and the Celestial Arts*, in *Marsilio Ficino: His Theology, His Philosophy, His Legacy*, cit., pp. 307-326.

[9] See M. FICINO, *Philebus Commentary*, ed. by M. J. B. ALLEN, Berkeley 1975, 29, pp. 270-271; M. J. B. ALLEN, *Synoptic Art. Marsilio Ficino on the History of Platonic Interpretation*, Firenze 1988, p. 35.

[10] *Ibid.*, pp. 35-40.

[11] FICINI *Opera omnia*, cit., p. 944.2; it immediately precedes the letter to Paul of Middelburg (see above, note 2).

perfect recipient of «the Platonic and the Dionysian Sun», meaning Ficino's comparison of the Sun to God as treated by Plato and by Dionysius the Areopagite and interpreted by himself.

In a subsequent letter to the Duke, «inclyto comiti Wirtembergensi & montis Peligardi seniori»,[12] Ficino adopts, with only a few adaptations, the concluding chapter of the *De Sole*[13] obviously deeming its solar theme particularly suitable as an emissary to a German prince. He begins by invoking Socrates as sun-struck, as someone who on his military service had often stopped motionlessly in his tracks to watch with wonder the rising sun, «his dazzled eyes fixed like those of a statue». His attendant daimon, Ficino's traditional identification of his «warning voice» (*to daimonion*), was a phoebean one, and Socrates had been used since childhood to venerating Phoebus and was thus accounted by Phoebus' oracle «the wisest of the Greeks»; his final act was to order a sacrificial cock to Apollo's son Aesculapius. Of course Ficino sees this figuratively. We should never forget, he writes, that the Sun is not the origin of the cosmos, but rather a shadow or reflection («umbra quaedam [...] potiusquam imago»). For it is daily in motion and the power of its rays are often weakened or impeded: by the opposition of the Moon, by clouds, by the density of earthly objects, by distance. Indeed it is only a small part of the world, narrowly confined, dragged round by its sphere, subject to the pull of other spheres and to planetary oppositions, weakened especially by the power of the malefic planets, Mars and Saturn. Whereas the Father can effect all things, the Sun does not create the spheres or overpower the cold, the wet or the dense. Nor do the other planets and stars take their origin from the Sun even if they seem to take their measure from it as their ruler. Yet this submission does teach us that all things in, under or above heaven, likewise refer to the one universal principle; and it admonishes us to venerate this principle as the celestial beings venerate the Sun.

The Sun Socrates had admired in his ecstasy («in eo mentis excessu») was not then the visible but the invisible Sun, called by Plato the son of God, the prime intellect and contemplatable by the intellect alone, since it was, in Socratic terms, entirely beyond the visible heavens. It was this supercelestial son that had moved Socrates to contemplate «the incom-

---

[12] *Ibid.*, pp. 946.2-947 – the second letter in the twelfth book of *Letters*: it too dates from 1492. Montbéliard (Mömpelgard) was territory west of the Rhine (on the borders of Alsace and Franche-Comté), which an ancestor, Eberhard IV (1388-1419), had acquired through marriage.

[13] *Ibid.*, pp. 974.2-975.

prehensible goodness of the father», who is unchanging and in whom there is no «shadow of change», not even the changing we predicate of the intellectual realm. Thus the human mind first contemplates the visible sun, then the invisible sun of the prime intellect, and finally the Sun beyond the Sun, the One itself, the Father of lights.[14]

It is a studied, clever letter. For it implicitly links Eberhard, as a prince, to the Sun with all the usual flattering implications, even as it subordinates such an earthly light to the resplendent intellectual light of the angels and beyond them to the effulgent light of the Father of all light. In other words, it underscores both the advantages and the dangers of analogy, praising a prince and yet reminding him of his subordinate if lustrous position in the great scheme of things.[15] Above all, it establishes Socrates the philosopher as the wise soul who can make constant use of the rising of a great celestial prince to venerate the supercelestial Mind; who can translate from the language of the one to the language of the other, because Socrates' mind is itself supercelestial in origin. We have therefore a complex portrait of the art of *comparatio* looking back to the great guide to analogizing (albeit we are now aware of Socrates' frequent exploitation, even abuse, of analogizing), and forward to the recipient of an analogy which contains its own critique, its own pointers to its own limitations, since «the Sun is infinitely far from the world's Author» even as it serves in a way as the author of all life. At this point we can see why, in the separate proem to Eberhard, Ficino had stressed that his *comparatio* was both «Platonic» and «Dionysian». For comparing the Sun to the Good is a famous Platonic analogy, while Dionysius the Areopagite had warned in his *Mystical Theology* that nothing can be truly analogous to the God beyond all likeness, a God whom we can only approach in «an ecstasy», a standing outside itself of the mind.

Such a philosophical, golden-age critique necessarily undermines the notion of any lead or iron age language being authoritative. For every postlapsarian language, be it Latin or a vernacular, or even the Greek of Plato and of the Areopagite and Plotinus his greatest interpreters, becomes the

---

[14] ST. JAMES, *Epistle* 1:17.

[15] It also implies that Eberhard should know the *De Sole* entire since he now has its conclusion, though there is nothing in the letter to suggest that it is in fact the last chapter of a larger work, a *comparatio solis ad Deum* that might remind Ficino's friends of the similar *Orphica comparatio* which is now a letter written in 1479 to Lotterio Neroni in Ficino's sixth book of *Letters* (FICINI *Opera omnia*, cit., pp. 825.2-826).

language of *comparatio*: the best it can do is to point to its own limitations, and to look beyond its own brightness to the supercelestial source of all brightness. One might even hazard the notion that the revival of this kind of Platonic critique of all language played a role, however indirectly, in undermining the authority, philosophical and even to a degree theological, of Latin and Greek, thus permitting the emergence of the vernaculars as being no more nor less tied to the structures and functioning of analogy, modern tongues that shared the same fundamentally provisional nature as the classical languages: stars to Latin's Sol but both pointing to an intellectual light and to a Father to which no sunshine could compare. Ficino's comparatist heliocentrism was pointing in fact to the need for a revolutionary displacement of all the planets as light-bearers, *phosphorai*, and by implication problematizing all language, even the planetary language of astrological prediction, influence, and magical invocation, and with it the German expertise in establishing star tables.

From the summer of 1488 on Ficino wrote a number of letters to Martinus Uranius (Martin Prenninger, Preninger or Brenninger) of Constance, a humanist-ecclesiastic in the service of Eberhard and a canon lawyer who wrote a commentary on the Decretals. Ficino almost invariably puns on Prenninger's Latin name: «Martine, amice Uraniae, revera coelitus mihi date»;[16] as well as, less often, on his German one: «praemia geres».[17] Of particular note is Ficino's reply of 11 June 1489 to Martin's request for some guide to Platonism.[18] For it enumerates Ficino's own Platonic works (Kristeller calls it the second catalogue),[19] and also adduces the chief Platonic authorities available in Latin: the Areopagite, Augustine, Boethius, Apuleius, Calcidius, Macrobius, Avicebron, Alpharabi, Henry of Ghent, Avicenna, and Scotus. It also specifically mentions the *Elements*, *Theologia platonica*, *De Providentia* and *De Fato* of Proclus, the *Defensio Platonis* of Cardinal Bessarion, and «certain speculations» of Nicolaus Caisius (apparently Cusanus, though this is the sole reference to him in Ficino's

[16] *Ibid.*, p. 912.2.

[17] *Ibid.*, p. 899.2: «Prennyngere praemia geres. Sed utinam Uranio, id est, coelesti donum aliquod, vel prope coeleste dare».

[18] *Ibid.*

[19] KRISTELLER, *Supplementum*, cit., I, pp. CXIII-CXIV.

writings). Also of note is another letter to Uranius which lists Ficino's intellectual friends and pupils («catalogus familiarium atque auditorum»),[20] those who were joined with him in the cultivation of the 'liberal disciplines', because it bears on the way we should think of the familiar but perhaps misleading notion of Ficino's 'Platonic Academy' as distinct from his circle of admirers.[21]

In a letter of 29 August 1489 Ficino gave Uranius a detailed account of his own horoscope and nativity signs and news of his completion of his astrologically keyed, three-book *De vita*,[22] a copy of which he sent him in April 1490 with a cover note in which he thanked him for the gift of a small knife-case with bejewelled gold handles.[23] Moreover, he dedicated the ninth book of his *Letters* to him referring to Uranius in a dedicatory proem as his guardian angel, what the ancients had referred to as his «good demon» and «genius», and as his alter ego.[24] He also sent him separately – as a numerologically appropriate conclusion of the tenth book of his *Letters*, since love, to which the tenth book is dedicated («consecratus»), should end in pleasure – the four pleasure fables that now form part of the appendix to the *Philebus Commentary*[25] (which Ficino despatched to Uranius in two parts in 1491).[26] And in a letter of 4 August 1492 he sent this «amicus unicus» some seven summary extracts of Latin notes he had made on the recently arrived first twelve treatises of Proclus' *In Rempublicam*, notes he called «little flowers from the most delightful meadows» and which he had waywardly gathered from the huge commentary.[27]

---

[20] Ficini *Opera omnia*, cit., pp. 936.2-937.

[21] For the continuing controversy over the nature of Ficino's '(Platonic) Academy', see J. Hankins, *Cosimo de' Medici and the 'Platonic Academy'*, «Journal of the Warburg and Courtauld Institutes», LIII, 1990, pp. 144-162; Id., *The Myth of the Platonic Academy of Florence*, «Renaissance Quarterly», XLIV, 1991, pp. 429-475; and A. Field, *The Platonic Academy of Florence*, in *Marsilio Ficino: His Theology, His Philosophy, His Legacy*, cit., pp. 359-376.

[22] Ficini *Opera omnia*, cit., p. 901.2.

[23] *Ibid.*, pp. 908.5-909.

[24] *Ibid.*, p. 893.1.

[25] *Ibid.*, pp. 921.2-924; see *Philebus Commentary*, appendix 2.

[26] *Ibid.*, pp. 928.2, 929.3 – letters of 20th July and 24th November 1491 respectively.

[27] Ficini *Opera omnia*, cit., p. 937.2, with the commentary notes on pp. 937.3-943.1. See M. J. B. Allen, *Nuptial Arithmetic: Marsilio Ficino's Commentary on the Fatal Number in Book VIII of Plato's* Republic, Berkeley 1994, pp. 37-39. Incidentally, Ficino never had access to the second half of Proclus' commentary.

In his last, undated, letter to Uranius in the twelfth book,[28] Ficino wittily writes that Castor and Pollux are not the only *gemini* in the night sky. For so are Saturn and his younger brother Mercury (being of the same brightness and both presiding over the intellect); and equally so are Jupiter and Venus (his *germana alma*), and Phoebe the Moon and Phoebus (her *germanus)* the Sun. Only Mars is solitary, a rival rather than a companion of the Sun. After playing with the notion of the two Suns among their respective patrons, Ficino then turns to the great Platonic theme of being led from the dimness of sensible knowledge up into the blinding light of the intelligibles, ending with an allusion to the notable passages in Plato's *Seventh Letter* 341cd and 344b, which describe the difference between the rational pursuit of lower forms of knowledge and the sudden *scintillatio*, the catching fire, that marks our perception of the Ideas, of the 'sparks' in the divine mind.[29]

But two letters to Uranius, given their themes, merit especial attention here. The first is a note of 9 June 1492[30] that accompanies Latin versions of a) the palinode that became in later antiquity the preface to the *Orphic Hymns*,[31] and b) the Orphic *Hymn to Jove* with Porphyry's explication of it.[32] Ficino declares that as a youth he had (he doesn't know how!) translated rather literally the *Hymns* and the *Argonautica* of Orpheus, the hymns of Homer and Proclus, the *Theogony* of Hesiod, but all for his own use alone (*mihi soli*), though Uranius had recently seen them when he was his guest. But Ficino had never wanted to publish them lest he «should appear to be recalling readers to the ancient cult of the gods and the demons which has been the subject of reprobation for a long time, properly so». Like the ancient Pythagoreans he is anxious to avoid the impiety of publication, and the same concern had led him to commit his youthful com-

[28] FICINI *Opera omnia*, cit., pp. 949.3-950; cfr. KRISTELLER, *Supplementum*, cit., I, p. CXIV.

[29] Cfr. *ibid.*, p. 1535 – Ficino's epitome for the letter.

[30] *Ibid.*, pp. 933.2-935.2.

[31] The first is known as the Aristobulus version (Kern's frag. 247) and Ficino encountered it in Eusebius' *Praeparatio evangelica*, 13.12.5, though it also appears in part in Clement of Alexandria's *Stromata* 5.14 (Kern, frag. 248). D. P. WALKER, *The Ancient Theology*, London 1972, p. 28, argues that this Latin version is by George of Trebizond.

[32] Once again, his source for both the hymn (Kern, frag. 168) and Porphyry's *expositio* of it is probably Eusebius's *Praeparatio evangelica* at 3.9; see WALKER, *The Ancient Theology*, cit., pp. 36-37.

mentaries on Lucretius to the flames as Plato had done his tragedies and elegies.[33] For noxious views are like poison! Nevertheless, he had promised to send Uranius «some of the safer songs of Orpheus», the palinode and the *Hymn to Jove* being examples.[34]

Unexpectedly, we see Ficino's profound reservations about texts that he had always admired and attributed to the third in the line of ancient sages which had culminated in Plato, a poet whom Plato himself had often quoted, and whose *Hymns* were revered by the later Neoplatonists (though we now suppose that the majority of the *Hymns*, as contrasted to earlier fragmentary quotations, are products of later antiquity). This is the odder in that the palinode is, as its name suggests, a retraction supposedly penned by Orpheus, who was recanting his earlier polytheism and testifying to his belief in the one god, Jove, the «beginning, middle and end of all things» as the penultimate line declares. But such a recantation was hardly necessary for a Neoplatonic exegete who would habitually interpret all polytheistic references monotheistically, since the many must always be referred to the One. And Christian exegetes had continually interpreted classical poetry in this way, though the pitfalls were recognized and the poets were often condemned or chastised for themselves not knowing what they really meant.[35] Ficino's curious acknowledgement of his own youthful folly in commenting on the seductive Epicurean poetry of Lucretius also speaks to the subordination of poetry to graver philosophy, as does his reference to Plato's rejection of his own songs. This anti-poetic stance is not, moreover, for the traditional Platonic reasons: that poets roused tumultuous passions in the young, that poets credited human passions and behaviour to the virtuous gods, that poets posited chaos as the first principle of cosmology.[36] Rather, it is because poetry is closely allied to demonic cult: much of it is 'unsafe' though certain bits were 'safer'. Uranius, being himself uranian, was therefore honoured by passages that had

———

ICINI *Opera omnia*, cit., p. 933.2: «For being older and judging with greater care often leads us to condemn what the levity of youth too rashly embraced or at least did not know to condemn».

[34] We only have two other such examples, a *Hymn to Heaven* (Uranus) and a *Hymn to Nature*, both in letters Ficino never published (one to Cosimo of 4 September 1462 and the other to Germain de Ganay, undated but c. 1495). See KRISTELLER, *Supplementum*, cit., II, pp. 87-88; ID., *Studies in Renaissance Thought and Letters*, Rome 1956, pp. 50-54, 96-97.

[35] See ALLEN, *Synoptic Art*, cit.

[36] *Ibid.*, pp. 111-114.

both come from a notable Church Father and long been subject therefore to Christian appropriation. In short, we are confronted by the fear of translation into Latin, particularly the translation of Orphic-Platonic poetic theology, and by a corresponding and requisite concern with interpretation. Hence the affixing of Porphyry's exposition which Ficino obviously feels is in accord with Christian cosmology, the Creator being both 'intellect' and 'vivific spirit'.

In another letter, in Ficino's twelfth and last book, Ficino takes up one of the most venerable of the ancient myths.[37] Given that Martin is a lawyer, Ficino addresses the bond between philosophy and the laws, mythologically the relationship between Saturn and Jupiter the author of laws. Astrologically this was important since it was thought that a conjunction of Saturn and Jupiter (which occurs every nineteen years) occasioned the promulgation of new laws, and especially when this occurred in the four cardinal signs of Aries, Cancer, Libra and Capricorn. «Didn't the ancient poets and the old theologians», he writes, «imagine Saturn as a contemplator in the innermost parts of shrines, excogitating laws and judgements after daily contemplation which he then handed on to Jove his son, the leader of actions who would issue mandates to the citizens on all they should obey». Hence King Minos in Homer withdraws for nine years into the cave of Jupiter and there receives the laws from the father of gods and men. But «nobody adept in the ancient mysteries would dedicate a cave to Jupiter as his property since he is always in the open». The cave «is obviously nothing other than the inmost shrine (*adytum)*, domicile or chapel of Saturn himself», where Jupiter, united now with Saturn, gives Minos the laws that he subsequently administers to the people. Ficino then proceeds to laud philosophy and philosophers citing Plato, the Stoics, and Daniel to the effect that philosophers blaze forth like the splendour of the firmament, not as Saturn, that is, and not even as the eighth sphere of the fixed stars, but as the entire collective mass of the celestial spheres.

This Saturn-Jupiter governed argument is interesting in that it duplicates elements in the golden age myth. There is a descent from Saturn the contemplator down through Jove the lord of action to the heroic man, King Minos, and on to the people; and an ascent from Saturn in his *adytum* up to the eighth sphere and thence to the cosmos, Saturn serving as the link between celestial philosophy and human law, the mean between the lan-

[37] FICINI *Opera omnia*, cit., pp. 947.2-948.

guage of sovereignty and the language of obedience, the language of grace and the language of prescription. For the paradigmatic gift is the gift of laws in classical mythology as in the story of Moses' ascent of Sinai, the Biblical equivalent to Homer's *adytum*. For Ficino's world certainly, Latin still owed its prestige, not so much to the humanists and poets, for all their yearning to revive the words of antiquity, as to law and theology. But interestingly, although Ficino acknowledges Jupiter's magisterial role as the god of law, he is responding to the political divisions of the ancient Greeks and to their own myths of the founders of each of the great city states, the men who had first given them their own peculiar laws, Solon to the Athenians, Lycurgus to the Spartans, Minos to the Cretans, and so on.

One suspects that this Saturn-Jupiter paradigm eventually serves as a model for the relationship between classical Latin and the vernacular with the implication being that Saturnian Latin is the language of contemplation, of the golden age, while the vernacular, and by implication Eberhard's German, is the language of the law. If so, the myth also implies an ideal relationship, a *cognatio*, between father and son, surely one of the enduring metaphors for the link between the classical languages and the vernaculars. This is ironic given the infanticidal impulses apparent in the myths of Zeus's birth, the vomiting up of the Titans, and the jovian revenge that imprisons Cronos not in the cave of contemplation but in a cell. But here too the metaphors map out the often parricidal aspects of a vernacular's relationship to its classical forbear, and certainly to the authority that is claimed for that forbear by its most ardent supporters, those who have most to gain by championing its preeminence and holding other language speakers to its norms. Here too the later confusion of Cronos with Chronos, of Saturn with the figure of old Father Time, speaks to the equating of the classical language, again one's own or another's, with a past age and its excellencies, and with the implication that the new language is a witness to lapse and degeneration, a falling away from the poetic and philosophical heights once occupied by masters of word and song. Ficino's letter to Uranius speaks, by way of contrast, to the legitimate transmission of philosophy and law from the old to the new, a *translatio* of the Platonic gold. And here surely Ficino's own acute sense that Latin was neither Greek nor Hebrew nor Egyptian nor Chaldaean (Aramaic) nor Persian, the languages of the *prisci theologi*, but rather the language of interpretation, of commentary, gloss and exposition, must have played a signal role. For all his massive investment in Latin translation and Latin commentary, Ficino was after all an hellenophile, someone who felt perpetually that the language he was speaking was not the language of the gods, even as he hoped that something of that language would be born again as a result in part of his scholarly travails.

Some speculative conclusions. Ficino's sympathetic attitude towards his own vernacular on the one hand, and his lifelong engagement with Greek on the other meant, I would argue, that he never privileged Latin in his own mind, even though the bulk of his scholarship and of his own theological and philosophical speculation is in the Scholastic Latin of the medieval school tradition (he tried his hand at fashionable Ciceronian ornamentation mainly in his letters). Indeed, his abiding sense that the ultimate mysteries had been unfolded in their most intelligible or accessible form in a foreign language, in Greek, furnishes us with an arresting model for mapping bilingualism in the context of a one-language supremacy (not necessarily conceived on the imperial model since Ficino did toy with the notion of *translatio studii*).

There is an interesting lesson to be drawn here. If English is the new Latin, then the philosophical and poetic mysteries, the *theologica*, of any other language (potentially at least) become like Greek, and specifically Platonic, texts for all but native speakers of that language. They become, accordingly, texts that increasingly require interpretation and mediation by way of English (and one thinks of the near hegemony of English in certain areas of literary criticism and literary theory, even for the native speakers of the language of the texts engaged by or in the criticism). The more authoritative the texts indeed, the more compelling their translation into, and their interpretation by way of, English.

Ficino's 1492 letters to his three German correspondents thus serve, albeit incidentally, as mirrors reflecting our own contemporary engagement with a universal interpretative language, even as interpretation itself (and its accompanying epistemology) is a singularly problematic activity in the life of any Platonist as we noted earlier. I would even hazard the argument that Latin remained for Ficino and most of Europe, primarily the language of interpretation, despite the best endeavours of the humanists to inculcate a love of Latin literature; and that this remains indeed the primary reason for its study today. Ficino's revival of Greek Platonism would certainly serve to underscore such a hermeneutical role for what was always in his mind, and despite Vergil, Lucretius and Boethius, the language of a subordinate philosophical tradition, and a language too that was already being challenged by three very different kinds of enemies: those who were championing the new vernaculars, those who were already recognizing the special nature of the languages of mathematics and astronomy; and those like Ficino who were yearning still for the classical golden language of revelation, the language of Plato's Ideas be it Greek, or Hebrew, or the pre-Babelic language of Enoch who walked with God.

10

The Birth Day of Venus

Pico as Platonic Exegete in the Commento *and the* Heptaplus

Giovanni Pico della Mirandola (1463–94) was the wunderkind among Italian Renaissance philosophers and a key figure, along with Cusanus, Bessarion, and Ficino, in the revival of Platonic metaphysics, though he was not a devout Neoplatonist like Ficino but rather an Aristotelian by training and in many ways an eclectic by conviction. Nonetheless, he plunged as hardly more than a youth into the works of Plato, Plotinus, Proclus, and other Neoplatonists, notably in the fifteen months or so he spent in Florence from the spring of 1484 to the summer of 1485, where he acquired a rare understanding of the Platonists' methodology, central postulates, and metaphysical distinctions. This Platonic education was succeeded by nine months in Paris (July 1485 to March 1486) and was subsequently harnessed to an encyclopedic, ambitious, essentially Aristotelian plan. This was to gather together an array of Egyptian, Chaldean, Greek, Hebrew (including Cabalistic), patristic, and scholastic (including Arab) propositions rather than arguments or proofs as such – an array which eventually amounted to 900 conclusions, 900 being the numerological symbol of the soul's ecstatic return to itself in philosophical study – and to defend them in Rome. The event would take place early in 1487 in what he called a "council" but which would be in effect a grand Parisian *disputatio,* and it would include, he hoped, the pope, the College of Cardinals, and a number of eminent theologians and philosophers (whose expenses he would cover!). While this breathtaking proposal by a brilliant twenty-three-year-old had a positivistic dimension to it inasmuch as a number of the theses either concerned nature or had implications for any consideration of the natural world, and a few even invoked mathematical and numerological ideas, yet it was at heart a hermeneutic enterprise exploring the necessity and the limits of Platonic interpretation – interpretation not so much of a scheme or a set of propositions as of any philosophical or mythological proposition whatsoever regardless of its provenance or original argumentative context.

The *Conclusiones* were published in Rome on December 7, 1486, notices were posted in all the universities in Italy, and Pico set about preparing an introductory Latin *Oration*, with its celebrated account of God's addressing the protoplastic Adam. Controversy immediately erupted, and in January Pope Innocent VIII appointed a commission to examine the conclusions. In early March the commission expressed reservations about just thirteen – those dealing, for example, with the real presence at the Mass and the role of magic and Cabala in determining the divinity of Christ, along with others possessing unorthodox theological implications. Pico rushed to defend the thirteen publicly in a Latin prose apologia, which appeared toward the end of May 1487, and the Pope condemned the whole enterprise on August 5, though publication of the papal brief itself was delayed, interestingly, until December 15.

To escape arrest, Pico left Rome and fled to France, where in January 1488 he was caught and briefly imprisoned at the pope's request by Philip of Savoy. But King Charles VIII and other influential voices took up his cause, and by June the pope had permitted him to return to Florence on condition he refrain from any more discussion of the *Conclusiones.* He settled in a villa at Querceto near Fiesole lent him by Lorenzo de' Medici, and in the remaining years of his truncated life, he wrote a short polemical treatise defending the Aristotelian thesis that being is the primary metaphysical hypostasis (1491) and labored at, but never finished, a series of commentaries on the Psalms and a long treatise directed against the claims of divinatory astrology (both of which remained unpublished in his lifetime). However, from the viewpoint of this essay, which aims to explore aspects of Pico's Neoplatonism, particularly his understanding of Platonic exegesis, his most interesting works are (1) a seven-part treatise on the six days of the Mosaic creation, the Latin *Heptaplus*, written and published in 1489 and dedicated to Lorenzo de' Medici, and (2) a youthful endeavor and his first work, the Italian *Commento.* This was compiled in 1486, though not published until 1519, and it has a very complicated history. Both these texts raise, in rather different ways, the *Commento* even more so perhaps, the problem of being a Platonic exegete and interpreter and thus of determining the parameters of explaining, allegorizing, and extrapolating and ultimately of theologizing itself.

Let us begin then with what is now known as the *Commento*, an unfinished series of notes Pico first compiled in the autumn of 1486 on his way to Rome, when he took refuge for a few weeks at his country retreat in Fratta near Perugia, after his escapade with Margherita (the unhappily married wife of a minor Medici *signore*, a tax collector in Arezzo).[1] Here he began to prepare in earnest for his council and was joined by two Hebrew scholars and by a close friend and admirer, Girolamo Benivieni (1453–1542).[2] Benivieni was a fine and subtle poet who was buried eventually in the same tomb with Pico in the Dominican church of San Marco – the church of the fiery Savonarola, who played a signal role in both their lives – and he had written a self-declaredly Platonizing love poem, a *canzone* beginning "Amor, dalle cui man sospes' el freno / Del mio cor pende." This was known as the *Canzona dell' amor celeste e divino*, and it summarized four brief passages (I.3, II.5,7, V.4, VI.4,6–7) from Ficino's commentary on the *Symposium*, the *De amore*, which had been composed in 1469 and was already becoming the most influential of Ficino's Plato commentaries.[3] Benivieni's poem was itself modeled on a famous poem, "Donna me prega," by Dante's contemporary, Guido Cavalcanti, which Ficino mentions in the *De amore* (even though it was Aristotelian, not Platonic, in inspiration!) in order to flatter his own friend Giovanni Cavalcanti, a descendent of Guido's.[4] Pico's notes on "Amor, dalle cui" consist of a general Platonizing introduction, divided into three unequal books, followed by a section of particular commentary on the canzone's nine stanzas, stanzas that Benivieni subsequently altered or added in various places to accommodate Pico's ideas or requests (he added what is now stanza 3, for instance).[5] Pico seems to have worked up the notes in just

[1] For details see Eugenio Garin, *Giovanni Pico della Mirandola: Vita e dottrina* (Florence: Le Monnier, 1937), 25–6.

[2] See the detailed entry by Cesare Vasoli in the *Dizionario biografico degli Italiani* (Rome: Enciclopedia Italiana, 1966), 8:550–5; see also Olga Zorzi Pugliese, "Girolamo Benivieni: Umanista riformatore (dalla corrispondenza inedita)," *La bibliofilia* 72 (1970): 253–88.

[3] See Olga Zorzi Pugliese, "Variations on Ficino's *De amore*: The Hymns to Love by Benivieni and Castiglione," in *Ficino and Renaissance Neoplatonism*, ed. Konrad Eisenbichler and Olga Zorzi Pugliese (Ottowa: Dovehouse Editions, 1986), 113–21.

[4] See Massimo Ciavolella, "Eros/Ereos: Marsilio Ficino's Interpretation of Guido Cavalcanti's 'Donna me prega,'" in *Ficino and Renaissance Neoplatonism*, 39–48.

[5] See Eugenio Garin, "Marsilio Ficino, Gioralamo Benivieni, e Giovanni Pico," *Giornale critico della filosofia italiana* 23, nos. 1–2 (1942): 93–9.

a few weeks, even as he was preparing his defense of the 900 theses, for he had already sent drafts of them to Girolamo's brother, Domenico, by November 10, 1486. Pico also sent a draft to Ficino, presumably for his reactions. In working through it, however, Ficino found several off-the-cuff attacks on his own views, either aimed at him directly or at "a distinguished Platonist" who was wrong on such and such an issue (clearly himself), and he was agitated enough to pen his own marginalia, with abrupt remarks such as "This is a bad mistake," before sending the draft back to Pico.

Nonetheless, this scholarly contention did not develop, as it well might have, into an academic feud or estrangement, even though Pico, in revising and reorganizing, took only partial, one might even say high-handed, account of Ficino's corrections, incorporating some of them and rebutting others, and also asseverated at the end of 2.2 that Marsilio had "made mistakes on every subject in every part of his treatise [i.e., the *De amore*]." Irenically, however, Ficino was one of the influential voices who defended Pico after the banning of the Roman disputation, and he helped Pico to obtain Medici patronage, even writing a letter dated May 30, 1488, on Lorenzo's behalf inviting Pico as another Saturnian to come to live and philosophize in Florence.[6] Pico in reply addresses Ficino as "father of the Platonic family" and as his life's "solace," his mind's "delight," conduct's "guide," and learning's "master" (*disciplinae magister*).[7] In any event, from the onset Pico had regarded his own commentary notes as preliminary speculations, and he says several times that he is going to write more about various topics in three future treatises: a commentary on the *Symposium*, a poetic theology, and a love treatise. None of these ever materialized, though he may have been drawing on notes that he had begun to compile for them. Very soon, understandably, he lost interest in the whole project, as his "council" and other issues became more pressing, though he did extract some formulations from the *Commento* in preparing his *Heptaplus*.[8]

Pico died on November 17, 1494, and in 1496 his nephew Gianfrancesco published his uncle's collected works in two volumes with a

[6] This is now in Ficino's *Opera omnia* (Basel: Heinrich Petri, 1576), 888–9, in his eighth book of *Letters*. This edition has been reproduced in modern times, most recently by Phénix Editions, Paris, 1999. See, too, Ficino's letter to Salviati and Benivieni in praise of Pico as Count of Concordia and as the child of the Graces possessed of wisdom, eloquence, and virtue (ibid., 890).

[7] Ibid., 889.

[8] Ibid., 98.

prefatory biography, but he did not include the *Commento*, though the table of contents lists an *In Platonis Convivium* lib. III. Benivieni too deliberately suppressed Pico's original version and eventually reorganized, expanded, and in places completely rewrote an expurgated version that omitted the references to Ficino and was stylistically and in other aspects much more polished. In the process, he collapsed books 2 and 3, inserted his poem at the end of the new book 2, and titled the particular commentary book 3. It seems that, like Gianfrancesco, he and other friends were anxious to conceal the disagreements with Ficino, lest these disagreements and indeed the relationship between the two luminaries be misunderstood. Moreover, since Ficino himself certainly considered the notes replete with youthful errors whose publication would not enhance Pico's reputation, as he had observed in a letter to Germain de Ganay in Paris dated March 23, 1495,[9] the circle of mutual friends may well have agreed with him, particularly if Pico himself had come to acknowledge some errors before he died. More problematically, at the turn of the century, Benivieni, now an ardent and devout *piagnone* who repented his earlier life as a love poet, cannibalized portions from Pico's notes when he decided to publish a prose commentary of his own to accompany a selection of a hundred poems, but not, remarkably, the canzone "Amor, dalle cui," that he had written earlier but had reworked and "reformed" in the light of his new spirituality. This commentary appeared in Florence in 1500 and was entitled *Commento di Hieronymo Benivieni sopra a più sue canzone et sonetti dello Amore et della Bellezza divina.*[10]

Finally, to compound the confusion, in 1518 a relative of Ficino's, Biagio Buonaccorsi, used Benivieni's expurgated version (but collated in part, it would seem, with a manuscript of the unexpurgated one!) to prepare another edition of Benivieni's poems that would include both the *Commento* as such and "Amor, dalle cui." This was the Giunta edition of Benivieni's *Opere* (it included an errata sheet), which was published in Florence in 1519 with the *Commento* as the first item and with the poem appearing between books 2 and 3. Occupying some 67 octavo leaves, Pico's work was now entitled *Commento delo illustrissimo Signore Conte Iohanni Pico Miradulano sopra una Canzona de Amore composta da Hieronymo Benivieni Ciptadino Fiorentino secondo la mente & opinione de'*

9 Edited by Paul O. Kristeller in his *Supplementum Ficinianum*, 2 vols. (Florence: Olschki, 1937), 2:91–3. The letter is dated March 23, 1494, Florentine style.

10 See Olga Zorzi Pugliese, "Benivieni's *Commento* and Bonaventure's *Itinerarium*: Autobiography and Ideology," *Rivista di storia e letteratura religiosa* 30 (1994): 347–62.

Platonici. Benivieni must have known all about the venture and about Buonaccorsi's attempt to rework the *Commento,* but he claims partial ignorance. The 1519 text was then reprinted in the Venice 1522 edition of Benivieni's *Opere,* with the errata corrected, and this 1522 version of the *Commento* was thereafter published in the three Basel editions of Pico della Mirandola's own *Opera omnia* (1557, 1572, and 1601), where it is listed in the table of contents as "three books on Plato's *Symposium,*" though properly entitled *Commento* in the text itself.[11]

Obviously the problems of editing the *Commento* and of deciding which version or versions to privilege are fraught with challenges, particularly since Benivieni's caliber as a poet makes his own contribution and his reworking both of the commentary and of the canzone important aspects of the story and since too he was in a position to analyze Pico's intentions better than any of his contemporaries, let alone modern scholars, however distinguished. And I am thinking here of Eugenio Garin in particular, who has done more than anyone else to enhance our understanding of Pico and his whole age and to uncover the various stages in the changes and cover-ups; it is he indeed who published the original unexpurgated version in his monumental 1942 edition of Pico's works, the standard edition we still refer to.[12]

In the *Commento,* Pico is concerned, broadly speaking, with poetic theology; he does not comment extensively on Plato's *Symposium* but discusses only selected bits and pieces of it. The work hardly compares to Ficino's *De amore,* either in length or breadth, though it raises a number of subtle points and has a rapid-fire brilliance to it. Nor indeed does it always persuade us that Pico is right in his series of contretemps with Ficino, and its combative mode of arguing has to be understood in the light of the conventions of Renaissance scholarly disagreements, which were voiced, as a rule, in pricklier terms than we usually adopt today. More surprisingly,

[11] It does not appear, incidentally, in the Venice 1557 edition.

[12] Giovanni Pico della Mirandola, *De hominis dignitate, Heptaplus, De ente et uno, e scritti vari,* ed. Eugenio Garin (Florence: Vallecchi, 1942); the *Commento* appears on pp. 459–81, with Benivieni's *canzona* preceding it on pp. 451–8. I shall also refer to the translation of the *Commento* usefully introduced and annotated by Sears Jayne as *Commentary on a Canzone of Benivieni by Giovanni Pico della Mirandola* (New York: Peter Lang, 1984). Sears Jayne used Garin's text but consulted two other (derivative) MSS – N.A. 1217 in the Biblioteca Nazionale in Florence and C. VI.16 in the Biblioteca Communale in Siena – and some of the readings of the various editions (see his stemma, 263–5). Of the surviving MSS, none is a Pico autograph. Another good English translation, by Stephen Salchenberger, was done as a Johns Hopkins University Ph.D. dissertation (1967).

Pico is not (yet) well acquainted with Platonic texts that have a bearing on the *Symposium*, especially the *Phaedrus*, along with Hermias's commentary on it; the *Charmides*; and various sections of the *Enneads*. And despite his protestations, he is not concerned with love theory except in a rudimentary form. What does concern him is metaphysics (which he thinks of as a dimension of theology), especially metaphysics as he sees it embedded in Greco-Roman myth and to a lesser extent in the myths of Egypt and the *Chaldean Oracles* (attributed to Zoroaster, though in fact deriving from the first centuries of the Christian era).

For Renaissance thinkers, myths were the stuff of ancient poetry. Pico, like Ficino (and like Proclus and the Neoplatonists before them), was committed, therefore, to analyzing the divine mysteries embedded especially in poetry and in the hexameters of such pre-Socratic philosophers as Empedocles and Parmenides. That is, he was committed to poetic theologizing on the assumption that the ancient poets and their tales of the gods were a veiled, cryptic unfolding of the fundamentals of religious belief. For Ficino and Pico, the myths indeed constituted a gentile scripture, a scripture revealed, rather than compiled, by a line of ancient theologians, and posing much the same kind of hermeneutical challenges as Solomon's Song of Songs. Collectively they articulated a metaphysics that was almost perfected by Plato (as seen anachronistically through the interpretative eyes of Plotinus) and then truly perfected in Christian theology. The Christian-Platonic philosopher was in their eyes the exemplary hermeneut, the interpreter who could interpret correctly the wealth of pre-Christian, non-Hebrew revelation bestowed by a loving God on the many peoples without access either to the laws of Moses or to the Mosaic books of prophecy, the Pentateuch. This was a revelation mediated by seers, sibyls, and priests but above all by such poets as Orpheus, Hesiod, and Homer – and this despite the fact that Plato had banned poets in general from the ideal city he had envisioned in the *Republic*.

One of the most controversial bits in the *Symposium* is Plato's denigration of Orpheus, otherwise a figure whom Plato seems to have revered and whose fragments he cited as possessed of religious authority. At 179A–D, Phaedrus is said to have called Orpheus a coward on the grounds that he "showed no spirit" when, while still a living person, he tried to "scheme his way into Hades" in order to rescue Eurydice. A "mere harp-player or minstrel," says Phaedrus, and a "lukewarm lover," he "did not dare to die for love," as Alcestis by contrast had dared. Accordingly, he was sent back from Hades empty-handed, having seen the mere wraith of a woman. As a consequence of his refusal to die for love, the gods had doomed him "to meet his death at the hands of women," for heaven itself has a peculiar regard for ardor and resolution in the cause of love (179D). At the pertinent moment in his *De amore* (1.4), Ficino had declined to venture an interpretation of this notable reference that Plato had put into the mouth, significantly, of the banquet's first appointed speaker, who was also the eponymous hero of Plato's other great dialogue on love and poetic theology. "At the moment," Ficino writes, "I do not intend to enquire into the allegory of Alcestis and Orpheus." Later, however, at 7.14, he did argue that Orpheus was subject to all four of the divine furies and not just to the amatory, while Socrates was especially subject to the amatory.[13] And in a letter to Braccio Martelli dated January 20, 1491, he eventually suggested that the etymology of Eurydice signified "amplitude" (*euros*) of the "judgment" (*dikê*) and that whereas Orpheus had to descend into hell to gaze upon his beloved again, Plato, in order to see the same Eurydice, was about to "ascend to heaven" (a reference apparently to Ficino's hopes for a revival in his own age of Christian Platonism and with it of the original union between religion and philosophy).[14] Given Ficino's youthful Orphism – his admiration for the Orphic hymns and fragments; his identification of Orpheus as third in the succession of the six principal ancient theologians that was to culminate in Plato; his elevation of Orpheus to the status of the gentiles' David; his sense of Orpheus as a great magician-magus who could enchant the world of nature; and his own musical and magical interests and his skills as a performer on an Orphic lyre, which led contemporaries to praise him specifically as an Orpheus reborn – given all these dimensions of his Orphism, it is not surprising that he was reluctant to tackle what seemed to be a defamatory passage, though he would surely have agreed with Phaedrus's conclusion that "the lover, by virtue of Love's inspiration, is always nearer than the beloved to the gods" (180AB).

Pico was more intrepid. In his particular commentary on Benivieni's poem's fourth stanza, specifically on the lemma *Da lui el foco,* he argues as follows:

> Plato says that although Orpheus wanted to go to see his beloved Eurydice, he was not willing to go to her through death, because he had been made soft and weak by his own music. Instead he tried to find a way of going to her alive, and therefore, Plato says, Orpheus was not able to reach the true Eurydice, but was shown only a ghost or apparition of her. It turns out the same way

[13] *Phaedrus* 244A–245C, the *locus classicus.*

[14] Ficino, *Opera omnia,* 918.3.

for anyone who thinks he is achieving true understanding of the intellectual Ideas without cutting himself off from the functions of the imagination and also the reason. For what he is seeing is not the Ideas themselves, in their true being, but only some fantasm or likeness of them, shining either in the passible intellect or in the imagination. Although this meaning is subtle and profound, it is nevertheless so consistent with the facts that it seems to me almost a wonder that neither Marsilio nor anyone else has understood it on the basis of Plato's text. My conscience is my witness, that the first time I ever read the *Symposium*, I had no sooner finished reading Plato's words in this passage than this interpretation came into my mind. I shall explain it more fully in my commentary on the *Symposium* and in my Poetic Theology.[15]

Interestingly, Edgar Wind argues that the notion that Orpheus was not prepared to die for his beloved must have been a widely diffused "doctrine" in the Medici circle.[16] Witness the testimony of Lorenzo the Magnificent himself, who died in 1492. In a commentary on his own love sonnet sequence, Lorenzo explains why he had commenced the sequence with a sonnet on death: "If love has in it a certain perfection, ... it is impossible to arrive at that perfection without first dying with regard to the more imperfect things. ... And because Orpheus did not really die, he was debarred from the perfection of felicity" and lost his Eurydice. Eventually, indeed, the Thracian bard was savagely dismembered, and for Orphic initiates this dismemberment became a metaphor for the violence of the descent from unity into multiplicity.[17] Our last Platonic view of the poet is in the myth of Er at the end of the *Republic* (10.620A), where Orpheus has become a misogynist and, from the lots that will determine his life in the next incarnation, selects the life of a swan that only sings as it dies; this was because he "was unwilling to be conceived and born of a woman" given his brutal death at women's hands.

Pico's enthusiasm for this Orpheus-Eurydice myth in the *Symposium* is notable, as the gloss above demonstrates: he is excited and self-congratulatory that he has come upon an interpretation that is both "subtle and profound" and that no one else has discovered beforehand, though it seems so obvious to him – indeed he is scornful that Ficino had

[15] *Commento*, 556; *Commentary*, 149; henceforth formatted as (556 [149]). In his translation, Sears Jayne introduced his own chapter numbering (with a persuasive justification), but, for convenience's sake, I have stayed with Garin's numbering. In 233 n. 45, he notes that Marsilio's name is omitted here in most MSS.

[16] Edgar Wind, *Pagan Mysteries in the Renaissance*, rev. ed. (New York: Norton, 1968), 157, citing Lorenzo de' Medici, *Opere*, ed. Attilio Simioni (Bari: Laterza, 1939), 1:24ff. See also my *Synoptic Art: Marsilio Ficino on the History of Platonic Interpretation* (Florence: Olschki, 1998), 120–2.

[17] Wind, *Pagan Mysteries*, 173–5.

not even attempted a reading (Pico was of course unencumbered by the multisided Orphism and Orphic commitments of Ficino). For him, the key is the theory of the Platonic Ideas. Orpheus gazed on the images purveyed to him through his imagination or passive reason alone, because he refused to die to these faculties in order to live in the Ideas. The psychological imperative, already articulated in an earlier paragraph dealing with the Alcestis myth, is that, in order to reach "the perfect sublimity of the Ideas," we have to cut ourselves off from the sensible world to the point of no longer living in it any more.[18] But is Pico denying the possibility of achieving this severance in living trance and ecstasy when the intellectual eye reigns supreme? Let us look at the section immediately following, where he turns to what he thinks of as the Cabalistic topic of the "death of the kiss" (in Hebrew, *binsica*).[19]

In the amatory ecstasy or frenzy – and Pico never deals with the other three Platonic ecstasies – which the soul experiences while it is in the body or more properly when the body is in it, the soul separates from the body in the sense that all its lower powers cease to function, but with one exception: the nutritive or vegetative soul continues in a subdued or minimal way to maintain the body's life. Otherwise the soul's intellect is supremely active and gazes upon the heavenly Venus, the Idea of Beauty, "talking with her face to face" and feeding upon her image with its eyes. Pico denominates this ecstasy the soul's "first death."[20] If, however, the activity of the intellect becomes so sovereign that it no longer stops at all, then the body falls totally away from the soul, and the soul joins with the heavenly Venus "in an intimate embrace" that is perfected in the union of the kiss, the two becoming "a single soul." This is the "second death." Pico adds, "Since the Cabalist wise men believe that many of the ancient fathers died in this kind of rapture of the intellect, you will find the Cabalists saying that those fathers died of *binsica* which in our language means death from kissing," and he lists Abraham, Isaac, Jacob, Moses, Aaron, and Mary (i.e., Miriam).[21] The death from kissing occurs "when the soul in intellectual rapture unites so completely with incorporeal things that it rises above the body and leaves it altogether." Solomon longs for such an amatory death, says Pico, in the verse "Kiss me with the kisses of thy mouth" (Canticles 1:2), and Plato too when he speaks of the kisses of

[18] *Commento particulare* (555 [148]).

[19] In general, see Nicholas J. Perella, *The Kiss Sacred and Profane* (Berkeley: University of California Press, 1969).

[20] *Commento particulare* (557 [150]): "la prima morte."

[21] *Commento particulare* (557–8 [150]).

Agathon.[22] This analysis is an opportunity for Pico to display his interest in the Cabalists and their candidates for the second death, including the prophetic sister of Moses and Aaron.

But has he really thought the situation through? Is he saying in effect that Orpheus should have died the second death, that Orpheus should have been a Jacob or a Moses? Or simply that he should have died the first death, that is, fled to Eurydice in intellectual rapture while his body remained alive, albeit in a kind of suspended animation? Or has he now forgotten Orpheus and been swept up by the idea of a total union with intelligible Beauty that cannot be obtained while we are sensible beings? But such a union means, as he had intimated earlier in glossing this same lemma, *Da lui el foco,* that we pass "from human existence to intellectual existence" and are by that death transformed into an angel, as the Cabalists declare Enoch was transformed into Metatron, "the angel of divinity." The heart is burned away in the fire of love as the soul is led, says Pico, by ineffable grace to the Temple of Solomon, "the true habitation of divinity" (I Kings 6:11–13): "O inestimable gift of love which makes men equal to the angels. O wonderful power, which by means of death gives us life."[23] To attain such a gift, the soul separates from the body, but, even more importantly, the body drops away entirely from the soul. We cease to be humans and become angels – the cherubim and seraphim of Ezekiel's great vision.

However, Pico goes on to raise two controversial points. First, in glossing the next lemma, *Per lui el fonte immortale,* he emphasizes that the soul's ecstatic intellectual vision, which is transcendent love of God, is not reciprocated by God; God, he says, does not love us, because such a love in God "would be an imperfection" in him.[24] This is a challenging statement that runs counter to the long tradition in both Platonism and Christianity of denominating God's providential care for his creation the highest kind of love. Presumably Pico is distinguishing erotic love, the love of the lower for the higher, from agapic love, the love of the higher for the lower, and focusing on erotic love on the grounds that Plato had defined love as "the desire for beauty." But if so, why doesn't he mention agapic love and clarify the distinction, especially given the traditional role of love terminology in defining the relationship of creatures to the creator? His

[22] The reference is to Plato's first epigram to Agathon in Diogenes Laertius's *Life of Plato* 32, though Wind also cites the *Greek Anthology* 5.78 (*Pagan Mysteries,* 131 n. 2).

[23] *Commento particulare* (554 [147]). Pico spells it "Matatron."

[24] *Commento particulare* (559 [151]).

intention at this point seems to be to shock the reader, or at least to refute Ficino, who is specifically cited as believing, incorrectly, that God loves us on the grounds that in the very notion of desire there is a Platonic basis for the complementary notion of reciprocation, of the beloved's returning of the lover's love in the threefold movement of giving and receiving and giving again that is figured in the three Graces and their intertwined dance.[25]

Later, in glossing the lemma *Che poi che in sè* in his particular commentary on Benivieni's seventh and eighth stanzas, Pico takes the further step of denying that our love for God is Platonically definable as "a desire for beauty" on the basis of the arresting argument that "there is no beauty in God, according to the Platonists, because of his infinite simplicity," beauty having been previously defined as an ordering of parts into a whole. Rather, says Pico, we can only love God "in Himself" and not "as the author of ideal beauty."[26] All this suggests that Pico has not yet arrived at a coherent theory of the relationship of God to Beauty and of the soul's transition from sensible love to divine love (despite the ladder of Diotima in the *Symposium* 201D–212B), defined as the splendor or radiance of the Ideas seen collectively as the outpouring of Goodness. This is another way of questioning whether Pico has mastered the complex problem, which he inherited from the scholastics, of integrating Beauty into the three other traditional transcendental attributes of God: Goodness, Truth, and Unity. This is especially important given the central role of Beauty in the *Symposium* and *Phaedrus* and indeed in Neoplatonic metaphysics (not to mention it was reinforced by Ficino in a number of arguments in the *De amore*), and it suggests that Pico is coming up against some fundamental contradictions in his own reading of the *Symposium* and its rearticulation in "Amor, dalle cui."

The soul's pure intellectual vision depends of course on a theory of the soul's ascent and necessarily on the role of its highest faculty and on the corresponding theory of the Ideas seen by that faculty. So let us turn now to Pico's presentation of Platonic psychology in the *Commento*, which is keyed, interestingly, to being and not, as in Ficino, to unity – though we should note that Pico is clearly indebted to the third book of Ficino's *Platonic Theology* and its exploration of God's attributes, including God's role in our understanding. The *Commento* begins with an ontological preoccupation by distinguishing among causal, formal, and participated

[25] Pico treats of the Graces in *Commento* 2.18 (508–9 [113–14]).
[26] *Commento particulare* (575 [164–5]).

being as a fundamental Platonic postulate and by defining God not as being per se but as the cause of being and not as an intellect per se but as the source and cause of all intellect.[27] This leads Pico from the onset to challenge the reaction of amazement by "un gran platonico" (clearly Ficino) to a passage in Plotinus's *Enneads* (5.6.3 or 6.7.37) in which God is said to understand nothing and to castigate him for not realizing that Plotinus merely intended that "the attribute of understanding exists in God in its causal not formal being [*secondo quello essere causale e non secondo quello formale*]."[28] This is demonstrably polemical. Ficino was well grounded in the intricacies of negative theology, the theology that denies the possibility of talking about God except in equivocal terms, and he was to devote some considerable time eventually to commenting on the works of the Dionysius the Areopagite, "the prince of Christian theologians" for him as for Pico,[29] especially *On the Divine Names*. Even more significantly perhaps, he was to compose his longest Plato commentary on the Areopagite's ultimate source and inspiration, the second part of Plato's *Parmenides*, where Plato has the aging Eleatic explore inter alia the consequences that would ensue were the One not to exist.[30] Therefore, Ficino, if amazed at all, as Pico claimed, must have been amazed not at the notion that God cannot be said to understand anything in the way we or even the angels understand (for this was an apophatic argument with which he was wholly familiar) but rather at its role in the particular passage in Plotinus.

One of Pico's most interesting contributions in the *Commento* is, I would argue, his account of the three hypostases, particularly of the second, which the ancient Neoplatonists had identified with Mind but which he identifies with Angel or Angelic Mind. Some of the Neoplatonists had maintained that between the first hypostasis, God or the One or the Good, and the third hypostasis, the World Soul, came a host of intelligible and intellectual creatures whom Christians call the "angels"[31] – and here Pico reveals his medievalism, since Plotinus had spoken simply of Soul and had argued that the World-Soul is the first instance of

[27] *Commento* 1.1 (461–2 [77]).
[28] *Commento* 1.1 (462 [77]).
[29] *Commento* 1.1 (462 [78]).
[30] See my *Icastes: Marsilio Ficino's Interpretation of Plato's* Sophist (Berkeley: University of California Press, 1989), chap. 1, "The Ficinian *Sophist* and the Controversy with Pico," esp. 39–41ff., 49, with further references.
[31] *Commento* 1.3 (464–5 [79]).

this generic Soul. For this view, Pico specifically cites Proclus, Hermias, and Syrianus (Proclus's teacher), along with the Areopagite and other Christian theologians, probably alluding to Scotus and Giles of Viterbo (since he adduces them later).[32] In his terminology, he is certainly drawing upon Iamblichian and Proclian distinctions between the Ideas (the pure intelligibles) and the highest spiritual beings contemplating them, who are in turn midway between the intelligibles and the host of intellectual beings below them. These are distinctions, incidentally, that postdate Plato and that an enthusiast who assumes the integrity of the Platonic tradition and its hermeneutics can easily read back into the Platonic text, as did the later Neoplatonists as a matter of principle. However, those Pico twice calls the "more perfect Platonists," Plotinus and Porphyry among them, had maintained that between the first and third hypostases there is only one Mind, not many minds, and they had even referred to it as the "son" of the father. This view, he says, is also closer to the opinion of Aristotle, and he prefers it because it enables him to explore the ground common to both Platonists and Aristotelians[33] (such as Avicenna, who is mentioned at the beginning of the next chapter, 1.4). This is an important issue for Pico and is worth looking at in detail.

From his eternity, God creates this single Mind, and since He is the perfect cause, it is a perfect effect and is unique. This is God's sole creation in the sense that it alone comes "directly" (*immediatamente*) from him.[34] And here Pico again attacks Ficino, this time for maintaining (presumably in *De amore* 4.4) that "according to Plato" human souls are also created directly by God, a view maintained by neither Plotinus nor Proclus nor their followers. But Pico is ignoring the problems generated by the Platonic account of the Demiurge in the *Timaeus,* where the creator God does create human souls directly, while leaving younger gods to fashion the human body; further, this Demiurge cannot be equated with the World Soul, since the *Timaeus* specifically says that the Demiurge creates the World Soul (30B, 34Bff.). Again either Pico is being precipitate and not acknowledging the complexity of the problems or else he is choosing radically to simplify them. At all events, this first unique creature had been variously called by the ancients "Wisdom" "the Son," "Mind," "Divine Reason," even "The Word,"[35] though Pico argues that we should not identify

[32] *Commento* 2.13 (502 [108]).
[33] *Commento* 1.3 (464–5 [79–80]).
[34] *Commento* 1.4 (465–6 [80–1]).
[35] *Commento* 1.5 (466–7 [81]).

this Platonic Word with the Christian Son of God (yet this is precisely what Ficino does do and is eager to do in the conviction that Plato had foreseen, at least in part, the mystery of the Trinity and the creative if not the redemptive power of the Son). Pico's grounds are twofold: there is the familiar theological definition that the Son is of one essence with, is consubstantial with, the Father, and there is the less familiar argument that the Christian Son is a creator whereas the second Platonic hypostasis is a creature and must therefore be identified with the first and noblest angel created by God.[36] God, in short, creates Mind as Angelic Being, as Angel.

Nonetheless, Pico has to dovetail this theory of the first unique creature into the Platonic account in the *Timaeus* (28A–29A) of the role of the Ideas and of the Ideas collectively as the model, exemplar, or paradigm to which the Demiurge turns when he creates the world. For the Neoplatonists, if not Plato himself, the first progression or emanation from the One (it is not a "creation" per se) is not the creation of the world but the emergence of thought and of thinking, defined as intelligible being. But since God has created the Ideas or Forms of all things in that first Mind, where they have their formal being, he has created in it the intelligible world, and our sensible world, governed in its entirety by the World Soul, is an image and likeness of this Idea world.[37] This seems clear enough, but Pico proceeds to introduce several complicating factors.

The ancient theologians, he says, had "concealed their mysteries under poetic veils," meaning in effect under the veils of mythology.[38] They had equated God with Uranus, Mind with Cronus (Saturn), and the World Soul with Jupiter, observing the following basic principle: Uranus must stand for anything that is preeminent (as the firmament is preeminent), Saturn for "the property of being intellectual," and Jupiter for "the property of being active" in ruling over inferiors.[39] This triple principle is derived in fact from the etymologies explored in Plato's *Cratylus*, where Uranus is the upward-regarding or contemplative power, Cronus the self-regarding or self-reflective power, and Zeus the downward-regarding or regulative power. Ficino sets out the same set of arguments in his *Phaedrus* commentary.[40] Both Florentine thinkers understood the Proclian-inspired equations that allow for Saturn to exercise at times a

36 *Commento* 1.5 (467 [81]).
37 *Commento* 1.6 (467–8 [81–2]).
38 *Commento* 1.8 (470 [83]).
39 *Commento* 1.8 (470–1 [84]).
40 *In Phaedrum* 10.6,12, 11.11. See my *The Platonism of Marsilio Ficino* (Berkeley: University of California Press, 1984), 124–6.

Uranian or a Jovian power or for Uranus to exercise a Jovian power, though Pico breaks with Ficino in denying that Uranus can exercise a Saturnian power on the grounds that he transcends the intellect entirely. For these equations presuppose that any deity can exercise any or all of these powers on the grounds that each deity is in its own way all other deities in what is in essence a monotheistic system concealed beneath a polytheistic rind. It also means that any reference to a deity, or indeed to the deity's attendant *daemons*, has to be interpreted with extreme care, since several readings are simultaneously possible and at times may even run in parallel.

But how do we dovetail this poetic-theological account of Saturn into his role as the signifier of Angel or Mind, and in what way is Mind preeminently and characteristically Saturnian? What happens in effect when one brings to bear all the various intractable aspects of the larger Saturn myth: his castrating his father, his cannibalizing his offspring, his imprisonment by Jupiter after Jupiter has usurped his throne, and so on?[41]

Pico is led to confront some of the key problems associated with the Platonic Mind, which he identifies as the first and "noblest" angel and as the intelligible world within it, that is, as the Ideas or Forms of all things that will be created subsequent to it.[42] Since it has been created, and created solely by God, it is a creature "as perfect as it is possible for a created thing to be."[43] It is the "perfect effect" of a perfect cause and is unique as God is unique; and yet it consists for Pico, who is thinking here in an Aristotelian way, of potency and act, the former being inferior to the latter. Potency he hastens to equate with "the unlimited" in the famous passage in the *Philebus* (23Cff.), and act he equates with "the limit," and then suggests that in some sense at least the former is a kind of matter (though matter differs with differing levels of being) and that the latter is form.[44] In regard to this being, Angel or Mind is compounded of two contrary principles, like every other created thing existing between the two uncompounded extremes of God and prime matter. But Pico moves into difficult terrain when he assumes that the potency of Mind is in some senses its imperfection, though he formulates

[41] On the "dark" side of Saturn, see Gianni Guastella, "Saturn, Lord of the Golden Age," in *Saturn from Antiquity to the Renaissance*, ed. Massimo Ciavolella and Amilcare A. Ianucci (Toronto: Dovehouse Editions, 1992), 1–22.

[42] *Commento* 1.6 (467–8 [82]).

[43] *Commento* 1.4 (465–6 [80–1]).

[44] *Commento* 1.9 (472 [85]).

this as follows: whatever imperfection Mind possesses is the result of its potency, and whatever perfection it has is the result of its act.[45] But Mind, identified hypostatically with Saturn, nonetheless has three functions – a Saturnian contemplation of (Ficino was to call this, more logically, a Uranian regarding of) things higher than itself (but such can only be God); a Saturnian contemplation "that stays within itself" (Ficino was to call this self-regarding), that is, a contemplation of itself as the first, most perfect creature; and a Jovian downward, providential regarding of the universe it creates.[46] But how can any one of these three functions, though grouped in a descending hierarchy, be deemed imperfect?

Pico performs a sleight of hand here by attributing Mind's Saturnian (Uranian) regard upward to its act, its Saturnian regard self-ward to its act and potency, and its Jovian regard downward to its potency.[47] But this distribution becomes untenable if we introduce his identifications of potency with matter and act with form. For Mind's Jovian regard downward is an extending downward not of its matter but of its form, an exercising not of its limitlessness but of its limit. Indeed, none of these three functions remains a potency: all three are exercised as acts. Moreover, since Mind is the first one-and-many and exists both as the first angel and as the plenitude of the Ideas, it is the first unitary composite and therefore the first beautiful thing: not so much the absolute, exemplary unique Idea of Beauty as the composite, manifold, universal beauty, the splendor, Ficino would consistently call it, of all the Ideas, the attractiveness or grace (*quello decore e grazia*), says Pico, which results from their diversity.[48] But such beauty, he argues in 2.8, is the result of both discord and concord, of unity and of contrariety, of Venus's companionship with Mars: "This can be taken as a true definition of such beauty: it is nothing other than a friendly enmity, or a harmonious discord." In addition, he cites Heraclitus on strife as the father of all things and Empedocles on the ever-during alternation of love and strife.[49] Only God is without contrariety or discord, whereas Angel and Beauty alike are composed of potency and act, of discord and concord. They constitute accordingly the *concordia discors* and *discordia concors* of the Renaissance choric ideal of harmony, which is at the same time the personal, the political, and the cosmic ideal of the entire European age.

45 *Commento* 1.9 (472 [85–6; but *ogni perfezione* is rendered as "every attribute"]).
46 *Commento* 1.9 (472–3 [86]).
47 Ibid.
48 *Commento* 2.13 (503 [109]).
49 *Commento* 2.8 (495–6 [102–3]).

For a Platonic elucidation of this fundamental metaphysical issue, Pico turns to an amalgam of the lemmata in the memorable account of Love's birth attributed by Socrates to Diotima in the *Symposium* (203Bff.): "Love was born in the gardens of Jupiter on the birth day of Venus, after Porus had joined with Penia, all the gods being seated at the banquet, and Porus himself, the son of counsel, being drunk with nectar." For it is these lemmata that constitute, I believe, the greatest mystery of the *Symposium* for Pico and that occasioned some of his most fertile ideas as a Platonizing hermeneut.[50] In 2.13, he asserts that after God Himself, there trailed "an unformed substance" (*quella natura informe*) that must originally have been prime matter; but when it was given form by God, it became Angel-Mind, the form consisting of the Ideas that emerge from God as their source and that collectively constitute Beauty.[51] But all things, he goes on, become imperfect as they move away from God and mix with the unformed substance of Mind, which till now had been completely untouched by the form-giving power of the Ideas (*in tutto disforme dalla formosità d'esse Idee*). This is at first glance a series of self-contradictory arguments, particularly so in light of the proposition at the end of book 1, namely, that the Ideas have (1) their causal being in God and are therefore not in God; (2) their formal being in Mind, who "is counseled" by God (meaning furnished with the Ideas needed to make this sensible world);[52] and (3) their participated being in (rational) Soul, where they are called rational principles or reasons.[53] But it underscores a real and enduring problem in the Neoplatonic emanatory system: Mind without the Ideas must have been not only unformed but also, in a way, in potency, unlimited, in a state (however we may define such a state) of imperfection, of what Pico here calls an "opacity."[54] Consequently, it must have been a quasi-matter.

Pico goes on to demarcate yet further intermediate stages: with the coming of the Ideas, Mind does indeed contain their beauty within itself, but problematically, since "that beauty is still imperfect and obscured by the darkness, the opacity of Mind's own substance." Hence, "there inevitably arises in angelic Mind a desire to possess the Ideas in their

50 They also intrigued Ficino, as his *De amore* 6.7 demonstrates, but that is a matter for another occasion.

51 *Commento* 2.13 (501 [107]). And Pico himself refers us to 1.9.

52 *Commento* 2.21 (513 [117]), on Porus the son of counsel. See Wind, *Pagan Mysteries*, 276–81.

53 *Commento* 1.13 (480 [92]).

54 *Commento* 2.13 (501 [107]).

perfect form," and this desire is a desire for beauty and constitutes therefore (though Pico never exactly says this) the first instance of love.[55] Though Mind is the first creature to love beauty, this beauty is the beauty of the Ideas as they are causally in God, who is without composition and without Ideas. Pico therefore adapts his argument. For desire could never arise in Mind if the Ideas were not there in it, since Mind's desire would not know what to desire, or if they were in it completely, in which case Mind would no longer desire but already possess the Ideas.[56] Thus Love is born when Porus (Plenty), meaning the multitude of the Ideas in Mind, is united with Penia (Need), meaning, not the essence per se of Mind, but the unformed, deficient, or imperfect state, the Jovian state, of that essence, which Pico sees Plato signifying in the *Symposium's* image of "the gardens of Jupiter" (203B). This birth moment is the uniting of act with potency, the planting of the Ideas in the garden of Mind, a planting that gives rise to Paradise, or rather to Mind as Paradise.[57]

Pico stumbles, however, when he goes on to declare that the desire was born from a union between the perfect state of the Ideas, signified by Porus, the son of Counsel, that is, of God,[58] and the Ideas' defective or imperfect state in the incomplete, unformed substance, signified by Penia. Love could only be born after ideal Beauty had been born in Mind; thus it was born on Venus's birthday, later defined as the day "when the beauty of the Ideas first descended into Angelic Mind."[59] This natal day of Venus, when the goddess was "still new-born," signifies that she had not yet reached perfection; thus her beauty lacked perfection, and the splendor of the Ideas that is Beauty lacked perfection.[60] Nonetheless, Love was born at that time in Mind, born as the desire "to possess more perfectly that beauty it already possessed in some measure [*già in qualche modo avea*]" but not fully. Awakened by this love, Mind turned toward God "and received from Him the perfecting of the beauty of the Ideas." And only then when Mind possessed the Ideas and their beauty did Venus become a fully grown goddess, "that is, reached perfection in Mind."[61] For at such a time, it would seem to follow, Mind is no longer in a state of desire but is at one with, and made perfect by, God. On this natal day, however, the

55 Ibid.
56 Ibid.
57 *Commento* 2.13 (502 [107–8]).
58 Isaiah 9:6 and Proverbs 8:14.
59 *Commento* 2.16 (508 [113]).
60 *Commento* 2.13 (503 [108–9]).
61 *Commento* 2.16 (508 [113]).

gods were seated at the banquet, the gods meaning, in the Pythagorean-Parmenidean manner, says Pico, the Ideas which precede Venus herself, since she is the beauty or grace, he reiterates, which results from all the Ideas.[62] She is therefore born after them – with the implication that for the gods she is not, or not yet, the goddess of beauty and of love but merely a divine child.

The banquet itself consists of nectar and ambrosia, the food and drink of eternity and immortality which the charioteer in the great mythical hymn of the *Phaedrus* gives to the soul's twin horses of concupiscence and irascibility when they return "home" (247E), having winged their way across the intellectual heavens to the utmost rim, where the soul could gaze out from afar at the intelligibles themselves. Pico takes Plato's description of Porus as drunk with nectar to signify "the sheer multiplicity of the Ideas" (*l'affluenzia universale d'esse idée*),[63] presumably the Ideas of all the other things that were there in Mind, or possibly all the Ideas not yet signified by the gods who were invited to the banquet and who formally and causally preceded Venus. For, he concludes 2.13 with the argument that "although the Ideas of other things existed in the Angelic Mind, Plato does not say that they were welcomed to the banquet, because the gift of immortality was not granted to them."[64]

In Plato's own dialogic banquet, Phaedrus's speech at 178A–B is keyed to the Orphic notion that Love, traditionally the child of Venus, is paradoxically the oldest of the gods, since he was "born from the bosom of chaos before all the other gods."[65] Moreover, writes Pico in 2.22, he was "the first of all the gods to achieve natural or perfected being," and he gave such being to the other gods. Countering Phaedrus at 195A–C, Agathon declares that Love is the most blessed and the loveliest of the gods, since he is the youngest and flees forever the ravages of time, shunning the very sight of senility. Pico resolves the apparent paradox by declaring that Love is the oldest god, because he existed before the other gods, who, as the Ideas, were to achieve their "natural" or "perfected" being only after Love had caused Mind to return to the One and in turn to receive its natural being; in other words, the Ideas were still in Mind

62 *Commento* 2.13 (503 [109]).

63 *Commento* 2.13 (504 [109]).

64 Ibid. In his *Commentary*, Sears Jayne argues, "This sentence is clearly a mistake. Pico has just explained that all of the Ideas are immortal, yet here he says that only some of them are. This confusion may explain why in his own MS he had deleted this passage" (204 n. 151).

65 See the Orphic *Argonautica* 419–25.

imperfectly (*secondo il loro essere ideale imperfetto*). But he is the youngest and the most beautiful god, because the other gods existed before him, not, as one might have anticipated from Pico's earlier arguments, in their cause, the One, but rather joined to the still unformed substance of Mind in an ideal but imperfect way. From this perspective, Love was not born in Mind until after Mind had been furnished, albeit imperfectly, with the Ideas.[66] An old-young god, therefore, though Pico does not pursue the paradox, he is a mysterious *paidogeron*, a child-father, who has not even been conceived on the day that Venus was born and the gods banqueted together in celebration of her coming. And yet on that very day in the gardens of Jupiter – that is, in "the unformed substance of angelic Mind" and from the mixing of the perfection of the Ideas, which is Porus, with their imperfection and their want of being perfect, which is Penia, "poor and indigent, being devoid of all being and all act" (*d'ogni essere e d'ogni atto priva*) – Love was born, even as his mother was still a babe.[67]

Interestingly, Ficino had confronted the same conundrums in his *De amore*, both at 5.10 and earlier at 1.3, when he attempted his own unfolding of the mystery of Mind and its threefold emanation from, turning back toward, and returning to the One. Both thinkers are struck by the Orphic notion of the "bosom of chaos" and argue that Mind was in a sense a chaos, a chaos waiting nonetheless to be a cosmos.[68] Pico adduces the Orphic verses in 2.14 and 2.22 and observes that Mind could "rightly be called a chaos" when it was first filled with all the Ideas and the Ideas were still "imperfect, indistinct as it were, and confused."[69] In it, Love was born, that is, Mind's desire to perfect the Ideas.[70] Since the Ideas can be perfected only when they are separated from what is alien to them, separated in effect from the as yet unformed chaos of Mind and returned to their source in the One, Mind must itself revert to God and unite with him. Thus Mind completes what Pico calls "the first circle" (*il primo circulo*) of returning to its own first and final cause and to the Ideas' first cause, namely, to the unity of God.[71] When it does so, it possesses the beauty of the Ideas in their perfection, and at that point Venus becomes adult, becomes a perfect, a sovereign goddess in Mind.[72]

66 *Commento* 2.22 (513–15 [117–18]).
67 *Commento* 2.13 (502–3 [108]).
68 *Argonautica* 419–25. See n. 62 above.
69 *Commento* 2.14 (504 [110]).
70 Ibid.
71 *Commento* 2.15 (505 [110]).
72 *Commento* 2.16 (508 [113]).

Despite this ideal triadic encircling of Mind and the notion of its return and perfection, eventually Mind succumbs to time in what seems to be the onset of a Saturnian aging and fatigue, succumbs, that is, to a new inferior order. In the Ancients' poetic mythology, Jupiter, the World Soul, escapes being consumed by Saturn, as thoughts are consumed by their thinker: in his stead, his father is given a stone (the stone of the sensible world, of sensible images and data) to swallow down. Timeless Mind is then overthrown in time by his youngest son, who has returned to cast his progenitor into the prison of materiality, to become by usurpation the new father of gods and men even as he continues to listen to the counsels of his own aged father.[73] The unitary, contemplative realm of Mind is subsequently divided into the three realms of heaven, earth, and Hades, which are ruled over respectively by Saturn's sons, Jupiter, Neptune, and Pluto, Neptune being the power who presides over the whole realm of generation and corruption, the ebb and flow of being born and dying.[74] For Pico and Ficino, this violent revolution or succession myth, like other such myths, speaks to a fundamental aspect of the Neoplatonic metaphysics of emanation: the mystery of the violence involved in the hypostatic succession, the wrenching descent of levels of being, and in Jupiter's particular case the violence integral to Soul's emergence from Mind. But it no longer seems to accommodate Pico's initial account of Love and Beauty.

Accordingly, he turned to the unfolding of another of the *Symposium's* mysteries: Plato's reference at 180D–E to another Venus, the daughter of Uranus. This, the heavenly Venus, had another birthday altogether, since she was never a babe but was born a perfect nymph, a Nereid from the sea's foam, when Uranus's sperm was cast by Saturn as he cut off his father's testicles into the waves of matter. These violent and disturbing images are an integral part of this, one of the most rebarbative of the Greco-Roman myths. But they pose the kind of interpretational challenge that Pico reveled in, particularly when we recall that he was well aware that Proclus and other antique interpreters had taught, following the lead of the mythological passages in Plato's dialogues, that all the traditional myths were theological at heart and that one had to exercise extreme subtlety and inventiveness rather than caution in their exposition. Indeed, the more repellent the myth, the more profound its hidden mystery and the greater the distinction-making skill and zeal expected of

[73] *Commento* 2.20 (511–12 [115–16]).
[74] *Commento* 1.10 (475–6 [88–9]).

its interpreter, as Dionysius the Areopagite had stressed in his work *On the Celestial Hierarchy* (2.3).[75] The myth of the Anadyomene certainly spurred Pico into boldly suggesting that the sea was the unformed substance that was first found in Mind and was the primal Oceanus or Neptune, as certain Platonists had maintained, and that in sense Venus was united with Mind.[76] He turns for confirmation to references in Moses, David, Origen, and Pletho to the effect that "waters" are a recurring image for the seas "upon which God founded the whole world."[77]

Since Uranus, as God, creates only the first angel, "whom the Platonists call Mind, and the poets, Saturn," who in turn creates the rest of the universe, God is figuratively sterile after he has created Mind, having been in a way castrated by Mind.[78] But Pico avoids reconciling the notion of Saturn as castrator with the notion of Saturn as himself the foam-flecked sea, the unformed matter or substance of Mind, which is impregnated by the sperm from Uranus's testicles, allegorized by Pico as "the plenitude of the Ideas."[79] Mysteriously, then, Venus is born as the Beauty or Grace which comes from the Ideas in their variety, the variety without which there can be no beauty and which they derive, Pico says, from being mixed with Mind's substance. Moreover, since he also identifies this substance with the Necessity of the *Timaeus* (47Eff.), he can argue that the Ideas first came into Mind during the reign of Necessity and were thus not yet in their perfect state; only in the succeeding reign of Love, when Mind turned to God, did the imperfect Ideas within it become perfected.[80]

In all these arguments, based as they are on the gift of the Ideas to a still imperfect Mind and on the identification of Venus with the collective splendor and yet variety of the Ideas, Pico treads a tightrope across the chasm, on the one hand, of inherited mythological contradictions and, on the other, of various Neoplatonic attempts to distinguish the stages in the emanation, not only of becoming, but of being itself, however envisioned and defined.

Behind all this Neoplatonic allegoresis, with its unveiling of myth-inspired notions of the emanation and procession of the Ideas, of Mind, of the two

75 See Wind, *Pagan Mysteries*, 133–8.

76 *Commento* 2.19 (510 [115]). See 3.1 (522 [122]).

77 *Commento* 2.19 (510–11 [115]). See Psalm 136:6: "Him that stretched out the earth above the waters."

78 *Commento* 2.20 (511–12 [115–16]).

79 *Commento* 2.20 (512 [116]).

80 *Commento* 2.23 (515–16 [118–19]).

Venuses, and of their accompanying Loves, there looms for Pico – and for Pico much more, I think, than for Ficino – the authority and the ever presence of Genesis. This is not only the definitive account for the Judeo-Christian tradition of the beginning of things, it excels, Pico declares in the proem to the second exposition of the *Heptaplus*, "all other progeny of the human mind in doctrine, eloquence, and genius," even as it is the product of Moses having to speak "with a veiled face" (*velata facie*).[81] For a consideration of what Genesis, or more particularly its first twenty-seven verses, meant to a Neoplatonizing Pico, we must turn to this *Heptaplus* of 1489, where he produced a sevenfold interpretation of the six days of the Biblical creation and of the seventh day of God's rest and added in an appendix a Cabalistic reading of the Bible's opening phrase. In this complex treatise, the Mosaic account of creation is approached by way of two dominant perspectives: the perspective, predictably for a Christian, of Christology and the perspective, once again, of Neoplatonic metaphysics and allegorizing which Pico and Ficino wished to reconcile with the lore of Moses and whose cosmological principles were embodied in Plato's *Timaeus*. For both, it and the biblical Genesis described the creation of nature by divine command and from a void or chaos that Christian commentators had traditionally interpreted as "from nothingness" (*ex nihilo*), a notion open to a number of interpretations and questions and definable perhaps only by reference to the contrasting notion of *cosmos*, which means in Greek that which is good and beautiful because ordered and structured. But whatever the allure for Ficino of Plato's *Timaeus*, for Pico Moses's first book took precedence, and eventually it dominated his attempt to understand the origin of things Platonically. Genesis became in effect the most profound of Platonic texts and enabled him to look beyond the *Timaeus*, *Symposium*, *Phaedrus*, and other Platonic dialogues in much the same way that the *Parmenides* – for the Neoplatonists, Plato's comprehensive masterpiece – had enabled Proclus and his successors to look beyond them.

[81] *Heptaplus*, proem 2. The Latin text is found in *De hominis dignitate, Heptaplus, De ente et uno, e scritti vari*, 222. The English translation cited here is that of Douglas Carmichael in Pico della Mirandola, *On the Dignity of Man, On Being and the One, Heptaplus*, trans. Charles Glenn Wallis, Paul J. W. Miller, and Douglas Carmichael (Indianapolis, IN: Bobbs-Merrill, 1965), 94–5. Hereafter references are formatted as *Heptaplus* (222 [94–5]). In general see Crofton Black's rich new study, *Pico's* Heptaplus *and Biblical Hermeneutics* (Leiden: Brill, 2006), which deals with a variety of patristic, Neoplatonic, scholastic and cabbalistic sources (though not with Ficino whose influence on Pico was, I would argue, pervasive).

In a proem to the *Heptaplus* which is addressed to Lorenzo de' Medici, Pico observes that Moses "most loftily philosophizes on the emanation of all things from God, and on the grade, number, and order of the parts of the world,"[82] and that beneath "the rough bark [*rudi cortice*] of its words," Genesis, and preeminently its opening, has divine depths requiring interpretation by those who have achieved maturity of judgment, just as Jerome had declared in his fifty-third *Epistle*.[83] In the proem to the fourth exposition, Pico exults that "every mode of speech in the whole work includes such hidden senses and deep truths about human nature," just as it does about the worlds man inhabits.[84] He is anxious to assert, furthermore, not merely that Moses is a deep philosopher, but more particularly, first, that Genesis requires "a self-consistent and coherent course of interpretation," despite its apparent "perplexity, ambiguity and variety," for it is planned in such a way that it interprets "the entire creation of the world continuously and without confusion in not merely one but seven senses,"[85] and, second, that it does not assert "anything strange or wonderful or alien to the nature of things as they are observed, or to the truths ascertained by the better philosophers."[86] In the proem to the second exposition, Pico defines Moses's aim, "truly carried out with divine rather than human diligence," as follows: "to use terms and to arrange his discourse so that the same words, the same context, and the same order in the whole passage are completely suitable for symbolizing the secrets of all the worlds and of the whole of nature."[87] The first book of Moses, "which in the fewest words both fittingly and deeply encompasses all things as well as single things,"[88] thus becomes the model of all nature. Correspondingly, nature becomes an image of Genesis, and its single objects become images of the "fewest" words of Moses.

In the second general proem, Pico proceeds to outline the ancient philosophers' doctrine of the three worlds which he also finds in Genesis: the ultramundane or supercelestial world, "which the theologians call

[82] *Heptaplus*, general proem 1 (176 [71]).

[83] *Patrologia Latina*, ed. J.-P. Migne (Paris: Garnier, 1844), 22:547.

[84] *Heptaplus*, proem 4 (268 [117]).

[85] *Heptaplus*, general proem 1 (180–2 [73–4]): "Secunda est difficultas, ut tenor idem sit interpretamenti sibi consentiens ex se aptus." See proem 5 (286 [127]). For a fascinating analysis of the work's structure, see Raymond B. Waddington, "The Sun at the Center: Structure as Meaning in Pico della Mirandola's *Heptaplus*," *Journal of Medieval and Renaissance Studies* 3 (1973): 69–86.

[86] Ibid.

[87] *Heptaplus*, proem 2 (222 [94–5]).

[88] Ibid.

the angelic and the philosophers call the intelligible world" of light and which is symbolized by fire; the celestial world of the stars and planets, of darkness and light together, which is symbolized by fire and water; and the sublunary world of darkness we inhabit, which is symbolized by water. Pico proceeds to assign eternal life and unchanging activity to the first, partaking as it does of the divine nature of mind; stability of life but change of activity and position to the second, partaking as it does of incorruptible body and of mind enslaved to that body; and perpetual alternation of life and death to the third, composed as it is of corruptible body. The third is moved by the second, while the second, whose outermost sphere is the prime mover, is governed by the first. But "these three worlds are one world" in that "whatever is in all the worlds together is also contained in each of the worlds separately."[89] Here, surely, Pico is invoking the two celebrated Neoplatonic formulas to the effect that the whole is in the part, though according to the capacity of the part, and that all things are in all things, though each in its own way or in a certain way. These formulas had been refined by Proclus in the belief that they were the key to our understanding of the unity of the world, of the oneness that makes the intelligible world a many and a one. For Pico continues, "Whatever is in the lower world is also in the higher ones, but of better stamp," and contrariwise "whatever is in the higher ones is also seen in the lowest but in a degenerate condition."[90] Thus our elemental world has the heat and fire which burns, while the celestial world has the heating power of the sun, which gives us life, and the supercelestial world has the Idea of heat, identified apparently with the love of the seraphic intellects. Similarly, what is water here is the Moon in the heavens and the understanding of the cherubic intellects in the supercelestial realm. The nine orders of the angels presided over by God's unmoving unity correspond to the nine revolving heavenly spheres presided over by the unmoving empyrean, and these correspond in turn to the nine spheres of ever-moving corruptible forms founded upon prime matter. These nine spheres are themselves divided into three triads. The three lowest spheres contain the four lifeless elements; things such as storms, which are unstably mixed; and other inanimate things that are stably mixed. The three vegetal spheres contain the three genera of grasses, shrubs, and trees. The

[89] *Heptaplus*, general proem 2 (188 [77]): "quicquid in omnibus simul est mundis, id et in singulis continetur." I have changed Carmichael's rendering here; see ibid., 194: "quae sunt in omnibus mundis contineri in singulis."

[90] Ibid. Cf. Black, *Pico's* Heptaplus, 164–6.

three spheres of sensitive beings contain imperfectly ensouled creatures such as zoophytes, lower animals governed solely by their irrational souls or fantasies, and higher animals capable of being instructed by man.[91]

Moreover, "bound by the chains of concord," writes Pico, "all these worlds exchange natures as well as names with mutual liberality."[92] Thus Nature herself is an allegory full of "hidden alliances and affinities" that enable an enlightened interpreter to work by way of the correspondences between the worlds.[93] By implication at least, Nature must also be riven by discord: countering every hidden alliance and affinity must be ruptures and oppositions. To every attraction of like to like – to invoke the ancient saw – there must be the corresponding repulsion of unlike from unlike. But such an Empedoclean vision seems to be foreign to Pico, perhaps because it is too dualistic. However divided our fallen world may be by the discord caused by a Helen or a Clytemnestra, the intelligible realm is governed by the concord of a Castor and Pollux, and in between are the conjunctions and oppositions that constitute the dance of the stars. Furthermore, we might have expected in the final, the sensitive, triad a division into zoophytes, beasts, and man rather than into zoophytes, lower animals, and higher animals. But Pico wants to postulate a separate, a fourth, world for man, in whom are found all those things in the three other worlds, the sublunar, the celestial, and the supercelestial.

Since the scripture of Moses is the "exact image of the world" and is arranged, as Exodus 25:40 had declared, "according to the pattern that God had shown him on the mountain,"[94] its every word can and must be interpreted in terms of the four worlds. Even so, a fifth kind of exposition is needed to explain how the natures are distinct and at the same time united "by a certain discordant concord" and knotted and linked together "by many kinds of interwoven chains," and a sixth kind is needed to explain the fifteen ways we can understand "how one thing is joined or related to another." Finally, Pico's interpretation comes to rest in a sabbatical exposition of "the felicity of all creatures and their return to God." For this book of Moses "is marked with the seven seals [*septem signaculis obsignatus*] and is full of all wisdom [*doctrina*] and of all mysteries."[95]

91 *Heptaplus*, general proem 2 (188–90 [77–8]).

92 *Heptaplus*, general proem 2 (192 [78–9]): "astricti vinculis concordiae uti naturas ita etiam appellationes hi omnes mundi mutua sibi liberalitate condonant."

93 Ibid.

94 *Heptaplus*, general proem 2 (192–4 [79]).

95 *Heptaplus*, general proem 2 (194–6 [80–1]).

In short, although Pico is confronting the challenges of the Mosaic text, he is also confronting the challenges of reading the world as text, the challenges of what we now think of as science but which for him were those of Neoplatonic metaphysics and mythology. Since "whatever is in any of the worlds is contained in each," Moses, as an "imitator [*aemulator*] of nature" and in effect as an adept in allegoresis and correspondence theory, necessarily "had to treat of each of these worlds in such a way that in the same words and in the same context he could treat equally of all."[96] Transposed into a Platonic key, this means that each reading must pertain to, and hence explain, both sublunar nature and the translunar heavens and be at the same time fully consonant with a theological account of the angelic realm and the realm of Mind. An enlightened interpreter must move back and forth harmoniously, that is, between the realm of nature and that of theology. Moreover, a proper understanding of man, an enlightened anthropology, will be consonant with such a concomitant natural science and theology, and the three disciplines will share the same fundamental methodology and hermeneutics. A reading in one discipline will not only set up resonances in another but be keyed, by way of the isomorphic structure of the analogies established by God at the creation, to a particular parallel reading in that other discipline. While such a perspective looks back to the ancient theologians, it also looks forward as Pico searches for a unitary methodology, a way of explaining all phenomena, a theory of everything.

Pico's *Heptaplus* may first strike one, for all its boldness, as an essentially medieval work in which the theological concerns take precedence over a concern with the recalcitrant variety of the physical world, though this is very much the theme of the first exposition. Furthermore, like other medieval and indeed ancient texts, and like Pico's own *Commento*, as we have seen, its central engagement is with another authoritative text, in this case the Bible's opening verses. Pico first wants to understand Genesis and then things as they are now in the time after creation; hence his concern with authorial intention, with the intricacies of Moses's formal design, and with the problems of correct, including numerologically correct, interpretation. The *Heptaplus* is also original, however, in its turning aside to the Cabala and in its fashioning out of Genesis a Christological text (and by implication an anthropological or anthropocentric one) and thus articulating a human-dominated worldview, for the seventh chapter of each of the seven expositions turns to the Son of Man as the definitive "law," the key to all physics, to all metaphysics, to all

[96] *Heptaplus*, general proem 2 (194 [80]). See n. 86 above.

theologies, the first and the final cause. It is also remarkable as a *summa* presenting on the eve of the scientific revolution a cosmology governed by the principles of harmony, correspondence, and consonance. In doing so, it may be harking back to Boethius and Aristotle, but more obviously it is still drawing on Plato's Pythagorean themes and on their elaboration by the Neoplatonists, including Dionysius the Areopagite, whom Pico, like most Renaissance scholars, still assumed was the Athenian disciple of St. Paul mentioned in Acts 17:34.[97] The *Heptaplus* is in effect a triumph of Platonically inspired analysis.

One more particularly striking creation or succession question requires consideration here, given various modern indictments of what is often misinterpreted as Renaissance anthropocentrism. A naive reaction to the famous opening sections of Pico's *Oration*, as indeed to the verses of Genesis itself, might interpret God's injunction to the prelapsarian Adam as an injunction to postlapsarian mankind to use, to exploit, to conquer nature. Certainly, read out of context, the famous apostrophe suggests a special role for humanity. Caught between steadfast eternity and changing time, original "protoplastic" man was and is the cosmic chameleon, the "great wonder," "the messenger between creatures," "the interpreter of nature," the bond, yea "the nuptial knot of the world," the animal especially blessed, Proteus as he appeared in "the secret rites" of old. The speech reaches its climax in an injunction to Adam "to have that which he chooses and to be that which he wills" and thus to elect his own determination. Whereas other creatures, including the celestial planetary souls and the angelic intellects above them, have "natures" which confine them to a particular realm of being, the first made man is not so confined. As the "molder and maker of himself," he can sculpt himself into whatsoever form he pleases, be it that of a beast or a seraph.[98] Adam is thus destined to pass up and down the ladder of nature without being confined to any one ontological rung or level, and in this respect he is unique among God's creatures – autonomous, self-choosing, free, not bound to and yet at the very heart of the order of nature, a shape-changing sea god invested in the mystery and the majesty of ancient cult and worship.

We should remember, however, that this famous speech is subject to a variety of interpretations, depending on which ancient or even medieval source or sources one feels Pico had in the forefront of his mind, and

97 Black, *Pico's* Heptaplus, 166–177, underscores the debt to the Pseudo-Areopagite.

98 The Latin text can be found in *De hominis dignitate, Heptaplus, De ente et uno, e scritti vari*, 102–6.

depending too on one's familiarity with parallel if not identical formulations in the *Heptaplus* and the *Commento.* In 1.12 of the latter, Pico had already defined "human nature" as "the tie and knot of the world,"[99] being located in the middle of the ontological hierarchy, and had asserted that man "through his various parts has some relation or correspondence to every part of the world," first his body corresponding to the material realm; his second, vegetative part to the plant realm; his third, sensitive part to the irrational animals; his fifth, intellectual part to the angels; and his sixth part, his unity, to God himself. His fourth rational part is peculiar to himself, or at least peculiar to rational animals. These correspondences underlie the very notion of man the microcosm,[100] though the Platonists had disagreed as to whether all these parts were mortal, the radical position (i.e., that all man's parts were immortal) being espoused by Numenius and Plotinus.[101] Interestingly, Pico had been content in the *Commento* with the asymmetry that results from postulating six parts or powers of the soul, for what is peculiarly man's is not in the exact center of his being, is not the faculty that constitutes the median tie and knot of himself. Though he may be the bond of the world, his rational part is not, mathematically speaking at least, the bond of himself. At all events, the notion of man as the little world and by predication of the world (or World Soul, as Pico seems to suggest in 2.6) as the great man, the *macroanthropos,* has rather different implications for our understanding of man's relationship both to nature in general and to his own human nature than does the image of Proteus. And this despite the fact that the world as a great man is also an ancient trope and for Pico at least a Mosaic one (as his gematria-based epilogue on Genesis's opening *Bereshit* makes clear).[102] The twin tropes point, I suggest, to a more than intricate sense of man's belonging to the world in its plenitude and continuity and it to him – of his being simultaneously its every part and its every part being him. No longer just a mirror that simply reflects the world's ontological levels or a Proteus that can swim or slither through them, man is not even a fourth world but "the bond and union of the other three," and his substance "encompasses by its very essence the substance of all natures

99 See Engelbert Monnerjahn, *Giovanni Pico della Mirandola: Ein Beitrag zur philosophischen Theologie des italienischen Humanismus* (Wiesbaden: Steiner, 1960), 15–25.

100 See Rudolf Allers, "Microcosmus: From Anaximandros to Paracelsus," *Traditio* 2 (1944), 319–407.

101 *Commento* 1.12 (478–9 [91–2]).

102 *Heptaplus, expositio primae dictionis* (380 [173]). See Black, *Pico's Heptaplus*, pp. 214–232, on Bereshit and the Sabbath.

and the fullness of the whole universe." Thus, if "God contains all things in Himself as their origin, man contains all things in himself as their center."[103]

This vision of man as "a great miracle" – and Pico again cites the famous expostulation from the Hermetic *Asclepius* – flows inevitably into a Christology. "Just as man is the absolute perfection of all lower things, so is Christ the absolute perfection of all men."[104] He is "the first born of all creation,"[105] the statue in the center of the city, in the striking image at the beginning of 5.6.[106] If Mosaic man is angelic only in an allegorical sense[107] – since the scriptures often use man, writes Pico in 2.6, to represent all angelic and rational creatures, "not because he is an angel but because he is the end and terminus of the angelic world," as Psalm 8:6 declares – then Christ as man, as the "newest Adam,"[108] is more eminent than the first angel: indeed, he perfects the angels.[109] In turn, he enables us to become more than the angels – to become, as Paul exults in Hebrews 1:4, not just the image and likeness but the sons of God.[110]

The trope of the human microcosm haunted Ficino too, though he was most drawn to the image of man's standing on the middle rung of the cosmic ladder, for insofar as man is soul, he is a participant in the realm or hypostasis of Soul, which is the middle and therefore mediating hypostasis in the pentadic scheme of hypostases Ficino inherited from Proclus and the late ancient Neoplatonic tradition, the scheme of the One, Mind, Soul, Quality, and Body (i.e., matter in extension).[111] Man as soul thus serves as the marriage knot, the nuptial copula of the world, mediating between the intelligible realm of Mind and the corporeal realm of sensible qualities. But his mediating role derives not from his being a particular entity or species, or even from his being the little-world-man, for arguably every creature is a necessary link in the hierarchical continuum, but rather from his being a part of, a participant in, Soul and

[103] *Heptaplus* 5.6 (302 [135]): "quod Deus in se omnia continet uti omnium principium, homo autem in se omnia continet uti omnium medium."
[104] *Heptaplus* 1.7 (220 [92]).
[105] *Heptaplus* 5.7 (308 [137]).
[106] *Heptaplus* 5.6 (300 [134]).
[107] *Heptaplus* 2.6 (240 [103]).
[108] *Heptaplus* 4.7 (286 [125–6]).
[109] *Heptaplus* 3.7 (266 [115–16]).
[110] *Heptaplus* 6.7 (324 [145]).
[111] See my "Ficino's Theory of the Five Substances and the Neoplatonists' *Parmenides*," now in my *Plato's Third Eye: Studies in Marsilio Ficino's Metaphysics and Its Sources* (Aldershot, England: Variorum, 1995), chap. 8.

thus a participant in the World Soul, which is the prime instance of Soul (and in a cosmological context the Neoplatonists often equated the two). Once again this implies an even greater recognition of connectedness than the microcosm trope allows, let alone the notion of man as Proteus, and it underscores the complexity and profundity of the Renaissance Neoplatonists' anthropology and cosmology alike and of their several and sometimes contrasting perspectives on nature, man in nature, and nature in man.

Ficino's emphasis on Soul and thus on the World Soul directs our attention away from the notion of particular entities and species toward the general concepts of life, of potentiality, of being, and specifically of being part of a greater whole while reflecting the whole in the part which is ourselves. Pico's Platonic anthropocentrism by contrast, along with his commitment to the Genesis myths of man's creation, serves in a way to underscore the uniqueness of man, and certainly of man in Christ and of Christ as the Idea of Man,[112] and it lends its Christological force to the notion that the world itself is a great man. Ficino's vision may be in a way more unitary, more panentheistic, since his metaphysics is attuned to his abiding fascination with harmony, with the antiphonal and responsive play of voices in the choir of creation, with the counterturns of the cosmic dance, and it looks, as we still do, to mathematics and particularly to the key notions of ratio and proportion as the initiatory discipline for our entry into this choir, into this starry dance. Indeed, this originally musical concern is arguably his most arresting imaginative legacy and makes him one of the Renaissance harbingers of our modern commitment to discovering fundamental and mutually corroborative and interacting laws, laws that are now the preoccupation of particle physics and astrophysics alike.

Pico's contribution, however, is interesting for different reasons. He has given us a rich, if not an internally consistent, set of speculations concerning the principles of the emanative process itself: the principles that underlie the birth of thought, of the world, of beauty, of love, of humanity, of Adam, of ourselves as particular beings, of ourselves in Christ as the Son of Man, and of God. Many of the problems that he encountered and that prevented him from arriving at consistency are demonstrably intrinsic

[112] See my "Cultura Hominis: Giovanni Pico, Marsilio Ficino and the Idea of Man," in *Giovanni Pico della Mirandola: Convegno internazionale di studi nel cinquecentesimo anniversario della morte (1494–1994), Mirandola 4–8 ottobre 1994*, ed. Gian Carlo Garfagnini (Florence: Olschki, 1997), 173–96.

to Neoplatonism itself and to Plotinus's iterated attempts to probe not so much into the genesis moment as into the emanative moment: the first flowing out of the One, the first manifestation of the dyad, whether or not this dyad is coincident with being or is already becoming. After all, this is the mystery investing the very idea that anything, let alone everything, exists, and it haunts us still as physicists, as cosmologists, as metaphysicians, as theologians. Certainly it haunted the Florentine disciples of Plotinus, who believed with him that this mystery had once been comprehended fully by Moses and by Plato and, in part at least, by the ancient theologians who preceded Plato and by the line of prophets who succeeded Moses. This fascination with the origin of existence, with the origin of the very thought of what does not yet exist in thought, constitutes for Pico and Ficino, I would argue, the fundamental allure of Plotinian Platonism. In particular, it accounts for Pico's most enduring and interesting contributions as a speculative philosopher and as one of the age's subtlest exegetes of what he invariably sees as the Platonic and Mosaic mysteries enveloped in the veils of ancient myth, divine hymn, and poetic invocation. In this important regard at least, we should continue to think of him as Ficino's fellow Neoplatonist, however Aristotelian or eclectic he may have been in many other respects; certainly he joined his older friend, however contentiously, in celebrating philosophically the birthday of Venus.

«QUISQUE IN SPHAERA SUA»: PLATO'S *STATESMAN*, MARSILIO FICINO'S *PLATONIC THEOLOGY*, AND THE RESURRECTION OF THE BODY

Dedicated to Professor Cesare Vasoli

As the subtitle *De immortalitate animorum* demonstrates, with its evocation of the titles of treatises by both Plotinus and Augustine, Ficino's eighteen-book *Platonic Theology*, which was eventually published in 1482, has as its avowed aim the task of proving the immortality of the soul.[1] But the immortality of the soul, though now embedded in Christianity as a dogma, was in origin a Greek notion and brought in its train a host of ancillary Greek conceptions that were elaborated and further refined by the Church Fathers and then by a succession of Greek and Latin Scholastics. Remarkably, Ficino's great work, itself a triumph of Scholastic argumentation though one deeply indebted to Plato, Plotinus and Proclus, was demonstrably responsible, if only in part, for the Fifth Lateran Council's declaration in 1513 of the immortality of the soul as a dogma.[2]

---

[1] Reference throughout is to M. FICINO, *Platonic Theology*, ed. and trans. M. J. B. ALLEN-J. HANKINS, 6 vols., Cambridge, Mass. 2001-06.

[2] The Council (1512-1517) discussed the doctrine in 1512 and then it was promulgated in Leo X's bull *Apostolici Regiminis* dated 19 December 1513. See G. DI NAPOLI, *L'immortalità dell'anima nel Rinascimento*, Torino 1963, pp. 179-181, 220-221; F. GILBERT, *Cristianesimo, Umanesimo e la bolla* Apostolici Regiminis *del 1513*, «Rivista storica italiana», LXXIX, 1967, pp. 976-990: 977; J. MONFASANI, *Aristotelians, Platonists and the Missing Ockhamists: Philosophical Liberty in Pre-Reformation Italy*, «Renaissance Quarterly», XLVI, 1993, pp. 247-276: 251 – now in his *Greeks and Latins in Renaissance Italy*, Aldershot 2004; and E. A. CONSTANT, *A Reinterpretation of the Fifth Lateran Council Decree* Apostolici Regiminis *(1513)*, «Sixteenth Century Journal», XXXIII, 2002, pp. 353-379, with further refs. The Council also condemned those Aristotelians who upheld the unicity of the intellect. Note that the Council of Vienne in 1311-1312 had already condemned the Averroistic proposition of Peter John Olivi «quod anima rationalis seu intellectiva non sit forma corporis humani per se et essentialiter». Note too that the Creeds simply affirm that we «look for the resurrection of the dead; and the life of the world to come». For excerpts of all pertinent doctrinal statements, see H. DENZINGER-A. SCHÖNMETZER, *Enchiridion symbolorum, definitionum et declarationum de rebus fidei et morum*, Barcinone 1963 (XXXII ed.).

Part of the *Platonic Theology*'s intellectual force as a *summa* derives from the sheer number of its arguments. For in it Ficino marshals numerous sections, proof after proof, sometimes concatenated and at other times free-standing, in defence of the notion that soul generically and individually cannot die, and that, if hypothetically it were to do so, then the entire chain of being would become unlinked. If that were to happen, the cosmos itself, the entire «world machine», would «collapse into immobility», as Socrates had argued in the *Phaedrus* 245DE.[3] It is as though Ficino sought solace in the notion that, if no one proof were to persuade us and each was found wanting in some respect, then certainly the cumulative impact of all the proofs must surely overwhelm us, given that they reinforce each other and compensate for each other's weaknesses, like overlapping pieces of armour.

Nonetheless, the work climaxes in books seventeen and eighteen with a defence not only of the immortality of the soul, but also, perhaps not surprisingly, of the resurrection of the body, another of Christianity's cardinal dogmas and certainly one that dominated the intellectual and theological horizons of the Middle Ages and the Renaissance, though nowadays it and its ramifications are neglected by the Church and are little understood by most of the lay public.

The resurrection of the body has its roots in later apocalyptic Hebrew writings, since earlier writings do not indicate any belief in a life after death.[4] When the belief did develop, as in *Isaiah* 26:19 and *Daniel* 12:2, it focused on the resurrection of the dead and not on the immortality of the soul, a resurrection that would take place at the end of time and for all human beings, and was not merely a resuscitation of an individual physical body. At that moment, Daniel declares at 12:3, in a verse that will have tremendous implications for Ficino and others, the dead will shine like stars.

The resurrection of Christ is the paradigmatic event for Christians who believe that God raised his Son, as Paul declares in *I Corinthians*

---

[3] In his *In Phaedrum* 6.6 (ed. ALLEN as *Marsilio Ficino and the Phaedran Charioteer*, Berkeley 1981, p. 97) Ficino glosses this as «will plunge to its ruin» (*ruitura*): see the analysis in my *The Platonism of Marsilio Ficino*, Berkeley 1984, pp. 82-84.

[4] For early ideas (including pseudepigraphal) of resurrection and immortality, see R. H. CHARLES, *Eschatology: The Doctrine of a Future Life in Israel, Judaism, and Christianity: A Critical History*, reprinted with *Introduction* by G. W. BUCHANAN, New York 1963 (1899; II ed., 1913). See also C. W. BYNUM, *The Resurrection of the Body in Western Christianity 200-1336*, New York 1995.

15:20-22, as a witness that in the end we will all rise together, and that we will do so precisely because Christ has risen before us and for us. His final ghostly ascension has less significance for us and our salvation than this initial resurrection. But Christ's recorded post-resurrection appearances raise some haunting and difficult questions. In Luke's Gospel, Mary Magdalene, Joanna, Mary the mother of James, and other women (24:10) had discovered that the stone wheel blocking the tomb had been rolled aside and had hastened away to tell Simon Peter (and also, John's Gospel adds, «the other disciple whom Jesus loved»). Christ then «appeared» to them and to other disciples, in a physical or quasi physical manner. Perhaps most memorably, Luke's Gospel says, he appeared to Cleopas and one other disciple on the road to Emmaus and «beginning at Moses and all the prophets, he expounded unto them in all the scriptures the things concerning Himself» (24:27). Later he showed them his hands and feet, enjoining them: «Handle me and see; for a spirit hath no flesh and bones as ye see me have». And to underscore the point that he was physically present, he straightway ate «a piece of broiled fish and of an honeycomb» (24:39, 42).

According to the Gospels of both Mark and John, he appeared in the midst of the disciples one evening when the doors were shut; and while eating and drinking with them «upbraided them with their unbelief and hardness of heart because they believed not them which had seen him after he was risen» (*Mark* 16:14). In John's Gospel he exhorted Thomas eight days later to stretch forth a finger and to thrust it into his side, though he had earlier told the Magdalene, who had first supposed him the gardener, not to touch him since he had not yet ascended to his Father. Later, John says, «he showed himself again to the disciples at the sea of Tiberias and enjoined them to cast their net once more so that "now they were not able to draw it for the multitude of fishes [...] a hundred and fifty and three"; and this was "now the third time that Jesus showed himself to the disciples after that he was risen from the dead"» (21:1-14). *Acts* 1:3 declares that Jesus «showed himself alive after his passion by many infallible proofs, being seen of them forty days» before assembling them together. Then, having commanded them that they should not leave Jerusalem, but wait for the promise of the Father, he was taken up «and a cloud received him out of their sight» as he ascended into heaven (1:4-10), an ascension to which three of the four evangelists also bear witness, Mark even declaring that Jesus sat on the right hand of God (16:19).

It has been argued that these witnesses were assembled in order to contradict the kind of argument eventually associated with the Docetist heresy, which declares (as its etymon *dokeô* implies) that Christ never fully descended into the physical world, was never incarnated and made man. Accordingly, he never really suffered, but retained his full antenatal spiritual essence throughout his 'life' on earth and at the end escaped death (some Docetists even argued that Judas Iscariot or Simon of Cyrene took his place before the Crucifixion). His 'body' as such was thus a ghostly phenomenon that only appeared or seemed to be like ours, while he remained a wholly divine, incorporeal and spiritual being.

What may be a heretical idea with regard to the life of Christ prior to his crucifixion, however, may well seem more persuasive, if not orthodox, with regard to his post-Crucifixion appearances, despite his own declaration in Luke that «a spirit hath not flesh and bones as ye see me have» (24:39). For the doppelganger element in the Emmaus road encounter; the haunting «Noli me tangere» to Mary Magdalene; the sudden materialization in a room where the door was closed; the iteration of the notion that he has already «showed himself»; his enigmatic command that his disciples should not leave Jerusalem – all become in effect a set of surreal preludes to the Ascension from a mountain top. They are real and simultaneously surreal events: the disciples are sighting, are encountering, not a savagely lacerated corpse, but an angel-like revenant, a teacher who has become a god, if not yet the whole, the living God, whom he will become after his ascension, though he has already ascended from the grave in a foreshadowing of it. These post-Easter narratives constitute in fact a Docetist last chapter at the end of each Gospel in that they underscore the problem of how to think about, and how to define, the notion of the risen, the post-mortem, body.

St. Paul's luminous meditation in *I Corinthians* 15, which anchors the traditional funeral service, also begins with Christ's resurrection on the third day and also focuses on Christ's post-Easter appearances. He uses the same Greek word *ôphthê*, the aorist passive of the verb «to see», that he uses elsewhere for visionary experiences: «he was seen of Cephas, then of the twelve. After that he was seen of above five hundred brethren at once [...]. After that he was seen of James; then of all the apostles. And last of all he was seen of me as of one born out of due time» (15:5-8). This personal witness underscores Paul's declaration: «if there is no resurrection of the dead, then is Christ not risen. And if Christ be not risen, then is our preaching vain» (15:13-14). «For as in Adam all die, even so in Christ shall all be made alive» (15:22). Paul is arguing for a resurrection of the body, albeit of a transformed body; and this prompts him to ask the critical question: How are the dead raised up? And with what body do they come? (15:35). This in turn leads to the postulation of two kinds of body, a celestial body and a terrestrial one; for what is sown as a natural body in corruption is raised as a spiritual body in «incorruption». The first Adam lived in the one and was an «earthy» man; the second Adam was made a «living soul» and became «a quickening spirit» – the «second man» is indeed the Lord from heaven (15:40-47). All of us can look forward to bearing the image of the heavenly man as we have borne the image of the earthly one. But this will happen only at the last trump, in «the twinkling of an eye». For then, and only then, «the dead shall be raised incorruptible and we shall be changed» as we put on 'incorruption'; and death, our death in the old earthly bodies, will be swallowed up in victory (15:49-54). Paul's vision of the resurrection of the body is thus dovetailed completely into his eschatological vision of the Resurrection of the Dead at the end of time on the Day of Judgement.

Later Christian theologians identified this Pauline spiritual body with a «glorified» body, «glory» having a long and complex history in the Old Testament. The term is frequently applied to the visible manifestation or presence of God to humans,[5] and by attribution to God-inspired men. At the giving of the Law on Mt. Sinai God's glory appeared as a cloud by day and as fire by night[6] and God will appear in glory at the end of time.[7] In the New Testament «glory» is again attributed to God;[8] and the Gospel of St. John develops the notion that Jesus had glory in his human existence too, since it was God's glory that appeared in him.[9] Glory is linked to Jesus' miracles, but above all it is associated with his death – «The hour is come that the Son of Man should be glorified» and «Father, the hour is come: glorify thy Son that thy Son may glorify thee»[10] – and then with his resurrection and second coming.[11] Such a glorified body, theologians postulate, is therefore going to be man's resurrected body too. But the

[5] E.g. *Num.* 16:19; *Ps.* 102:16; *Ezek.* 10:4; cf. 28:22, 43:2-5.

[6] Cf. *Exod.* 16:10, 24:16-17.

[7] Cf. *Isa.* 4:5, 60:1-2.

[8] Cf. *Luke* 2:9; *John* 11:40; *Acts* 7:55.

[9] Cf. *John* 1:14, 13:31, 17:5.

[10] *John* 12:23, 17:1.

[11] Cf. *Matt.* 25:31; *Mark* 8:38; *I Cor.* 2:8; *Heb.* 2:7, 9; *I Pet.* 1:11; *Rev.* 5:12-13.

most striking implication is that Christ's post-Easter appearances were in such a glorified body, one that had already been witnessed by certain of his Apostles at the time of his Transfiguration on Mt. Tabor.

In all of this argumentation, the Biblical assumption is that any life after the grave, postponed as it might be until the last trump sounds, must be lived in a body, though a body that is «celestial» or «spiritual», not subject to the decay, to the corruption of the physical world. Indeed, for Christianity the Resurrection is not a raising up of the soul alone, but rather of the soul in a body, the two constituting the unity which is man, man who is neither just a disembodied soul nor just a material body, but an incarnated soul in an ensouled body.[12] Such a lifting up, furthermore, is an apocalyptic universal event that ends the reign of death over us all. Such is the Christian legacy Ficino inherited and was intimately, indeed professionally, familiar with, based as it is in the main on the Gospel of St. John and St. Paul's First Epistle to the Corinthians.[13]

Famously, Ficino's central project in his great 1482 *summa* was to reconcile Christianity and Platonism or rather the Neoplatonism of Plotinus, following, but only in part, the example of Augustine, who had singled out the books of the Platonists as the ones that had restored him at last to the embrace of the Christian beliefs of his mother and his childhood.[14] In all but his later works, the saint had accorded them a special distinction.

Now Plato's metaphysical and psychological principles, given his idealism generally, are profoundly anti-materialistic, except perhaps in the *Timaeus*. In the *Phaedo*, admittedly one of the most dismissive of the dialogues in its attitude towards the realm of the corporeal, Socrates asserts, in a memorable series of arguments against fearing death, that the body is a prison from which the soul yearns to escape, a tomb from which it will eventually ascend. In the *Platonic Theology* 17.4.8, Ficino readily adopts this Platonic assumption that the body is lost or surrendered.[15] But the implications are important: «In the *Phaedo*», Ficino says, «Plato

---

[12] For Ficino's interest in Athenagoras' views, see E. LUPIERI, *Marsilio Ficino e il* De resurrectione *di Atenagora*, «Studi storico-religiosi», I, 1977, pp. 147-163.

[13] The question of Ficino's familiarity too with Byzantine iconography awaits exploration; see G. PEERS, *Subtle Bodies: Representing Angels in Byzantium*, Berkeley 2001.

[14] See my *Synoptic Art: Marsilio Ficino on the History of Platonic Interpretation*, Firenze 1998, chap. 2, on the un-Augustinian aspects of Ficino's programme.

[15] Cf. FICINO, *Platonic Theology* 18.3.5.

adds that souls, purged by way of lawful philosophy, will live with God for eternity without bodies. He confirms this in the *Epinomis* when he declares that a righteous, thinking soul separated from the body will spend the rest of time in the contemplation of the most beautiful of all things». Ficino then goes on to argue that «what Christians call purgatory Plato understood to mean the place where the person awaiting purgation takes [his] soul, and time and again leads it on a circle through lower things», not through the bodies of beasts but through their lives and their mutual dealings. «Finally, after purgation his soul is restored to heaven». In other words, purgatory itself is not a series of Dantean terraces where an individual is bodily punished, albeit in an aerial purgatorial body,[16] but rather a succession of alternate lives in which an impure soul is purged by way of circuiting through them.

Indeed, Ficino feels bound to attack, even as he is fascinated by, the hallowed Platonic notion of soul-circuits, meaning reincarnation in some form or other. «We conclude from all this evidence», he says, «that Plato only affirmed facts about matters divine that he sanctioned in the *Letters* and the *Laws*. But in these works the infinite circuits of souls are not approved and the things that he reviewed only in the remaining dialogues as inventions of the ancients he held as being probable rather than certain. And if anyone contends that Plato also affirmed them, then we too will concede that perhaps for the sake of discussion he did affirm them. Nonetheless, we shall maintain the opinion that they have to be explained in a sense far different from their literal one» (17.4.14). Ficino is especially anxious to reject the radical or literal notion of transmigration into the bodies of other life forms, and to exculpate by way of reinterpretation any Platonic passage, or any passage by the pre-Platonic theologians of antiquity, that seems to affirm it.[17]

Furthermore, he is not prepared at this point, despite his fascination with the myth of Er at the end of the *Republic* and with other mythological and figurative passages in Plato's dialogues, to entertain what would

---

[16] Ficino's *Phaedo* epitome (*Opera omnia*, 2 voll., Basilea, Heinrich Petri, 1576 [repr. anast. Torino 1959 and Paris 1999], p. 1392) explicitly identifies the airy body as the purgatorial one.

[17] FICINO, *Platonic Theology* 17.4.7-11. For two penetrating analyses, though differently oriented, see R. KLEIN, *L'enfer de Ficin*, in *Umanesimo e esoterismo*, Atti del V convegno internazionale di studi umanistici, a cura di E. CASTELLI, Padova 1960, pp. 47-84; and J. HANKINS, *Ficino on* Reminiscentia *and the Transmigration of Souls*, «Rinascimento», II s., XLV, 2005, pp. 3-17.

seem to be the corollary notion of our soul's ante-natal existence without a body. In the *Platonic Theology* 18.3 he sets out the necessary arguments for the orthodox theory that souls were not created before their bodies even though this would seem to require that God create souls daily: «Why are new souls daily created by God? Could not God, having constructed the world, create all the souls at the same time, just as He procreated all the angels at the world's beginning?» Ficino advances the argument that this was not appropriate; «For had the souls lived freed from the chains of bodies for a long time, they would in all honesty have judged how much more precious this freed life was than another, and would never have wished to enter bodies». As a consequence «this middle part of the temple divine would lack divine priests and be without divine hymns. And yet the individual circles of this temple deserve to be occupied by their own priestly choirs singing hymns to God» (18.3.1).

Ficino underscores two further scholastic arguments keyed to Aristotle's hylomorphism, the first being that «soul is the form and act of body». While it is true that «in the universe and according to the order of nature act is prior to potentiality, yet in one and the same subject, and according to time, act is posterior to it, since motion is achieved from potentiality into act». Hence «the seed that is living in potentiality is prior to the soul that is living act» (18.3.2).[18] The second argument is that «it is natural to each form, furthermore, that it be united to its own matter; otherwise what results from compounding matter and form would be an unnatural clump. But to each thing is given what naturally accords with it and only then what is unnatural to it. For what naturally accords with it is intrinsic to it *per se*; but what happens to it unnaturally results from something extrinsic. Therefore, by very reason of its being soul, it is proper that soul should be bound to body before being separated from it» and therefore could not have lived before body (18.3.2).[19] These two proofs seem to counter any notion of an ante-natal existence, and underscore the successive creation of souls and their accompanying bodies in time.

---

[18] This undermines, or at least complicates, the notion, held by Origen for example, that the soul precedes the body; see HANKINS, *Ficino on* Reminiscentia, cit., pp. 3-5. We should note, however, that it also complicates the opposite notion, espoused by the Ecumenical Council of Constantinople in 543, that soul comes into being with the body.

[19] Cf. FICINO, *Platonic Theology* 15.12.2-3; see P. O. KRISTELLER, *The Philosophy of Marsilio Ficino*, New York 1943, pp. 195-196, 390-391. We should recall that the Fourth Lateran Council of 1215 had defined the human being (*humana creatura*) as «quasi communem ex spiritu et corpore constitutam».

However, the situation is not so scholastically defined and oriented for Ficino,[20] given his encounter with a signal ancient Neoplatonic notion, which he then read back into Plato himself and into what were for him such pre-Platonic texts as the *Chaldaean Oracles*, the *Hermetica*, and the *Orphic Hymns*, namely the notion of the soul's spiritual envelope, vehicle or chariot (*ochêma*), in the notable imagery of the *Phaedrus* and *Timaeus*.[21] This was thought to be compounded either from Aristotle's fifth essence (usually identified with the aether), or more suggestively, as we shall see, from light itself. Indeed, it was the ancient Neoplatonists and their predecessors who supplied Ficino with a number of insights into this arcane topic of what is often called the astral body, a topic which has a number of occult and yogic associations that even now continue to interest historians of religion and the esoteric, and to bewitch theosophists and new age devotees.

In the *Platonic Theology* 4.2.10, Ficino speaks of the soul's aethereal envelope as if it were a planet's sphere,[22] and notably Saturn's sphere; and he formulates the arguments that the soul is present at this envelope's every point; and that, since the soul is never at rest in the sense of not moving, the body too never stops, but revolves around its soul as a planet revolves on its axis. The soul in turn is forever revolving around God as its centre, though of course there are higher beings who do not move at all but contemplate God and the intelligibles in rest.[23] Ficino thinks of

---

[20] We should bear in mind that Ficino deploys a number of methodologies: he is not committed only to Scholastic proofs. On Scholasticism's commitment, by contrast, to a unity of method, see R. SCHÖNBERGER, *Was ist Scholastik?*, Hildesheim 1991 – I have used the Italian translation by L. TUNINETTI, *La Scolastica medievale. Cenni per una definizione*, Milano 1997, p. 22.

[21] *Phaedrus* 247B ff. and *Timaeus* 41DE, 44DE, 69C; also *Phaedo* 113D and *Laws* 10.898E-899B. Cf. FICINO, *Platonic Theology* 18.4.1-7. For the history of this complex topic, see PROCLUS, *The Elements of Theology*, ed. by E. R. DODDS, Oxford 1963 (II ed.), app. 2; R. C. KISSLING, *The* ochêma-pneuma *of the Neo-Platonists and the* De insomniis *of Synesius of Cyrene*, «American Journal of Philology», XLIII, 1922, 4, pp. 318-330; P. MORAUX, *'Quinta Essentia'*, in PAULY-WISSOWA-KROLL, *Realencyclopädie der classischen Altertums-wissenschaft*, XXIV.1, 1963, pp. 1171-1263: 1251-1256; G. VERBEKE, *L'évolution de la doctrine du pneuma du stoïcisme à saint Augustin*, Paris-Louvain 1945, esp. chap. 6; and various papers in *Spiritus*, IV Colloquio internazionale del lessico intellettuale europeo (Roma, 7-9 gennaio 1983), a cura di M. FATTORI-M. L. BIANCHI, Roma 1984. For Ficino, see KRISTELLER, *The Philosophy of Marsilio Ficino*, cit., pp. 371-373. We should be alert to the important distinction between materiality and corporeality; see my *The Platonism of Marsilio Ficino*, cit., pp. 13, 91, 97.

[22] Cf. FICINO, *Platonic Theology* 15.12.2: «It is natural for this eternal soul to be joined to an eternal and heavenly body forever» as each of the planets to its own sphere.

[23] Cf. *Ibid.*, 17.3.3.

Zoroaster as the ancestral source of this formulation. Resembling a planetary sphere, however, is more than just a simile: in a profound way, a risen soul is a planetary, is a celestial soul; and its spiritual body is its planetary sphere, a sphere forever perfect in its axial motion. This implies that its ideal or original shape is spherical and that its natural motion is circular. Our angular earthly bodies are the result of the distortions incurred as we plunged immediately prior to birth down through the seven planetary spheres to earth, losing our sphericity until we became imprisoned finally in an extended earthly body.[24]

In considering the question in 18.4.1 as to whence exactly the soul departs in order to descend into body, Ficino turns to Zoroaster and Hermes with the seemingly playful but disingenuous remark that «Now and then it is pleasant to converse with the ancients».[25] The soul in its descent is like a sunbeam or a ray of sunshine, and it is «poured» first into the highest body which is then united to grosser bodies. This vehicle of the soul is «the little aethereal body received from the aether, as the soul's immortal garment» (18.4.3).[26] It is naturally «round» because the aethereal sphere is round, though in entering the human body it «transforms itself» into our human shape, and only returns to its original shape when it leaves the human body, presumably at death or in spiritual trance. The soul's «familiar body» comes from the aether and thus from the celestial sphere; and Ficino adduces the obvious sources: the *Phaedrus's* references to the chariots of the gods and souls, and the *Timaeus'* reference to the vehicle's «utmost purity». Once again, Zoroaster is given the final word but in a manner that adds yet another critical term, the «spirit» (*pneuma*): «Do not sully the spirit: do not extend what is planar into depth» (18.4.3).[27]

In glossing these cryptic verses in 18.4.4 Ficino writes that the spirit «is almost not a body given its extreme tenuity and radiant purity». And

---

[24] Cf. Proclus, *In Cratylum* 35, 72; see my *The Platonism of Marsilio Ficino*, cit., p. 13 and notes.

[25] A sentiment he repeats in 18.5.1: «yet it is delightful to play poetically for a while with the ancients». But to play as a philosopher is «to study most seriously»; see Ficino's remarks in the proem to his *Parmenides* Commentary, in *Opera omnia*, cit., p. 1137: «Pythagorae, Socratisque et Platonis mos erat [...] iocari serio et studiosissime ludere». See also E. Wind, *Pagan Mysteries in the Renaissance*, London 1968 (II rev. ed.), p. 236 and notes.

[26] Cf. 18.5.1. For 18.4 in general, see Allen, *The Platonism of Marsilio Ficino*, cit., pp. 218-220, and Hankins, *Ficino on* Reminiscentia, cit., pp. 4-6.

[27] *Oracula Chaldaica* frag. 104 (ed. Des Places).

yet the soul's «rational part» is not in contact with this vehicle. The intermediary is rather «a life-giving act» which Ficino here identifies with what the Neoplatonists had called the «idolum»: it is the soul's «mortal species», not because it dies of itself, but because it «would tumble, some think, to its ruin» if the vehicle were ever to be withdrawn. As similes Ficino adduces the luminescence the moon produces in a cloud or a comet in its tail. Since the vehicle will never in fact be withdrawn, Zoroaster was able to declare that «there is a place too for the idolum in the region of clarity»[28] as it returns with its rational soul to heaven.

In Ficino's view Plotinus had thought that the idolum is unconditionally immortal just as the light of the sun is independent of the air (the reference is probably to *Enneads* 4.4.29); but that other philosophers had supposed that an irrational and troubled phantasy, and even hearing and seeing, dwell in the idolum (18.4.5-6). For, if someone can «gather himself again into his celestial body, having cast aside for a time his earthly body», then he will often perceive through the idolum's senses «the marvellous harmonies of the heavens and the voices and bodies of daemons» (18.4.6). And Ficino briefly outlines the ancient theory of the soul's gifts to the three vehicles: on the first bestowing an irrational but immortal life, on the second an irrational but long-lasting life, and on the third an irrational and mortal life (18.4.7).

Ficino does not endorse all these views as such but presents them as the views of the Platonists. Even so, his extended «playing with the ancients» effectively valorises them; and it often becomes difficult to determine in the following analyses when Ficino is speaking as an ancient and when *in propria persona* as a *Quattrocento* Florentine. Effectively he appears to be endorsing the ancient views despite some caveats or qualifications This is even true of the ancient description – found most obviously in Macrobius and deriving from the *Timaeus'* account of the demiurge sowing souls in the stars and their becoming the stars' companions[29] – of the soul's descent through Cancer, «the portal of men», and its subsequent re-ascent through Capricorn, «the portal of the gods». And this is despite his assertion that the constellations here are not to be interpreted as places but rather allegorically, Cancer being «the instinct that is lunar and vegetative», and Capricorn «the instinct that is saturnian and intel-

[28] *Ibid.*, frag. 158.

[29] Cf. Ficino, *Platonic Theology* 18.5.1.

lectual» (18.5.2). In describing the gifts the soul receives from the planets as it descends, Ficino again compares the soul to a sunbeam and notes that some of the ancients supposed that souls first dwelt in the planetary spheres and for many centuries lived a life in their vehicles appropriate to their own sphere before their journey down into a demonic, and finally into a human life, a journey all souls will eventually undertake again in reverse. It is only at this point when he has raised the complex issue of an extended ante-natal existence in the planetary spheres, despite his earlier rejections of that very notion, that Ficino introduces his one and only disclaimer within the domain of the *Platonic Theology* as a whole, namely, «We want to affirm, and others to affirm, only what may appear acceptable to a council of Christian theologians» (18.5.4).[30]

Theologically speaking, many of these notions of the 'ancients' are next to impossible to reconcile with the account in *Genesis* 1:26-27 of Adam's creation in the image and likeness of God, unless we entertain the heretical notions that prelapsarian Adam was a perfect sphere made in the image and likeness of God Himself as a sphere; and that, moreover, he revolved in a perfect circle around God, instead of wandering across the glades and through the coverts of Paradise in what we assume was something other than an orbital manner. This theocentric motion would imply that the requisite mathematical and geometrical formulae for measuring the ideal man and measuring in a way God Himself would in turn involve the Pi that accounts for the ratio of the circumference of a circle to its diameter. And we recall the famous Hermetic formulation (at least it was Hermetic to Ficino) that God is a circle whose circumference is nowhere and whose centre is everywhere.[31] To introduce the prelapsarian Eve would be to complicate the problem still further: Did she revolve epicyclically as a satellite moon around Adam while he revolved around God; or did they revolve around each other in a binary system; and so on?

Interestingly, this notion of circular or spherical man has temporal as well as spatial dimensions. The linear course of our bodily lives here can be seen as distorted in time in a way that parallels the distortion of our

---

[30] The whole summa is bracketed by the general disclaimer: «In all I discuss, either here or elsewhere, I wish to maintain only what meets with the approval of the Church». On the intriguing possibility of a 'council', see HANKINS, *Ficino on* Reminiscentia, cit., pp. 3-4.

[31] FICINO, *Platonic Theology* 18.3.12 and note 24.

angular bodies in space: earthly life is thus limited to the narrow span for the most part of threescore years and ten, whereas it should be lived in a perfectly, eternally circular or cyclical manner. This is the mystery Ficino saw adumbrated in the ancient theologian's concern with a cyclical world time. In the *Platonic Theology* 4.2.5, for instance, he affirms that Zoroaster believed «that when exactly the same causes will have returned at some point in time, the same effects will recur». Similarly, the Platonists had claimed that «to be completed the circuit of the universe takes an interval of 36,000 solar years, designated the Great or Cosmic Year» (Plato had referred to this in the *Timaeus* 39CD without assigning it a number of solar years).[32] Ficino also adduces the hermetic reference in the *Asclepius* 26 to «the old age of the world» and finally Plato's comment in the *Statesman* that the end of the Cosmic Year is the moment of the world's «restoration» (269C-270D).

Ficino is interested in the *Statesman* for reasons other than determining the precise count of solar years in the Great Year, however significant that might be. What the dialogue 'celebrates' at 269C-274D, he says in 18.8.7, is an «ancient mystery» in the form of a divine myth about Cronus, about time-in-eternity, and about rebirth with its host of religious and spiritual associations. The Eleatic Stranger who is conversing with the younger Socrates tells him of the time when God Himself guides the world and helps to roll it on its course; and of the other time when, «at the completion of a certain cycle», He lets it go and the world turns around and «by an inherent necessity revolves in the opposite direction». It can do so independently because it is a «living creature» which «has received intelligence from its author and creator» (269CD). The Stranger insists that «we must neither say that the world turns itself for ever; nor again that God causes it to turn as a whole and forever in two opposite directions; nor finally that two gods with contrary purposes make it revolve». Rather the world is guided at one time by the divine power external to it, receiving new life and indeed immortality from «the renewing hand of the Creator»; but when He lets it go, it moves of its own accord and does so «for millions of revolutions» perfectly balanced and turning on the smallest pivot (269E ff.). The reversal is the greatest of conceivable changes and thus it occasions the greatest change for mankind. At first there is destruction; but for those who survive, the mortal nature ceases

[32] CICERO, *De natura deorum* 2.20.51-52, says the number of years was «hotly debated». Another calculation was 15,000 years as in Macrobius.

to age and people begin to grow younger again and more delicate, to the point even of becoming newly born children, mentally and physically. In the absence of sex and procreation, the fabled «earth-born» race rises out of the ground and at the same time «the dead who are lying in the earth return to life». And all «rise and live in the opposite order, unless God has borne any of them away to some other lot» (271AB).[33]

Ficino refers admiringly to this Platonic myth on a number of occasions, in addition to summarizing it in his argumentum for his Latin version of the dialogue in his monumental *Platonis Opera omnia* edition of 1484. I wish to confine myself here, however, to four interesting passages of exegesis in the final two books of the *Platonic Theology*, and more particularly since they bear on the problems both of the Resurrection itself and of Plato's wonderful anticipation, as Ficino saw it, of Christian dogma.

Ficino addresses Platonic views on the theory of the soul's pre-existence in 17.3.5, citing as an instance Pythagoras' claim to have lived a number of lives. Pythagoras did so, his argument goes, by his donning, not a new body as we might expect from tales about his being a cockerel and so on, but rather the same body «at the end of fixed cycles of time», just as the world's spheres «re-enact their own returns». Ficino adduces Zoroaster's use of the word *palingenesis* – a word which *Matthew* 19:28 strikingly attributes to Christ Himself: «ye which have followed me in the regeneration when the Son of Man shall sit in the throne of glory»[34] – and also Hermes Trismegistus' account of rebirth in the *Pimander* 13.1 and 13.10-16.[35] He then turns to the *Statesman*, where, he says, «Plato describes this resurrection as something that is going to occur at the end of a cosmic revolution [*in fine mundanae revolutionis*] under the commandment of God and with the aid of ministering daemons». Elsewhere Ficino consistently identifies these benign daemons with the dialogue's reference to the «shepherd» daemons at 271DE.[36]

---

[33] See K. MORGAN, *Myth and Philosophy: From the Presocratics to Plato*, Cambridge 2000, pp. 253-261. I am using Jowett's translation of the *Statesman*.

[34] Cf. *Titus* 3:5, «the washing of regeneration».

[35] See WIND, *Pagan Mysteries*, cit., pp. 256-258, on Bessarion's letter on palingenesis to Pletho's sons upon their father's death. Wind reminds us that the Church taught the second coming not only of Christ but of Enoch, of Elijah – whose perfect form, following *Matthew* 3:3; *Luke* 3:4 and *John* 1:23, was held to be present in St. John the Baptist – and of Jeremiah.

[36] Cf. *Statesman* 275A-276D and *Laws* 4.713CD. His authority here was Proclus.

In 17.3.11 he turns to Plato's deployment of such large numbers as 1,000, 3,000, and 10,000 in the *Phaedrus* 248C-249B and the *Republic* 10.615AB, since he interprets them as signifying, albeit figuratively, souls' «transmigrations» and «reincarnations» (*restitutiones*); and specifically those referred to in the myth of Er. Each of these numbers is both large and «perfect» insofar as it is a value of 10 (and not in the more restricted sense of being a truly perfect number, like 6, which is both the sum of its parts and the product of its factors). And Ficino takes these millennial numbers to imply that perfect purgation for Plato, but also by implication for Christian souls, is achieved in an extended but fixed span of time. We return to our original selves, therefore, only when «the whole course of the world has been at last fulfilled», as the *Statesman* had decreed – a course computed by the astronomers, as we saw, to terminate after 36,000 solar years.[37] Now this seems very much a Platonic, i.e. a pre-Christian, astronomical concept concerning Time itself and its recycling or renewal, even as Ficino is obviously assuming that it can be subjected to a Christian (re)interpretation focused on the dogmas of the final Day of Judgement and of the «fullness» of Time as it crosses over into eternity.

Plato's celebration of the ancient mystery concerning the two circuits of the world is likewise adduced at 18.8.7. The present circuit passes from east to west under Jupiter and Fate, and the future circuit will return from west to east under Saturn, so that men will be born «of their own accord», parentlessly, as we saw, and their lives will revert to youth in a spring made bountiful with autumnal fruits. But now Ficino plumbs deeper. He identifies Jupiter here with the World-Soul «by whose fatal law this manifest order of the manifest world is disposed», the jovian life being devoted to the life of action and of the senses (as active or perspicacious instruments). But Saturn is «the supreme intellect among the angels» and his rays illuminate souls so that they are more illuminated even than the angels: the rays set our souls on fire and continually waft them upwards to the life of the intellect. Hence souls live under Saturn «to the extent they live by understanding»; and in that saturnian life they are «regenerated of their own accord», because they themselves choose to be «reformed». Under him they are daily renewed and «blossom more and more»; and the fruits they consume in abundance are the «spectacles

---

[37] Cf. Ficino, *Platonic Theology* 4.2.5.

of truth» referred to in the *Phaedrus* 247A4-5.[38] These spectacles Ficino identifies not just with the intelligible Ideas at the apex of Plato's metaphysical hierarchy but with the source of an «inner light» that brings us the «deepest tranquillity» and the «loftiest pleasure», a pleasure we can, as it were, both scent and taste when we become totally divorced from the physical world. And Ficino alludes first to the *Symposium*'s reference to the «sea» of divine beauty at 210D4, in which the soul immerses itself after it has been purged of earthly affections; and then to the *Epinomis* 992BC's reference to the soul at the summit of beauty, gathering itself entirely into its own unity, a unity which is loftier than its intellect; and transferring itself thence into the unity divine which entirely transcends the intelligible world. Saturn in other words takes us to the threshold of the empyrean and beyond, offering us the opportunity, it would seem, to escape the alternating cycles of time altogether.

Ficino returns to the *Statesman*'s myth for the last time in the *Platonic Theology* in 18.9.4 in order to draw an explicit connection between Platonic and Christian conceptions of the resurrection of the body. When the present, fatal course of the world ends, then, «with God commanding them and giving them life again», the souls of men will receive the bodies they have lost in this fatal course, «with the result that, just as human bodies once succumbed to fate on earth, so under the rule of divine providence they will rise from the earth and live again».[39] And Ficino boldly declares that «these mysteries of the ancient philosophers do not much differ from the mysteries of the Hebrews and Christians, mysteries that have been confirmed even by the Muslims» (and he is probably thinking of Avicenna whom he introduces a paragraph later). He ends this part of his argument by asserting: «At length when the sky's course (wherein all things are begotten) is completed, nothing is to be generated further; but men's individual bodies, for whose sake all things were first generated, will rise again from the earth at God's command».

His grand conclusion, however, is that God's infinite power is such that He «can take the bodies that have been dissolved into the elements, and at a particular moment – i.e. at the Resurrection – reassemble them again from the elements that remain» (18.9.10). Although men will not

[38] Cf. Ficino's *In Phaedrum*, summa 19 (ed. Allen, pp. 150-151).

[39] Ficino interprets Plato here as referring to both the celestial and the elemental or earthly bodies as is clear from his later commentary on the Areopagite's *De divinis nominibus* «[animas] terrenum quoque corpus terrae tandem non relicturas» (*Opera omnia*, cit., p. 1031.1).

reacquire the very same elements, they will get the same body «rewoven», because «the same form will exist as before, that is, the soul»; and the elements will come from the same prime matter and be subject to «the same undetermined dimension that accompanies this matter», i.e. to spatial extension. In this regard it will be no different from our having the «same» body in our age as in our youth, even though its elements have forever been renewed *(ibid.)*. Even so, this later body will be «entirely immortal» since the body will be totally congruent now with the soul (18.9.11). Ficino calls this Resurrection after the world's motion ceases the «re-creation» or the «second creation», and insists that God will make each individual soul and body immortal and not just mankind as a species (for ordinary earthly generation already ensures for post-diluvian mankind a biological immortality) (18.9.12).

It is interesting, however, that Ficino once again moves to adopt a Neoplatonic viewpoint, and with it the controversial but familiar notion, which elsewhere he seems to have argued against as we have seen, of the soul's ante-natal existence in an aethereal body. This body is not only the glorified body of the ultimate Resurrection of the Bible but also, from a Neoplatonic perspective, both its original ante-natal body and the spiritual body it assumes in its individual resurrection immediately after the death of the elemental body – the notion of a distant universal Resurrection at the end of time being foreign to Neoplatonism as is the notion too of a long sleep or suspension prior to that Resurrection. In other words, the soul has a corporeal, albeit an aethereal existence before its birth in its elemental body and after its leaving that body at death,[40] though strictly speaking it has not existed for ever, given the traditional Aristotelian and Christian arguments for man's composite nature and given Judaeo-Christian arguments for a beginning to the created world. It was thus created in and not before time.

In this regard it is kin to the angels, whether the human soul is forever a little lower than the angels (*Psalm* 8:5), or equal to them (*Luke* 20:36), or eventually set above them as «gods» (*Psalm* 82:6, cited by Christ himself in *John* 10:34).[41] In both Origen and Augustine the angels

[40] The *Phaedo* epitome suggests that a dead person sometimes returns in his airy body to haunt his physical remains as a ghost, the airy body being «a sort of veil» (*involucrum quoddam*) «compounded [*conflatum*] from the spirits and vapors of the body or materialized [*congregatum*] from the surrounding air» (FICINO, *Opera omnia*, cit., p. 1392 [misnumbered 1390]).

[41] «Ye are gods and all of you are children of the most High»; cf. *Heb.* 1:4, 2:16; *I John* 1:3, 3:1-2, 4:4; also FICINO, *Platonic Theology* 13.4.12: «The person who commits himself en-

too have aethereal bodies, a position denied of course by Aquinas who thought of them as subsistent forms, but reaffirmed in a way by Scotus who argued for their composite nature, though their matter was incorporeal in the sense of not being like our earthly bodies.[42] But the more one believes that man in his original state was like the angels, and can reacquire that angelic state and so return to the angelic choirs, then the less can one credit the argument Ficino turned to briefly in 18.3.2, namely that human souls are created «daily». Rather, the more convincing becomes his alternative vision: that human souls were created at the time the angels were created, and therefore acquired the same kind of eternal glorified body that was bestowed on the angels. The presence of the angels thus raises both the fundamental issue of our own angelic nature, given Christ's promise in *Luke* 20:36 that as «children of the resurrection» we will be equal to the angels, and the notion that the angelic body is an aethereal body that we too have possessed or do possess or will possess. In short, Christian angelology, and especially Scotist angelology, opened up the possibility for Ficino of drawing upon the ancient notions of the star vehicle or body of light and accommodating it to the theology of man's return to the angelic choirs. Indeed, the more compelling the notion of the angelic life of the redeemed soul, the more compelling the notion of an aethereal body in that life, and the more compelling therefore the notion of a prenatal life extending back to the sixth day of Creation and the beginning of time.

At all events, Ficino argues that in the Resurrection, in the second rising, the body will again conform to, or be congruent with, its soul, and not the reverse as is the case in this mortal life; for at that time they will both be raised «lest souls remain forever imperfect» (18.9.13). This «congruence» argument can obviously apply equally to an aethereal or to an elemental body; and Ficino believes not only that such a congruent body is going to be our immortal body (though it had a beginning), but also that it was our original immaculate body, our glorious envelope of aether. God's measureless power is the efficient cause of the resurrection of this immaculate body and His omnipotence will make the everlasting life of the soul «flow everlastingly» into the body (*sempiterne quoque exundet*) at that moment

---

tirely to God's inspiration ceases to be a soul and becomes, being reborn from God, a son of God, an angel».

[42] See my *The Absent Angel in Ficino's Philosophy*, now in my *Plato's Third Eye: Studies in Marsilio Ficino's Metaphysics and its Sources*, Aldershot 1995, as essay no. I.

of resurrection, whether this is in time or at the end of time (18.9.15).[43] At this juncture, any distinction between an aethereal and an elemental body loses its significance; for the two have become one and the same glorified body, as Paul had declared in *Philippians* 3:21 «[Jesus] shall change our vile body that it may be fashioned like unto his glorious body».[44]

In the general Resurrection, therefore, or in an individual resurrection prior to that, an immaculate soul will once again be clothed in its immaculate aethereal body that was created with it in time and will last with it to eternity. The intellect, which will be «full to overflowing with divine light», and the will, which is going to be filled with gladness and with «incomparable power» to move, together will transmit their «wonderful splendour» and their wondrous power into the resurrected body. Consequently, our bodies too will be given «the clarity and power» of the celestial bodies, meaning of the planets and the stars. In fact, it should come as no surprise, given our body's natural resemblance to the heavens (*caelo*), that, when it is clothed once again in «a kind of celestial or heavenly form», it will, of a sudden, be raised on high to «the region of the heavens», following the soul which is borne up by the infinite, the supercelestial power of God. The soul will lead the body to the highest region of the aether and there it will itself become «aethereal in power and quality» (18.9.15) and hardly distinguishable, if at all, from an angel.

Plato's *Statesman*, or rather its great myth, is thus made into a work anticipating and conforming to Christian dogma and bearing witness to the belief both in a personal resurrection, at least for the purified philosopher, and in a final, or rather the final Resurrection of all men. In particular, Plato's Stranger is made into a voice championing not only the soul's immortality, but the resurrection of the body – and this despite: a) Plato's negative accounting of the body in the *Phaedo* and elsewhere; b) the *Statesman's* core vision of (endless?) temporal cycles or alternations, which Ficino redesigns to refer to just two ages – the present fatal tem-

[43] Irrelevant here is the fine-spun Proclan distinction which Ficino had nonetheless carefully noted between «sempiternity» in general, meaning «duration without beginning or end», and «eternity» and «perpetuity» as subcategories: «eternity» meaning «interminable duration that is wholly present», and «perpetuity» meaning «interminable duration that flows on and on». See H. D. SAFFREY, *Notes platoniciennes de Marsile Ficin dans un ms. de Proclus, cod. Riccardianus 70*, «Bibliothèque d'Humanisme et Renaissance», XXI, 1959, pp. 161-184: 174; also my *The Platonism of Marsilio Ficino*, cit., p. 81 and notes.

[44] Cited by Ficino in his *De divinis nominibus* commentary (*Opera omnia*, cit., p. 1031.1): «The Lord will change the body of our humility that it may be fashioned into the body of his clarity». Ficino's debts to Origen on this issue await investigation.

poral age, and the coming golden age of eternity; and c) the problematic implications of having Saturn, either the ancient pre-Olympian god or the planetary deity, as the ruler of that golden age, implications which Ficino avoids by substituting God and God's command. In these regards he deliberately misreads or misinterprets the dialogue's mystery in order to make it conform to the Christian dogma of a final Resurrection. At the same time he is implicitly rejecting (or subordinating) the traditional Christian notion of the final Resurrection of the ordinary elemental body in order to embrace the heterodox, if not completely unorthodox, notion of each liberated soul in its own ascendant resurrection reacquiring after corporeal death its original spiritual envelope. This notion he assuredly found adumbrated in Plato and indeed in some of the earlier Church Fathers, but it had been fully elaborated in the commentaries of the Neoplatonists and in the various compilations (and pious forgeries) of later antiquity that he supposed of very ancient origin, and notably those purporting to contain the dicta of Zoroaster and Hermes. It also quite distinct from most of the popular views of the afterlife – Dante springs to mind – that Christians have traditionally held, however confusedly and confusingly, about each human being's having to await the last trump, whether it be in the grave, in the long sleep, in hell, in purgatory, in paradise, or in the angelic choirs themselves.

The whole vision, in sum, is set against the backdrop of the ancient doctrines of the twin portals of Cancer and Capricorn, however allegorically conceived, and of the soul's planetary descent and re-ascent via these portals, even though Ficino is careful to reject the hallowed Egypto-Pythagorean doctrine of soul-circuits, in the sense of a series of reincarnations. The result is an unorthodox but characteristically Ficinian compromise, a subtly articulated positioning between the Aristotle-anchored orthodoxy of the schools on the one hand, and his own profound and innovative engagement with Plotinus and his followers on the other. It is a positioning, moreover, that assuredly provides a paradigmatic case for maintaining the distinctiveness of Renaissance philosophy, or, at the very least, for maintaining the notion of a Renaissance moment in the history of philosophy, one that is characterized by what Edgar Wind has aptly called a «transvaluation of values».[45]

---

[45] Cited by A. Brown, *Reinterpreting Renaissance Humanism: Marcello Adriani and the Recovery of Lucretius*, in *Interpretations of Renaissance Humanism*, ed. by A. Mazzocco, Leiden 2006, p. 269.

The supreme validation of the soul-body ascent to the aether is Ficino's account in the *Platonic Theology* 13.4.15 of levitation.[46] Ficino writes that the Magi believed that the soul can of itself perform a marvel or miracle in that it «can surround its own body with light drawn from scattered rays of light» and thereby raise on high not only itself but its own body;[47] and the «father» of the Chaldaean Magi, Zoroaster himself, was reputed to have mastered this luminary feat. Ficino speculates that the nature of light itself is six-fold: it begins with the trans-intelligible light of God Himself, and passes down through the angels where it becomes intellectual light. Thence it passes into the soul as rational light, and thence into the soul's idolum (the «life» of the aethereal vehicle as we have seen)[48] as sensitive but not yet corporeal light. Thereafter it enters into the vehicle itself, where it becomes corporeal but still invisible light, until finally it crosses over into the elemental body and becomes visible light. This six-fold nature of light, he believes, is the true if hidden meaning of Homer's six-linked golden chain in the *Iliad* 8.18-25, pendent from the heavens, a chain whereby «men who have seized hold of it can raise themselves to the heavens». When we contemplate and worship God, we are filled with His overflowing light: its radiant abundance brims over into our aethereal vehicle, and thence, via the airy body, into our elemental body. At that moment, «with the copiousness of the rays», this lower body «is set ablaze, rarefied and lifted up» accompanied by the aethereal vehicle and the airy vehicle, like tow wafted through a flame. «In such a fiery chariot», Ficino imagines the Magi and Platonists maintaining, «Elijah and Paul were swept up into heaven».[49] After the Last Judgement, the body that Christian theologians call «the glorified body» of the resurrection «will be similarly enraptured». At this pivotal moment in the argument,

[46] For a more detailed analysis, see M. J. B. ALLEN, *Marsilio Ficino, Levitation and the Ascent to Capricorn*, in *Éducation, transmission, rénovation à la Renaissance*, ed. by B. PINCHARD - P. SERVET, Genève 2006, pp. 223-240.

[47] The role, if any, of Al-Kindi's treatise on rays in Ficino's thought has yet to be carefully documented. Ioan P. Couliano's enthusiastic speculations in his *Eros and Magic in the Renaissance*, tr. M. COOK, Chicago 1987, pp. 119-123, *passim*, are often very wide of the mark.

[48] See KRISTELLER, *The Philosophy of Marsilio Ficino*, cit., pp. 371-375.

[49] *II Kings* 2:11-12; *II Cor.* 12:2-4. D. P. WALKER, *The Astral Body in Renaissance Medicine*, «Journal of the Warburg and Courtauld Institutes», XXI, 1958, pp. 119-133: 123, points out that the chariots of Ezekiel and Elijah were also going to be equated with the astral body, albeit tentatively, by Nicolaus Leonicus in a 1524 tract that he dedicated to Reginald Pole and entitled *Alverotus sive de tribus animorum vehiculis*.

Ficino in 13.4.16 assembles three separate verses from the *Chaldaean Oracles*, namely 96 (line 1), 112, and 158:

Because the soul becomes resplendent fire through the power of the father,
May the soul's immortal profundity dominate you. Raise all eyes on high as one,
And then you will not abandon even the material body to the precipice.[50]

He takes this to be referring – and he glosses the various lemmata carefully – to the ascent of the soul, dominated by its unity, and bearing with it both its celestial body and its earthly «material» body. Does the latter ascend too precisely because Ficino is thinking of ecstatic levitation during this and not the next life? Or does it ascend with the soul at death because it too becomes light-filled? In either event, Ficino's metaphysics of light fully accommodates such levitation to Platonic interpretation, even though levitation (as contrasted with *mania* or trance in general) does not appear in Plato, and though it has not been a much discussed or attested phenomenon in western spirituality, despite the «glory» of the Transfiguration and the witness of the odd levitating saint, and despite too its intermittent appearance in occidental folklore and carnival. Nonetheless, it serves as the ultimate witness to the nature, power, and divinity of light [51] In his late commentary on Dionysius the Areopagite's *De divinis nominibus*, Ficino dramatically envisions the Resurrection as an event caused by the radiant splendour of Christ's own body: «Just as the sun in the spring awakens the seeds hidden in the entrails of the earth and adorns the majority of them with flowers of exceeding beauty, so Christ's most splendid body, at the appointed time, with its rays far-flung everywhere will awaken the bodies of men; and will adorn many of them, moreover, with the splendours [of his body] [...]. So when we become the children of the resurrection [*Luke* 20:36], that is, when we are reborn from him who has already risen first and are reborn in his likeness, and when we are brought into heaven, we will enjoy the light of Christ. Through our sight, we will enjoy the visible light of Christ's body, but through our intellect, now freed from all corporeal contagion, we will enjoy his intelligible light by way of our intellectual light, that is, enjoy the soul of Christ ablaze in our understanding».[52]

---

[50] Ficino could just have well added the last line of 158: «But the image (*eidôlon*) too has its part in the region bathed in light», since he quotes it several times elsewhere, equating the «image» with the aethereal vehicle!

[51] Cf. Ficino, *Platonic Theology* 18.8.9-10

[52] «Profecto quemadmodum sol in vere terrae visceribus condita semina suscitat et pleraque pulcherrimis floribus ornat, ita splendidissimum Christi corpus, statutis temporibus, conie-

The ultimate Resurrection of the body, of all bodies, of Body itself has become, in Ficino's eyes, the ultimate levitation, one quickened by the very radiance of Christ's body and then borne upwards on the shafts of his intelligible splendour to a union with the Father who transcends all light and darkness.

To conclude, the finale of the *Platonic Theology: On the Immortality of Souls* is also triumphantly concerned with the resurrection of the body. Not only is Ficino clearly invoking, if indirectly, St. Paul's memorable fifteenth chapter in *I Corinthians*, and the themes of Christ's Transfiguration, post-Resurrection appearances, and final Ascension, he is also deliberately twinning and intertwining the notion of our before-birth and our post-death body with that of light, and arguing that our resurrected body will become visible once again as light, like a starry or planetary sphere, like an angel even, in the world to come.[53] In this nice sense, the *Platonic Theology* is pre-eminently a luminary work, one that focuses, not on our penitential imitating of Christ as we walk here through the valley of the shadow of death, but on an almost Gnostic concern (or is it Eastern Orthodox inspired?) with our souls as sparks of divine light in aethereal, transfigured, light-filled and translucent bodies, soaring, as if we were already blessed and among the blessed, to join the hymning choirs of the angels in the luminous empyrean which was and will again be our natural home. Indeed, Ficino's ponderous eighteen book *summa* is, in the last analysis, a philosophical *levitatio*, a book of transfiguration and ascension that focuses on the hope of man's soul and body uniting once more, at some point after physical death, but assuredly before the final Resurrection, to become pure resplendent light, returning like radii to an incandescent centre, to what the Epistle of St. James calls «the Father of lights with whom is no variableness, neither shadow of turning» (1:17).[54]

Only a few decades later this auroral Platonic-Christian vision of

---

ctis usque quaque radiis, hominum corpora suscitabit, multaque preterea splendoribus exornabit [...]. Quando igitur ita filii resurrectionis erimus, id est ex eo qui primus iam resurrexit in similitudinem eius renati fuerimus, celoque donati, eterno Christi lumine perfruemur: per visum quidem visibili corporis Christi luce; per intellectum vero, iam ab omni contagione corporea liberum, intelligibili lumine ex intellectuali, videlicet Christi anima in nostram intelligentiam emicante» (*Opera omnia*, cit., p. 1031.1). Note that «intellectual light» is what we then share with the angels.

[53] Cf. *I Cor.* 15:40-44.

[54] For the Areopagite God is also the Father of darkness, or rather of what is beyond light and darkness.

man's almost angelic being was going to be eclipsed by the crepuscular emphases of the Protestant Reformers on sin, temptation and the devil, on man's perverted if not diabolic will, on his need for unmerited and even prevenient grace, and on his justification, if any, by faith alone. Luther was roundly to reject St. James' Epistle, not for its reference to the «Father of lights», but for its several declarations that «faith, if it hath not works, is dead, being alone», and that it is «by works a man is justified, and not by faith only» (2:17, 24). The Reformer was to turn instead to the contrary formulations in Paul's Epistle to the Romans where at 13:12 the Apostle to the gentiles exhorts mankind to cast off the works of darkness and to put on the whole armour of light. This armour Luther and the other Reformers were to interpret, moreover, in a fideistic sense at two, and at more than two removes from the many overlapping senses of Ficino's poetic and metaphysical theologizing, and his ardent belief in the salvific work of the light, of the angelic light, within.

12

At Variance: Marsilio Ficino, Platonism and Heresy

Heresy in Greek antiquity meant a choice, or what is chosen, particularly a tenet. But heresy takes many forms. When orthodoxy is not yet established, an heretical opinion may still represent a proto-orthodox or a not yet heterodox option. When orthodoxy is too well established, another point of view can become branded as heretical even if it is in fact a speculative possibility, an adumbrated option with regard to an issue that still invites, and may even deserve, further examination. Upholders in the first category may be 'material' but not yet 'formal' heretics, since they are innocent choosers. Many of the great heresies are of course Christological and revolve around the definition, in Greek initially and later in Latin as well, of such terms as being, substance, nature, person and so forth.

The central heresies of Renaissance Neoplatonism were sandwiched uneasily between the past orthodoxies of Scholasticism and the coming orthodoxies of the Reformation, and its child, the Counter Reformation. In its entirety this Neoplatonism appeared reconcilable with orthodoxy to only a few, even though it received the support and indeed advocacy of such important champions of orthodoxy as Cardinals Cusanus and Bessarion and the approval, at least in part, of Augustinians.[1] By the many, however, it was constantly eschewed or viewed with suspicion given Plato's treatment of the community of goods and wives, of homosexuality, of reincarnation, of cyclical time, and so on. From later antiquity, moreover, the metaphysical framework that articulated the primacy of the One and the descent or emanation of being into corporeal becoming,

[1] See Dennis F. Lackner, 'The Camaldolese Academy: Ambrogio Traversari, Marsilio Ficino and the Christian Platonic Tradition', in Michael Allen and Valery Rees, with Martin Davies (eds), *Marsilio Ficino: His Theology, His Philosophy, His Legacy* (Leiden: Brill, 2002), pp. 15–44; Anthony Levi, 'Ficino, Augustine and the Pagans', ibid., pp. 99–114.

31

D. Hedley and S. Hutton (eds.), *Platonism at the Origins of Modernity: Studies on Platonism and Early Modern Philosophy*, 31–44.

material extension and, ultimately, non-being had been interpreted, because of its series of subordinations of the lower to the higher, at least potentially, as an Arian system. Marsilio Ficino, the most eminent of the Renaissance Platonists, had to exercise all his subtlety to argue that two passages at least in Plato's *Letters*, one in the second letter at 312E, the other in the sixth at 323D, were interpretable as Trinitarian in content, and only then in the elliptical and enigmatic manner of a prophet—necessarily so, since the full Trinitarian revelation was bestowed on mankind only by Christ.[2] Ficino felt entitled, that is, to read back into Plato meanings which Plato had not fully articulated himself but only seen 'through a glass darkly' in the famous metaphor of St. Paul's first epistle to the Corinthians 13:12.

Besides the Trinitarian, other heresies haunt Renaissance Neoplatonism. Most notably there is the Pelagian heresy with its insistence, central indeed to the tradition of the sage and the philosopher, the holy men of the academy, the lyceum and the stoa, that one's own moral effort can lead to mental clarity and thence to illumination; can lead, that is, to the flight of the charioteer of the soul, in the imagery of the famous mythical hymn of the *Phaedrus*, to the very rim of the intellectual heaven, thence to gaze from afar at the pure intelligibles, the Ideas in their collective splendour as the Truth. Though ancient Neoplatonism, beginning with Plotinus' successor, Iamblichus, had reintroduced the notion of mediation, of soteriology, of the importance of prayer and theurgy, of ritual and of inner emptying,[3] the true hero of Plotinus himself, the founder of Neoplatonism, is the empowered philosopher, the self-liberating mystic who embarks on the ultimate flight of the alone to the alone, in the memorable phrasing of the sixth *Ennead's* conclusion.

The positions taken by Renaissance Neoplatonists with regard to heresy are in fact complex and manifold, and predictably they depend upon whom one focuses. Take the controversial Byzantine theologian, George Gemistos Plethon, who was one of the Byzantine emperor's chief advisors and who made a great impression on the Florentines during the ecumenical council of Ferrara/Florence in 1438–1443, the abortive attempt to reconcile the Roman and Greek churches. He was probably a Neoplatonising monist but he was accused by rabid enemies of being a polytheist, and a crypto-Moslem (hardly compatible positions);[4] and he did compose and perform some remarkable hymns to the sun and light and to abstractions in imitation of the ancient Neoplatonic hymns by Proclus, Synesius

[2] See my 'Ficino's Theory of the Five Substances and the Neoplatonists' Parmenides', *Journal of Medieval & Renaissance Studies* 12 (1982), 19–44, now in *Plato's Third Eye: Studies in Marsilio Ficino's Metaphysics and Its Sources* (Aldershot: Variorum, 1995) as No. IX.

[3] Christopher Celenza, 'Late Antiquity and Florentine Platonism: the "Post-Plotinian" Ficino', in Allen and Rees, *Marsilio Ficino*, pp. 71–98.

[4] C.M. Woodhouse, *George Gemistos Plethon: The Last of the Hellenes* (Oxford: OUP, 1986); Milton Anastos, 'Pletho's Calendar and Liturgy and Pletho and Islam', *Dumbarton Oaks Papers* 4 (1948), pp. 183–305; and John Monfasani, 'Platonic Paganism in the Fifteenth Century', in his *Byzantine Scholars in Renaissance Italy: Cardinal Bessarion and Other Emigrés* (Aldershot: Variorum, 1995) as No. X, with further references.

and others. Or take Giovanni Pico della Mirandola who made his egotistical entrée into the intellectual world by inviting all comers to papal Rome to challenge his defence of 900 theses in the manner of a Parisian university debate (though it was usual in Paris to defend just one or two propositions). Included in these 900 were 13 propositions which a committee appointed by the Roman Curia found questionable and some as heterodox. Pico, headstrong, brilliant and aristocratic, rushed to a defence of these 13 propositions which the committee then condemned as unquestionably heretical. They included items that dealt with the real presence in the Mass and the magic of sacramental transformation, with the questions of whether Christ really descended into hell and whether we can truly worship the Cross, and with the role for a Christian, and specifically in Christology, of Cabala.[5] Or take as a third and final example the strange prophetic figure Giovanni 'Mercurio' da Correggio, a Platonic-Hermetist, who rode on a white ass through the streets of Rome on Palm Sunday 1484, the year of a grand conjunction between Saturn and Jupiter. Clothed in a blood-stained linen mantle and with a crown of thorns topped by a silver disc in the shape of the crescent moon, and accompanied by crowds of people bearing palm branches, he made his way first to St. John's in the Lateran and then via the Campo dei Fiori to the high altar amazingly of St. Peter's itself, urging repentance before the coming millennium, while striking a skull in a basket with a reedstaff, and proclaiming that he was the Angel of Wisdom, Pimander, the divine being who appears to the Egyptian Hermes Trismegistus, the thrice great Mercury, at the beginning of the *Corpus Hermeticum*.[6]

The Florentine Marsilio Ficino (1433–1499), however, is a particularly interesting case since he was charged late in his immensely productive scholarly and philosophical career by detractors in the Curia with resurrecting the world of the pagans, their mysteries, magic and demonology, and this despite the fact that he was a priest, a venerable canon of Florence's cathedral, and at one point a Medicean candidate for the bishopric of Cortona. For Ficino spent his

[5] See Brian P. Copenhaver, 'Number, Shape, and Meaning in Pico's Christian Cabala: The Upright *Tsade*, the Closed *Mem*, and the Gaping Jaws of Azazel', in Anthony Grafton and Nancy Siraisi (eds), *Natural Particulars: Nature and the Disciplines in Renaissance Europe* (Cambridge, MA: MIT Press, 1999), pp. 25–76. For Pico in general, see now Leonardo Quaquarelli and M.V. Dougherty, *Piciana: Bibliografia del XIX e XX secolo* (Florence: Olschki, 2007).

[6] Paul Oskar Kristeller, 'Marsilio Ficino e Lodovico Lazzarelli: Contributo alla diffuzione delle idee ermetiche nel Rinascimento', now in his *Studies in Renaissance Thought and Letters*, vol. I (Rome: Edizioni di storia e letteratura, 1956), pp. 221–247; 'Ancora per Giovanni Mercurio da Correggio', ibid., pp. 249–257; and 'Lodovico Lazzarelli e Giovanni da Correggio, due ermetici del Quattrocento e il manuscritto II. D. 4 della Biblioteca comunale degli Ardenti di Viterbo', now in his *Studies in Renaissance Thought and Letters*, vol. III (Rome: Edizioni di storia e letteratura, 1993), pp. 207–225; also David B. Ruderman, 'Giovanni Mercurio da Correggio's Appearance in Italy as Seen Through the Eyes of an Italian Jew', *Renaissance Quarterly*, 28 (1975), 309–22; and Wouter J. Hanegraaff and Ruud M. Bouthoorn, *Lodovico Lazzarelli (1447–1500): The Hermetic Writings and Related Documents* (Tempe, AZ: Arizona Center for Medieval and Renaissance Studies, 2005), with further references. In the Renaissance the first fourteen treatises of the *Corpus Hermeticum* were known collectively, following Ficino, as the *Pimander*.

whole Neoplatonising life on the very borders of heterodoxy, even though his work strikes us at first glance as massively Christian and as being in the direct line of the great Scholastics and their *summae*.[7] His magnum opus, the *Platonic Theology* (first published in 1482), is just such a *summa*, albeit a *summa platonica*; and it invokes at every turn medieval premises and argumentation, *quaestiones* and *quodlibeta*.[8] Yet, its very title also invokes the magisterial work of the fifth-century Proclus, who, though an enemy of the Christians and the last of the pagan Neoplatonists, shaped in many fundamental ways, ironically so perhaps, the later Augustinian tradition. Even Ficino's subtitle for the *Platonic Theology*, 'on the immortality of the soul', is not without its Janus faces since it looks to the title of an early treatise of Augustine and simultaneously to that of a treatise (*Enneads* 4.7) by Plotinus—Plotinus who was in Ficino's eyes almost, or in all but name, a Church Father.[9]

For all his pastoral and educational reaching out, Ficino was locked, however, into the elitism intrinsic to the notion that knowledge, a secret and difficult knowledge, a gnosis, is the key to enlightenment and therefore to salvation. But the path to gnosis, though perfected by Christ, had a distant origin, and Ficino was one of the first Renaissance authors to champion the notion of a secret, esoteric, and perennial wisdom (as Agostino Steuco would later call it) that preceded and prepared the way for Christianity as the climactic Platonic revelation. As such it paralleled the Mosaic wisdom transmitted to the Hebrews by the Pentateuch, by the secrets of the Mosaic oral tradition later inscribed in the books of the Cabala, and by the revelations of Moses' successors, the psalmists and the prophets.[10]

For symbolic and numerological reasons Ficino propounded the idea that Plato was the sixth in a succession of gentile sages, six being the sum of its integers and the product of its factors and thus, according to the arithmological tradition, the perfect number.[11] It was also the number of Jupiter, of the days of biblical creation, of the links in Homer's golden chain from which hangs the pendant world (which the Neoplatonists interpreted allegorically), and of the six primary ontological categories in the *Sophist* (essence, being, identity, alterity, rest

[7] For a lucid introduction to Ficino's non-Scholastic embrace of pagan wisdom, see James Hankins, *Plato in the Italian Renaissance*, 2 vols (Leiden: Brill, 1990), pp. 280–287; idem, 'Marsilio Ficino as a Critic of Scholasticism', *Vivens Homo* 5 (1994), 325–333, reprinted in his collection *Humanism and Platonism in the Italian Renaissance*, Volume II: *Platonism* (Rome: Edizioni di storia e letteratura, 2004), pp. 459–470.

[8] See the introduction to the new six-volume I Tatti edition and translation by James Hankins and myself (Cambridge, MA: Harvard University Press, 2001–2006)—all *Platonic Theology* references are to this edition.

[9] See H. D. Saffrey, 'Florence, 1492: The Reappearance of Plotinus', *Renaissance Quarterly* 49 (1996), 488–508; and my *Synoptic Art: Marsilio Ficino on the History of Platonic Interpretation* (Florence: Olschki, 1998), pp. 90–92.

[10] Ibid., pp. 1–49. In the following sections, I am drawing upon my Ficino entry in Wouter J. Hanegraaff (ed.), *Dictionary of Gnosis and Western Esotericism*, 2 vols. (Leiden: Brill, 2005), pp. 360–367.

[11] Allen, *Synoptic Art*, pp. 25–26.

and motion). Indeed, the hexad was such an authoritative category for charting the gentile succession of sages that Ficino had to adjust its members, since he had many more sages than slots available for them; but eventually he decided on Zoroaster, Hermes Trismegistus, Orpheus, Aglaophemus, Pythagoras and Plato. This is remarkable on several counts. It insists on the primacy of Zoroaster as effectively the first Platonist *avant le mot*, with a number of implications as we shall see. It omits such important figures as Socrates, Timaeus, Parmenides and Empedocles whose dicta Ficino often quoted as Platonic; it also omits the sibyls whose authority he accepted and in whose company he included Diotima, Socrates' teacher in the metaphysics of love.[12] And in the Neoplatonic manner, it underscores Plato's Pythagorean wisdom, a wisdom embodied in the *aurea dicta* and *symbola* which Ficino found in Iamblichus's *Life of Pythagoras*.

Let us turn, however, to Orpheus whom Ficino knew from the many fragments quoted in Plato's works and in the works of his commentators, and from the 87 *Orphic Hymns* now thought to be products of later antiquity but that he and his contemporaries believed authentic. From early on, when he first translated them, he treated these *Hymns* as sacred but dangerous texts.[13] Certainly they testified to Orpheus being the David of the gentiles, and his hymns, their pagan psalms; and they invoked the attributes of the deities they addressed in an aretology, a listing of virtues, hiding under a polytheistic rind a monotheistic core (a much revered prefatory palinode explained away the polytheism). But they also appeared to invoke demonic powers; and Ficino was careful to circulate only a few fragments in his Latin translation to his close friend, Martinus Uranius.[14] Orpheus himself, though Plato's *Symposium* 179D condemns him as faint-hearted for his refusal to die for Eurydice (etymologised as 'breadth of [the] judgment'), had been the master of incantation, the paradigmatic magus who bent the natural world to his will and whose music derived from the fundamental harmonies of the cosmos. Ficino was himself flatteringly addressed by various poet-friends as another Orpheus, and the figure of Orpheus was painted on an 'Orphic' lyre he played in his Platonic hymn recitals—apparently to great effect, since onlookers describe him as musically entranced and entrancing. At the onset of his career as a Medicean teacher and sage he seems indeed to have presided over a kind of neo-Orphic revival.[15] Orphic incantation became the key to his conception of Platonic or Platonizing poetry and, in general, of musical images and models, and the affective bearer, the perfect medium effectively of philosophy, of worship and of trance.

Nonetheless Orpheus was subordinate to the two most ancient of the sages: first to Hermes Trismegistus, whose *Pimander* (*Corpus Hermeticum*) Ficino

[12] Ibid., 24ff.

[13] Ibid., pp. 98–100.

[14] See my 'Summoning Plotinus: Ficino, Smoke, and the Strangled Chickens', in Mario A. Di Cesare (ed.), *Reconsidering the Renaissance: Papers from the Twenty-Sixth Annual Conference of the Center for Medieval and Early Renaissance Studies* (Binghamton, NY: MRTS, 1992), pp. 63–88 at 73–74, now in *Plato's Third Eye* as No. XIV.

[15] Ibid., pp. 82–86.

continually cited and whose *Asclepius* he knew from the Latin translation attributed to Apuleius, as well as from hostile notices in Augustine and more sympathetic ones in Lactantius. However, while Hermes' personal authority remained intact, Ficino retained a guarded approach to Egypt's religious tradition. This may have been partly because Egypt appears in the Bible as the land of exile even though Moses could have taught or been taught by the Egyptian priests (and here determining whether Hermes was coeval with Moses or succeeded him was critical, though Ficino never entertained a later view that Hermes preceded Moses!). Egypt was also known, however, for its zoomorphic deities and pagan rites, and Hermes had devised a sacred, hieroglyphic alphabet utilizing animals, birds and plants to convey his wisdom.[16] The strange little myth of Theuth and Ammon in Plato's *Phaedrus* 274B ff may have played a decisive role here; for it portrays Ammon (Jupiter) rebuking Theuth (identified with Hermes) for inventing writing and thereby opening up the possibility of debasing or profaning teachings that should only be transmitted orally, in the fullness of time, by a master who has properly prepared his disciples for their reception and comprehension. An apotropaic story also attributed to Pythagoras, it created a dilemma for a committed interpreter such as Ficino, who was faced with voluminous texts of, and commentaries on, a wisdom that from the outset he felt impelled to explain to everyone and yet considered sacred, and thus needing protection from the eyes of the vulgar. It set private, esoteric teaching steadfastly against public exposition, and so went to the very heart of his commitment to educating and converting the elite, the *ingeniosi* of Florence.[17]

Prior even to Hermes, however, was Zoroaster. Ficino must have derived this notion in the first instance from Pletho. But he was also following the odd sympathetic references to Zoroaster in Plato's works, notably in the *First Alcibiades* 121E ff, and in the works of such Platonising thinkers as Plutarch. He was responding too to the authority of the *Chaldaean Oracles*, a late antique compilation, which he and others deemed authentically Zoroastrian and whose derivative and eclectic Middle Platonism was therefore assumed to be the original Platonism.[18] For Ficino, however, Zoroaster's primacy was pre-eminently something that highlighted the centrality of the Epiphany and the Magi.[19] The three wise Chaldaeans who had come from the East, following a star, were the followers of Zoroaster, whose very name in Greek has the word 'star' in it, and who was supposedly the founder of both astronomy/astrology and the magic associated with it. Thus they symbolised the coming of the ancient wisdom to the cradle

[16] Allen, *Synoptic Art*, pp. 26–31, 35.

[17] Ibid., pp. 17–24.

[18] For the status and history the *Chaldaean Oracles* for Ficino and his contemporaries, see Karl H. Dannenfeldt, 'The Pseudo-Zoroastrian Oracles in the Renaissance', *Studies in the Renaissance* 4 (1957), 7–30; also his 'Hermetica Philosophica' and 'Oracula Chaldaica' in Paul Oskar Kristeller, *Cataloguus Translationum et Commentariorum*, vol. 1, (Washington DC: Catholic University of America Press, 1960), pp. 137–151, 157–164.

[19] Allen, *Synoptic Art*, pp. 31–41.

of a new philosopher-king-magus: the new Zoroaster. Moreover, having set out from the very land from which Abraham had first departed, they symbolised the reunion of the two ancient branches of wisdom, the Hebrew and the Zoroastrian, stemming from Noah's sons (since the Ark had come to rest allegedly in a province of Persia—and Persia, Chaldaea and Babylon were often confused). Insofar as Zoroaster was also, in Ficino's view,[20] the discoverer of writing, since he used the stars and constellations, and not animals, birds, and plants, as the 'letters' of his sacred alphabet, he was, in a way, the sage who had transcribed the wisdom of the stars and had brought the stars into men's language, indeed had taught men to write with the stars. Hence, the Magi were primarily astronomer–astrologers and practitioners of a star-based magic, whose knowledge of the heavens had enabled them to follow a star, or rather for Ficino a comet,[21] and to find the Christ child in order to worship him as the Lord of the stars and constellations, the Zoroastrian sage, the supreme Platonic guardian in Bethlehem.[22] Thus, to Plato's Pythagorean, Orphic and Hermetic predecessors, we should add Zoroaster as the original *priscus theologus*, the founder of the ancient gentile wisdom that Ficino himself was dedicated to reconciling with the theology of Abraham as perfected in Christ.

The history of gnosis after Plato was also subject to revision by Ficino, since he believed that the Proclus-inspired writings nowadays attributed to the Pseudo-Dionysius of the late fifth century had been composed by the Dionysius mentioned in Acts 17:34 as an Athenian converted by St. Paul's preaching on the Areopagus, in other words by a thinker of the first century.[23] Since one of the Dionysian treatises is a masterpiece of a negative theology inspired by the second part of Plato's *Parmenides* as interpreted by Plutarch of Athens, Syrianus and Proclus, this had the effect of transferring the fully fledged late Neoplatonism of Proclus back to the time immediately following the Ascension. Suddenly the opening of St. John's Gospel, the epistles of St. Paul, and the Pseudo-Areopagitian treatises all coalesced to form an impressive body of Christian–Platonic writing, a body that indeed signified the perfection of the Platonic wisdom in the Christian revelation, though it was articulated anachronistically in terms of Proclan metaphysics and its host of distinctions and subdivisions.[24] Given the centrality of the *via negativa*, moreover, it had the effect of foregrounding Platonic dialectics as a mystical rather than a logical instrument, and thus of transforming the old Socratic scepticism or agnosticism into a kind of super- or supra-gnosis.[25]

[20] In his *Philebus Commentary* 1.29 Allen (ed.), p. 271.

[21] See his sermon on the *Stella Magorum* in his *Opera Omnia* (Basel: Heinrich Petri, 1576) pp. 489–491.

[22] Allen, *Synoptic Art*, pp. 37–38.

[23] For an introduction to the situation in fifteenth-century Italy, see John Monfasani, 'Pseudo-Dionysius the Areopagite in Mid-Quattrocento Rome', now in his *Language and Learning in Renaissance Italy* (Aldershot: Variorum, 1994), as No. X.

[24] Allen, *Synoptic Art*, pp. 67–72.

[25] Ibid., pp. 187–190.

This pivotal pre-dating of the Pseudo-Dionysius in turn impacted Ficino's perspective on the centuries we now assign to the Middle Platonists, and led him to embrace the notion that the Ammonius Saccas who was Plotinus' teacher had been a Christian Platonist, and that the Origen whom Porphyry mentions as Plotinus' fellow disciple was the Christian heresiarch, author of the *De principiis* and *Contra Celsum*.[26] Consequently, Plotinus emerges as a Christianised Platonist, if not as a Christian. This was all-defining given the centrality of the *Enneads* in Ficino's own understanding of Plato, and his belief that Plotinus was Plato's beloved intellectual son 'in whom'—thus Ficino imagines Plato using the very words used by God according to the Gospels—'I am well pleased'.[27] Ficino's supreme scholarly achievement indeed was to render the 54 treatises of Plotinus into Latin, and to devote his interpretational life to arguing that Plotinian and Christian metaphysics were almost one and the same: that Plotinus had written a *summa platonica* just as Aquinas would later write a *summa theologica*. Moreover, succumbing to a temptation common to many historians and interpreters, Ficino read most of Proclus' subtle distinctions back into Plotinus too, and thence into Plato, the *Hermetica*, the *Orphic Hymns* and the *Oracula Chaldaica*, thus creating an ancient Platonic, but in effect an heretical Proclan, theology that had begun with Zoroaster but had been perfected in the works of Plato, of the Christian Dionysius, and the crypto-Christian Plotinus. Finally, since so much of Proclus's metaphysics had become incorporated into medieval theology by way of the Pseudo-Areopagitian writings—and, indeed, had become embedded in the Augustinian mystical traditions of the Middle Ages—Ficino was able to argue with conviction that the time was ripe for a Christian–Platonic revival that would unite wisdom and faith, philosophy and revelation, as they had once been united in the golden age,[28] the pre-Noachian time of Enoch himself who had walked with God. Interestingly, this whole fabric is built on some fundamental mistakes in attribution and dating; but they were mistakes that the vast majority of Ficino's learned contemporaries also shared. Accordingly, Ficino was able first to present a Neoplatonic view of the history of philosophy and of Christianity, and then to propel that history back into the remotest past, into the time recorded in Genesis itself.

Ficino was also familiar with a number of medical, pharmacological and medical-astrological texts, some of them of Arabic provenance, that formed part of his intellectual training as a doctor—a role he never abandoned, since he regarded himself, in the Socratic sense, as a doctor of souls, a *medicus* even to the Medici. Many of these were pregnant with heresies. His adventurous *De vita libri tres* of 1489 in particular provoked a Curial investigation, though it was called off. It is a treatise in three books on regimen, diet, abstinence, salves, beneficent powders and sprays, aromas, psychosomatic exercises, meditation and mood-elevation

[26] Ibid., pp. 68–74.

[27] In the closing exhortation of his preface to his Plotinus Commentary, *Opera*, p. 1548.1.

[28] Hankins, *Plato in the Italian Renaissance*, pp. 289–291.

techniques and astrological and demonological attuning.[29] The third book, however, entitled *De vita coelitus comparanda* ('On bringing one's life into harmony with the heavens'), is a rich and complex exploration of scholarly melancholy, holistic medicine, psychiatry and demonology. It makes continual reference to zodiacal and planetary influences, to stellar oppositions and conjunctions, to astrological election, to the theory of universal sympathies and to synastry, the assumption that particular people who are born under the same planet, under the same astral configurations and under the same higher demons, are therefore star twins. Additionally, Ficino treats of the therapeutic powers of talismans and amulets when properly made and inscribed; but he is careful to draw both upon scholastic notions of acquired form and the hylomorphic structuring of corporeal and (contra Aquinas) incorporeal entities,[30] and upon the Galenic and subsequently medieval notions of the vital, vegetable and animal spirits that can be refined, like sugar, into the pure spirit. The spirit's health is the goal of all the various interlocking therapies, since the body will be well, that is, perfectly tempered, if the *spiritus* is well. But this is a troubling because ambivalent concept: (a) because it attempts to mediate between the intelligible and sensible worlds as the ultimate copula, and (b) because it has a rich set of occult and magical associations.[31]

Ficino sees this spirit both as an image of the soul (like the meteor's tail) and as an envelope, vehicle or aethereal quasi-soul quasi-body linking soul to body, or rather animating body or corporealizing soul. It functions as the soul's chariot, first as the 'body' in which we endure the cleansing purgatorial fires, and then as the 'glorified body' of the resurrection and of entry into paradise. Ficino believed that Zoroaster had been referring to this spirit or pneuma in such Chaldaean oracles as no. 104, which exhorts us not to add depth (that is, three-dimensional corporeality) to what is plane (that is, to the planar two-dimensional spirit); and no. 158, which asserts that even the pneuma (*idolum*) will be with us 'in the region of utmost clarity',[32] with the implication for Ficino that Zoroaster is affirming the resurrection of the glorified body.[33]

Governing the amulets, talismans, salves and drugs, and the aethereal spirit alike are the astrological powers and influences, ever-changing in their dance; and governing these in turn are the musical consonances and harmonies that rule the

[29] It has been well edited and translated by Carol V. Kaske and John R. Clark (Binghamton, NY: MRTS, 1989).

[30] Brian P. Copenhaver, 'Scholastic Philosophy and Renaissance Magic in the *De vita* of Marsilio Ficino', *Renaissance Quarterly* 37 (1984), 523–554.

[31] See the various papers in Marta Fattori and Massimo Bianchi (eds), *Spiritus: IV° Colloquio internazionale del lessico intellettuale europeo* (Roma, 7–9 gennaio 1983) (Rome, 1984).

[32] Brian P. Copenhaver, 'Iamblichus, Synesius and the *Chaldaean Oracles* in Marsilio Ficino's *De vita libri tres*: Hermetic Magic or Neoplatonic Magic', in James Hankins, John Monfasani, and Frederick Purnell Jr. (ed.), *Supplementum Festivum: Studies in Honor of Paul Oskar Kristeller* (Binghamton, NY: MRTS, 1987), pp. 441–455.

[33] See my 'Marsilio Ficino, Levitation, and the Ascent to Capricorn', in Bruno Pinchard and Pierre Servet (eds), *Education, Transmission, Rénovation à la Renaissance* (Geneva: Droz, 2006), pp. 223–240 and especially pp. 232–236.

universe. Plato had described these in the *Timaeus*, in a famous passage at 35B ff. (cf. 43D ff.) on the two quaternaries of 1–2–4–8 and 1–3–9–27 (traditionally seen as a Greek *lambda*) used by his Demiurge to create the mathematical-musical structure of the World-Soul, both Demiurge and World-Soul being difficult to integrate as concepts into Christian creationism. This Soul itself, in Ficino's speculative view, animated a World-Spirit that mediated between it and the World-Body; and to this World-Spirit our own spirit was originally attuned, or rather tuned literally to the point of vibrating with it like a violin string. An integral part of the healer's training therefore consisted in learning to understand a complex pneumatology with reference both to the cosmos (the great man, according to the famous Macrobian phrase), and to the human being, the little world. Indeed, rather than being a soul chained to or entombed in a body, according to the hallowed Platonic and Christian images, man is to be identified here with his spirit in this non-Pauline, quasi-physical or medical sense: a spirit imaged as a talismanic inscription, an airy powder, an attar of roses, a musical chord, a diffused light, a planetary ray even, and subject to the influences of salves, songs, spells, incantations and prayers. Ficino often responds to this world of 'spiritual' therapies in fact not as a realm of insidious evil or of base matter but as a bountiful pharmacopoeia of lenitives and cures, a musical, a magical *concordia discors*.

Other ancient or medieval texts Ficino studied carefully treat of aspects of arithmosophy and arithmology (Theon of Smyrna), oneirology (Synesius), angelology and demonology (Porphyry, Proclus and Psellus), and the occult (Iamblichus), all of which raise heretical issues or call at least upon ambiguous terms and metaphors. Iamblichus in particular was an authority whom Ficino encountered at the onset of his Platonic studies; and among his first attempts at translating philosophical Greek were the four Iamblichian treatises that constitute a kind of Pythagorean handbook, dealing with Pythagoras' life and with various mathematical and numerological issues. The *De Mysteriis* probably served as his basic introduction to occult lore and to the notion of theurgy, of god-making, that is, converting oneself and others—even wood, clay and stone statues—into gods.[34]

While he identified the highest order or chorus of demons in ancient theology with the angels of Christianity, he also inherited a hierarchy of lower orders of demons who were principally beneficent spirits caring for the earth. Said by Hesiod to be 30,000 in number, they were divided into as many legions as there are stars in the night sky and with as many individual demons again in each legion, and were ruled by the 12 princes in the 12 zodiacal signs.[35] By virtue of their intermediate nature between the gods and men, they dwelt in the intermediate zone of the air, particularly of the upper or fiery region of air often identified with the aether; and their mandate embraced the airy realm of sleep and the production of omens, oracles and portentous dreams. Essentially airy

[34] Celenza, 'Late Antiquity', pp. 77–80, 94–97.

[35] Ficino, *Platonic Theology* 4.1.15.

beings, though they could be found throughout elemental creation, the good demons were called by the ancients 'genii', writes Ficino, because 'they were the tireless leaders of men's ingeniousness', being 'agile in their motion, perspicacious in their sense, and endowed with a marvellous knowledge of things'.[36] They were apportioned and linked to the seven Ptolemaic planets, and assigned the guardianship and ministration of lunar, venerean, mercurial, solar, martian, jovian and saturnian entities (collective or individual) such as kingdoms, institutions, homes, places, people, animals, plants, and stones. The Jews, for instance, along with melancholics, were supposedly saturnian; all scribes, keen-scented dogs and the city of Hermopolis were mercurial; Socrates, lions and cockerels were solar; and so on. Their airy nature meant they were particularly sensitive to aromas, mists, fumes and smokes. Thus the fumigation instructions accompanying many of the *Orphic Hymns*, quite apart from having other invocatory dimensions, would make the chanting of such hymns attractive to the class of demons attending the deity who was the subject of the hymn, since they could materialise, if only momentarily, in the wafts of burning aromatics ascending from the thuribels, hearths, altars or lamps used for igniting fumigants. A solar demon for instance would be drawn to the eighth *Hymn to Helios*, which was sung to the smoke of incense and manna; and a jovian demon would be drawn to the nineteenth *Hymn to Zeus the Thunderer* sung to the smoke of styrax (while some of the hymns have identical fumigant instructions, the majority prescribe 'aromatics' generally, and some lack any instructions at all).[37]

However, as creatures essentially of light, the beneficent demons were most drawn to, and acted as, mediums of, light: light scintillating from the faceting of gems and crystals, reflecting from pools and mirrors (natural or man made), refracting through lenses, beaming from lamps and lanterns, haloing clouds and in shimmering mirages. Indeed the entire realm of optics was theirs, and necessarily so, given that Ficino thought of light as in some ways the spirit, or as linked to the spirit, of the natural world, its source being in the sun but its essence radiating through the length and breadth of the cosmos as life itself, as visible animation. In the *Platonic Theology* 8.13.1, citing the followers of both Orpheus and Heraclitus, Ficino actually calls light 'visible soul' and soul 'invisible light'. Hence, the importance for him of Zoroastrian and Hermetic light worship or of light in worship; and the haunting significances too of the reference to God in St. James' Epistle 1:17 as 'the father of lights' and of the noonday setting with the stridulating cicadas of Plato's *Phaedrus*. These harmonising insects Ficino identified with demons, in the particular sense now of men who had entered, after philosophising for the requisite three millennia, a quasi-immaterial, light-filled, demonic condition, being ruled entirely by their intelligences and about to repossess their glorified spirit–star bodies as their envelopes or vehicles.[38]

[36] Ibid., 16.7.17–18, 18.10.3.

[37] Allen, 'Summoning Plotinus' passim.

[38] In his *Phaedrus* Commentary summa 35 Allen (ed.), pp. 192–197.

All light demons, whether erstwhile philosophers or planetary spirits, were benevolent, intellectual, even musical presences, higher pneuma-borne souls whom we will ultimately accompany in the universal cavalcade Jupiter leads across the intellectual heaven, thence to gaze from afar at the intelligible beings, the Ideas in their collectivity as both the unfolding or radiance of Beauty, and the enfolding or incandescence of Truth.[39]

This demonological world is not confined, furthermore, to aromatic, musical or intellectual invocation in hymns or prayers at such threshold times as dawn, noonday, and dusk. For Ficino was also fascinated by ancient *idolum* theory. On the one hand, he could look to the materialist view, articulated most memorably by Lucretius that effluvia or material images, idola, emanated from all objects, and were seen most obviously in mirrors (hence, the Aristotelian story that mirrors bled in the presence of menstruating women).[40] On the other hand, he could look to the enigmatic references in Plotinus, Proclus, the *Orphica* and the *Chaldaean Oracles*, to the idolum as the densest and most visible form of the spiritual body, to its being in some respects the shadow self or the other residual self. Plotinus' references to Homer's account of the shade, the idolum, of Hercules in the *Enneads* 1.1.12 and 4.3.27 were especially notable since they pointed to his readers' own demonic duality, their condition not so much as souls tied to bodies, but as higher souls tied to lower secondary souls, that is to say, to images or reflections of themselves. Life was seen now as the Platonic mirror, however distorting, to which Socrates alludes in the *Republic* 596DE when he speaks of the sophistical or 'easy way' in which the created world might be reproduced catoptrically:

> You could do it most quickly if you should choose to take a mirror and carry it about everywhere. You will speedily produce the sun and all the things in the sky, the earth and yourself and the other animals.

Following Plotinus, Ficino interpreted this as an enigmatic reference to the World Body as it reflects the idolum of the World Soul, an idolum that is in turn identified with the twice-born Dionysus, lord of ecstasy and dance. Optics, accordingly, and its accompanying plane geometry, and especially—given the section 53C–55C in the *Timaeus*—the geometry of right triangles and the Pythagorean theorem that determines the squares and square-roots, the 'powers' of their sides, became the key to understanding the nature of our reflected, catoptric demi-lives as Dionysian images tied to images, to idola and effluvia. It also became the key to understanding the demons and, by implication, our own ascending, philosophical, Apollonian selves, as beings who can pass like Alice through the terpsichorean illusions of the mirror plane into the world of intellectual, of uranian light.

39 Ibid., Chapter 11.

40 See his *Sophist* Commentary summa 46 Allen (ed.), pp. 270–277; also his *De amore* 7.4 Marcel (ed.), p. 247 and his notes from the twelfth treatise of Proclus' *Republic* Commentary (*Opera*, pp. 941–942), with a reference to Aristotle's *On Dreams* 2.459b27 ff.

In such an ascent, man will again become the Hermetic and Orphic 'spark', the 'colleague' of a star that we once were, before our precipitation from Cancer, the Moon's constellation and 'the gate of mortals', down through the nest of planetary spheres.[41] As man ascends again towards Capricorn, Saturn's constellation and 'the gate of the gods', he assumes the demonic, stellar, luminous body that is eternally his, and that Zoroaster had assumed when he devised an astral 'alphabet'. For man, so Ficino writes in a generic letter to the human race, is an earthly star enveloped in a cloud, while a star is a heavenly man.[42]

Ficino was voyaging through the straits of unorthodoxy out into the open seas of the ancient Gnostic heresies, including Manicheanism, which had been attacked by various Church Fathers, pre-eminently Augustine, and interestingly by Plotinus before him, Ficino's greatest Platonic authority next to Plato himself. That such esoteric and magical speculations did not land him in serious trouble is a measure both of his personal diplomacy (testifying to his commitment to accommodation) and of the authority and weight of his other philosophical and theological works. A century later Giordano Bruno was burned at the stake for notions that were no more revolutionary. Ficino bequeaths us both the venerable Christian emblem of man as *viator* and such pagan emblems of him as a cicada, an Orpheus with his lyre strung to the planetary modes, a Hermetic talisman or seal, a Zoroastrian magus, a spark struck from the flint of dionysian matter, a starry charioteer in a *biga* or *quadriga*. For his audacious attempt to reconcile Platonism with Christianity in the event went far beyond Platonism: it became a life-long ecumenical quest to introduce into orthodoxy an encyclopedic range of unorthodox spiritual, magical, and occult beliefs keyed to the theme of the soul's ascent from the cave of illusion, and keyed too to what was always a fundamentally Plotinian search for the 'flower' in the mind, the oneness that is for him the object of intellectual and of spiritual ascent.

This meditative ideal, a strange blend of Plotinian and Proclan metaphysics and Iamblichan daemonism, has now been completely lost to Christianity and one might well argue that Ficino's whole Platonic endeavour was heretical. Its goals after all were to become a sage not a saint, a magus not a worshipper, a choiring angel not a sinner praying for forgiveness; and accordingly to achieve the ascent from human depth into daemonic and spiritual planarity, a corporeal levitation even from the void of darkness into the purity, into the mystical 'glory' of light.[43] For Ficino, predictably, one of its most important consequences was to draw our attention to Christ's Transfiguration on Mt. Tabor, as recounted by Matthew 17.1–9 and Mark 9.2–9, as the supreme Platonic moment in the Christian New Testament.[44] For his transfiguration on that 'high mountain', when 'his face

[41] Ficino, *Platonic Theology* 18.5.2, citing Macrobius, *In Somnium Scipionis* 1.12.1–2 (ed. Willis); also his letter to Lorenzo in the tenth book of his *Letters* (*Opera*, p. 917.1). See Allen, 'Marsilio Ficino, Levitation', pp. 224, 227 and 239.

[42] Ficino, *Opera*, p. 659.

[43] Ficino, *Platonic Theology* 13.4.15 analyzed in Allen, 'Marsilio Ficino, Levitation', pp. 232 236.

[44] Allen, 'Marsilio Ficino, Levitation', pp. 239–230.

did shine as the sun, and his raiment was white as the light' and when Moses and Elias appeared with him, offers us the hope of our own transfiguration, of our eventual return via saturnian Capricorn, the sign of contemplation, into the world, not just of the stars, but of light itself, whence originally we descended into the ever darkening, sublunar realms of generation and the elements. By that very token, however, Ficino also bears witness both to dimensions of the Christian experience quite other than those that are currently fashionable or even imaginable,[45] and to the insistent call of an intellect-based philosophy that we must live in order to understand and understand in order to believe, and not, as in Anselm's famous dictum, the reverse.

[45] For an interesting but very different view, see James Hankins, 'Religion and the Modernity of Renaissance Humanism', in Angelo Mazzocco (ed.), *Interpretations of Renaissance Humanism* (Leiden: Brill, 2006), pp. 137–153.

13

SENDING ARCHEDEMUS: FICINO, PLATO'S SECOND LETTER, AND ITS FOUR EPISTOLARY MYSTERIES

Though now relegated to the status of being a spurious, or at best, a dubious text of Plato's, the *Second Letter* has had a distinguished history,[1] particularly and predictably so among the ancient Neoplatonists and those they inspired in the Renaissance.[2] Most notably Plotinus's *Enneads* invoke its enigma at 312DE three times (1.8.2, 5.1.8, 6.7.42); and Proclus glosses it in detail in his *Theologia platonica* 2.8-9, as does Marsilio Ficino, their Florentine disciple, on several occasions. For a mere letter it has made a signal contribution and this in itself should give us pause: perhaps our whole notion of a letter as a medium for philosophical formulation is in need of some revision, and particularly when we recall the extraordinary contributions in antiquity of St. Paul's and Seneca's letters (real and spurious) and in the Quattrocento of Ficino's letters, not to mention those of Leibniz and of many other thinkers subsequently.

This paper dedicated to Eckhard, our distinguished peripatetic colleague and friend, is going to examine Ficino's introduction (*argumentum*) for his translation of Plato's *Second Letter*. There are several reasons it deserves our scrutiny: first it not only takes up the most famous enigma in the canon (or certainly one of the most famous), but also identifies three other enigmas or mysteries in the same letter. Next it provides us in the process with four

1 Scholars now seem agreed on its inauthenticity; see Norman Gulley, "The Authenticity of the Platonic Epistles," in *Pseudepigrapha* 1, Entretiens sur l'antiquité classique 18 (Vandoeuvres-Geneva, 1972), pp. 103-143; and Luc Brisson, *Platon: Les Lettres* (Paris: Flammarion, 1987), introduction. Even so, some have pointed to its being a valuable witness to the ancient context, e.g. J. Stannard, "Plato, Epistle II, 312A," *Phronesis* 5 (1960), 53-55; R. S. Bluck, "The Second Platonic Epistle," ibid., 140-151; and J. M. Rist who has argued for its Neopythagorean origins, "Neopythagoreanism and 'Plato's' Second Letter," *Phronesis* 10 (1965), 78-81. In the past some distinguished scholars have argued for its authenticity, e.g. L. A. Post, "The Date of the Second Platonic Epistle," *The Classical Review* 41.2 (1927), 58-59. The Quattrocento bore witness to the same debate. Among those who translated some, or in Ficino's case all, of Plato into Latin, Leonardo Bruni thought it and the other letters genuine, holding them in greater esteem than the dialogues because "they were far from irony and phantasy (*figmentum*)"; Ficino thought it genuine (even as he ascribed the first and fifth of the other letters to Dion); while Pier Candido Decembrio thought it and all the other letters false. See Edgar Wind, *Pagan Mysteries in the Renaissance* 2nd rev. ed. (New York: Norton, 1968), pp. 2-3.

2 For its lustrous Neoplatonic history, see the long introductory section in the second volume of H. D. Saffrey & L. G. Westerink's splendid six volume edition of Proclus' *Theologia Platonica* (Paris: Belles Lettres, 1968-1997), pp. xx-lix, with an array of further references.

perfect instances of Neoplatonic interpretative over-reading, long sanctioned though that over-reading may be, and is therefore methodologically interesting. And thirdly it underscores Ficino's twin beliefs that only in the *Letters* and the *Laws* was Plato speaking *in propria persona*, rather than through the mouths of Socrates or of a Pythagorean such as Parmenides or Melissus; and that only in these texts of his old age was he sanctioning what he had to say about matters divine.[3]

The argumentum would seem to have a straightforward function. Ficino wrote it as an epitome of the letter as it appeared in his great Latin translation of Plato, the 1484 *Platonis Opera Omnia* volume; and it is in line with all his epitomes for the dialogues and other letters. It is therefore meant to be a prefatory essay for the general learned public and not the occasion for an abstruse or speculative scholarly analysis, or for pleading a difficult special case or exploring a recondite methodology or hermeneutics. None the less, he managed to cull a tetrad of mysteries (and one cannot dismiss the possibility of there being an evangelistic or a numerological significance to this) from what would at first sight appear to be just a covering letter which Plato had sent, along with a defective orrery, to Dionysius the Younger, ruler of Sicily, by way of Archedemus, a Pythagorean disciple of Archytas of Tarentum,[4] who was to act as the intermediary.

***

The first mystery concerns the complementary relationship, the interdependence even, of wisdom — and hence of the *vita contemplativa* — and of power — and hence of the *vita active* — the interdependence in other words of the philosopher and the ruler. For "immense power seeks out wisdom with a natural instinct, and wisdom in turn seeks out power so that they may consort together [310E]." In the very beginning, Ficino argues, God's measureless wisdom accompanied His infinite power; and Plato recognized this. Witness his decision here to link together the names of Jupiter and Prometheus [311B], Jupiter being power, and Prometheus being the wisdom that underlies God's providence.[5] Plato argues that "the fountain of divine understanding" has power as its reflecting mirror image. Having the power to understand, it does understand, and in understanding it understands the power

3 See the preface to his Plato translation, *Opera*, p. 766.2, and his *Platonic Theology* 17.4.14, and on the Eleatics as Pythagoreans 17.4. 4, 10 (ed. and tr. in six volumes by Michael J. B. Allen & James Hankins, Cambridge, Mass: Harvard University Press, 2001-2006). See also Allen, "Marsilio Ficino on Plato's Pythagorean Eye," *Modern Language Notes* 97 (1982), 174-175, now in *Plato's Third Eye: Studies in Marsilio Ficino's Metaphysics and Its Sources* (Aldershot: Variorum, 1995) as No. VII.

4 Archytas was the recipient, incidentally, of the ninth and twelfth Platonic letters.

5 Ficino has already linked them together in his *Philebus* Commentary 26 (ed. Allen, Berkeley, 1975, pp. 240-247).

it has to understand. We find a like union in nature; for with all compounded things — whether it be stones, metals, plants, animals or the celestial spheres themselves — philosophers agree that "from the innermost power of nature a certain order proceeds, and it does so with a natural vigour."[6] The order is witnessed both in the forms themselves of these natural objects and in their actions and effects, where, as an external order accompanying "the internal force of power," it seems to manifest "a kind of wisdom." For wisdom governs all the progressions of nature, and establishes an order in them. Finally in human art too, whether private or public, there seems, says Ficino, to be a like coming together (*congressus*) of power and of wisdom. For the natural virtue or capacity innate in our natural intelligence (*ingenium*), memory, and will pertains to power; from this arises the wisdom we acquire; and this in turn results in the ordering itself of actions which pertain to wisdom.

Plato provides Ficino with examples of this first mystery as we initially encounter it in patrician social intercourse,[7] that is, in the mutual companionship (*in mutua familiaritate*) of the powerful and the wise, and in the practical necessity, as it were, of their natural union or linkage. For the very heavens alert us to the mystery insofar as God has set the ruler planets closest to the wise planets: Jupiter is next to Saturn, and the Sun never departs from Mercury or barely so. Hence Ficino sees Plato enunciating in effect a moral precept or *sententia*: "Princes should honour the wise, and the wise should gladly deliberate with princes." For wisdom without power only profits a few, and power divorced from wisdom actually brings injury to the many. Indeed, "the more power functions without wisdom the more pernicious it is, whereas wisdom apart from power seems impaired or crippled."[8] The grand conjunctions of the planets Saturn and Jupiter are especially instructive here. For Jupiter is the ruler or lord, but Saturn, the philosopher. However, "unless they are in conjunction, they occasion nothing great or lasting" on their own.[9] To bring the powerful man and the wise man together produces a happy conjunction. But the happiest of all conjunctions is when power and wisdom are conjoined in the same rational soul. For sitting in that soul is the very divinity of Pallas Athene who in herself unites power with wisdom. For Pallas alone both understands the arts, writes Ficino, being the goddess of wisdom,

6 "ut ex intima naturae potentia naturalique vigore procedat ordo quidam" (*Ficini Opera Omnia*, Basel, 1576, p. 1530).

7 Ficino refers to it with the phrase *in consuetudine eleganti* [310E].

8 "Potentia quidem expers sapientiae quo maior est eo perniciosior, sapientia vero procul a potential manca videtur" (*Opera*, p. 1530.)

9 Such a conjunction of Saturn and Jupiter occurred in 1484, and Ficino delayed publication of his Plato edition to that year in order to take astrological advantage of the possibility of uniting power and wisdom, the wisdom of his reviving Plato and the power of the princes who were in a position to initiate and expedite it.

and at the same time brandishes a spear in her capacity as the martial goddess of governance and rule.[10]

In sum, Ficino has elaborated on 310E-311B, and more particularly on Plato's observation at 310E that "It is natural for wisdom and great power to come together, and they are for ever pursuing and seeking each other, and consorting together." But why does he regard this as a mystery? Fundamentally it is because he sees Plato referring, albeit cryptically, to the basic metaphysical, or what for him is the basic theological, principle governing the very notion of understanding, which is triadic and which governs the relationship of power and understanding in God, in nature, and in men. This is seen at its most profound in God who perpetually exercises His power to understand and understands His power to understand. This self-reflecting Augustinian argument enables Ficino to subordinate the binary Aristotelian distinction between potentiality and act, and to refer instead to the Neoplatonic "mystery" of the endless procession or emanation of essence into power, thence into understanding, and finally into the dual understanding of both essence and of the power itself to understand essence. This is a divine or transcendent version of the triad resulting from the combination of two fundamental Neoplatonic triads: the triad of procession, rapture (or conversion), and return, and that of being, life, and intellect. This threefold combination poses of course a number of problems, but it has obvious Trinitarian implications, and, for a Christian, a Trinitarian validation.[11] Significantly, it is the first "mystery" referred to in the letter and it gives rise to the remainder of the analysis where Ficino exhorts the powerful to recognize their role in the triadic cosmic and social structure and to play their part in what is the "processing" phase of it, even as the philosopher must enact his part in the "converting" phase, in order that individuals, that society, that nature itself may return to the One, to God who forever is and proceeds from and returns to Himself.

***

In a passage that Ficino identifies as the second mystery [311B-D], Plato simply adverts to the fact that "the most slavish" men have no regard for their posthumous reputations, whereas "the most upright do all they can to ensure that they will be well spoken of in the future," and then adding as a proof that the dead have "some perception of things here on earth" [311C].[12]

---

[10] For other invocations of Athena, see the fable accompanying his *Philebus* Commentary (ed. Allen, pp. 468-479) and her role as Wisdom, the mother of philosophy, in his preface to his great Plato edition (*Opera*, p. 1129). See, more generally, Rudolf Wittkower, "Transformations of Minerva in Renaissance Imagery," *Journal of the Warburg Institute* 2.3 (1939), 194-205.

[11] Wind, *Pagan Mysteries*, pp. 37-41.

[12] Cf. Plato's *Menexenus* 243FC and *Apology* 40C ff.

For Ficino, however, this demands expatiation: "The soul excelling in goodness rejoices most of all in the divine, that is, in the greatest good." But such a good is what profits the most people and for the longest time; and this can only be "virtue in all its true glory," which leads men, men of later generations as well as of the present, to embrace true "doctrine" and virtuous customs and habits (*mores*). Human beings endowed "with the best genius or intelligence (*ingenio optimo*)" delight most of all in this virtue for two reasons: first "because, just as they love the inmost light of virtue, so do they also love virtue's outermost splendour," meaning, I take it, the splendour of virtuous deeds; and second because with this splendour, this exercise of external virtue, they always elect to confer some good on as many people as possible. They rejoice in leaving a lasting benefit to mankind (insofar, that is, as they can perceive the benefit). But while they study to benefit posterity and acquire "sempiternal glory" for their virtuous deeds in the future, they meanwhile hope to enjoy virtue's splendour in the present as well. They foresee that they will learn of their fame posthumously. But they "are prompted by the impulse of a diviner nature" to foresee in this way, not so much that they may rejoice in the prophecy's fulfilment now, as that they may rejoice in its future fulfilment. If many species of animals, Ficino argues, in making nests and seeking food with nature prompting them, strive to foresee the future, and do not do so in vain, so it is even less in vain that divine souls hope to enjoy a like office in eternity. And he turns to the prophet Daniel because he sees him bearing eloquent witness to the splendour and benefit of possessing such a glorious virtue both in doctrine and in moral behaviour: "The wise will shine out as the splendour of the firmament and they who teach many to be just will shine as stars for ever and ever (12.3)." Obviously in certain souls who fall away from their divinity, the desire to enjoy true glory with all its concomitant beneficence is extinguished, or else it is transmuted into a desire for vain glory.

Once again Ficino has Neoplatonized his text. At the heart of this second mystery is the notion of virtue and its radiance which is completely absent from this section of Plato's letter, and which derives from Augustinian light metaphysics that distinguishes between the radiance of pure light in itself and the splendour of that light as it is seen by others. Moreover, woven into the analysis is the central Biblical notion of a "glory" which signifies the presence of light divine in some visible form, as a halo or nimbus or aura or aureole, as the glory of the Lord that shone about the shepherds that they were sore afraid. The term is frequently applied to the visible manifestation or presence (in Hebrew *shekinah*) of God to humans,[13] and by attribution to God-inspired men. At the giving of the Law on Mt. Sinai God's glory appeared we recall as a cloud by day and as fire by night[14]; and God will appear in glory at the end

---

[13] E.g. Num. 16.19, Ps. 102:16, Ezek. 10:4; cf. 28:22, 43:2-5.
[14] Exod. 16:10, 24:16-17

of time.[15] In the New Testament, "glory" is again attributed to God[16] but also specifically to the risen Christ and his Second Coming.[17] It is the Gospel of St. John, however, which develops the notion that Jesus had glory in his human existence too, since it was God's glory that appeared in him.[18] Glory is linked to Jesus' miracles, but above all it is associated with his death and the events following upon it: witness Christ's assertion that "The hour is come that the Son of Man should be glorified" and his prayer: "Father, the hour is come: glorify thy Son that thy Son also may glorify thee."[19] Such a glory accompanied Christ's post-Easter appearances in a body that certain of his Apostles had already witnessed at the time of his Transfiguration on Mt. Tabor when he appeared with Moses and Elias, and that was to become the glorified body of the Ascension. Furthermore, these are the grounds, theologians postulate, that enable us to believe in the possibility of our own future glory, and in the resurrection of our glorified bodies at the Last Judgement. And it is a state we can experience now in that when we become wholly suffused with the light of virtue, we too will be enveloped in both an inner radiance and an outer splendour, and shine like the stars for ever and ever.

Plato's concern with a posthumous reputation for piety and good deeds has been transformed into our hope both for glory in the mystical Biblical sense of spiritual brightness, of angel-like luminosity, and for acquiring at last the glorified body of the resurrection, and more — our original ascended divinity. Daniel's verse has become the key to a mystery that no ancient Platonist could have completely unravelled; and it raises once again the issue of Plato's role as a seer, who, in the tradition of pagan seers and rhapsodes, was not in a position always to foresee the full import of what he himself was prophesying. Only a truly Christian hermeneut would be in a position to interpret the most mystical statements of Plato, or indeed of any ancient theologian, entirely and correctly: would be able, that is, to bring in the interpretative harvest of what their ancient words could mean to a later believer, regardless of what they may have originally meant to the author and his auditors.[20]

***

15 Isa. 4:5, 60:1-2.
16 Luke 2:9, John 11:40, Acts 7:55
17 Matt. 25:31, Mark 8:38; I Cor. 2:8, Heb. 2:7, 9, I Pet. 1:11, Rev. 5:12-13.
18 John 1:14, 13:31, 17:5
19 John 12:23; 17:1.
20 See Allen, *Synoptic Art: Marsilio Ficino on the History of Platonic Interpretation* (Florence: Olschki, 1998), pp. 102-107, for the problems of the reader/listener's role in determining poetic meaning and in negotiating what is now called the intentional fallacy.

The third mystery [312D-313A], which I have analyzed elsewhere in light of its anticipation of the doctrine of the Trinity,[21] has been dismissed by some modern Plato scholars as "wilful mystification."[22] But for Ficino it was even more profound, since from the 1460s, if not earlier, he knew that it had beguiled the most illustrious of the Platonic interpreters of antiquity, notably Plotinus and Proclus as we have observed; and moreover, that in his own age it had fascinated the Byzantine sage Gemistus Pletho, who had devised a Zoroastrian interpretation of it based in turn on Plutarch's *De Iside et Osiride* 46 (*Moralia* 369DE).[23]

Ficino takes up this "most sublime" mystery about the nature of "the First" with the declaration that he has already dealt with it in his *Platonic Theology* at 11.4.6-7 and 14.10.4 (though neither constitutes a detailed analysis) and in his *De Amore* 2.4 (his first and most deficient account).[24] When we diligently consider the forms made by the artificer, he argues, we gradually come to understand the reasons or rational principles why they were made; and when we understand these reasons, then through them we can approach with ease the Ideas themselves in the Artificer's mind. For at creation the Ideas had served as His exemplars and they had guided Him as He drew upon the various rational principles He needed to make the forms in nature. But as we ascend in the case of created forms themselves to their rational principles, and from these to the exemplary Ideas, so in contemplating the order of natural things, we come to know that they are beautifully compounded by the Artificer's most intricate rational principles, and therefore by the exemplary Ideas, according to the likeness of which the Artificer's reason has produced and is producing forms in the order of nature.

Thus we have three orders in the universe: the orders of forms, of reasons or rational principles, and of Ideas. The order of forms, which we perceive with the senses, derives from the World Soul, which, as the principle of motion, generates forms in matter, even as it generates different things with different rational principles and seeds. But the order of reasons is in the World Soul and derives in turn from Mind which is higher than Soul, for Soul receives its rational principles for governing things from the Ideas of Mind. Finally, the order of Ideas is in Mind and in turn derives from the immense splendour of the divine and simple Good, since God needs only one Idea of men and one Idea of goods, though subsequently these are poured into Angelic

---

21 "Marsilio Ficino on Plato, the Neoplatonists, and the Christian Doctrine of the Trinity," *Renaissance Quarterly* 37 (1984), 555-584, and esp. 571-580; now in *Plato's Third Eye* as No. IX.

22 See, for example, R. G. Bury's severe comments in his Loeb translation of the epistle (in vol. 9 of the Loeb Plato), pp. 400 and 410n.

23 Commentary on the *Chaldaean Oracles* no. 34 (ed. Brigitte Tambrun-Krasker, *Oracles chaldaïques: recension de Georges Gémiste Pléthon* [Athens: Academy of Athens, 1995], p. 19).

24 Cf. Ficino, *Platonic Theology* 4.1.25 (and note 28), which also refers to the Zoroastrian trinity and to the *Second* Letter.

Mind as various Ideas of various goods. Thus the three universal orders are led back to the three princes or fountains: the order of forms to the World Soul, the order of reasons to the Angelic Mind; and the order of Ideas to the Good. And since all are referred to the Good by way of the Ideas, Plato observes in a triple formula: a) that "around the king of all are all things," that is, around the Good itself are the Ideas, and all things through the Ideas; b) that "around the second," that is, Mind, "are the second things," that is, the rational principles which follow the Ideas; and c) that "around the third are the third things," that is, around the World Soul are the forms. But Plato signified that God is the universal exemplary cause when he spoke of things being "around" (*peri*) God; likewise that God is the final cause when Plato said "for His sake" (*heneka* 312E); and that God was the efficient cause when Plato added "He is the cause of all beautiful things." For though some things are ugly or ill-formed (*deformis*), their *deformitas* derives, not from their being derived from God, but from their having degenerated from Him.

Though Plato has named each of these three principles, and though he has named each of them in a similar way, Ficino observes, he does not hold that they are equal. God Himself exists as one and good through Himself; and since unity and goodness are comprehensive attributes, are "most ample" that is, it follows that God exists entirely in and through Himself. Mind, which is second to God as the First, exists through God to the extent it is one and good; but Mind also exists through itself insofar as it is Mind and is thus the order of "the second nature." Finally the World Soul is triply "produced": it is produced by God insofar as it is one and good; it is produced by Mind too which is next after God insofar as it is or has mind; but it is produced by itself insofar as it mobile in and through itself. Up to this point Plato has spoken about the origins of divine things and about the procession of the universal principles. For Ficino, however, Plato goes on to say that our human soul is divine when it aspires to things divine; but when it yearns for those things which are alien to itself, that is, for the senses and sensibles and the forms of their objects, forms conceived by the soul, then it does not comprehend the True. For such sensibles are completely contrary to the divine, and in attending to them the soul is compelled both to see and to declare false or misleading things about the divine.

Again, the mystery Ficino discovers here is theological and metaphysical. He takes the famous enigma and from it derives Plato's core metaphysical system with its apex in the One and its emanation (or pouring forth) into Mind and then into Soul, in a subordinationist scheme that is Plotinian rather than strictly Platonic.[25] Interestingly, however, he would return twice more to the enigma in the hope of accommodating its wording to orthodox Trinitarian formulae and thus to underscoring the perfective or climactic nature of Plato's prophetic role as the last and greatest of the *prisci theologi*. First of all in his

[25] Allen, "Ficino and Doctrine of Trinity," pp. 571-580.

In Timaeum 8 he would take up the threefold nature of divine causality, identifying God's efficiency with His Power, His exemplarity with His Wisdom, and His finality with His Goodness. Finally, in the seventh chapter of his Commentary on St. Paul's Epistle to the Romans, a commentary he was working on at his death, he would concentrate still more circumspectly on Plato's precise wording. This he now interpreted in light of St. Paul's famous formulation in Romans 11:36, a formulation which had been interpreted by Augustine, Aquinas and others as referring respectively to the three persons of the Trinity, and which in the Vulgate translation reads "Quoniam ex ipso, et per ipsum, et in ipso omnia." St. Ambrose had emended the last phrase, however, to "in ipsum omnia," thereby introducing the notion of "returning to" God. Ficino would eagerly adopt this Ambrosian reading because it obviously echoed or paralleled the triadic rhythm of *emanatio-conversio-remeatio* which was so fundamental to Neoplatonic metaphysics and its analysis of any kind of descent or issuance or process.[26]

Ficino's dedication to this enigma, in sum, or rather his obsession with it as the most profound, the *dictum mirabile*, of all Platonic dicta, is the result, for all his indebtedness to Plotinus and Proclus, of his commitment to reconciling Platonism with the hallowed dogmas of Christianity. He is doing so by reinterpreting and subordinating Platonism; and specifically by reinterpreting Plato's most intricately wrought triadic dictum as being concerned not only with the highest mystery of the relationship of the three Platonic hypostases, but also with the three divine causes, and ultimately, he would decide in his commentary on St. Paul, with adumbrating the nature of the Trinity, *ex ipso et per ipsum et in ipsum*. For the present, however, we should bear in mind that his analysis in this argumentum for the *Second Letter* is not his final word on the matter of its celebrated enigma.

***

The fourth mystery [313Aff.] deals with our perception of matters divine; and it is the one, significantly, most elaborated in the letter, in part, I believe, because it is concerned with the very nature of our response to a Platonic mystery, to its articulation, comprehension, and transmission. It is the mystery of how we can best approach the mysteries themselves. Ficino's premise is that "an incorrectly performed investigation of matters divine — that is, one that is not instructed in the proper steps of purification or the modes of instruction — is the cause of all evils." This is because those who seek God without instruction arrive at the point either of denying that God exists or else of affirming things of God that are not God's. As a result "true religion" perishes, and when religion perishes all the ills flood in upon us. Therefore the

26 Wind, *Pagan Mysteries*, pp .37, 123, 243-244. *Conversio* is sometimes replaced by *vivificatio* or *raptio*.

impulse to investigate things divine, if we abuse it or use it indifferently, is the cause of evils. For when we yearn for the higher things, our yearning does not permit us to enjoy the present delights of earth, or to rest content in this life. Ficino takes Plato to imply this when he declares in the letter: "Unless a person roots out from his soul this incitement [to seek delight on earth], he will never attain the truth" (313A). Plato certainly argues that we cannot arrive at the truth concerning things that are dependent on God unless we know the truth concerning God Himself.

Still straying from the epistle's text, Ficino deduces from what follows that Plato was customarily and continually committed to investigating things divine; and that those who first heard him as he contemplated such things were usually straightway blinded by their dazzlingly unbearable splendour. For a long time they were troubled, until, finally, they were able to separate their minds both from the passions of their senses and from the images of their fantasy. When they had achieved this, they were filled with a blaze of light and discovered the truth they had never found before. Pythagoras, "whom our Plato venerates in all things," accordingly approached the sacred mysteries of doctrine only after a most careful "expiation" or purging of his mind. He commanded his followers, and Plato similarly commands us, Ficino believes, never to divulge the mysteries to the crowd, lest the rabble, having understood them incorrectly, were either to despise them or to lapse into errors. For if we do tell the crowd that God possesses in Himself nothing that is visible to us, it will either laugh and hoot at us, or else deny that God exists. Hence the force of the comment of Lysis the Pythagorean to Hipparchus, which Ficino recalls from Iamblichus' *De vita pythagorica* 75: "It would be impious to take the mysteries of philosophy and to make them familiar to people who could not even dream about purifying their souls."

Furthermore, there are several mysteries held by the theologians concerning God "which may fatigue not only the ordinary crowd but the majority too of the elite (*elegantes plerosque fatigent*)." One of them is that nothing derived from our realm of understanding should be affirmed absolutely of God. For whatever has been defined or limited by the understanding must exist below God, who is the infinite beyond all such limiting. So the majority of the learned are as yet unprepared for the greater "more secret" mysteries, just as the crowd is unprepared for the lesser mysteries. And to the extent even that many who have excellent acumen, memory, and judgement, and who have been acquainted with these mysteries for a long time, still cannot comprehend them perfectly, it is because, although they have been born to think about many other matters, they have not been born to contemplate the matters of theology. Or if they have been so born, Ficino adds, they have not yet become learned or instructed enough to do so; or if they have become educated and instructed enough, nonetheless they are not yet separated from their passions and able to enjoy the benefit of maturer years. Because passion uses diverse things to move us, to distract us, and to drag us down towards matter, it alienates our mind from God — and one cannot suppose anything further removed from God, Ficino emphasizes, than movement, diversity, and matter. It is not without justice therefore that the said Lysis admonished Hipparchus with these words: "It is worth reconsidering how much time we will have spent in removing the stains which were branded unjustly in our hearts, before we were able to understand the precepts of Pythagoras as they deserve" (ibid. 76).[27]

Furthermore, Ficino continues, even if someone does transport himself in his intellect to God, when his intellect is calm and instructed, nonetheless he is deceived by his very understanding with regard to God in almost the same way as the crowd is deceived by its senses and imagination; and even the majority of the learned are driven back by their passions. For when our understanding sets out to form a judgement in its natural way, the intellect compels us to assert that God Himself is either an intellect or something intelligible. But the Good in its immensity is not an intellect that turns in its need as it were towards the intelligible as towards a good from whose illumination it can profit. Nor can the Good be called something intelligible, which indeed shares a common nature with the intellect, and by virtue of this nature even has a certain congruent proportion with its understanding. But with the Good in its immensity there is no proportion or communion at all with the finite goods of nature.

In the *Parmenides*, Ficino continues, Plato proves that we have no name, no definition, no knowledge about God insofar as He is above the limits of understanding. Mercurius [Trismegistus] had affirmed the same thing before Plato; and Dionysius the Areopagite the same after him, when he shows that we must not call God either an entity or an intelligible, since He is above both. Wherefore, since God exceeds the intellect and the intelligible by an infinite distance, nobody can attain the divine substance by any act of the understanding, though we can attain it sometimes by way of our understanding's passivity or receptivity — in other words, by way of our own benign passivity and of the beneficent action of the infinite good which enters us. This good enters into the unity which is our mind's head, when the mind has gathered itself wholly and completely into its own unity, which is the express image of the divine simplicity. To the mind clothed with this unity, the truth glows under the divine Sun, but the truth virtually disappears when the mind doffs its unity and dons multiplicity again. Plato's key maxim here is therefore: Divine matters are not found by us; rather they are revealed to us from above.

Nor can the substance and property of matters divine be comprehended by our mind, much less unfolded in words or letters. So we should only raise or

27 "Operae pretium est recensere quantum temporis abstergendis maculis, quae nostris iniuste pectoribus erant, consumpserimus antequam praecepta Pythagorae percipere digne possemus" (*Opera*, p. 1532).

describe these matters using the mind in the hope that we can use words and letters to exhort and prepare our souls for things divine, but not because they can demonstrate such things to us. Thus Plato never writes anything down by way of defining the divine substance or property. Yet he writes much that might contribute at some point to inducing in the mind a state of rest or receptivity, and he does so by way either of negations or of comparisons. And he exhorts or instructs us to acquire that receptive state of mind "to which the house of omnipotent Olympus is at last revealed from on high."[28] After the mind has withdrawn from lower things into itself, and then having withdrawn from itself turns towards higher things, straightway, in what is now one simple and receptive state, it attains as it were unity itself, stability, and simplicity. St. Paul says, however, that what it has attained it is not lawful for a man to utter (II Cor. 12:4); and Plato says that still less are we permitted to write it down, lest what is sacred be tossed to the dogs. But in the unfolding of matters divine, although Plato puts his trust in neither words nor writing, he deems it safer to commit himself nevertheless to words rather than to writing; for writing make things common to just anyone at all. Yet men who are most chosen[29] are allowed to hear the secrets told them orally, though Plato supposes they will acknowledge the dignity of matters divine by communicating mind to mind, and by using words alone rather than writing them down as we do with external matters. For this reason, Ficino believes, the Jews maintained that the mystical sense of their law was not so much divinely handed down through Moses in writing as it was entrusted to souls by way of oral teaching. In this *Second Letter* Plato himself promises that he will learn many things by talking to Archedemus rather than by confining himself to just reading Dionysius' letters (cf. 313DE). Ficino notes that the Pythagoreans observed this prohibition on writing, and that Plato, for all his commitment to writing, none the less abided by the prohibition insofar as what he chose to write down were Socrates' words in the main not his own, because Socrates' "proper office" was to purify, that is, to prepare his auditors to receive instruction and to create in them a proper spiritual preparedness, rather than to instruct them per se.

Ficino asks why Plato had subjoined that Socrates was also beautiful in youth (314C's "become fair and young")[30] and takes him to mean that Socrates was divinely illuminated: "in the perfection of his first upbringing as in the happiness of his nature, he had suddenly[31] received from God and by way of a

[28] "cui tandem ex alto panditur domus omnipotentis Olympi" (ibid.)

[29] For philosophy as being only possible for the elected few, cf. *Republic* 494A, *Seventh Letter* 341E.

[30] This is R. G. Bury's rendering. L. A. Post's translation is "embellished and modernized" (*Thirteen Epistles of Plato: introduction, translation, and notes* [Oxford: Clarendon Press, 1925])!

[31] On the suddenness in Plato of the vision of the Idea, see his *Seventh Letter* 341CD: "[knowledge of the divine] is brought to birth in the soul on a sudden, as light that is kindled

familiar spirit what other men can scarcely attain after many labours." Subsequently, the same mysteries, having been received by Socrates by way of divine revelation, were transmitted to Plato; and by way of Plato's "exhortations" they can now be transmitted to men who are "similarly affected." Here Ficino cites Proclus on the need for faith: "Those who yearn to arrive at the highest good do not need knowledge or to exercise their wit and ingenuity. Rather they need steadfastness, quietness, tranquillity, which indeed is divine faith which draws us towards, and with ineffable reason joins us to, the highest good and all matters divine."[32] Indeed, we should not seek out and aspire to the highest good by way of knowledge or of any action that derives from cleverness; rather we should offer and commit ourselves to the divine light, and, having rejected the senses, take our repose (*quiescere*) in that unknown and hidden unity of all beings. For this genus of faith is more ancient than all doctrine; and "it is well known" (*constat*), Ficino asserts, that Proclus received it from Plotinus and his predecessors.

"But should anyone consider this matter carefully," he continues, "he would not exact that doctrinal order from Plato in his dialogues as disputants customarily do; rather he would be content with that style alone which can lead to God by the more correct path. But a style or an order such as this consists in purging and converting. For the mind's eye must be purged from the shadowy mire of matter, and then, having been purged, it must be duly directed towards the light of the divine sun. But one should not seek or strive further. For the immense light which is everywhere present entirely by its own nature pours itself into the mind's eye which has been created for it, and it does so as soon as, duly purified, it looks back at the light. But if the intellect continually uses its own action to approach God, action which is an accidental thing and multiple and in its way mobile, then through that action it is certainly separated in a way from the substance of God which is most simple and absolutely removed from every image of motion. It is enough, after the appropriate inquiry, just to have purified and directed the mind. Mercurius [Trismegistus] leaves the remainder to the mind's sacred silence. For he thinks that God is pronounced by the mind in a silence of its own rather than in its speech.[33] Thus all Plato's dialogues turn on this one consideration, and some consist in purging only, others in converting, and yet others in both."[34] These

by a leaping spark" (cf. 344B); see also Plato's *Symposium* 210E and *Republic* 6.509ff. and Ficino's *Platonic Theology* 11.3.21 and 18.8.5. Ficino may owe a debt here to Hesychasm; but the fascinating topic of his relationship generally to the Eastern Orthodox community and its tradition awaits exploration.

32 "His qui ad summum bonum pervenire cupiunt non scientia & exercitatione ingenii opus est, sed firmitate, quiete, tranquillitate, quae quidem divina fides est, quae nos ad summum bonum divinaque omnia ineffabile ratione trahit atque coniungit" (*Opera*, p. 1532). This is summarizing Proclus, *Theologia Platonica* 1.25 (ed. Saffrey & Westerink 1:111.2-112.24).

33 *Asclepius* 20, 41.

34 "Siquis autem haec diligenter consideravit, non exigit a Platone in dialogis suis consuetum illum apud humanos disputatores ordinem doctrinalem, sed eo duntaxat stylo contentus erit

mysteries Ficino sees reconfirmed in the letter to the Syracusans, i.e. the *Seventh Letter* 341C-344C; and for him they serve "in a marvellous way" to reinforce the precepts of the Gospels.

This too is a remarkable analysis in that it reads back into Plato's letter the Proclan notion that it is quiet "faith," not busy understanding, that is the right mental "set" that impels us to search for the good and enables us "suddenly" to see the divine and to unite with the good. And it launches an attack essentially on the search for intellectual understanding, for the "doctrine" that dominates scholastic disputes. Socratic debate — and Ficino refers to "all of Plato's dialogues" whether they are cathartic or conversionary — aims by contrast, not at acquiring knowledge or doctrine, but at "purging" the mind's eye and at "converting" it to gaze upon the light of the sun (with the shadowy cave of the *Republic* as the presiding image): it is "the more correct path." For the mind's eye sees suddenly and intuitively or unitively, not discursively; the eye being created in a way for the light, and indeed, after purification, being made one with the light. The intellect that relies on its own activity which is "accidental" and "multiple" and "mobile" in order to attain God is inevitably still separated from God's substance which is unitary and motionless. We should aspire, rather, not to intellectual understanding but to intellectual activity that is purgative, and that leads ultimately to a kind of intellectual quiescence, to the trans-intellectual state of "faith" and "sacred silence" which is "more ancient" than doctrine. By doing so we can entertain the paradoxical notion that at that moment the mind will be able to "pronounce" God, in the literal sense I believe of pronouncing His ineffable name or names, as in the Hebrew Scriptures, though it will pronounce it in silence not in speech, pronounce it, that is, in the speech of silence.[35] This silence is not the simple faith of the shepherd watching his flock by night but rather the sudden moment of Proclan meditation that one arrives at only after the intellectual exercise of "the ways" of negating and of analogizing, and then of abandoning even these ways, given that any kind of negating and analogizing is

---

qui rectiori tramite perducat ad Deum. Eiusmodi vero stylus sive ordo in purgando & convertendo consistit. Oportet enim mentis oculum & purgare a caliginosis materiae sordibus & purgatum in ipsam divini Solis lucem rite dirigere. Ulterius vero perquirere aut contendere non oportet. Immensa enim lux ubique praesens sua prorsus natura creato ad ipsam mentis oculo, cum primum in eam purus rite respexerit, se infundit. Ac si ad suscipiendum Deum intellectus assidue actione utatur propria, quae & accidens quiddam est & multiplex & modo quodam suo mobilis, profecto per ipsam a Dei substantia simplicissima & ab omni motionis imagine remotissima quodammodo disiungetur. Sat ergo fuerit post convenientem inquisitionem purificasse mentem atque direxisse. Reliquum Mercurius sacro mentis silentio tribuit. Deum enim a mente suo quodam silentio potiusquam sermone suo censet pronunciari. Omnes itaque Platonis dialogi in hoc ipso versantur & alii quidem in purgando solum, alii vero solum in convertendo, alii in utroque consistent" (*Opera*, p. 1532).

[35] See Ficino's *Philebus* Commentary 11-12 (ed. Allen, pp. 140-145) on pronouncing the name(s) of God; also Allen, "*In principio*: Marsilio Ficino on the Life of Text," in *Res et Verba in der Renaissance*, ed. Eckhard Kessler and Ian Maclean (Wolfenbüttel: Herzog August Bibliothek, 2002), pp. 11-28 and esp. 26-28.

fundamentally at odds with, or disproportionate to, the divine. This kind of transcendental meditation — and it is a method rather than an analysis — Ficino associated above all with the negative theologizing of Dionysius the Areopagite;[36] but it is in fact Plotinian as well in that its goal is a unitive experience beyond understanding and beyond willing, beyond even the awareness of faith or hope or charity.

***

Let me conclude if I may on a somewhat personal note. It is profitless not to say anachronistic to castigate Ficino either for misunderstanding Plato's riddling irony and playfulness (to which in other contexts he was often ingeniously sensitive), or for being a mystagogue, and particularly since it is by no means clear that the *Second Letter* is not itself a consummate piece of mystagoguery, whether it is forged or authentic. After all, the letter's famous enigma — and one can surmise that it governed Ficino's response to the other three — like many other enigmas in Plato, had long been the focus of attention for the Neoplatonists, and most obviously so for Proclus. Indeed, the whole explicatory tradition which Ficino inherited and revived stems from the Middle Platonists;[37] and it has its deepest roots in particular exegetes in the Old Academy itself. An historian's responsibility is surely not just to unravel or explicate Ficino's analysis or to lay out its systemic workings and dynamics along with its various debts to earlier interpreters and its deployment of other Platonic passages, or even to establish its all-embracing, all-explaining argumentative imperatives. He should also try to convey something at least of why this was all so fundamental to Ficino, and why it spoke to his larger philosophical, theological, and spiritual vision, and indeed to the values that underlay his whole mission in effecting a Platonic instauration. After all, he could have ignored or marginalized the letter, or simply glossed over the four enigmas. Instead he responded to it with the same complex intellectual enthusiasm with which he approached what is demonstrably the greatest of all the dialogues in the later Neoplatonic tradition, the *Parmenides,* and along with it the *Sophist*, the *Philebus*, the *Timaeus*, and the *Phaedrus*. These were the five dialogues to which he devoted his longest commentaries (leaving aside the youthful commentary on the *Symposium*, the *De amore*); and eventually he published them together, along with his treatise on the nuptial number in the *Republic's* eighth book, in a single remarkable volume, the 1496 *Commentaria in Platonem*. In sum, one might even go so far as to say that meditating on the cynosure of the Platonic enigma, and especially as it is

[36] See Ficino's translation of the *Mystical Theology* (*Opera,* pp.1013-1024).

[37] John Dillon, *The Middle Platonists 80 B.C. to A.D. 220* (Ithaca, N.Y.: Cornell University Press, 1977).

quadruply demonstrated in the *Second Letter*, constituted the supreme challenge, the ultimate contemplative moment, of Ficino's Neoplatonism.

If this kind of philosophical-theological exegesis and methodology is in fact typical of the Renaissance, and it is certainly characteristic of Ficino, then doing intellectual history in this field clearly requires launching oneself similarly into a kind of sacred text where the limits of interpretation are difficult to define or are definable only by reference to the practices of earlier "theological" exegetes, Christian and non-Christian. None the less Ficino's account of Plato's *Second Letter* raises a number of interpretative questions that are absolutely central for an understanding of his methodology and metaphysics, and even more so of his whole notion of what it was to do philosophy as a Christian Platonist and to explicate not just avowedly sacred texts, but any text, even that of a private letter, if it contained or encapsulated a "mystery" or a sacred formulation of some sort. His account is the more remarkable too because he was convinced that he was listening to Plato himself in his extreme old age, at his most venerable and authoritative. If for nothing more august, therefore, it put Ficino in the privileged ancillary position of being another Archedemus, mediating between the most sublime of the ancient Greek philosophers and the Italic princes of his own Quattrocento's Magna Graecia, even as he prepared the introductions and the translations of his 1484 *Platonis Opera Omnia* edition in the abiding hope that the *signori* would help him to achieve the revival of Plato that he considered his life's work — a revival that would bring with it the golden age reunion of philosophy and belief, of reason and faith, and once again unite the loftiest wisdom with the sway of beneficent power. For such was his Minervan dream.

14

TO GAZE UPON THE FACE OF GOD AGAIN: PHILOSOPHIC STATUARY, PYGMALION AND MARSILIO FICINO

Dedicated to the memory of Father Ed Mahoney

There is nothing novel or arresting about declaring that philosophy and theology are both deeply indebted to myth. However, I would like to take this occasion to explore the mythological underpinnings in Florentine Quattrocento Platonism of man's attempt to envisage the nature of God, even when every effort was being made to guard against the encroachments or even contaminations of myth; or at least to guard against re-mythologizing the mysteries of theology (as against theologizing the ancient myths themselves). For we must bear in mind that there is always a permeable membrane between theological abstraction and the figurative language that holds that abstraction in solution – indeed a permeable membrane between abstraction and figuration more generally; and this despite the fact that the human mind in reflection is often well aware of the rooted nature of mythological language and its limitations, and may even embark on a concerted effort to transcend them: to outwit, to outfigure itself and its own instinctive myth-making or myth-resorting tendencies.

The implications of the *Genesis* assertions in 1 : 26-27 that man is made in the image and likeness of God include the obvious complementary reverse notion that we continue to make God, however much we may try not to do so, in the image and likeness of man, though variously conceived and reconceived over the centuries. But the insistent anthropomorphism in theological enquiry has not been accepted uncritically. Following the ancient prophets themselves, we are often acutely aware that we are confusing man and God, or superimposing the one on the other, or creating a divine idol out of an ideal man, trying indeed to infuse that idealized idol with a superlative but still human animation, and hoping to breathe life itself into the conceptual statue we have made, and have always been making it seems.

Let me focus on the Renaissance. Frances Yates was one of the first modern scholars both to underscore the role of statues, and of statue magic and statue animation in the Hermetic treatise, the *Asclepius* 23-24, 37-38, and to speculate about the invasive force of its impact – and with it of Augustine's notable condemnation in the *City of God* 8.23-26 – specifically on Renaissance mages such as Ficino, Agrippa, and Bruno, and, more generally on the Renaissance sense of Egypt and its daemonological and religious mysteries.[1] More recently, Moshe Idel and Wouter Hanegraaff have separately delved into the notions of magical soul-making by way of bringing life to statues, and in particular they have turned to the complementary though not cognate subjects of the animated Hermetic statue and the kabalistic man-made golem.[2]

Haunting these scholarly enquiries and the mythopoetic history of statuary itself is Ovid's unforgettable telling in the *Metamorphoses* 10.243-297 of the myth of Pygmalion, the Cypriot king and sculptor who, having rejected consorts of flesh and blood, was granted the power by Aphrodite to infuse life into an ivory statue which he had carved and with which he had fallen desperately in love. It was not until the eighteenth century that this beloved statue became generally known as Galatea, and thereafter she was often confused with the sea nymph of the same name, the beloved of Acis, earlier representations of whom already adorned Renaissance *palazzo* and *villa* walls, the most breathtaking being Raphael's depiction in the Farnesina in Rome.

We might adduce as further confirmation the well known references by Pliny and others to the ancient artistic goal of achieving life-like images, painting grapes that the birds would peck at, or sculpting a mare that would excite a stallion; and more particularly of animating a portrait, or seeming to do so, by making the painted eyes for instance appear to follow us as we look at them from various angles. This goal of rendering something so life-like obviously haunts Shakespeare's depiction of Hermione at the close of *The Winter's Tale*, even as she would have appeared some sixteen years or so after King Leontes' rejection of the oracle and her sudden apparent death. Such was the skill, the «carver's excellence», of Julio Romano, the mannerist sculptor and painter, in anticipating the ageing of the virtuous Sicilian queen, or so declares Paulina, her lady in

---

[1] Cf. F. A. YATES, *Giordano Bruno and the Hermetic Tradition*, London 1964, chap. 1, esp. pp. 1-19.

[2] See M. IDEL, *Golem: Jewish Magical and Mystical Traditions on the Artificial Anthropoid*, Albany 1990; and Wouter J. Hanegraaff's interesting introduction to his and R. BOUTHOORN, *Lodovico Lazzarelli (1447-1500): The Hermetic Writings and Related Documents*, Tempe-Arizona 2005, esp. pp. 84-96.

waiting, as part of her orchestration of the suspense and wonder of the final reconciliation.

However, there is another dimension entirely of statue magic that has a major bearing on theology and philosophy but little, it would first seem, to do with Pygmalion or the Hermetic *Asclepius*.[3] Let us look closely at three remarkable passages in Ficino's works, where the notion of a statue is not linked to the controversial *Asclepius* but is fundamental to a larger argument about man's ascent to some kind of knowledge, and indeed love, of God.

In his *Platonic Theology* 9.3.2, Ficino turns to what he calls the soul's two principal «offices», namely its contemplative and deliberative functions (both being independent of bodies); and he commences with the traditional role of, and the epistemological ascent of, the phantasy.[4] This effort by the phantasy initially deludes the rational soul, when the soul desires to find out what God is and first resorts to this faculty and to the other lower faculties: «Immediately the phantasy, which is too rash a teacher and artisan, fashions a statue from five materials which the external senses have presented to it». These five materials are of course the gifts of the five physical senses, even if we predicate that they are «the most beautiful of all gifts». The phantasy has received these materials from the world, yet in such a way, Ficino argues, that it renders them «more excellent in some measure than it received them through the senses». The phantasy «offers us a light which is so clear that nothing seems brighter, so immense that nothing seems more immense», a light which is «diffused as it were through the infinite void and is decked with countless colors and revolves in a circle», that is, revolves like the nest itself of heavenly spheres. On account of this revolution, the light comes «with the most dulcet of measures filling and charming the ears» with the music that is traditionally known as the harmony of the spheres.[5] Moreover, the phan-

[3] For Ficino's account of the Asclepian statue magic in three different texts – the *Commentary on St. Paul* (that is, *Romans*) chap. 8, the *De Vita* 3.26, and the *Apology* epitome (FICINI *Opera Omnia*, Basel 1576, pp. 440, 571, 1388) – see my *Marsilio Ficino, Hermes Trismegistus and the* Corpus Hermeticum, pp. 38-47 at 43-45, now in *Plato's Third Eye: Studies in Marsilio Ficino's Metaphysics and its Sources* (Aldershot-Brookfield 1995), as number XII.

[4] *Marsilio Ficino: The Platonic Theology*, ed. and trans. M. J. B. ALLEN and J. HANKINS, 6 vols., Cambridge, Mass. 2001-2006, 3 : 16 ff. The threefold refs. are to book, chapter, and paragraph.

[5] For the classical background, see S. K. HENINGER JR., *Touches of Sweet Harmony: Pythagorean Cosmology and Renaissance Poetics*, San Marino 1974, pp. 3-5, 31, 124, 178-187.

tasy imagines the statue «as redolent of the most fragrant odors, abounding too with all the tastes, the sweetest of all imaginable, and as being wonderfully soft to the touch, delicate, smooth, and duly tempered». In short, it imagines the statue as the perfection of all sensation; and it proclaims both that this perfection is God and that the world's body «can offer us nothing more beautiful and that corporeal sense cannot come into contact with anything better». The phantasy has reached its epistemological limit, its ceiling if you will, and cannot conceive of anything being more excellent. A friend still of the senses, it can fashion nothing «more sublime» than this witness to the five sensations at their most refined and their most intense.

Even so, for all its beauty – and Ficino is imagining the phantasy as receiving like Pandora the most exceptional of gifts – the statue formed by the phantasy is a false idol that ensnares us in perilous delusions. Its creator is a sophist in that it is constructing a model of God, not by contemplating Him, but by refining the data it receives from the senses and arriving eventually at a work of sensuous art that may be technically superlative – indeed conform to Zeuxis' ancient formula for depicting perfect beauty by selecting what is best from a variety of options – but is nonetheless anchored to this world and to the sophistries of a false, a deceptive beauty.[6] This beautiful idol imagined by the phantasy is a kind of composite delusion even though it enables us to hear the music of the spherical revolutions, and even though its creator is a superlative artist who can cull the best data from the lower world and redesign a composite sensuous ideal. This sensuous ideal, nonetheless, is a derivative artifact, an empty cornucopia. If not erotic per se, it remains a merely sense-derived triumph, not a foam-born Aphrodite perhaps, but certainly an ancillary nereid or siren.

To counter and transcend the phantasy meanwhile, the reason proposes a more subtle strategy, a mental exercise or experiment that moves us away from the notion of creating a statue to that of exploring the possibility of achieving, like some alchemist, an ultimate reduction, a stripping away of any trace of the sensible. Ficino's authorities here are two inter-related Pythagorean notions: a) of arriving at the notion of a geometric point by stripping away dimensions and ascending from solid to

---

[6] See my *Icastes: Marsilio Ficino's Interpretation of Plato's* Sophist*: Five Studies with a Critical Edition and Translation*, Berkeley-Los Angeles 1989, chaps. 3-5 and Epilogue, for the ambiguities investing Ficino's notions of Platonic sophistry.

plane to line to point;[7] and b) of thinking of a point as being at the very center of a circle from which countless lines radiate out to the circumference. The faculty of the reason goes beyond the phantasy, interestingly, by first accepting the data of the senses and then either denying them outright or modifying them. Ficino imagines the reason meanwhile «from the height of the mind's watch-tower» looking down on the phantasy's childish games and exclaiming to the soul, «Be careful little soul, beware of the tricks of this idle sophist». In seeking God, we must, he says, «take a light which is brighter than the sun's light to the same degree that the sun's light is brighter than the shadows» (9.3.3). For if we compare it to the sun's light, the latter, even if it is a thousand times clearer, appears as a shadow. We must next take a light «which is so much more refined that it eludes the eye's gaze», but we must not extend it through some sort of space or emptiness, lest it be compounded from parts and so need the props of parts and of space. Rather we must gather the whole, he exhorts us, into a point, «so that from this infinite union it can be infinitely powerful».

Ficino imagines this point as everywhere present, not scattered in space but omnipresent, «wholly present in any point in space». It is no longer dyed with the endless variety of colors, pure light being more splendid than polychrome light. And this time the light is neither revolving nor resounding, «for I do not wish this point to be moved or to be struck or to break, and I deem rest more perfect than motion». He also imagines it as devoid of odors, tastes, and tactile qualities, «lest it be compounded of too gross a nature». At this juncture we arrive, he rhapsodizes, «at a refulgence no space contains, a resonance no time bears away, a fragrance no gust of wind dispels, a savor no gluttony deadens, an intimate softness that satiety never strips away». We arrive, that is, at a conception that transcends our ordinary sense-based perception and everything that derives from the senses, and transcends even sense perfections, the superlative perceptions, in other words, that we must utterly abandon if we are to embrace the divine conception.

In 9.3.4 Ficino's advice to the little soul continues: «Do you want to gaze upon the face of God again?». If so, we must look at the universal world full of the light of the sun, a light that dwells in the world's matter and is forever changing even as it is full of all the universal forms. If

[7] Cf. Aristotle, *Topics*, 6.4.141B5-22; *Metaphysics*, 3.5.1001B26-1002B11, 13.9.1085A7-B3.

we can subtract matter from this light, then suddenly we will have soul itself, that is, incorporeal light, replete with all the forms, yet still changing and changeable. If we then subtract change from this soul-light, we will arrive at last at angelic intellect, at an incorporeal light which is filled with all the forms but is now unchanging. If we in turn subtract from this the difference by means of which each form is different from the light and introduced into the light from elsewhere, then we will reach the essence of the light as identified now with its unchanging forms; for here the light is forming itself and through its forms informing all. The light shines out infinitely, since it is naturally radiant, and it is neither sullied nor constrained by the admixture of anything else. Because it dwells in no one thing, it is poured through all things: «it dwells in no one thing in order that it may blaze in its fullness through all things». It lives from itself even as it gives life to all, since its shadow, in Ficino's suggestive phrasing, is like the sun's light; for it alone gives rise to life in bodies. This light senses all and gives sense to all, because life, its shadow, awakens the five senses in things. Finally, this light «loves individual things if they are preeminently its own». Accordingly, Ficino concludes rhetorically: «What is the sun's light? God's shadow. So what is God? God is the Sun of the sun». Hence the sun's light, that is, God's shadow, is God in the body of the world. But God Himself is the divine Sun far above the angelic intellects».

Ficino next turns to the notion that everything here is but a shadow to God's radiance; that all light is shadow to His light; and he breaks into meditative prayer:

> O soul, here, here is your God! The phantasy shows you His shadow. The shadow of God is such that it is the most beautiful of sensible things. What do you think God's light is like? If God's shadow shines so dazzlingly, how much more intensely does God's light shine? You love the sun's light everywhere before all else, or rather you love it alone. Love God alone, His light alone, O soul. Love infinitely the infinite light of God in His beneficence. You will then be radiant and experience infinite joy.[8] So, I beseech you, seek His face and you will rejoice for eternity. But do not move, pray, in order to touch it, because it is stability itself. Do not perplex yourself with things various in order to apprehend it, because it is unity itself. Cease motion and take the many and bind them into

[8] «Dei faciem rursus intueri [...] oblectaberis infinite»: (repeated, with variations, in Ficino's *Dialogus inter Deum et animam theologicus* in his *Letters* 1.4.80-103; ed. S. Gentile, Firenze 1990, p. 15 = Ficini *Opera*, cit., pp. 610-611) a letter to Mercati.

one. Straightway you will comprehend God, God who long ago utterly comprehended you.[9]

At this juncture the reason effectively surrenders to the mind's intuitive gaze, a gaze totally liberated now from images and from contemplating intelligible form, and more than form. The mind in a way is momentarily comprehending God, even as God is eternally comprehending the mind.

In this quest, 9.3.5 continues, the mind withdraws from all bodies, dispelling their images and deceits and condemning the phantasy and the senses as the bodies' companions! In truth, just as the mind is a substance in itself, and therefore does not derive from any body, so it performs its own work at various times through itself without the assistance of any body, or rather – and this is even more wonderful – it performs it in opposition to all the apparatus of bodies. In doing its work, it would never be able to cut itself off from all corporeal blemish, Ficino argues, unless it were in its own essence completely severed from all corporeal roots. And because the mind cannot oppose by way of any partial bodily power the universal nature of all bodies – on the principle that «a tiny part does not rebel against the whole» – it necessarily follows that the mind must operate in the present via its own mental power, and without the aid of anything corporeal. In the future it should be able to do this to an even greater degree.

In this entire analysis we can see Ficino involved in a kind of mind game exploring the limits of abstraction and the possibility of escaping not only sense data but rational categories and even such intellectual abstractions as superlatives. However, while the paragraphs here help to advance the arguments pursued in the *Platonic Theology*, they are nonetheless anchored in Ficino's early *Dialogus inter Deum et animam theologus*; and their roots lie, as the title indicates, in a traditional contemplative exercise: in listening to an imaginary dialogue between soul and body. The role of a statue here is limited to the description of the superlative but still inadequate fabrication of the sense-based and sense-monitoring phantasy.

By contrast, in commenting on the *Phaedrus* 252C ff., Ficino encountered a striking passage that suggests that statues and statue-worship are

---

[9] «Quare igitur, obsecro, faciem [...] penitus assecutum»: (*ibid.*, 1.4.54-58; ed. GENTILE, p. 14).

an integral part both of a divine mystery and of the disciple's eventual initiation into it. Plato has Socrates declare that the lover treats his beloved as if he were a god, a god that he fabricates and adorns for himself «as an image» (252D6: *ekeinon*). Ficino translates «as an image» here to mean «as a statue» (*quasi statuam*) inasmuch as the beloved is «to be honored and sacrificed to».[10] Accordingly the worshippers who think of Jupiter as their particular god «seek out someone to love whose rational soul is jovian». But this statue which they fabricate as lovers is mysteriously within: Lovers track «their own god's nature from within themselves; and they obtain their wish at last because they are compelled at the peak of their attention as it were, to elevate their mental gaze towards the god». Plato thus suggests, at least in Ficino's understanding of the passage, that the lover begins with, indeed must begin with, fashioning within himself a sort of conceptual statue of the beloved; for only then can the beloved become the object of the kind of desire that will bring him to his own divine ruler. However, in this making of a statue of the beloved, the lover is in fact trying to make a perfect threefold likeness: of himself as lover, of the beloved, and of the god whom they both worship. The statue becomes in effect a daemonic intermediary between the lovers themselves and their presiding god.

This interpretation of statue worship effectively legitimizes it. For a lover, idolatry in this special Platonic sense[11] becomes the only way of finding the tutelary god who is within himself and within the beloved, of ensuring that they love each other as worshippers of the same deity. And Plato's subsequent argument suggests that the lover is taken prisoner by his beloved even as the beloved is taken prisoner by the lover, with the result that they both share in the frenzy of love (253C). Indeed, the fabricating and adorning of the statue is equated with drinking down the Dionysian draughts of wine that transform us all into Bacchantes, nay, into Bacchoi, into the enraptured avatars of the god himself. The statue

[10] For Ficino's translation of these passages from the *Phaedrus*' mythical hymn, see my *Marsilio Ficino: Commentaries on Plato*, I, Phaedrus *and* Ion, Cambridge, Mass. 2008, pp. 26-27.

[11] The sixteenth century Reformers were to mount an attack on idolatry that became an attack on all images. The Elizabethan «Homily Against Idolatry and Superfluous Decking of Churches», for example, was to explicitly identify idolatry with image worship and call all images used in church and in worship «vanities, lies, deceits, uncleanliness, filthiness, dung, mischief, and abomination before the Lord» (*ibid.*, pp. 270-272), equating them with dead things that aroused a kind of necrophilia (*ibid.*, p. 188) and prompted «spiritual fornication» (*ibid.*, p. 246)!

is now the bearer of grace: it is what enables us to become the object of our love, and, in the mystery's completion, to become the god who is ourselves, who is both the object and the subject of love. Hence the erotic statue is not a statue of wood or ivory or stone, however reconfigured within ourselves; rather it is a good daemon whom we have created in a way, but whom we have also summoned up as our own semi-divine intermediary between ourselves and God. This indeed is Love, the greatest of all daemons, the *magnus daemon*, the very desire, that is, for Divine Beauty which is itself Platonically the splendor of all the Ideas. In venerating their daemon, lover and beloved become their god, become the absolute Beauty that they unwittingly first desired when they were captivated by the individual physical and personal beauty of each other. For the end of love, Ficino declares at the close of summa 30 of his *Phaedrus* Commentary, is to worship together the god whom we know to be our own and to be united jointly with him («cumque illo communiter copulari»).[12]

In the last decade of his life, Ficino turned to translate and comment on two works of the sixth century Neoplatonist Dionysius, whom the medieval tradition inherited by Ficino and his contemporaries confused both with the Dionysius whom St. Paul had converted on the Areopagus in Athens (as noted in *Acts* 17 : 34) and, incidentally, with another Dionysius, the patron saint of France. The Neoplatonist was revered as the greatest of the Greek Church Fathers and was almost invariably known until the late sixteenth century, when doubts began to surface, as Dionysius the Areopagite. The works in question are the long *On Divine Names* and the brief but profound *On Mystical Theology*. In chapter nine of his commentary on the latter,[13] Ficino once more set up a thought experiment involving a statue and reminding us again of the famous verses in *Genesis* 1.26-27.

He advances the arresting argument that if God made man in His own image, then there has to be a statue of God – meaning a human likeness of Him – embedded in us, however encompassing and multi-layered the accretions hiding it. But how do we liberate this divine statue? Ficino suggests a sevenfold contemplative ascent by way of subtraction. It is imperative that first we banish body from our soul; second, banish

[12] *Ibid.*, pp. 160-161.

[13] Now in his *Opera omnia*, cit., p. 1020.2, where the treatise is referred to by its alternative title as the *De trinitate*.

corporeal passions from this same soul; third, banish imagination's images from its reason; fourth, banish reason's discursive arguments from its intellect; fifth, banish intellect's multiformity from our soul's unity; and sixth, from this unity banish the condition of being either soul or intellect. We must come to rest, he says, only on the seventh step. For there we will always find the absolute Unity itself, that is, God, lying concealed beneath our own soul's particular unity, a unity the ancient Neoplatonists had denominated the crown or the flower of the soul.

In the world too, God has made His statue, but «wrapped in many veils». Again we must undertake the discipline of first taking matter everywhere away from the world in order to gaze upon the celestial realm of the heavens. Next we must subtract dimension from this celestial world, but save all the forms and «the motions of forms». At this point we will have acquired «the universal soul», the soul of the world. If we then remove the motions, as it were, of the forms and leave just the motionless forms, we will immediately be in possession of the universal intellect, the intellect of the world. If we subtract from this intellect the rays of the forms (the rays which are divided among themselves), we will then receive light in itself, light as the rational principle of the rays but no longer dispersed through them and no longer confined to particular species of them. This light in its utterly absolute and simple immensity is the Good itself, Ficino declares, the goal of every attempt of the understanding and the will. Therefore, by stripping away stage by stage as we ascend the ontological and epistemological hierarchy, ultimately we will approach God Himself, chiseling His likeness so to speak within ourselves, first in the little world of ordinary man, then in the great man, in the macrocosm itself.

Ficino turns finally to a third option. For we can similarly extract God's statue from the sun if first we think of all things' colors and lights as radiating out from the sun and always being preserved in such a way that «nothing virtually exists other than the light of the sun itself hidden in things». Hence, if we take the colors everywhere on earth itself and systematically subtract from these colors «the earthly grossness» that is mingled in with them; and then if we subtract the watery and earthy vapors from the colors of the clouds when they are suffused with light; and if finally we subtract the fiery mixture and the starry property from the light of fire and the light of the stars, then, at the end of this process of subtraction, we will have discovered the source of all light in this elemental world. We will have found the light of the sun itself, the light that is transcendently prior to the four elements.

Furthermore, if we detach the sun's mass and property but retain the light, we will, Ficino asserts, «win God [Himself] from this sun»; for God is truly the Sun of the sun,[14] reigning everywhere over the immensity of creation without circumscription or limitation. Such a beneficent light, the light of the prime Good, is infused from God in all good, beautiful, and desirable things, just as the sun's light is diffused in all things that have light and color. And there is an almost perfect analogy between the two. With regard to the stages in the ascent, Ficino refers us to earlier comments in his second book of *Letters*,[15] in the *Platonic Theology*,[16] and in his treatise on St. Paul's rapture to the third heaven.[17]

At this point we can see that the abstraction of the earlier text has been brought to bear in a way that reminds us inevitably of the statue conceit in Michelangelo, both in some of his most famous poems (see for instance his famous meditation in 151, but also in 152, 236, 237, and 239), and as it is visually manifested in his Florentine slaves: namely the conceit that we can uncover an embedded sculptural form by way of hammering away the encompassing rock and liberating the figure within. But Ficino has brought the notion to bear on three levels: on man, on the world, and on the sun (i.e. on the human, the terrestrial, and the celestial). And once again he ends up with a light mysticism, a mysticism combining the notion of a geometrical point with that of concentrated light.[18] For God's image in man is ultimately the image of light, since God is the Father of lights in the famous phrasing from St. James' Epistle. Thus the most perfect statue of God we can ever fabricate in our minds is that of God as an intense point of light lightening our darkness. Or alternatively we could say that the life in all the statues that we fabricate of God

---

[14] Cf. *Platonic Theology* 9.3.4.

[15] I.e. in the *Argumentum in Platonicam Theologiam*, now edited and translated by James Hankins and myself in the appendix to volume six of our edition of the *Platonic Theology*, pp. 220-271 (= Ficini *Opera*, cit., pp. 706.4-716). This introduction explores the theme of «tres contemplationis gradus».

[16] E.g. *Platonic Theology* 8.1, 10.8.4, 12.1.1, 12.2-3, 15.16.10.

[17] The *De divino furore* is the sixth letter in Ficino's first book of Ficino's *Letters* (ed. Gentile, pp. 19-28 = Ficini *Opera*, cit., pp. 612-615); see S. Gentile, *In margine all'epistola «De divino furore» di Marsilio Ficino*, «Rinascimento», II s., XXIII, 1983, pp. 33-77.

[18] See my *Marsilio Ficino, Levitation, and the Ascent to Capricorn*, in *Éducation, Transmission, Rénovation à la Renaissance*, éd. par B. Pinchard and P. Servet, Geneva 2006, pp. 223-240; and *«Quisque in sphaera sua»: Plato's* Statesman, *Marsilio Ficino's* Platonic Theology *and the Resurrection of the Body*, «Rinascimento», II s., XLVII, 2007, pp. 25-48. See also the texts translated and annotated by Julie Reynaud et Sébastien Galland in their *Marsile Ficin, Métaphysique de la lumière (1476-1492)*, Paris 2008.

is His light – *fiat lux* being the prime and necessary condition of the six days of creation. Of course there is always the terrible irony that Satan was once a prince of light, a light-bearer; and the ensuing irony that we too are in the penumbra of the darkened Lucifer – some of us despairingly fallen, some of us yearning still to return as Lucifers redeemed to our source in the divine radiance.

At the end of his commentary on the Areopagite's *Mystical Theology*, Ficino confronts the failure of any kind of mind game or strategy to guide our final accession to God, when, like Moses on Sinai, we face the radiant darkness of God's unknowability.[19] For at this juncture language itself becomes the stone that is chipped away as we attempt to carve out, neither man's statue, nor the world's, nor even the sun's, but rather the statue at last of God Himself, the ultimate conceptual statue to which we long to give the gift of life so that we ourselves might live everlastingly as worshippers of His transcendent form. Mystically, however, even as we try to sculpt Him conceptually, He recedes from the very language by which we attempt to conceive of the divine; and we find that in the very process of trying to sculpt Him that He is mysteriously sculpting us. As sculptors we will become indeed, in the climactic Pygmalion moment, the sculpted, the living stone under the awful majesty of God's living hand. For at that moment, as God's animated statues, we will be more fully, more intensely, more transcendently alive than we were ever alive in our own earthly bodies, alive even as sculptors, as Pygmalions enamored of the beauty of our own artifacts.

To conclude, Ficino's engagement with the image of a statue demonstrates how complex and how rich the notion of a statue-magic had become in the Renaissance. From the *Genesis* text that declares we are in the image and likeness of God, the notion naturally follows that we are creative sculptors like God. But Ficino was able to explore the paradoxes attending the notion that we are sculptors who are in turn sculpted: that the ultimate creative moment is the gift of eternal life, not only to the sculpture but then, even more miraculously, to the sculptor, who is paradoxically dead until he has carved a living statue of his beloved in himself. For this is a gift that can be received only if we acknowledge that we are sculptural forms in the rock responding to God's awakening

[19] Ficini *Opera*, cit., pp. 1023.3-1024.

of our limbs and of our very soul. At all events, the permutations on the Pygmalion theme suggest a number of intricate and arresting possibilities; and Ficino's notions of philosophizing, of meditating, of prayer itself are wonderfully informed by the image of human beings as God's statues awaiting life, even as they are sculptors both of their own souls, and of a concept, however inadequate, of God in their souls. At the close, we are left with the haunting contemplative image of the sculptor himself as a moribund statue, even as he prays that his own form may be liberated from the marble of mortal and corporeal life.

Paulina's exhortation to Hermione «'tis time descend» is the prelude to one of the most admired of all Shakespearean coups de théatre, and as bardolaters we would not wish it otherwise. But for a Renaissance Neoplatonist, I believe, a higher magic would have focused rather on Leontes: it would have urged him at last, after his years of heart sorrow, to step up to Hermione's stone plinth, as Paulina prayerfully intones, «'tis time ascend, be human; stone, no more». The king would then miraculously take his place beside his faithful wife and queen, his long lost daughter's mother, who is still a living statue, but carved by a master more divine, incomparably so, than any Italian mannerist, however rare, «The very life seems warm upon her lip. / The fixure of her eye has motion in't / As we are mock'd with art» (5.3.66-68). And like Hermione herself, he too would stand as a living statue, a husband and king, who after sixteen long years of penitence for having enmeshed two royal families, and with them the Sicilian and Bohemian courts, in the spidery death of jealousy, is now required to «awake» his faith and gaze upon an action that is as holy, Paulina says, as her spell is lawful: «Do not shun her / Until you see her die again, for then / You kill her double» (5.3.105-107).

The statue for Ficino, at least in certain mystical or poetic contexts, is therefore the symbolic nexus between man and God, ironically so given its traditional associations with idolatry. Hence the divine imperative that we must, with purity of heart, fabricate statues of ourselves, of our beloveds, of the world, of God Himself; and that we must do this if we are ever to escape our own post-lapsarian limitations and isolation; ever to understand and participate in the nature of love. However, it is not the fabrication of statues as such that is our goal as self-transcending intellects; rather it is the search for the power, the gift, the faith to animate them. For without animation the universe is a universe of death. Locked within corporeality, and more, behind the bars of our own psychological and mental cells, we are the walking dead, are prisoners in a dungeon, even though we may appear to be alive. The religious injunction that we must be born again means in effect that we must first fabricate, and then animate, the statue not only of ourselves – and not of our former selves but of the selves we should become – but also of what we must successively pursue as the supreme object of our desire: first a beautiful beloved, then Beauty as an Idea, and then at last the one God of our idolatry and of our image-making and our image-breaking powers alike.

15

MARSILIO FICINO ON SATURN, THE PLOTINIAN MIND, AND THE MONSTER OF AVERROES

Summary

This article explores some striking aspects of Marsilio Ficino's many-sided engagement with Saturn. It focuses, however, not so much on the old god's traditional mythological and astrological associations, though these played important roles for Ficino for both personal and medical reasons, as on Ficino's deployment of Saturn in his exploration of Platonic metaphysics. In particular I am concerned with two interrelated problems: 1) with Ficino's analysis of the theology of the *Phaedrus'* mythical hymn with its cavalcade of gods under Zeus as the World-Soul traversing the intellectual heaven, the realm of Saturn as Mind; and 2), more startlingly, with Saturn in the context of the long and intricate rejection of Averroism in Ficino's *magnum opus*, the *Platonic Theology*, and notably in the fifteenth book which has hitherto received little scholarly attention. His goal there was to reject what he saw as the capstone of Averroes's metaphysics and psychology as articulated in the commentary on the *De anima* (which he only knew in Michael Scot's Latin version): namely the theory of the unity (unicity) of the agent Intellect, even as he identified this Intellect too with Saturn. Combined with other Saturnian motifs and interpretations, we can now see that Saturn played a signal role in Ficino's account of ancient Neoplatonism, in his own Christian transformation of it, and in his polemical attack on the great Moslem commentator on Aristotle.

English speakers have always associated saturnian melancholy with that incomparable compilation by the hypochondriacal Robert Burton in the seventeenth century, *The Anatomy of Melancholy*,[1] though the problem of the black humour goes back to antiquity and to the Pseudo-Aristotelian *Problemata*.[2] Academic study of melancholy's complex history in the Re-

* I am especially indebted in this essay to conversations with Brian Copenhaver, Stephen Clucas, Peter Forshaw, Guido Giglioni, Dilwyn Knox, Jill Kraye, and Valery Rees.

[1] Now edited and annotated by J. B. Bamborough *et al.*, 6 vols., Oxford, Clarendon Press, 1989-2000. See A. Gowland, *The Worlds of Renaissance Melancholy: Robert Burton in Context*, Cambridge, Cambridge University Press, 2006; and J. Hankins, *Malinconia mostruosa: Ficino e le cause fisiologiche dell'ateismo*, «Rinascimento», 2nd s, xlvii, 2007, pp. 3-23, which deals inter alia with some of Burton's Ficinian sources. See also J. Schmidt, *Melancholy and the Care of the Soul: Religion, Moral Philosophy and Madness in Early Modern England*, Aldershot, Ashgate, 2007.

[2] *Problemata*, xxx.1.953a10-955a39. See H. Flashar, *Melancholie und Melancholiker in den medizinischen Theorien der Antike*, Berlin, De Gruyter, 1966; J. Pigeaud, *La maladie de l'âme: étude sur la relation de l'âme et du corps dans la tradition médico-philosophique antique*, Paris, Belles

naissance, however, is the work of a number of distinguished twentieth-century scholars, beginning effectively with Fritz Saxl and Erwin Panofsky's penetrating investigation of Dürer's great woodcut, *Melencolia I* (1514), and of Dürer generally.[1] This was followed by the pioneering studies of Don Quixote by Harald Weinrich[2] and Otis Green,[3] and of Elizabethan drama by Lawrence Babb in *The Elizabethan Malady.*[4] Then in 1963 appeared Rudolf and Margot Wittkower's remarkable *Born under Saturn;*[5] and barely a year later appeared what would turn out to be the commanding work in the field Klibansky, Panofsky and Saxl's *Saturn and Melancholy: Studies in the History of Natural Philosophy, Religion, and Art,*[6] which linked *melancholia generosa* (with its roots in the medieval vice of *acedia*) to the emergence of our modern notion of genius. These foundational books were followed by Judith Gellert Lyons's arresting *Voices of Melancholy: Studies in Literary Treatments of Melancholy in Renaissance England,*[7] Winfried Schleiner's wide-ranging *Melancholy, Genius and Utopia in the Renaissance,*[8] and indeed a number of other studies by historians of art, literature, music, medicine, the melancholic Dane,[9] mad Timon,[10] and Don Quixote, which have enhanced our understanding of the history and iconography of this complex cultural and medico-psychological phenomenon.[11]

Lettres, 1981; and J. MONFASANI, *George of Trebizond's Critique of Theodore of Gaza's Translation of the Aristotelian* Problemata, in *Aristotle's* Problemata *in Different Times and Tongues*, edited by P. De Leemans and M. Goyons, Leuven, Leuven University Press, 2006 («Mediaevalia Lovaniensia», 1st s., XXXIX), pp. 273-292.

[1] E. PANOFSKY, F. SAXL, *Dürers 'Melencolia I': eine quellen- und typengeschichtliche Untersuchung*, Leipzig-Berlin, Teubner, 1923. This was followed by Erwin Panofsky's magisterial *Albrecht Dürer*, Princeton, NJ, Princeton University Press, 1943; subsequent editions in 1955 and 1971 were entitled *The Life and Art of Albrecht Dürer.*

[2] H. WEINRICH, *Das Ingenium Don Quijotes*, Münster, Aschendorf, 1956.

[3] O. GREEN, *El Ingenioso Hidalgo*, «Hispanic Review», XXV, 1957, pp. 175-193.

[4] L. BABB, *The Elizabethan Malady: a Study of Melancholia in English literature from 1580 to 1642*, East Lansing, MI, Michigan State College Press, 1951.

[5] R. and M. WITTKOWER, *Born under Saturn: the character and conduct of artists: a documented history from antiquity to the French Revolution*, London, Weidenfeld & Nicolson, 1963.

[6] R. KLIBANSKY, E. PANOFSKY and F. SAXL, *Saturn and Melancholy: Studies in the History of Natural Philosophy, Religion, and Art*, London, Nelson, 1964. On pp. 18-41 the authors provide the Greek text, a translation and a commentary on Aristotle's *Problemata* XXX.1.

[7] J. GELLERT LYONS, *Voices of Melancholy: Studies in Literary Treatments of Melancholy in Renaissance England*, London, Routledge & Kegan Paul, 1971.

[8] W. SCHLEINER, *Melancholy, Genius and Utopia in the Renaissance*, Wiesbaden, Harrassowitz, 1991.

[9] See esp. LYONS, *Voices of Melancholy...*, chapter 4.

[10] R. SOELLNER, *Timon of Athens: Shakespeare's Pessimistic Tragedy*, Columbia, OH, Ohio State University Press, 1979.

[11] See now N. L. BRANN's *The Debate over the Origin of Genius during the Italian Renaissance. The Theories of Supernatural Frenzy and Natural Melancholy in Accord and in Conflict on the Threshold of the Scientific Revolution*, Leiden, Brill, 2002.

There is a Ficinian chapter to this history, however, that still remains to be written, and this despite the central role Ficino already plays in Klibansky, Panofsky, and Saxl's study as the theorist who linked melancholy and frenzy and confronted the pathos they constituted;[1] and despite too the signal role he also plays in the work of two other eminent art historians, André Chastel[2] and Edgar Wind.[3] In this essay I shall attempt in part to contribute to the history of the Renaissance Saturn, a history for which a lively collection of essays edited by Massimo Ciavolella and Amilcare A. Iannucci, *Saturn from Antiquity to the Renaissance*,[4] has established some of the main parameters.

Astrologically speaking, Saturn, as furthest, slowest, and by implication the most aged, driest, and coldest of the seven planets, has traditionally been linked with the seventh and last decade of the biblical span of human life, and thus on the one hand with slippered pantaloons, sans eyes, sans teeth, sans everything, and on the other with otherworldly contemplation. More actively, as the 'highest' of the planets, it has also been seen as causing mutations in human life every seventh year, unlike the Moon, say, which causes mutations every seventh day.[5] But in addition to his astrological, pharmacological and medical roles – the three are of course intermingled – Saturn as a deity has a special status in the Platonic tradition; and chiefly on the following four counts.

1. First, he figures prominently in the Platonic vision of the zodiac – in this regard most familiar to Ficino via Macrobius's commentary on the dream of Scipio. Macrobius envisages human souls descending to earth from the fixed stars at birth by way of Cancer, the domicile of the Moon, and then at bodily death re-ascending by way of Capricorn, the 'night abode' of Saturn (Aquarius being his 'day abode'). In his 1482 *Platonic Theology* Ficino argues at XVIII.1.12 that the Egyptians had supposed that the light of the world's first day dawned when Aries was in mid-heaven and Cancer was rising. At that primal hour the Moon was in Cancer, the Sun in Leo, Mercury

[1] Klibansky, Panofsky and Saxl argue that Ficino was the figure «who really gave shape to the idea of the melancholy man of genius» (p. 255).

[2] A. Chastel, *Le mythe de Saturne dans la Renaissance italienne*, «Phoebus», I, 3-4, 1946, pp. 125-144; Idem, *Marsile Ficin et l'art*, Geneva, Droz, & Lille, Giard, 1954 («Travaux d'Humanisme et Renaissance» XIV); Idem, *Art et humanisme à Florence au temps de Laurent le Magnifique: études sur la Renaissance et l'humanisme platonicien*, Paris, Presses universitaires de France, 1959.

[3] E. Wind, *Pagan Mysteries in the Renaissance*, London, Faber & Faber, 1958; revised edition, New York, Norton, 1968. And we should now add Brann's section on Ficino in his *Debate over the Origin...*, pp. 82-117.

[4] *Saturn from Antiquity to the Renaissance*, edited by M. Ciavolella and A. A. Iannucci, Ottowa, Dovehouse Editions, 1992.

[5] M. Ficino, *Platonic Theology* XVII.2.12, ed. and tr. by M. J. B. Allen and J. Hankins, Cambridge, MA, Harvard University Press, 2001–2006 («I Tatti Renaissance Library»), vol. VI, p. 23.

in Virgo, Venus in Libra, Mars in Scorpio, Jupiter in Sagittarius, and Saturn in Capricorn. Furthermore, the Egyptians had supposed that the individual planets were lords of these signs because they were situated in them when the world was born.[1] The Chaldeans, on the other hand, had believed that the world's nativity occurred when the Sun was in Aries not in Leo. The Chaldeans and the Egyptians had both assumed, Ficino maintains, that the world was created at some point in time; and both had called Aries, either because the Sun was in it or because it was itself coursing through mid-heaven (*quod ipse medium percurreret caelum*), the head of the zodiacal signs. Hence astronomers had come to judge the fortune of the whole year principally from the entrance of the Sun into Aries, as if everything virtually depended on it. Moreover, the Egyptians had assigned Leo alone to the Sun and Cancer alone to the Moon,[2] while assigning to the other planets, in addition to the signs in which they were then dwelling, the five extra signs in reverse planetary order. Hence they had allotted the sign of Aquarius (which immediately succeeds Capricorn) to Saturn as the last and furthest of the planets, but Pisces to Jupiter, Aries to Mars, Taurus to Venus, and Gemini to Mercury.[3] In short, they had bestowed on five of the planets two zodiacal signs each, while giving the Sun and Moon just one each.

In the *Platonic Theology* XVIII.5.2 Ficino observes that since souls descend principally (though not apparently exclusively) from Cancer according to the Platonists, and ascend in turn through Capricorn, the sign opposite to Cancer, Cancer had been denominated by the ancients (meaning the ancient theologians) «the gateway of men», and Capricorn, «the gateway of the gods».[4] Yet nobody should be deceived, Ficino warns us, to the point of accepting the descent and ascent in this Platonic tradition as referring to an actual place or celestial region. Because the Moon, the mistress of Cancer, is closest to generation, but Saturn, the lord of Capricorn, the furthest away, the souls are thought to descend «through the instinct that is lunar and vegetative», but to ascend through «the instinct that is saturnian and intellectual». For the ancients call Saturn «the mind by which alone we seek higher things». The «dry power» that is common to both Capricorn and Saturn, «since it internally contracts and collects the spirits», will incite us ceaselessly to contemplation if we succumb to its dominance, whereas the wetness of the Moon will, to the contrary, disperse and dilate our spirits and drag our rational soul down towards sensibles. However, in the soul's descent from Cancer it has received from the divinity of Saturn directly, and

[1] MACROBIUS, *In somnium Scipionis*, I.21.23-25, in *Ambrosii Theodosii Macrobii Saturnalia apparatu critico instruxit In somnium Scipionis Commentarios selecta varietate lectionis ornavit*, edited by J. Willis, Leipzig, Teubner, 1970 («Bibliotheca scriptorum Graecorum et Romanorum Teubneriana»), vol. II, pp. 88-89. [2] *Ibidem* I.21.25. [3] *Ibidem* I.21.26.

[4] *Ibidem* I.12.1-2 (ed. Willis, p. 48).

from Saturn's light as well, certain «aids or incitements» to the more concentrated or focused pursuit of contemplation. And the soul has received them by way of its *idolum*, which is the 'foot' of the soul or rather reason's image, containing the phantasy, sense, and vital force and serving as «the ruling power of the body» in that it inheres in the ethereal body or vehicle as its life.[1] Likewise, the soul receives a stimulus to the governing of civic affairs from Jupiter's divinity and light; while from Mars's it is roused to the magnanimity that battles against injustices, from the Sun's, to the clarity of the phantasy and the senses, from Venus's, to charity (i.e. to the gifts of the Graces),[2] from Mercury's, to interpretation and eloquence, and from the Moon's, to generation.[3] Nonetheless, though the individual planetary gifts are bestowed in this beneficent way, they may degenerate in the earthly mixture and become evil for us.

Given Ficino's own horoscope – he was born on 19 October 1433, with Aquarius on the Ascendant and Saturn and Mars in Aquarius[4] – this all points, as Klibansky, Panofsky, and Saxl's book so richly demonstrates, to the special impact of «the seal of melancholia» in the life of the philosopher. He regarded it as a «divine gift», as he says at the conclusion of a letter to his beloved Giovanni Cavalcanti,[5] recalling the famous passage in the [Pseudo-] Aristotelian *Problemata* xxx.1. However, a close look at Ficino's *Platonic Theology* xiii.2 is in order here, since it casts considerable light on the unique role for him of Saturn. He argues, following medieval astrological lore,[6] that since the melancholic humour is associated with earth which is not «widely diffused» like the other three elements «but contracted tightly into itself», it both «invites and helps the soul to gather itself into itself». The earthy melancholic humour has in other words a contractive or concentrating power. He continues obscurely: «If the soul frequently

[1] *Platonic Theology* xiii.2.15–20. See P. O. Kristeller, *The Philosophy of Marsilio Ficino*, New York, Columbia University Press, 1943, pp. 371-5; also, interestingly, S. Toussaint, *Sensus naturae, Jean Pic, le véhicule de l'âme et l'équivoque de la magie naturelle*, in *La magia nell'Europa moderna: Tra antica sapienza e filosofia naturale*, edited by F. Meroi and E. Scapparone, Florence, Olschki, 2007 [2008] («Istituto Nazionale di studi sul Rinascimento. Atti di convegni», xxiii), vol. i, pp. 107-145; and B. Ogren, *Circularity, the Soul-Vehicle and the Renaissance Rebirth of Reincarnation: Marsilio Ficino and Isaac Abarbanel on the Possibility of Transmigration*, «Accademia», vi, 2004, pp. 63-94 at pp. 64-79.

[2] With a play on *Charites*, the three Graces, Aglaia, Euphrosyne, and Thalia.

[3] Macrobius, *In somnium Scipionis* i.12.14-15 (ed. Willis, p. 50).

[4] See his letters to Giovanni Cavalcanti in the third book of *Letters*, and to Martin Prenninger in the ninth; also his *De vita* iii.2 in his *Opera omnia*, Basel, Heinrich Petri, 1576, reprinted Turin, Bottega d'Erasmo, 1959, pp. 533, 732.3-733, 901.2 respectively. See O. P. Faracovi, *L'oroscopo di Ficino e le sue varianti*, «Bruniana & Campanelliana», vi, 2000, pp. 611-617.

[5] See note 4 above.

[6] See Klibansky-Panofsky-Saxl, *Saturn and Melancholy*..., p. 252, for instance, on Jacopo della Lana.

gathers the very spirits into itself, then because of the continual agitation in the liberated and subtle parts of the [other] humours», it takes the body's complexion, compounded as it is from the four humours in various proportions, and «renders it much more earthy than when it had first received it». This is especially because, by gathering itself in or concentrating itself, the soul «makes the body's habitual condition more compressed».[1] Ficino then identifies such a compression with the nature both of Mercury and of Saturn. For these two planets especially use their nature to «gather our spirits round a centre», and thus in a way to summon «the mind's attention from alien matters back to its own concerns, and to bring it to rest in contemplation, and to enable it to penetrate to the centres of things».[2] For the soul to accomplish this contemplative goal, the planets do not act as efficient causes but simply provide the occasion: they are hosts, but the soul is a guest who can come and go as she pleases. We have crossed over here from psychological or humoural concentration to mental concentration. And the underlying imagery involves not so much compression per se as contraction to a point, the geometrical point being closest, indeed immediately proximate, to the intelligible world of non-extension, since it is at the summit of the scale that descends through the line and the plane down to the three-dimensionality of the sensible world.[3]

II. Second, Saturn figures prominently in the famous mythical passage in the *Statesman* 269C-274D, which Ficino takes up on a number of occasions. Let us consider the convolutions of the argument in the *Platonic Theology* XVIII.8.7:

Here is unfolded that old mystery most celebrated by Plato in the *Statesman*: that the present circuit of the world from East to West is the fatal jovian circuit, but that at some time in the future there will be another circuit opposed to this under Saturn that will go from the West back again to the East. In it men will be born of their own accord and proceed from old age to youth, and in an eternal spring abundant foods will answer their prayer unasked. He calls Jupiter, I think, the World-Soul by whose fatal law the manifest order here of the manifest world is disposed. Moreover, he wants the life of souls in elemental bodies to be the jovian life, one devoted to the senses and to action, but Saturn to be the supreme intellect among the angels, by whose rays, over and beyond the angels, souls are set alight and on fire and are lifted continually

[1] *Platonic Theology* XIII.2.2.

[2] *Ibidem* XIII.2.3.

[3] On the Pythagorean notion of the progression of the point to line to plane to solid, see ARISTOTLE, *Topics* VI.4.141b5-22; *De caelo* I.1.268a7-a28; *De anima* I.2.404b16-b24; *Metaphysics* I.9.992a10-b18, III.5.1001b26-1002b11, XIII.9.1085a7-b3. In general see J. DILLON, *The Middle Platonists: 80 B.C. to A.D. 220*, Ithaca, NY, Cornell University Press,1977, pp. 5-6, 27-28; and, for Ficino, M. J. B. ALLEN, *The Platonism of Marsilio Ficino*, Berkeley & Los Angeles, University of California Press, 1984, p. 105 and n. 34; IDEM, *Nuptial Arithmetic: Marsilio Ficino's Commentary on the Fatal Number in Book VIII of Plato's* Republic, Berkeley & Los Angeles, University of California Press, 1994, p. 93 and n. 39.

as far as possible to the intellectual life. As often as souls are turned back towards this life, and to the extent they live by understanding, they are said correspondingly to live under the rule of Saturn. Consequently, they are said to be regenerated in this life of their own accord, because they are reformed for the better by their own choice. And they are daily renewed, daily, that is, if days can be numbered there, they blossom more and more. Hence that saying of the apostle Paul: 'The inner man is renewed day by day.'[1] Finally foods arise spontaneously and in good measure, and in a perpetual spring are supplied them in abundance. This is because the souls enjoy the wonderful spectacles of the truth itself, not through the senses and through laborious training, but through an inner light and with life's highest tranquillity and pleasure. The fragrance of such a life is perceived by the mind that has been separated as far as it can be separated; but its taste is tasted by a mind that has been absolutely separated.

In this suggestive passage Saturn is invoked as the ruler and guardian, not only of the golden age when mankind was in harmony with a beneficent and plenteous nature, but of an age to come when we will become young again even as we become wise and enjoy what the *Phaedrus* 247a, 4-5 calls «the spectacles» of truth.[2] Wisdom is now being conferred on youth not on old age, given that saturnian philosophy is being linked, however paradoxically, with the powers, not of the Titans, but of the youngest gods, those of the third Olympian generation. This gives us a special perspective on Socratic and Platonic philosophy's love affair with adolescents and their education, their *paideia*; and with the more mysterious but no less central idea of a returning time, of a reversal in the jovian ordering of things. There are further complications that need not concern us here but include the Ficinian notions that the saturnian return itself is governed mysteriously by Jupiter;[3] and that the *Statesman*'s myth concerns, *inter alia*, our ability to recover in the future, under the saturnian rule of providence, the pure immortal bodies that were corrupted at the Fall, when, under the rule of Jupiter, we succumbed to fate.[4]

III. The third aspect of Saturn's special status in the Platonic tradition involves his middle position in the generational triad of Jupiter, Saturn (Cronus) and Uranus, a position that is open, from Ficino's viewpoint, to four interconnected methods of Platonic allegorizing. He addresses these in the tenth chapter of his *Phaedrus* Commentary.[5] Methods one and three are of special significance.

[1] 2 Corinthians 4:16.

[2] See summa 19 of Ficino's *In Phaedrum* now in *Marsilio Ficino: Commentaries on Plato:* Vol. I: Phaedrus *and* Ion, ed. and tr. M. J. B. Allen, Cambridge, MA, Harvard University Press, 2008 («The I Tatti Renaissance Library» XXXIV), pp. 122-125.

[3] See ALLEN, *Nuptial Arithmetic...*, pp. 128-129, 134-135, 138.

[4] *Platonic Theology* XVIII.9.4. See ALLEN, *Nuptial Arithmetic...*, pp. 125-136; IDEM, *Quisque in sphaera sua: Plato's* Statesman, *Marsilio Ficino's* Platonic Theology, *and the Resurrection of the Body*, «Rinascimento», 2nd s., XLVII, 2007, pp. 25-48.

[5] For a detailed exposition of these four methods, see ALLEN, *Platonism of Ficino...*, chapter 5.

The first method of arranging or 'compounding' the gods is via substances: and here Saturn is the son of the Good and the One and identified therefore with the First Intellect which is pure and full (with a double pun: on *satur* meaning 'full' and on *sacer nus* meaning 'sacred intellect').[1] He presides over the hosts of the intellectual gods and the supermundane gods led by the twelve leading gods in Proclan theology,[2] and also over the World-Soul (identified with Jupiter) and all subordinate souls. As such he is the first to emanate from the One and he is to be identified both with absolute unitary Being and with the dyad of thinking and of thought. Thus for Plotinus and all subsequent Neoplatonists in antiquity he became identified with the second metaphysical hypostasis in Plotinus's system, namely with Mind. Insofar as Mind then became identifiable in Christian metaphysics, or at least in its Arian version, with the Son – the Logos who was in the beginning with God and was God in the famous opening formulations of St. John's Gospel – we might have predicted that Saturn would be used, at least in contexts where classical deities were a legitimate rhetorical recourse, to signify the Son. But the Latin West's constant cooptation of Jupiter to signify the Deity in such contexts, combined with the many negative or problematic associations of Saturn, obviously militated against this, even as Christian philosophers coopted aspects of the Plotinian Mind to account for aspects of God on the one hand and aspects of the angel, God's first creature, on the other.[3]

The second and fourth methods, which Ficino only passingly mentions, identify the gods first with various Platonic Ideas – and he makes no specific equations, though Saturn is presumably the Idea of Being as Uranus is the Idea of the Good – and then with the gods' attendant daemons. In this latter case one has to make room for many Saturns, since the daemons traditionally take the names of their presiding deities.[4] Such flexibility, indeed, enables a Neoplatonic interpreter to take any and every reference to a deity in classical mythology, and especially if it is introduced by one of the *prisci theologi*, the ancient theologians, and to interpret it monotheistically, provided it serves his argument. But it also enables him to acknowledge the multiple

[1] Cicero, *De natura deorum* II.25.64 derives Saturn's name from his being «saturated with years» (*quod saturaretur*) in the sense that «he was in the habit of devouring his sons as Time devours the ages and gorges himself insatiably with the years that are past». That the name was derived from *sacer nus* comes from Fulgentius, while Varro's *De lingua latina* V.64 derives it from *satum*, the past participle of *sero*, meaning «what has been sown». All three etymologies were entertained for centuries. Additionally, Romans identified Saturn's Greek name *Kronos* with the like-sounding *Chronos* (as in Cicero's work cited above).

[2] See esp. Proclus's own *Platonic Theology* IV.1.16; and Allen, *Platonism of Ficino...*, pp. 115-121, 249-251.

[3] For these transferences, see Kristeller, *Philosophy of Ficino...*, pp. 168-169.

[4] *In Phaedrum* X.5,12–13 (ed. Allen, pp. 84-85, 90-93).

roles of Saturn himself and of subordinate Saturns in what he calls, because polytheistically constructed, the poetic theology and daemonology of the ancients. We should bear in mind, moreover, that Ficino personally exorcised two saturnian daemons, presumably poltergeists, in October 1493 and December 1494 as we learn from two late inserts in his *Timaeus* Commentary.[1] In fact, Saturnian daemons would probably be the most troublesome of all daemons to exorcise given their complex nature, their recalcitrance and their malevolence. And one senses the especial relevance here of the astrological and occult lore associated with Saturn as an inimical planet, rather than the story of the god's castration of his father Uranus, which Ficino read allegorically as a mythical description of the radical nature of Mind's descent from, or procession from, the One.[2]

This takes us to the most important method for elaborating the gods, the third method via properties or powers.[3] Saturn is now interpreted as the turning of the prime understanding towards its own essence. Here Ficino relies in particular on the famous enigma in Plato's *Sixth Letter* 'To Hermias' 323D which postulates the intellect, i.e., Saturn, as the «cause» of Jupiter, and postulates the Good as «the lord and father» of both Saturn and Jupiter.[4] In the intelligible world Saturn's wife, Ops/Rhea, is the «vital power» with whom Saturn begets Jupiter, the All Soul. As the self-regarding one, Saturn himself is effectively the self-regarding or self-reflecting principle at any ontological level, though the first and exemplary instance of this is the self-regarding of the First Intellect, that is, of the pure separated Intellect.[5] As such it represents the 'turn' in the fundamental Neoplatonic triad of procession-turn-return, where the jovian glance downwards is the procession, and the uranian gaze upwards is the return. In this third method Saturn is the father who swallows his intellectual offspring in eternal contemplation of the intelligible realm – an act that symbolizes for Ficino the identity of thinker, thinking, and of thought.

This 'turning', noetic Saturn obviously is not the same as the old, slow, melancholic, contemplative Saturn of the astrological model, who reigns over every seventh year, or over the seventh age of the philosopher still tied to the world, still providing for his body, and still exercising jovian govern-

[1] *In Timaeum*, summa 24, in FICINO, *Opera omnia*..., pp. 1469-1470.

[2] WIND, *Pagan Mysteries*..., pp. 133-138, has an interesting section on violent myths and their interpretation. DIONYSIUS the Areopagite, *On the Celestial Hierarchy* II.3, suggests that the more rebarbative the myth, the profounder its core.

[3] *In Phaedrum* X.6-12 (ed. Allen, pp. 84-91).

[4] See Ficino's epitome, *Opera omnia*, p. 1533.4. For the theology of this enigma, see M. J. B. ALLEN, *Marsilio Ficino on Plato, the Neoplatonists and the Christian Doctrine of the Trinity*, «Renaissance Quarterly», XXXVII, 1984, pp. 555-584 (at pp. 568-571).

[5] *In Phaedrum*, summa 28; cf. X.6 (ed. Allen, pp. 154-155; cf. 86-87).

ing powers as well as saturnian reflective and speculative powers. Nor is he the same exactly as the «supreme intellect» who presides over the cyclical return of the golden age in the great *Statesman* myth, when all things spin back towards their youth, towards the East, towards indeed the Resurrection. But Plato arrives at a complementary elaboration nonetheless. For Saturn is now identified with the first metaphysical and, concomitantly, dialectical principle to issue from and to return to the One: that is, with Mind and with the self-regarding of Mind; and thus with the dyadic principle that is the very corner stone of Neoplatonism and of Ficino's Christian-Neoplatonic metaphysics. Even so, Saturn remained a troubling figure for Ficino, not, I think, because of his associations with parricidal and infanticidal violence as such, and not because of his baleful astrological and melancholic associations (which Klibansky, Panofsky and Saxl successfully explained and qualified in 1964). Why then? For an answer let us turn to a fourth aspect.

IV. It is my contention here that the figure of Saturn was inextricably entangled for Ficino in the problems generated by Averroes's great commentary on Aristotle's *De anima*, which he knew only in the thirteenth-century Latin version by Michael Scot,[1] and indirectly by way of Aquinas's refutations of its arguments.[2] More specifically Saturn was entangled in the controversial doctrine, one that Averroes and the Scholastics traced back to Aristotle himself, of the unity of both the agent and the possible intellects in all men.[3] The whole of the formidable fifteenth book of Ficino's eighteen book summa, the *Platonic Theology* – the longest book by far – is devoted to a thorough refutation of Averroes's positions; and not always on the basis of Ficino's own Neoplatonic convictions as we might have anticipated. The book is so extensive indeed, so packed with argument and detail, so combative in its refutation that it leaves us in no doubt that refuting the great Arab's arguments, and particularly what he saw as Averroes's denial of the soul being the substantial form of the body, was still an abiding concern for Ficino and presumably for his sophisticated Florentine readers.[4] But why

[1] For the dating, see R. A. GAUTHIER, *Note sur les débuts (1225–1240) du premier averroïsme*, «Revue des sciences philosophiques et théologiques», LXVI, 1982, pp. 321-374.

[2] In his *Summa contra gentiles* and *De unitate intellectus contra averroistas*. See D. BLACK, *Consciousness and Self-Knowledge in Aquinas' Critique of Averroes' Psychology*, «Journal of the History of Philosophy», XXXI.3, 1993, pp. 349-385; and B. P. COPENHAVER, *Ten Arguments in Search of a Philosopher: Averroes and Aquinas in Ficino's Platonic Theology*, «Vivarium», XLVII, 2009, pp. 444-479, which demonstrates convincingly that the position Ficino attributes to Averroes, namely that the intellect is not the substantial form of body, is not Averroes's own but derives from Aquinas's arguments against Averroes in the *Summa contra gentiles*.

[3] J. MONFASANI, *The Averroism of John Argyropoulos* in *I Tatti Studies: Essays in the Renaissance*, vol. V, Florence, Villa I Tatti, 1993, pp. 157-208, calls this doctrine «the distinguishing mark of Averroism» (p. 165).

[4] Ficino's summary refutation continued to be influential: it was the basis for Pierre Bay-

such a concern, given their familiarity with the Thomist and post-Thomist refutations that had authoritatively established the Christian position; and given that there seems to have been no well defined group or school of doctrinaire Averroists, Paduan, Bolognese or otherwise, as we were once led to believe?[1] Indeed, most of the leading Italian Aristotelians understood but certainly rejected Averroes's signature doctrine – at least it was signature for them – of the unity of the intellect.[2]

This is not the occasion to explore the entire topic of Ficino's own engagement with Scot's Latin version of Averroes's *De anima* commentary, which itself awaits detailed study. But a preliminary survey of Ficino's understanding of Averroes' views, however incorrect, and of his rejection of them is in order.

Having dealt with many questions and doubts concerning the soul in the preceding books, Ficino turns in Book xv to five objections still needing clarification. The first of these I shall return to shortly but the next four are recurrent and familiar questions: 2) Why are souls, if they are divine, joined to such lowly bodies? 3) Why are they subsequently so troubled in these bodies? 4) Why then do they abandon them so reluctantly? And 5) What is the status of the soul before entering the body, and what after it departs from it? Ficino's answers to questions 2, 3, and 4 constitute Book xvi and his answer to question 5 commences with the first chapter of Book xvii. But

le's entry on Averroes in the *Dictionnaire historique et critique*, third edition, Rotterdam, 1720, p. 383, which in turn shaped Leibniz's account of the history of monopsychism in his *Theodicée* as well as Johann Franz Budde's view of Averroes in his *Traité del'Athéisme et de la superstition*, Amsterdam, 1740, vii.2, p. 271. Even more tellingly the first 'modern' history of philosophy, Johann Jacob Brucker's *Historia critica philosophiae*, Leipzig, 1766, has a long passage in vol. iii, pp. 109-110 on Averroes. But Brucker took this from Lodovico Celio Rodigino's *Lectionum antiquarum libri xvi*, Basel, 1566, iii. 2, p. 73, which in turn reproduced Ficino's summary in xv.1 (see below)! See E. Coccia, *La trasparenza delle immagini: Averroè e l'averroismo*, Milan, Mondadori, 2005, pp. 22-27.

[1] See E. Renan, *Averroès e l'Averroïsme*, Paris, 1852; third revised edition, Paris, 1866; P. O. Kristeller's two masterful essays: *Paduan Averroism and Alexandrism in the Light of Recent Studies* in his *Renaissance Thought ii*, New York, Harper & Row, 1965, pp. 111-118; and *Renaissance Aristotelianism*, now in his *Studies in Renaissance Thought and Letters iii*, Rome: Edizioni di Storia e Letteratura, 1993, pp. 341-357; and C. B. Schmitt, *Aristotle and the Renaissance*, Cambridge, ma, Harvard University Press, 1983. See also M.-R. Hayoun and A. De Libera, *Averroès et l'Averroïsme*, Paris, Presses Universitaires de France, 1991; D. Iorio, *The Aristotelians of Renaissance Italy: A Philosophical Exposition*, Lewiston, me, Edwin Mellen, 1991; V. Sorge, *L'Aristotelismo averroista negli studi recenti*, «Paradigma», xvii, 1999, pp. 243-264; Eadem, *Profili dell'averroismo bolognese: Metafisica e scienza in Taddeo da Parma [fl. 1318/25]*, Naples, Luciano, 2001; Coccia, *La trasparenza delle immagini...*; and D. N. Hasse, *Arabic philosophy and Averroism* in *The Cambridge Companion to Renaissance Philosophy*, edited by J. Hankins, Cambridge, Cambridge University Press, 2007, pp. 113-133.

[2] See Monfasani, *The Averroism of John Argyropoulos...*, p. 165, with further references; and p. 20, note 3 above.

his answer to the first and seminal question raised by Averroes – Is there one intellect for all men? – constitutes the whole of Book xv.

The architecture of the Book is set out in chapter one. It begins with an account of Averroes's view that intellect is not body (with or without the definite or indefinite article), is not something composed, that is, of matter and form. Nor is it a quality divisible in or dependent on body; nor a form 'such that it can perfect, give life to, and govern body, and adhere to body so that a single composite results from matter and from the intellect's substance'. And here he sees Averroes denying that intellect is 'the life-giving act' perfecting body.[1] Averroes's (in)famous conclusion is rather that a / the human mind (or perhaps one should drop the article and simply say human mind), has no link with matter at all and is unitary (i.e., not peculiar to each individual). Thus it has always existed, and will always exist. Nevertheless, it is the lowest of all minds and it is confined to this subcelestial sphere, whereas higher single minds are assigned to each higher celestial sphere. Furthermore, since it is a single intellect, it is properly called the intellect not of this or that man's mind but of the whole human species; it is thus «wholly and everywhere present in this lower sphere».[2] So man as we encounter him here on earth consists of a body and a sensitive soul, but not of an intellective soul, although his sensitive soul is the most perfect of its kind and different from that of the beasts. Finally, according to Ficino, Averroes maintains that as many such sensitive souls exist as there are bodies of men, and that they are born and die with these bodies.[3] Hence there are many human sensitive souls, each of us being individually such, but there is only one generically human intellective soul.

The highest power of the sensitive soul Averroes calls the cogitative power (while the Greeks, Ficino is well aware, had placed such a power in the phantasy, broadly defined as preserving the images collected by the common sense from the five particular senses). This power is a particular reason in that it is not guided by nature still, and it seeks to weigh issues and after deliberating to choose. But it can perceive nothing universal: instead it is thinking discursively about particulars. Nonetheless, as queen in Averroist psychology of the brain's middle part between the phantasy (more narrowly defined now) and the memory, the cogitative power is of all the faculties «closest to» the unitary mind in that this mind is everywhere present to it. With the help of this cogitative power and of the images ablaze in it – and this is the key Averroistic innovation – the unitary mind above it 'perfects its own understanding'.[4] This is the only 'communion' any human being has with mind or with the mind. For mind is not a part of man or a life-

[1] *Platonic Theology* xv.1.3-4. [2] *Ibidem* xv.1.12. [3] *Ibidem*.
[4] *Ibidem* xv.1.13.

giving form for his body; and it is completely separate in both essence and existence – in Aristotelian terms in both potentiality and actuality. Yet mind is everywhere present in a way to all human cogitation, for it derives from the images of any man's particular cogitation the universal species that are its own. As such, any man's cogitation provides the universal mind with an 'occasion' for contemplating, just as coloured light, Ficino says, offers an occasion for seeing to the eye.[1] Given the cogitative occasion, «a single operation occurs», namely one act of pure understanding that is not in us at all, but in mind alone, prompted as it were by an individual's discursive thinking. Nothing passes over from this Averroistic mind to a man; the entire act is accomplished in mind. Consequently, in himself a man does not understand anything, but the Averroistic mind in a way understands in and through the man. While the cogitative power or the cogitative soul is joined to us at birth, the unitary mind only becomes «present» to us when we are older, when our sensitive soul's images, simulacra or phantasms are «pure enough» to move the mind, or more accurately to provide the occasion for moving it.[2]

To complicate matters still further, Ficino argues in XV.1.14, that the Averroists – and notice that he has switched here from Averroes to his followers[3] – affirm that mind is compounded not only from two powers but from two substances: the agent power is one substance, the receptive power another. The first, in accordance with its own nature, is «bright and formative», while the second is «wholly dark and formable»; and from the eternal bonding of these two substances comes, «with respect to its being», a unitary soul. For «in nature a single thing is similarly compounded, with respect to its being, from matter and form». The Averroists call the first substance the agent intellect, the second, the formable or receptive or possible intellect; and they suppose that the agent intellect, «since it is self-existing act, always understands itself through itself in such a way that in regarding its own essence it sees itself, and through itself the celestial minds too». Such understanding, so runs the argument of Averroes and his disciples, is its very essence. But since its essence is always united to the receptive intellect, they suppose «it is through this same intellectual essence that the receptive intellect always understands the agent intellect», whose essence is alike both essence and the act of understanding. It understands too «the higher minds». Hence this understanding is «a single, stable, and eternal act in the universal intellect or

[1] Occasionalism plays a key role in medieval philosophy and is especially linked to Avicenna's epistemology.

[2] *Platonic Theology* XV.1.13.

[3] It is difficult to determine who these Averroists might be, particularly given the later reference in XV.17.9 to «Averroists of more recent times». Among the possibilities are John of Jandun, Paul of Venice, Niccolò Tignosi, and Nicoletta Vernia; but there must be other, more plausible candidates. See COPENHAVER, *Ten Arguments...*, pp. 448 ff.

soul»; and the soul/intellect distinction is blurred here, indeed is unimportant, since the soul is intellective soul.

In this one intellect's formable part, however, there exists another understanding also, «everlasting indeed but changing, temporal, and manifold, which is borrowed from us (*mutuatur a nobis*)». Because it adheres more closely to the agent intellect than it does to our phantasy but is allotted «a temporal cognition» on account of its union with our temporal phantasy, the Averroists regard it as obvious, Ficino says, that, «on account of its union with that eternal intellect», this changing and manifold understanding of the receptive intellect is also eternal. It sees more clearly than our merely temporal cognition to the degree it is more akin to the impersonal agent intellect than to our personal phantasy.[1]

In us, however, the Averroists suppose that «only a doubtful and changeable knowledge is being individually pursued».[2] Ficino gives an example. When Pythagoras was alive, the single intellect «would have garnered the assemblage of Pythagorean knowledge by way of the images of things ablaze in Pythagoras's cogitation». But when he died and the images had faded away, that intellect «would have lost both the species culled from the images» and the Pythagorean knowledge itself, for «the species were created and sustained by these images». Even when Pythagoras was alive, in fact, «as often as his own cogitation ceased its activity, that intellect would have ceased acting in, or in the presence of, Pythagoras (*apud Pythagoram*)». It would – absurdly in Ficino's view – «have received, forgotten, and received again». And it would have done the same in the case of Plato and similarly with other individuals day after day. «Everywhere and at every time», the Averroistic argument goes, this unitary mind «is replenished in various ways through the various souls of men», and thus it is variously nourished. «It receives as many species as there are images in us» – just as a mirror, in the idola-based optics familiar to Ficino, receives images from bodies – and moreover «it produces as many acts of understanding». It also produces in itself, apparently, the diverse habits, that is, the potentiality we have for exercising the disciplines which deal with, and correspond to, the diversity of human studies. And since men in their numberless multitudes «daily apply themselves to the understanding of all things», that unitary intellect «daily learns all things from this multitude». Thus, through the species it culls from our images, the receptive intellect comes to know inferior things; and «eventually, in all men and in the wisest of men, it comes to know itself».[3]

This emphasis on self-knowledge is remarkable given the centrality of the notion in classical ethics; and it suggests that the Averroistic mind is in some haunting respects a great man, at least on occasions, seeking to know him-

[1] *Platonic Theology* XV.1.14. [2] *Ibidem* XV.1.15. [3] *Ibidem*.

self, even as, from the opposite perspective, it is also the lowest of the planetary intellects that already know themselves. But why should such a mind be dependent on us at all, however fleetingly, given the insufficiency and transience of our knowledge? And does its duality as an agent and a passive intellect mirror a complimentary duality in the higher, celestial intellects? And how and why does this mind continually forget what it has learned? These and other such questions point to Ficino's realization that the Averroistic mind was vulnerable to many of the problems and contradictions confronting us in treating of the human mind. Hypostasizing the human mind, that is, only transfers familiar epistemological and ethical problems from the individual or particular to the general, but without, from Ficino's viewpoint, resolving them.

The Averroists argue finally, writes Ficino in xv.1.16, that «the marvellous connection of things» is founded on this complex interactive process between mind and ourselves as essentially sensitive souls with cogitative powers. For forms exist that are wholly free of matter, and these incorporeal forms are the angels, the pure intellects themselves, amongst whom we find, Ficino adduces on Thomist grounds, not many angels existing in one angelic species, but rather as many species of angels existing as there are individual angels. Completely corporeal forms also exist, «hosts of them in the same species», as in the case of the irrational souls of animals, for instance, and of the forms inferior even to them. But interposed, so the Averroists falsely maintain, is «a compound made from man and from mind – from the many human souls and from one mind – like an enormous monster consisting of many limbs and one head, where the absolute form joins with things corporeal and things corporeal in turn with it». Whereas what is absolutely one remains in itself, as is right and proper, «what is corporeal becomes manifold, while one mind suffices for numberless souls». The Averroists designate that compound made from mind and from each one of us «the intellectual man». But they call each of us, when we are separated from mind, just a «cogitative man», affirming that «the first, the intellectual man, temporarily understands something, because a part of him, his mind, understands»; but that the subordinate kind of man, the cogitative man, understands absolutely nothing.[1]

This is Ficino's own preliminary one chapter summary of the complex set of Averroistic propositions he is setting out to refute in the course of book fifteen,[2] though in the end he will be prepared to offer the following eclectic compromise: to accept from Averroes the notion that the receptive or

[1] *Ibidem.*

[2] For this nexus of arguments, see O. LEAMAN, *Averroes and His Philosophy*, Oxford, Clarendon Press, 1988, pp. 82-103; and more generally H. A. DAVIDSON, *Alfarabi, Avicenna, and Averroes on Intellect: their Cosmologies, Theories of the Active Intellect, and Theories of Human Intellect*, Oxford, Oxford University Press, 1992. Ficino of course is presenting his own account.

possible intellect is immortal; and to accept from Alexander of Aphrodisias the notions that such an intellect is a power naturally implanted in the soul and that there are as many receptive intellects as there are souls. Platonic, Christian and Arab theologians can agree at least, and this is Ficino's conclusion for the whole book, that human souls are immortal, just as the original Aristotelians (i.e., not the later Averroists) had also argued.[1] Even so, the length of this book, twice that of any other, and the fact that it is dense with *quaestiones disputatae* as Ficino attacks one after another of Averroes's major propositions and pursues their consequences, speak to two intensely held convictions: on the one hand that our soul is both immortal and essentially intellectual and that our highest mode of existence is therefore ultimately as serene intellects in the act of contemplation; and on the other, that the notion of a unitary soul or a unitary intellect of the kind that Ficino interpreted Averroes as postulating is anathema ethically and psychologically, as well as being intellectually unacceptable.

v. However, this labyrinthine rebuttal, perhaps like other labyrinthine rebuttals, speaks, if not to a fascination with, then surely to an inability or reluctance to let go of the problems and challenges presented by the great commentator on Aristotle. Yet it is in my view neither the occasionalism, nor the peculiarly critical role of images or phantasms in occasionalism, *pace* Coulianu,[2] nor some of the other intricacies of the Averroistic system that continued to attract and to repel Ficino. Rather, I suspect, it was the core theory of the one separate intellect for all human beings, even if this is categorized as the 'lowest' of all intellects. For the theory of a unitary intellect per se has far-reaching implications, since mono-nousism (or mono-noeticism) or mono-psychism[3] is not just the hallmark of Averroism: it is also fundamental to the metaphysical notion of the hypostasized *nous* in Middle Platonism, and above all in Neoplatonism, as the influential studies of Philip Merlan,[4] John Dillon,[5] and others have amply demonstrated.[6]

[1] *Platonic Theology* XV.19.11.

[2] I. P. Couliano, *Eros and Magic in the Renaissance*, translated by M. Cook, Chicago, IL, University of Chicago Press, 1987; this was originally published in French as *Eros et magie à la Renaissance, 1484*, Paris, Flammarion, 1984. Though provocative, Couliano's claims with regard to Ficino are often over-stated and should be approached with considerable caution. On phantasms in Ficino, see M. J. B. Allen, *Icastes: Marsilio Ficino's Interpretation of Plato's Sophist*, Berkeley & Los Angeles, University of California Press, 1989, chapter 5.

[3] Again, one could distinguish between mono-psychism and mono-nousism, but not surely when the highest soul is intellective as is the case in Platonism and Aristotelianism alike.

[4] P. Merlan, *Monopsychism, Mysticism, Metaconsciousness: Problems of the Soul in the Neo-Aristotelian and Neoplatonic Tradition*, The Hague, Nijhoff, 1963; second edition, 1969; Idem, *From Platonism to Neoplatonism*, The Hague, Nijhoff, 1953, second edition, 1960.

[5] Dillon, *Middle Platonists…*, *passim*.

[6] The term monopsychism has a history that goes back at least to Leibniz; see p. 20, note 4 above.

For Ficino, I suggest, Averroes became in several unsettling ways not so much the perverter of the central propositions in Aristotle's *De anima* 3.5.340a10-25 as a subtle advocate – though perforce indirectly and inadvertently, since he would not have acknowledged or recognized this himself in the twelfth century – of some of the central propositions that Ficino had continually encountered and enthusiastically embraced in Plotinus's analysis of *nous*. And this is even as Plotinus was, like the Middle Platonists before him and the Neoplatonists he inspired after him, a thinker who had systematically subordinated Aristotle to Plato.[1] Consequently – and this is perhaps a psychological, or even a mono-psychological hypothesis – it was critically important for Ficino to discredit Averroes. This was in part at least because of the baleful, or at least misleading, implications of his doctrines for a study of the central Plotinian hypostasis that Ficino had so long and so carefully sought to accommodate to Christian thought – and specifically to accommodate to the Christian notion of ourselves, not as individualized aspects of a single impersonal intellect, the *nous*, but as many created intellectual beings, *noes* indeed like the angels, who yearn to contemplate our Creator. In this regard Averroes, *malgré soi*, must have posed an insidious threat. For he was the spokesman for an austere, impersonal, Idea-oriented intellectualism that closely resembled – perhaps too closely resembled – the austere intellectualism of Plotinus's own ethics and metaphysics, keyed as they were, not to a Logos theology of the incarnate Word, but to a unitary intellect as the prime intelligible being.[2] Indeed, Averroes's unitary intellect as Ficino understood it – though quite distinct metaphysically and epistemologically from Plotinus's *nous* since it is at the opposite end of the scale of intellects – must have appeared to Ficino – at least during the early 1470s when he was composing his *Platonic Theology* – as a kind of dangerous Plotinian look-alike, a noetic similar or revenant that had to be exorcised as one exorcises saturnian poltergeists.

Nonetheless, the situation was fraught with contradictions. Ficino thought of Plotinus himself, for all his noeticism, as the «beloved son» in whom Plato was well pleased – to use his own quasi-sacrilegious biblical phrasing. He revered Plotinus, moreover, as one of the first and greatest of the Church Fathers in all but name, supposing him acquainted not only with Johannine and Pauline theology, but, confusingly, with the apophatic theology of Proclus' great sixth century disciple, Dionysius the Pseudo-Ar-

[1] We must leave aside the intricate story of Averroes's own development and his prior encounter with various Neoplatonic texts and propositions in the work of his predecessors, notably Al-Ghazali and Avicenna.

[2] A cognate problem is the extent to which Averroes is in effect a Plotinian commentator, or one influenced by the Plotinian formulations of his Arab predecessors, when it comes to interpreting the famous Aristotelian passage on *nous*.

eopagite. This was only possible because Ficino, like the vast majority of his predecessors and contemporaries, mistakenly attributed the works of the latter to St. Paul's Athenian convert, the first century Areopagite, and thereby crowned him (to use his own image) as the king of a first century but already fully articulated Platonic-Christian theology that Plotinus had then inherited.[1] Most importantly for my thesis here, we should constantly bear in mind that Ficino's whole lifetime endeavour was focused on elaborating a Plotinian-Christian metaphysics centred upon *nous* and *noes*: *nous* in God, in the angels, and in souls.

By way of conclusion, let me hazard two tardy saturnian speculations.

The first is to wonder whether the antagonistic encounter with Averroes in Book xv of the *Platonic Theology* was not another chapter in Ficino's many-sided and evolving response to Saturn. In the war against Averroes's doctrine of the unicity of the intellect, was he not also waging war, albeit undeclared, against a manifestation or species of Saturnianism, a Saturnianism with something still of its cold, remote, contemplatively slow astrological history; and of its ancient infanticidal associations –and the more so, given that self-reflective thinking in abstractions is traditionally deemed to be hostile, since it feeds upon its own succession of offspring, to the consideration of mundane particulars? We recall that in Ficino's own horoscope Saturn was on the Ascendant in its «day abode» of airy Aquarius; and that as a planet it fascinated, attracted and repelled him, as we learn from a letter to his «unique» friend Cavalcanti,[2] though it never totally eclipsed his lifetime's companionship as a scholar-interpreter with Mercury.

The second speculation, conversely, is to suggest that Saturn as the unitary hypostasis *nous*, the self-regarding intellect as we have seen from Ficino's *Phaedrus* Commentary, is the god who mythologizes and at the same time planetizes (if I may coin the term) one of the more troubling dimensions for a devout Christian of ancient Neoplatonic metaphysics. This is its universal, impersonal, aloofly abstract conception of Mind and of the *vita contemplativa*. Undoubtedly, Saturn continued to haunt Ficino intellectually long after his body and his temperamental complexion, and thus his corporeal and emotional life, had achieved a balancing – an obviously successful balancing given his immensely productive career – of the humours and their dependent moods. For a self-regarding Plotinian, or alternatively

[1] See M. J. B. Allen, *Synoptic Art: Marsilio Ficino on the History of Platonic Interpretation*, Florence, Olschki, 1998, pp. 90-92, and in general chapter 2. The appropriation of God's words «This is my beloved son», to describe Plotinus is Ficino's own choice in the closing lines of his preface for the Plotinus commentary (*Opera omnia*, p. 1548.1); see Wind, *Pagan Mysteries*..., pp. 23-24.

[2] *Opera omnia*, p. 732.3: «Omnes omnium laudes referantur in Deum».

an Averroistic Saturn remained, I would suggest, the «familiar compound ghost» of Ficino's own philosophical journey to Emmaus. This journey was a search not just for personal salvation, but for the ancient union of theology and philosophy that was the hallmark of the golden age of the seventh, most aged, and most distant planet both of traditional astrology and of the poets and their multiplying theogonies and cosmogonies. For Saturn had devoured his own offspring, just as Ficino imagines Averroes's single intellect, if it were ever to exist, would be continuously devouring the thoughts of all men. For in preying upon them merely as phantasy-anchored cogitators of the divine, it would be denying them the opportunity to come into their own as discursive and independent rational souls and in their own right finally as liberated, immortal, and contemplative intellects.

Does Ficino's work culminate, however, in «a glorification of Saturn» at the very time when he hypothetically became, in the claim of Klibansky, Panofsky, and Saxl's triumphal conclusion to their second chapter of *Saturn and Melancholy* «the chief patron of the Platonic Academy at Florence»?[1] Prescinding from the issue of whether there was anything even remotely resembling a Florentine Platonic Academy – a Medicean propaganda construct which James Hankins in a series of five essays has brilliantly called into question from a variety of perspectives[2] – the answer is probably in the negative, given the kaleidoscopic permutations of Ficino's poetic theologizing throughout his career. But is there one saturnian intellect, one *insenescibilis intellectus* with its «dry light», as the Heraclitus maxim denominates it,[3] for all men? For Ficino at least, the most ardent of the anti-Averroist epistemologists and metaphysicians of the fifteenth century, the answer is certainly a resounding No.

[1] *Saturn and Melancholy...*, p. 273.

[2] Now collected in J. HANKINS, *Humanism and Platonism in the Italian Renaissance*, Rome, Edizioni di Storia e Letteratura, 2004 («Raccolta di studi e testi», 220), vol. II, pp. 187–395. Another version of one of these essays, *The Invention of the Platonic Academy at Florence*, has appeared as *The Platonic Academy of Florence and Renaissance Historiography*, in *Forme del Neoplatonismo: Dall'eredità ficiniana ai platonici di Cambridge*, edited by Luisa Simonutti, Florence, Olschki, 2007, pp. 75-96. For a contrary view, see A. FIELD, *The Origins of the Platonic Academy of Florence*, Princeton, NJ, Princeton University Press, 1988; IDEM, *The Platonic Academy of Florence*, in *Marsilio Ficino: His Theology, His Philosophy, His Legacy*, edited by M. J. B. Allen and V. Rees, with M. Davies, Leiden, Brill, 2002, pp. 359-376.

[3] Fragment 118 in *Die Fragmente der Vorsokratiker. Griechisch und Deutsch*, edited by Hermann Diels, 3 vols., Berlin, Weidmannsche Buchhandlung, 1903, fourth edition, 1922, vol. I, p. 100. This fragment was much quoted by Ficino: see, for example, *Platonic Theology* VI.2.20.

16

EURYDICE IN HADES: FLORENTINE PLATONISM AND AN ORPHIC MYSTERY

Song – Philomel in her sweetest, saddest plight – has traditionally been linked both with melancholy and with therapy. The Florentine Quattrocento eagerly revived the iconic attributes of Orpheus, the archetypal enchanter-poet-singer and the first Greek mystagogue,[1] along with his haunting story or stories, and here we should stress the plural.[2] It interpreted him as being subject to the divine frenzy, a frenzy that had been definitively analyzed, it was argued, in Plato's *Phaedrus* 244A-245C – indeed establishing a link between the poet and this important passage went back to antiquity itself.[3] In the early 1420s Leonardo Bruni ren-

---

[1] PROCLUS declares in his *Theologia Platonica* 1.5.26-27 (ed. and tr. by Henri D. Saffrey and Leendert G. Westerink, 6 vols., Paris, Les Belles Lettres, 1968-1997, pp. 25, 26-27) that «all Greek theology is the daughter of the mystagogy of Orpheus»; cf. PROCLUS' *In Timaeum* 3.168.8-20 (ed. Ernst Diehl). The idea is very ancient, see H.D. Saffrey and L.G. Westerink's long note 3, and the testimonia assembled by Otto Kern in his edition *Orphicorum fragmenta*, Berlin, Weidmann, 1922, pp. 244-252.

[2] See AUGUST BUCK, *Der Orpheus-Mythos in der italienischen Renaissance*, Krefeld, Scherpe, 1961; DANIEL P. WALKER, *The Ancient Theology: Studies in Christian Platonism from the Fifteenth to the Eighteenth Century*, London, Duckworth, 1972, chap. 1: *Orpheus the Theologian*; *Orpheus: The Metamorphoses of a Myth*, ed. by John Warden, Toronto and Buffalo, University of Toronto Press, 1982 – and notably Warden's own contribution *Orpheus and Ficino*, pp. 85-110; and MARIO MARTELLI, *Il mito d'Orfeo nell'età laurenziana*, in *Orfeo e l'Orfismo*, Atti del Seminario Nazionale (Roma-Perugia, 1985-1991), a cura di Agostino Masaracchia, Roma, GEI, 1993, pp. 319-351. For Ficino, Orpheus was third in the succession of ancient sages, the *prisci theologi*, being preceded by the Persian Zoroaster and the Egyptian Hermes Trismegistus.

[3] See EUGÈNE N. TIGERSTEDT, *Plato's Idea of Poetical Inspiration*, Helsinki, Helsingfors, 1969 («Commentationes Humanarum Litterarum: Societas Scientiarum Fennica», 44.2); ID., *The Poet as Creator: Origins of a Metaphor*, in «Comparative Literature Studies», V (1968), pp. 455-488. We should note that some of the original Church Fathers, Clement

dered the passage into Latin in the course of his partial, essentially bowdlerized version of the *Phaedrus* (up to 257C),[4] and in the 1460s it was competently re-translated and carefully analyzed by Ficino when he tackled the whole dialogue and when he too invoked Orpheus in the context of the divine poetic frenzy.[5] Such frenzy was connected, furthermore, as Klibansky, Saxl and Panofsky's remarkable book, *Saturn and Melancholy*, has so richly demonstrated,[6] with the noble *melancholia generosa* described in the *Problemata* 31 of Aristotle (now the Pseudo-Aristotle).[7] And this despite the fact that for most people the *generosa's* ignoble

---

of Alexandria in particular, had laid out the parallels between Orpheus and Christ, and that fascination with the notion lasted into the seventeenth century. See ANDRÉ CHASTEL, *Marsile Ficin et l'Art*, 3rd corrected ed., Geneva, Droz, 1996, p. 194, n. 11; ELEANOR IRWIN, *The Songs of Orpheus and the New Song of Christ*, in *Orpheus: Metamorphoses* cit., pp. 51-62; and, for the medieval story, PATRICIA VICARI, *«Sparagmos»: Orpheus among the Christians*, *ibid.*, pp. 63-83. We should note too that the Christian catacombs have many arresting depictions of Orpheus singing, where he seems to be identified with Isaiah 9.6's famous reference to the Prince of Peace.

4 See JAMES HANKINS, *Plato in the Italian Renaissance*, 2 vols., Leiden, Brill, 1990, I, pp. 66-72, for an account of this *Phaedrus* 'compilation' (p. 66). Hankins observes that «In his anxiety to bowdlerize, Bruni so mutilated the text that the sense was often difficult to follow» (p. 68): in fact, the dialogue was «beyond his powers as a translator» (p. 69).

5 MARSILIO FICINO, *Commentaries on Plato: Volume I: Phaedrus and Ion*, ed. and tr. by Michael J.B. Allen, Cambridge (MA), Harvard University Press, 2008 («I Tatti Renaissance Library», 34), pp. 2-7, 50-55, 114-119; MICHAEL J.B. ALLEN, *The Platonism of Marsilio Ficino*, Berkeley and Los Angeles, University of California Press, 1984, chap. 2: *Poetic Madness*; ID., *Summoning Plotinus: Ficino, Smoke, and the Strangled Chickens*, now in ID., *Plato's Third Eye: Studies in Marsilio Ficino's Metaphysics and its Sources*, Aldershot, Hants and Brookfield, Vt., Ashgate-Variorum, 1995, pp. 73-84. Bruni's notions of the divine frenzy must have certainly influenced the young Ficino: see AUGUST BUCK, *Italienische Dichtungslehren vom Mittelalter bis zum Ausgang der Renaissance*, Tübingen, M. Niemeyer, 1952, pp. 88-91; ROBERTO CARDINI, *La critica di Landino*, Firenze, Sansoni, 1973 («Istituto Nazionale di Studi sul Rinascimento. Studi e Testi», 4), pp. 100-103; and SEBASTIANO GENTILE, *In margine all'epistola* De divino furore *di Marsilio Ficino*, in «Rinascimento», n.s. XXIII (1983), pp. 33-77.

6 RAYMOND KLIBANSKY – ERWIN PANOFSKY – FRITZ SAXL, *Saturn and Melancholy: Studies in the History of Natural Philosophy, Religion, and Art*, London, Nelson, 1964. See now NOEL L. BRANN, *The Debate over the Origin of Genius During the Italian Renaissance. The Theories of Supernatural Frenzy and Natural Melancholy in Accord and in Conflict on the Threshold of the Scientific Revolution*, Leiden, Brill, 2002, and esp., pp. 82-117 on Ficino.

7 *Problemata*, XXX.1.953a10-955a39. See HELLMUT FLASHAR, *Melancholie und Melancholiker in den medizinischen Theorien der Antike*, Berlin, Walter de Gruyter, 1966; JACKIE PIGEAUD, *La maladie de l'âme: étude sur la relation de l'âme et du corps dans la tradition médico-philosophique antique*, Paris, Les Belles Lettres, 1981; and JOHN MONFASANI, *George of Trebizond's Critique of Theodore of Gaza's Translation of the Aristotelian* Problemata, in *Aristotle's* Problemata *in Different Times and Tongues*, ed. by Pieter De Leemans and Michéle Goyons, Leuven, Leuven Uni-

counterpart had always been a debilitating 'humor' or condition linked to the coldness, dryness, slowness, and distance of old solitary Saturn, the terrible infanticidal father whom Jupiter had deposed.[8] However melancholic himself, Orpheus was the singer, it might first appear, who could effect melancholia's cure, or rather its translation into *melancholia divina*, into the *furor divinus*,[9] whose 'saintly visage', in the iambs of *Il Penseroso*, 'is too bright / To hit the sense of human sight'.

Let us recollect that there was once a time, before gangster rap became the normative song of our i-Podal children, when music, theology and philosophy were the three central preoccupations of gifted men, the triple tiara of learning. Furthermore, in the Pythagorean and Platonic traditions, interchangeable as they often were, musical harmonies, proportions or consonances – and the terms were usually synonymous – and notably the fourth, fifth, and octave, were the keys to cosmology, since they governed the music of the cosmos and of the encircling spheres.[10] The *loci classici* in Plato are the *Timaeus* 35B-36D (on the lambda intervals) and 47C-E (on the harmony of motion) and the passage in the *Republic* 616B-617E on the Sirens, each singing one of the eight notes of the octave. But there are many other less familiar passages from later antiquity that speak to a time when music and music theory, and especially harmony theory, were part of the core preparatory discipline for any initiate

versity Press, 2006 («Mediaevalia Lovaniensia», 39), pp. 273-292. See also ERWIN PANOFSKY – FRITZ SAXL, *Dürers 'Melencolia I': eine quellen- und typengeschichtliche Untersuchung*, Leipzig und Berlin, Teubner, 1923. This was followed by Erwin Panofsky's magisterial *Albrecht Dürer*, Princeton (NJ), Princeton University Press, 1943, subsequent editions in 1955, 1971 and 2005 were entitled *The Life and Art of Albrecht Dürer.*

8 See the interesting studies in *Saturn from Antiquity to the Renaissance*, ed. by Massimo Ciavolella and Amilcare A. Iannucci, Ottawa, Dovehouse Editions, 1992. The iconography of Saturn as the god of agriculture and of the golden age was positively elaborated by, or rather for, the Medici dukes; as one can immediately see in the decoration of the Medici apartments in the Palazzo Vecchio; see ANDRÉ CHASTEL, *Le mythe de Saturne dans la Renaissance italienne*, in «Phoebus», I, III-IV (1946), pp. 125-144.

9 J. WARDEN, *Orpheus and Ficino* cit., pp. 98-99, observes that melancholy, «induced by the planet Saturn» and «as a physiological condition necessary in order to achieve exceptional mental states», was «a prerequisite for *furor*».

10 SIMEON K. HENINGER JR., *Touches of Sweet Harmony: Pythagorean Cosmology and Renaissance Poetics*, San Marino (CA), Huntington Library, 1977; JAMIE JAMES, *The Music of the Spheres: Music, Science, and the Natural Order of the Universe*, New York, Grove Press, 1993; and, more speculatively, STEPHEN GERSH, *Concord in Discourse: Harmonics and Semiotics in Late Classical and Early Medieval Platonism*, Berlin and New York, Mouton de Gruyter, 1996, esp. Part V.

into the highest mysteries, even as they served as the key to attaining psychological temperance and concomitantly physical health and well-being.[11]

Ficino was the first Renaissance thinker – though the significance of this has not been generally recognized – to read in detail, to mine for musical information, and to translate, paraphrase and epitomize a remarkable treatise entitled *On the Pythagorean Life* written by the eminent late third and early fourth century Neoplatonic philosopher and theurgist, Iamblichus.[12] Ficino was thus responsible for making the treatise's invaluable account of Pythagoras and the Pythagoreans, including their profoundly influential notions of musical therapy, known to the learned world for the first time since antiquity.

Predictably, Iamblichus Neoplatonizes Pythagoras and the writings later associated with the Pythagorean tradition,[13] even as he describes Pythagoras as a sage dedicated to the notion of purification and healing by music. This healing was especially effective apparently in the season of spring: «a lyre player was seated in the centre, and those who were good at singing sat round him in a circle and sang paeans, to his accompaniment, which they believed raised their spirits and established inner harmony and inner rhythm» (110). At times they also used music as a component of medicine, indeed as a kind of medicine. «Some songs were designed to ameliorate the afflictions of the soul, to counter depression and anguish of mind, others to soften anger and bursts of indignation

---

[11] See the range of texts in ANDREW BARKER, *Greek Musical Writings*, 2 vols., Cambridge, Cambridge University Press, 1984-89; ID., *The Science of Harmonics in Classical Greece*, Cambridge, Cambridge University Press, 2007. See also THOMAS J. MATHIESEN, *Apollo's Lyre: Greek Music and Music Theory in Antiquity and the Middle Ages*, Lincoln (NE), University of Nebraska Press, 1999.

[12] IAMBLICHUS, *On the Pythagorean Life*, transl., with intr. by Gillian Clark, Liverpool, Liverpool University Press, 1989. The references are to the traditional section numbers, not to pages. See especially CHRISTOPHER CELENZA, *Pythagoras in the Renaissance: The Case of Marsilio Ficino*, in «Renaissance Quarterly», LII (1999), pp. 667-711.

[13] There is of course a long history devoted to assessing the debts of Plato himself to Pythagoras and even to promoting the notion of an eclectic Pythagorean-Platonism in antiquity. See, for example, CORNELIA J. DE VOGEL, *Pythagoras and Early Pythagoreanism*, Assen, Van Gorcum, 1966; WILIAM K.C. GUTHRIE, *A History of Greek Philosophy*, 6 vols., Cambridge, Cambridge University Press, 1962, 1, pp. 161-169; 5, 426-442; and, for later antiquity, DOMINIC J.O'MEARA, *Pythagoras Revived: Mathematics and Philosophy in Late Antiquity*, Oxford, Clarendon Press, 1989.

and the soul's every perturbation; and yet others to counter the soul's desires» (111). Ficino discovered in fact that the entire Pythagorean community daily practiced what was called 'arrangement' or 'composition' or 'treatment' or 'attuning' (64 and 114), in order to alter and then stabilize its members' individual moods, and to balance their temperamental and mental states by way of the beneficial use of appropriate songs and their musical accompaniments. When going to bed, they again used selected songs and tunes 'to clear their minds of the day's troubles and preoccupations, and to make sleep calm and visited by few dreams, and those pleasant ones' (65). And directly they arose the next morning, they used another set of songs, accompanied or unaccompanied, to banish lassitude and torpor, and to instill order in the individual self, and peradventure to imitate, invoke or mediate the universal harmony divine. At such moments song became 'more complete' than any human melody, since it was composed of «subtly varied sounds [...] organized in a logical and harmonious relation to each other and producing a 'circuit' of exceptional beauty» (65).

All this suggests the Pythagoreans' songs not only did away with the need for words themselves, but were in effect uplifting auroral vocalizations using the voice purely as an instrument, a practice Ficino may have imitated in his own Orphic lyre recitals.[14] For they healed individuals' various afflictions and diseases by singing over those who were suffering from them; and from this curative singing originated, Iamblichus had surmised, the very notion of 'incantation' (114). They also used dancing for the same holistic purposes. It seems, indeed, that the Pythagorean day was not so much punctuated or interrupted as continually governed or

---

[14] DANIEL P. WALKER, *Spiritual and Demonic Magic: from Ficino to Campanella*, London, Warburg Institute, 1958, chap 1: *Ficino and Music*, pp. 3-29: 20. In general see his *Music, Spirit and Language in the Renaissance*, ed. by Penelope Gouk, London, Variorum, 1985, chap. 7: *Le chant Orphique de Marsile Ficin*, pp. 17-28, chap. 9: *Ficino's Spiritus and Music*, pp. 131-150; GARY TOMLINSON, *Music in Renaissance Magic: Towards a Historiography of Others*, Chicago and London, University of Chicago Press, 1993, pp. 84-89, 101-136; FRANK D'ACCONE, *Lorenzo the Magnificent and Music*, in *Lorenzo il Magnifico e il suo mondo*, Convegno internazionale di studi (Firenze, 9-13 giugno 1992), a cura di Gian Carlo Garfagnini, Firenze, Olschki, 1994, pp. 259-290: 272-273; and ANGELA VOSS, *Marsilio Ficino, the Second Orpheus*, in *Music as Medicine, The History of Music Therapy since Antiquity*, ed. by Peregrine Horden, Aldershot, Ashgate, 2000, pp. 154-172; EAD., *Orpheus redivivus: The Musical Magic of Marsilio Ficino*, in *Marsilio Ficino: His Theology, His Philosophy, His Legacy*, ed. by Michael J.B. Allen and Valery Rees with Martin Davies, Leiden, Brill, 2002, pp. 227-241, hereafter *Ficino: His Theology*.

orchestrated by instrumental and choral music and a litany of songs. That is, the devotees lived *sub specie musicae* in a way that must have reminded Ficino of monastic communities intoning the canonical hours. And this is notwithstanding the fact that he was well aware that the Greek term *mousikê* denoted a range of meanings centered on the ancient educational notion that music and its harmonies prepared men in a threefold manner: to know themselves, to serve their city-states, and to worship the gods.[15]

Iamblichus also informed Ficino that the Pythagorean musical instrument *par excellence* was the lyre, because Pythagoras had thought the *aulos* – the double Phrygian flute with a sound apparently more like that of an oboe and associated with corybantian dance and Anatolian cult – too assertive, though he had himself used an aulos one night when he was out star-gazing to pacify a drunk from Tauromenion (112). The lyre was variously stringed, and ended up eventually as an octachord, though analysis began apparently with the simple tetrachord. Its different combinations of intervals gave different scales, the most natural being, predictably for Ficino, the diatonic, (he disapproves of the chromatic and enharmonic as being unnatural). Even so, he knew that their tones and semitones and the scales as such were not the modern ones; and that later Pythagoreans such as Archytas had added more ratios in order to accommodate the enharmonic scales.[16] In his *Philebus Commentary* 1.28, Ficino claimed that Orpheus introduced the tetrachord on the grounds that in the 'Hymn to Apollo' 21-23 Orpheus attributes to Apollo a lyre with four strings, each signifying one of the four seasons;[17] and in his introduction to Plato's *Ion* he elaborated on the notion.[18] This in turn suggests that Ficino's own

---

[15] See Warren D. Anderson, *Ethos and Education in Greek Music: The Evidence of Poetry and Philosophy*, Cambridge (MA), Harvard University Press, 1966.

[16] I am culling from Clark's note, Iamblichus, *On the Pythagorean Life*, p. 53 n, which refers us in turn to Barker's *Greek Musical Writings*, vol. 1. I am much indebted here to Dr. Jacomien Prins.

[17] Marsilio Ficino, *The Philebus Commentary*, ed. by Michael J.B. Allen rev. ed., Tempe (AZ), Medieval and Renaissance Texts and Studies, 2000, pp. 266-267. In Wilhelm Quandt's edition, *Orphei Hymni*, iteratis curis edidit Guilelmus Quandt, Berlin, Weidmann, 1955 this Hymn is no. 34 (hereafter *Hymni*), cf. Marsilio Ficino, *Platonic Theology*, 2.9.7, 6 vols., ed. and tr. by Michael J.B. Allen, James Hankins *et alii*, Cambridge (MA), Harvard University Press, 2001-2006.

[18] Marsilio Ficino, *Commentaries on Plato*, I *Phaedrus and Ion*, ed. by Michael J.B. Allen, Cambridge (MA)-London, Harvard University Press, 2008 («The I Tatti Renaissance Library», 34), pp. 206-207. Ficino makes the startling proposal here that, since Apollo is the

Orphic lyre was a tetrachord, even though a lyre is usually seven stringed, and thus the ideal instrument for imitating the harmonies of the seven planets and for invoking the eighth, the universal harmony.[19]

In later antiquity, Orpheus had been attributed a number of divine hymns – 86 or 87 depending on who's counting what – addressed to various gods in the age's expanding pantheon,[20] including both such godlike abstractions as Nature, Nemesis, Death and Memory, and such memorable dicta and invocations as the *Hymn to Apollo's* «You possess the limits of the whole world [...] You tune the whole sphere with the sound of your lyre»;[21] the *Hymn to Nemesis's* «You see all within, you hear all within, you distribute all»;[22] or the *Hymn to Saturn's* «You who dwell in every part of the world, prince of generation».[23] Though compiled originally, it would appear, as pious forgeries or imitations, the hymns were soon generally deemed authentic and became the models of Pythagorean-Platonic music and song, more particularly since they acquired an important poetic preface, a renunciatory palinode that looked beyond the outward polytheism of the hymns and argued for their monotheistic core. Notable features include fumigation instructions – Zephyrus was invoked for instance by the burning of incense, Hygeia of manna, and Demeter of styrax[24] – and a list of laudatory epithets and attributions that allude to the deities' origins, to their idiosyncratic narratives and above all to their powers, their blazon of virtues (*aretai*). Moreover, the opening palinode underscores the link between the purest kind of Orphic music and true monotheism despite the flagrant polytheism and emotionalism of the hymns themselves.

Sun's soul and his lyre the Sun's body, the four strings represent the four motions of the Sun: annual, monthly, daily, and oblique; and that its four voices (i.e. tones) – acute (high), grave (low), the Hyperdorian and the Hypodorian – represent the four trinities of the zodiacal signs which preside over the four seasons.

19 See Ficino's own *Timaeus* Commentary 30 and 32 (Marsilii Ficini *Opera Omnia*, Basel, Heinrich Petri, 1576, pp. 1453, 1457); and J. Warden, *Orpheus and Ficino* cit., pp. 93-94. Warden assumes, following Gafurius, that Ficino's Orphic lyre was seven-stringed.

20 For a study, see Martin L. West, *The Orphic Poems*, Oxford, Oxford University Press, 1983.

21 *Hymn* 34.14-17. Ficino cites it, for instance, in Marsilio Ficino, *Platonic Theology* cit., 2.9.7.

22 *Hymn* 61.8. Cited in Marsilio Ficino, *Platonic Theology* cit., 2.13.9.

23 *Hymn* 13.8. Cited in Marsilio Ficino, *Platonic Theology* cit., 2.6.4.

24 For the role of fumigation here, see my *Summoning Plotinus* cit., pp. 79-86.

We know that Ficino translated the hymns into Latin – though the translation has not survived or at least been identified[25] – and that he never published them, for fear, it would seem, that the hymns in their entirety (as contrasted to lines selected from them) could be used as a means, however inadvertently, for provoking or invoking the daemons, and thus, indirectly at least, for furthering their cult.[26] Nonetheless, three correspondents, Cosimo de' Medici himself, Germain de Ganay, and Martinus Uranius (Prenninger), did in fact get to see Ficino's versions of four of the hymns: those to Heaven (Ouranos), to Nature, to Universal Jupiter, and the opening palinode.[27] But were, and how were, they sung or in some way performed?

Ficino was the only major Quattrocento philosopher, so far as I know, who was also an accomplished musician. Trained as a medic, moreover, he was inevitably involved in the practice of astrology and pharmacology, much of which was traditionally tied to music and its performance and not just to music theory. We have a number of testimonies to his skill as a lutanist and singer, though some are doubtless benevolent flattery or amicable exaggeration.[28] Several of the testimonies, including Lorenzo's own *L'Altercazione* 2.2-4, a notable letter to Ficino from a John

---

[25] See Ilana Klutstein's introduction to her edition, *Marsilio Ficino et la théologie ancienne: Oracles Chaldaïques, Hymnes Orphiques, Hymnes de Proclus*, Firenze, Olschki, 1987, pp. 21-52; also my *Summoning Plotinus* cit., pp. 73-74.

[26] And this is to leave aside the issue of whether Ficino thought of music itself as daemonic or even as a succession of airy daemons transforming themselves into notes or chords. See Tomlinson's *Music in Renaissance Magic* cit., chap. 4, with a detailed examination of earlier scholarship on this fascinating theme.

[27] For the *Hymn to Heaven* (*Hymn* no. 4), see Ficino's letter to Cosimo dated 4 September 1462 (and punning on cosmos). It has been edited by Paul Oskar Kristeller in his *Supplementum Ficinanum*, 2 vols., Firenze, Olschki, 1937, II, pp. 87-88; and it survives in just a single manuscript, the Laurenziana's 54.10, fol. 81r-v, which contains, importantly the *Collectiones Cosmianae* assembled by Bartolomeo Scala to celebrate Cosimo's memory. For a paraphrase of, and commentary on, the *Hymn to Nature* (*Hymn* no. 10) dated after 1494, see Ficino's letter to Germain de Ganay; this has been edited by Kristeller in his *Studies in Renaissance Thought and Letters*, 4 vols., Roma, Edizioni di Storia e Letteratura, 1956-96, 1: 50-54 (commentary), 96-97 (text). In a June 1492 letter to Uranius (Prenninger), he included the *Hymn to Universal Jupiter* (*Hymn* no. 15; Kern's frag. 168), along with Porphyry's commentary, and an extremely free rendering of the Palinode (without the recantatory warning to Musaeus). It is now in MARSILII FICINI *Opera*, cit., pp. 934-935.

[28] Ficino's nemesis, Luigi Pulci, predictably ridiculed him (notably in Sonnets 90 and 145). See NESCA A. ROBB, *Neoplatonism in the Italian Renaissance*, London, Allen & Unwin, 1935, pp. 163-166.

of Hungary (Johannes Pannonius),[29] and a poem and an epigram by Naldo Naldi, speak of Marsilio as another Orpheus or as one who had brought Orphic song back to life – «Hinc rigidas cythara quercus et carmine mulcet /Atque feris iterum mollia corda facit».[30] Ficino had the figure of Orpheus painted on what he called his «Orphic lyre», and his recitals consisted of Orphic-Platonic songs, modeled after, if not actually performing, the hymns of Homer, Proclus and Synesius, but preeminently the hymns attributed to Orpheus, the very hymns, according to the biographer Marinus, that Proclus had also sung.[31] The Byzantine intellectual Gemistus Pletho, who had caused such a stir at the Church council of Ferrara/Florence held to unite the Eastern and Roman churches in 1438-45, may also have inspired Ficino as a performer, for he was reputed to have treasured hymn-singing as a Platonic discipline – we recall Socrates' own hymn to Apollo in the *Phaedo* 60D and 61B. He had certainly copied out fourteen of the Orphic Hymns, and had written on the theme of *Hymns to the Gods* in his lost work, the *Laws*, a work burned by a bigoted ecclesiastical opponent.[32]

However, we can only imagine what Pletho's and Ficino's hymn-singing was actually like, given that the hymns' musical accompaniment is, alas, lost to us, though it has long been the subject of scholarly research and speculation. We know that Ficino accompanied himself on a *lyra da braccio*; that he addressed hymns to Light, the Good, Beauty, and other Platonic abstractions; and that he induced a state of trance or rapture (in Greek *mania*) both in himself and apparently in others. Predictably

29 Pannonius' letter is now in Marsilii Ficini *Opera* cit., p. 871; see my *Synoptic Art: Marsilio Ficino on the History of Platonic Interpretation*, Firenze, Olschki, 1998 («Istituto Nazionale di Studi sul Rinascimento. Studi e Testi», 40), chaps. 1 and 2, for a detailed analysis of this letter and of Ficino's interesting reply.

30 For Naldi's testimonies, see P.O. Kristeller's *Supplementum Ficinianum* cit., II, pp. 262-263. The epigram *Orpheus hic ego sum* is entitled *Ad Marsilium Ficinum de Orpheo in eius cythara picto*. The Latin verses cited are the last two lines of Naldi's *Panthoidem priscum* which were also addressed to Ficino. In general, see D.P. Walker, *Spiritual and Demonic Magic* cit., chap. 1, and J. Warden, *Orpheus and Ficino* cit., pp. 85-88.

31 *Vita Procli* 20. Corsi, Ficino's first biographer, declares that Ficino «presented the Orphic hymns and with a wonderful sweetness (they say) he sang them to the lyre in the manner of the ancients» (*Vita Marsilii Ficini* 6). We should recall that Cosimo had told him in a letter now at the beginning of his *Epistulae* «not to forget to bring his Orphic lyre», Marsilii Ficini *Opera* cit., p. 608.1.

32 Milton V. Anastos, *Pletho's Calendar and Liturgy*, in «Dumbarton Oaks Papers», IV (1948), pp. 183-305.

his friends likewise referred his Marsilian *furor* to the passage already cited in Plato's *Phaedrus* 244A ff. on the four divine frenzies, the amatory, poetic, priestly and prophetic, even as they toyed with the flattering conceit that he was an *Orpheus redivivus*.[33] Where these recitals took place is likewise unknown, though it is possible that several occurred in the church of Santa Maria degli Angeli which was under the jurisdiction of the Camaldoli brothers who played such a signal role in Ficino's early Christian-Platonic career.[34] Whether his singing was aureoled in incense smoke, if not in the smoke of poppies, manna, styrax or other precious fumigants, is also unknown but not impossible, or even unlikely, given the traditional role of incense in Byzantine worship and in the solemn masses of the Latin West. But Ficino was obviously wary, as we have seen, of broadcasting any of the ancient Orphic Hymns, even the four mentioned above, without his being present to furnish a proper musical and philosophical accompaniment and thus to provide a watchful mediation. He seemed especially fearful of rousing musically sensitive daemons associated with particular lunar, martian, and saturnian places, people, and situations. And here we should bear in mind that he was personally responsible for exorcising, with fumigations, two saturnian poltergeists, one in October 1493, the other in December 1494.[35]

What was he attempting to do by way of this Orphic *carminatio*, this singing or chanting or intoning of divine verses? His preliminary goal was to master the unruly passions, the wild beasts which Orpheus had traditionally enchanted, an achievement which Iamblichus had likewise attributed to Pythagoras.[36] For Ficino and his contemporaries, and not just for those interested in Platonism, this entailed calling upon music both to temper inner mood and to propitiate outer influences – those of time, place, and starry configuration – by way of inducing attunement, harmony and concord in an audience. And this is especially in light of the fact that the musical manipulation or enchantment of listeners – though

---

33 We should note that in his *De amore* 7.14, Ficino claims that Orpheus was subject to all four frenzies, while Socrates was subject especially to the amatory.

34 Dennis F. Lackner, *The Camaldolese Academy: Ambrogio Traversari, Marsilio Ficino and the Christian Platonic Tradition*, in *Ficino: His Theology* cit., pp. 15-44.

35 See his *Timaeus Commentary*, summa 24 (Marsilii Ficini *Opera* cit., pp. 1469-1470), and M.J.B. Allen, *Summoning Plotinus* cit., p. 85.

36 Iamblichus, *On the Pythagorean Life* cit., section 62.

this was always it seems an elite group – was the primary aim of medicine as well as of performance, even as it was ultimately taken to be the primary aim of ethics as well. Here we should note that the imagery of music is especially appropriate for articulating notions keyed to health: health at the personal level as temperance, and health in the body politic as justice, the overarching theme of Plato's second longest work, and particularly so for Ficino (we recall his reiterated punning on the Medici as *medici*, and on Cosimo as the cosmos).[37] But let us turn to what I see as his two primary goals in actually singing or at least imitating the Orphic hymns.

I. The first, clearly, was to induce inner ascent. This was not just to bring the *spiritus* of man into accord with the World-Spirit or in particular to make him open to the influence of the *spiritus* of a particular astral body, as Warden has argued, following D. P. Walker.[38] Rather it was to enable the soul's flight in the train of the World-Soul up through the heavens themselves, a flight that for Ficino and his circle was modeled on Plato's famous myth of the jovian cavalcade in the *Phaedrus* 246E ff. For in that myth Jupiter as the World-Soul, as the World-Intellect even, takes both gods and men to the very threshold of the intellectual realm, thence to gaze from afar at the splendor of the Ideas as the light collectively of Truth in the intelligible beyond.[39] Again one would like to know what such sublime Phaedran music would sound like, and particularly given that it is not keyed now to inducing health, attunement or *temperatio*. Rather, it is in effect the wings that enable us to soar away from the terrestrial and the human, and to join the spirits and the angels in their ascending chorus of enraptured meditation and praise far removed from earth's discordant din of words and images and sounds. In this it was linked at the time to the sacred goals of traditional Christian psalmody and worship, David the Psalmist being identified as the Biblical counterpart to Orpheus, an analogy that was easier to elaborate certainly than any analogy, however guarded, between Orpheus and Christ.[40]

---

37 See n. 27 above; also Marsilii Ficini *Opera* cit., p. 608.2.

38 *Orpheus and Ficino* cit., pp. 94-95.

39 For Ficino's commentary on this cavalcade, see his *In Phaedrum* 10-11 (ed. by M.J.B. Allen, pp. 80-103), with analysis in M.J.B. Allen, *Platonism* cit., chaps 4 and 5.

40 See n. 3 above.

II. The second primary goal of his Orphic, or Orphic-Platonic hymn singing was, I would argue, to regain the lost Eurydice. And herein lies a sequence of mysteries that I now wish to pursue.

Orpheus' most famous and haunting exploit has always been his descent into the caverns of the underworld, down to the court of Hades and Persephone; witness the well-known accounts in Virgil, Ovid and Boethius.[41] Having propitiated these dreadful deities by way of his thanatos-defying enchantment and song, he had been allowed to return with her to the very threshold of the upper world where the darkness meets the light. However, his quick glance backwards, as a prisoner of uncertainty and fear, to see if she was following him lost what the music of enchantment had earlier won, even as he had almost attained his goal. At the end he emerged as someone who has lost: he is no longer the empowered enchanter-singer-magus who had once moved the mighty oaks, the very stones, and the ranks of the infernal gods.

While the Renaissance did indeed revive the notion of enchanting song, of an Orphic music that could move the natural world,[42] and of Orpheus himself as a Platonic sage, third in the succession of *prisci theologi*,[43] it delved at the same time into the theological and philosophical problematics of his great failure.[44] It accordingly brought into question,

---

41 Notably Virgil's *Georgics* 4.454-527; Ovid's *Metamorphoses* 10.1-85 and *Culex* 268-295; and, most importantly perhaps for Ficino, Boethius's *Consolation* 3.12. See William S. Anderson, *The Orpheus of Virgil and Ovid*: flebile nescio quid, in *Orpheus: Metamorphoses*, pp. 25-50; Charles Segal, *Orpheus: The Myth of the Poet*, Baltimore, Johns Hopkins University Press, 1989, pp. 155 ff.; and John B. Friedman, *Orpheus in the Middle Ages*, Cambridge (MA), Harvard University Press, 1970, pp. 90-117.

42 In particular see Iain Fenlon, *Music and Patronage in Sixteenth-Century Mantua*, Cambridge, Cambridge University Press, 1980; Nino Pirrotta – Elena Povoledo, *Music and Theatre from Poliziano to Monteverdi*, trans. Karen Eales, Cambridge, Cambridge University Press, 1982.

43 While endorsing the Proclan notion that Orpheus is a theologian, Warden argues, following Horace's *Ars Poetica* 391 ff., that «the most familiar image of Orpheus to the Italian Renaissance is that of Orpheus the civilizer» (*Orpheus and Ficino* cit., p. 89). While this may be true for Landino (see his commentary on Dante's *Inferno* 4, pp. 139-141, a cura di Paolo Procaccioli, Roma, Salerno editrice, 2001, 1, p. 440), it is not true for Ficino; see below Orpheus' later retreat into the wilds of Thrace also militates against the notion of a 'civilizer'.

44 Lucretius presents us with a failure of a different but not unrelated kind: a great poet afflicted by melancholy, he not only went mad for love but embraced the wrong philosophical principles. See Ficino's *Platonic Theology* 14.10 *passim*, esp. 14.10.1-2 and 6; and James

at least indirectly, the role of a melancholic temperament and its relationship to a music that was the source of illusion and loss, even as it was the vehicle, Ficino assuredly believed, of liberation, of ascent and ultimately of divine union. But here we are confronted unexpectedly by the transference of what is in effect the symbolic power and authority of Orphic song from the poet himself, in his all too human frailty, to a re-conceptualized figure: that of a transcendent and all powerful Eurydice; and to this we should now turn.

In the Platonic tradition, Orpheus was never just the supreme lyrist whom Socrates in the *Apology* 41A-C had anticipated meeting in Hades along with Musaeus, Hesiod and Homer,[45] whose fragments (the so-called *Orphica*)[46] Plato himself had regarded as authoritative and had occasionally quoted. For Plato had also depicted one of his principal and most attractive speakers in the *Symposium* as contemptuously dismissing the Thracian bard. The young Phaedrus, the hero of the splendid eponymous dialogue that for Neoplatonists is the sister dialogue of the *Symposium*, designates Orpheus at 179D as someone «who showed no spirit». In ancient faculty psychology, that is, he is someone who lacked the courage, conviction and assertiveness we associate with the hot, dry humor of choler; and who was by contrast too tardy, too timid and too melancholic.[47] As a consequence he suffered «a divine punishment for his cowardice» by dying at the hands of maenads who dismembered him and flung his head into the swift Hebrus where it continued to sing, until eventually it was carried across to the Lesbian shore.[48] This story, in addition to the well known reservations Plato had expressed in general about Homer, Hesiod, and other passion-arousing poets, musicians and

---

Hankins, Malinconia mostruosa: *Ficino e le cause fisiologiche dell'ateismo*, in «Rinascimento», XXVII (2007), 2, pp. 3-23.

45 Agostino Masaracchia, *Orfeo e gli 'Orfici' in Platone*, in *Orfeo e l'Orfismo* cit., pp. 173-197: 179-180.

46 *Orphicorum fragmenta*, edidit Otto Kern, Berlin, Weidmann, 1922.

47 For this Platonic take on the myth, see Cecil M. Bowra, *Orpheus and Eurydice*, in «Classical Quarterly», XLVI (1952), pp. 113-126: 120 ff. We might note that, although he was the son of the Muse Calliope and of Apollo, Orpheus did not share in their divinity (hence some assert that in actuality he was the son of Oeagrus). Legend has it, however, that his lyre was immortalized by the Muses as the constellation Lyra.

48 Neither Plato nor Ficino toy with the allegation that Orpheus was a pedophile and that his death, which was always variously explained, was at the hands of infuriated Ciconian mothers.

rock-stars being allowed inside the ideal Platonic city, points to Plato's having divided the 'bad' from the 'good' poet-musicians on the grounds, not of their musical competence and affective pathos, but rather of their moral commitments, their right-thinking, and their ethos.[49] And where do we position Orpheus in this seemingly straightforward distinction, given his supreme skills as a musician but his failures as a human being?

In his *Comento* on his own love sonnet sequence, in explaining why he had commenced with a sonnet on death, Lorenzo de' Medici contends, echoing St. Paul,[50] that it is impossible to arrive at love's perfection (*alla perfezione della felicità sua*) without first dying, since «the beginning of the true life is the death of the untrue life»; and that was why Orpheus, «who did not really die» but had merely tricked his way into Hades, had lost his beloved bride.[51] Given, in Phaedrus's words, that «heaven itself has a peculiar regard for ardor and resolution in the cause of love», it was the gods and not just the infernal gods, Phaedrus says, who had sent Orpheus away from Hades empty-handed, and had showed him instead «the mere shadow of the woman he had come to seek».[52] Eurydice herself, he continues, they would not let him take away, because he would not die for her love, «mere minstrel that he was», and had chosen rather «to scheme his way, living, into Hades» instead of loving her, as Alcestis had once adored her husband, in pure self-abnegating, death-defying ardor.[53]

Furthermore, for Lorenzo and for other Medicean poets and interpreters – and here was yet another dimension of the Platonic mystery – the authentic Eurydice was not in Hades awaiting Orpheus at all, but

[49] For the many interesting problems, see Robert Lamberton, *Homer the Theologian: Neoplatonist Allegorical Reading and the Growth of the Epic Tradition*, Berkeley and Los Angeles, University of California Press, 1986; and, for Ficino, my *Synoptic Art* cit., chap. 3: *Poets Outside the City*, with further refs.

[50] Notably I. Cor. 15.21-22, 36.

[51] In Lorenzo De' Medici, *Opere*, 2 voll., a cura di Attilio Simioni, Bari, Laterza, 1939^2, I, pp. 24-25; Edgar Wind, *Pagan Mysteries on the Renaissance*, rev. ed., New York, Norton, 1968, p. 157, argues that the doctrine that Orpheus was not prepared to die was 'widely accepted' in the Medici circle. This again testifies to the impact Ficino's translation of the *Symposium* was already having. Cf. M. Martelli, *Il mito d'Orfeo* cit.

[52] *Symposium* 179D.

[53] This whole perspective obviously runs counter to Warden's concluding argument that 'above all', Orpheus is the lover and prophet of love (*Orpheus and Ficino* cit., pp. 101-103).

already dwelling serenely among the gods in heaven as her name indeed signified. Drawing on the etymological tradition stemming from the *Cratylus*, Ficino wrote in a letter to Braccio Martelli dated 20 January 1490 that the name of the half-regained Eurydice, signified «amplitude or abundance or breadth (*euroia* or *euros*) of judgment (*dikê*)».[54] By extension she was not the naiad she had been in the mythological tradition, but the Platonic Justice which is the overarching theme of the *Republic* and one of the primary manifestations of the Good, if not the primary manifestation for human beings as citizens. In a complimentary reference to Ficino midway through the last entry of his *Miscellanea*, Angelo Poliziano toyed with the same etymological conceit glossing Eurydice as «the Platonic wisdom of judgment at its amplest».[55] We should contrast this 'secret', though well established etymology,[56] with Boccaccio's casual note in his *Genealogie deorum gentilium* 5.12 that Eurydice merely symbolized 'natural concupiscence'.[57] In other words, there had always been, for the cognoscenti, two conflicting interpretations of Eurydice just as there had always been, for Plato's readers, two opposing manifestations of Aphrodite, given Pausanias' distinction in the *Symposium* 180D ff. between the heavenly Uranian and the earthly Pandemos, daughter of Zeus

---

[54] MARSILII FICINI *Opera* cit., p. 918.3, but 1490 is Florentine style and thus from our viewpoint 1491. The letter is in the tenth book of Ficino's *Epistolae*.

[55] In the *editio princeps* of 1489 the ref. is to be found on register 'pii'. I was lucky enough to examine the splendid incunabulum owned by Curt and Doug Dombeck of Los Angeles. In Poliziano's, ANGELUS POLITIANUS, *Opera Omnia*, Basel, 1553 – see the anastatic reprint (3 vols.), ed. by Ida Maïer, Basel, Bottega d'Erasmo, 1970-1971, it is on p. 310. See P.O. KRISTELLER, *Supplementum* cit., II, p. 281; J. WARDEN, *Orpheus and Ficino* cit., p. 86; and M. MARTELLI, *Il mito d'Orfeo* cit., p. 344. Poliziano, the author of his own marvelous poem *Orfeo*, writes that Ficino, «cuius, longe felicior quam Thracensis Orphei, cytharam veram, ni fallor, Eurydicem, hoc est amplissimi iudicii Platonicam sapientiam, revocavit ab inferis». In his excellent Yale diss. of 2010, «Orphic Poetics and the Intellectual Life of Lorenzo de' Medici's Circle», James K. Coleman points out that Poliziano had already dramatized the darker aspects of the Orpheus *fabula* in the *Orfeo* (pp. 148-149). His take on Ficino, however, is different from mine, given his concern with the poetics of *furor* in the *De amore* and his Piconian view that Ficino was too 'discomfited' by Phaedrus' 'problematic' comments at 179CD to read them allegorically: I am coming to them from a later, Plotinian perspective.

[56] J. WARDEN, *Orpheus and Ficino* cit., p. 104, n. 7, argues that Eurydice as 'broad judgment' (*eureia dikê*) derives from FULGENTIUS, *Mythologies* 3.10, and was a 'commonplace' in the Middle Ages. This needs scrutiny. The famous poem at the close of Boethius's *Consolation of Philosophy* 3.12 does not adduce this etymology.

[57] GIOVANNI BOCCACCIO, *Genealogie deorum gentilium*, 2 voll., a cura di Vincenzo Romano, Bari, Laterza, 1951, I, p. 245.

and Dione. For the Neoplatonists indeed, Jupiter too is doubled, given the *Philebus* 30D's reference to his royal soul (*psyche*) and his royal intellect (*nous*); and we might even go so far as to say that their sensitivity to the notion of divine duplication (even at times of divine multiplication, as we can see in the case of the reference in Ficino's *Platonic Theology* 4.1.28 to the nine Bacchoi) is one of the keys to their understanding of Platonic theology.

Now in the *Phaedo* 80D-81A, Plato had made an equally arresting distinction between the Hades of the twittering and shadowy dead and 'the place of the true Hades' which is «invisible, pure, and noble». And this is reinforced by evidence from the *Cratylus* where Socrates declares that the name Hades does not derive from *aeides* (invisible), as «people in general appear to imagine» (403A), because they continually make «various mistakes about the power of this deity and fear him without good reason» (403B). Rather, because a name «is really most expressive», says Socrates, «of the power of the god» (404E), it derives from the subterranean king's «knowledge of all noble things» (*apo tou panta ta kala eidenai*) (404B) and the fact that he is «the perfect and accomplished sophist».[58] Furthermore, Socrates asserts, he is «the great benefactor» not only of the inhabitants of the other world but of those still on earth to whom he extends «exceeding blessings». Hence his other name quite properly is Pluto (*ploutos*), meaning spiritual wealth (403E). Indeed, «he will have nothing to do with men while they are in the body, but only when their souls are liberated from the body's evils and desires». This marks Hades out as truly a philosopher-king, as the ideal Platonic ruler who can bind men in their liberated state not to the body but «to the desire for virtue» (*têi peri aretên epithumiai*) and, like himself, to the knowledge of all noble things (403E-404B), to the wealth of the mind. In the light of these Cratylean perspectives did Ficino assume then that Eurydice as Judgment in all its amplitude dwelt in the «pure and noble» Hades of the *Phaedo* and the *Cratylus's* «correct» etymology,[59] a realm of truth in which she, not Minos or Rhadamanthus or Aeacas, was the pure and invisible Judge?

---

[58] See my *Icastes: Marslio Ficino's Interpretation of Plato's Sophist*, Los Angeles, University of California Press, 1989, pp. 28-29, 111.

[59] For Ficino indeed the *Cratylus* was exemplary in its exploration of alternative etymons, and its contrasting of a deity's common with his or her secret names. What may seem merely playful to us was pregnant with arcana for him, as for Proclus before him.

While evidence for Ficino's knowledge of the double Hades, the true and the false, can be found in his *Sophist* commentary;[60] though not connected in any way with a Neoplatonic exegesis of two Eurydices, even more pertinent are Plotinus' well known allusions, in four separate passages in the *Enneads*;[61] to another subterranean mystery involving a second mortal who had once descended into Hades and returned to the upper air. This is of course the hero of the active life and the twelve labors who, though apotheosized at death, yet remained mysteriously twinned to another darker self. Plotinus was responding to the ««mystery» in the *Odyssey* 11.601-604 and ff., where Homer sings of Odysseus's encounter in Hades with the shade (*eidôlon*) of Herakles: whereas the lion-skinned hero had gone to feast with his father and the other gods, this terrifying idolous phantom had been left to be in a way the Herakles below, «surrounded by the dead crying like affrighted birds».

Now as a general principle, Plotinus refused to believe that the soul had ever descended in its entirety into matter.[62] Rather, here in this material world we live a double life among the shadows, as Plato had so memorably set forth in the *Republic's* parable of the Cave. In glossing this passage, Plotinus therefore argues that there are two Herakles's possessed respectively of two kinds of soul. In 4.3.27 and 32 he says that the authentic feasting Herakles on Olympus possessed the 'higher' soul which soon began to forget the deeds it had performed on earth and its life here; but that the terrifying shade in Hades possessed 'a lower' soul which clung to its memories much longer.[63] This subtle Plotinian exeg-

---

60 M.J.B. ALLEN, *Icastes* cit., pp. 96-98, 115, 206. The theme of the two Aphrodites was, on the other hand, a Platonic commonplace, as was the notion of a twin Jupiter.

61 *Enneads* 1.1.12.31 ff., 4.3.27, 4.3.32-4.4.1, and 6.4.16. Note that 4.3 and 4.4 (and 4.5) are all part of one long treatise that Porphyry divided in mid sentence; hence 4.3.32 runs directly on to 4.4.1.

62 As noted, for instance, by HENRI D. SAFFREY, *Theology as Science (3rd-6th centuries)*, Papers presented at the Twelfth International Conference on Patristic Studies held in Oxford 1995, in «Studia Patristica», XXIX, ed. by Elizabeth Ann Livingstone, Leuven, Peeters, 1997, pp. 321-339: 333.

63 Mirroring, reflecting or copying in general is of course a fundamental Platonic concept. Invaluable is JACQUES PÉPIN's *Héracles et son reflet dans le Néoplatonisme*, in *Le Néoplatonisme*, Actes du Colloque international (Royaumont, 9-13 juin 1969), éd. par Pierre M. Schuhl and Pierre Hadot, Paris, Centre national de la recherche scientifique, 1971, pp. 167-199. See also my *Life as a Dead Platonist*, in *Ficino: His Theology* cit., pp. 159-178: 169-173. One should adduce too the ancient notion of the double or look-alike deployed in battles; and notably the *tenuis umbra* in Virgil's *Aeneid* 10.636 ff. which was fashioned by Juno – *visu mirabile monstrum* – to look like Aeneas in order to deceive (and thereby rescue)

esis, complementary as it is to the references to the two Hades's in the *Phaedo* and *Cratylus*, therefore served as an exemplary guide for Ficino, and presumably for a Neoplatonizing Pico also. It taught both of them to interpret certain key mythological or legendary figures that appear in the Platonic dialogues in a double, essentially antithetical way that calls radically into question who the figures really are and what they signify both to the ordinary multitude and to the initiated few.

Be that as it may, whereas Orpheus had believed, so the revisionist Phaedran-Medicean argument went, that in order to gaze upon Eurydice again he had to descend into darkness, Plato and his disciples knew to the contrary that any true philosopher had to ascend into the light of heaven in order to see her as the very breadth of judgment, as the luminous principles by which we judge. And there indeed he could claim her, not as an infernal, but as a supernal bride.

The interpretation of Pico is equally unexpected. In his gloss on Benivieni's fourth stanza in the third book of his *Commento*,[64] he went so far as to argue that Orpheus had been unwilling to die in order to pursue his beloved «because he had been made soft and weak by his own music», the music, he adds enigmatically, that had been taught him by the very same serpent that had stung Eurydice. That is, the serpent had prevented Orpheus from dying for love by making him into a musician (though the chronology of this escapes me)! By way of partial clarification, Pico asserts that the poet had succumbed to his imagination; and this had led him down to Hades to beg for a fantastic or imaginary Eurydice, the insubstantial wraith, the *eidôlon* of his beloved. Instead, he should have cut himself off, Pico argues, from the functioning of his lower faculties, and summoned his intellect to wing its way upwards to heaven in order to gaze upon the authentic Eurydice in the midst of the intelligible Ideas.[65]

Turnus. Ficino must have had such doubling in mind when he postulated a true and a false Pleasure in a fable he originally attached to his *In Philebum* (Marsilio Ficino, *The Philebus Commentary* cit., pp. 472-479), but eventually dedicated as the last of four pleasure fables to Martinus Uranius (Prenninger) at the end of the tenth book of his *Letters* (Marsilii Ficini *Opera* cit., pp. 923-924).

[64] Giovanni Pico della Mirandola, De hominis dignitate, Heptaplus, De ente et uno, *e scritti vari*, a cura di Eugenio Garin, Firenze, Vallecchi, 1942, pp. 554-556. See E. Wind, *Pagan Mysteries* cit., p. 157. The *Commento* was first compiled in 1486 but not published till 1519 after a complicated series of expansions and changes.

[65] See my *The Birth Day of Venus: Pico as Platonic Exegete in the* Commento *and the* Hep-

Pico then self-congratulatingly complains that no one, including Ficino, had ever understood this «subtle and profound» mystery, whereas its interpretation had instantly occurred to him the first time he read the *Symposium*. By way of counter evidence, however, we must again recall that Plotinus's subtle and profound analysis of the twin Herakles's must have been just as familiar to Pico as to Ficino, and that both were also well acquainted with Plato's *Cratylus*, and surely with its memorable dual etymologizing of Hades. All this suggests that Pico was simply responding to Ficino's brief remark in the 1460s in his *Symposium* Commentary 1.4 (the *De amore*) that «for the moment» (*in praesentia*) his intention «was not to delve into (*perscrutari*) the allegorical meaning of Orpheus or Alcestis». We should bear in mind, incidentally, that in the *Commento* Pico never seems to refer to anything of Ficino's except the *De amore* (and only intermittently to that), despite the fact that by the mid 1480s the older scholar had already produced a massive body of translation, analysis, and commentary that the young prince could have referred to, whatever his interpretative reservations.

Platonic song, with all its attendant mysteries and paradoxes, is thus the hallmark, I would argue, not of a failed enchanter, a lukewarm lover, and eventually a singing severed head in the swift Hebrus, but of the philosopher about to join Eurydice herself, her breadth of judgment and her intelligible Ideas, as if she were an Orphic Athena or Astraea, a goddess of pure wisdom. One can only attain her in all her radiant intelligibility, however, not by scheming one's way into the realm of the dead as a living musician, but by dying wholly to the world, as Socrates in the *Phaedo* had exhorted the philosopher to die in the quest for his own soul and its immortal life[66] – to die as Orpheus himself, after his second loss of Eurydice, would also die in effect to the world by adopting a life, Ficino observes, of chastity, of seclusion, and of emptying (*vacatio*).[67] For it was only

taplus, in *Pico della Mirandola: New Essays*, ed. by Michael V. Dougherty, Cambridge, Cambridge University Press, 2008, pp. 81-113: 87-91.

66 *Phaedo* 61C, 64A, 67E ff., 77CD. We might note, incidentally, that one of Socrates' arguments in the same dialogue at 85E-88D and 91C-95A is that the soul is not a harmony, not a lyre.

67 Marsilio Ficino, *Platonic Theology* cit., 13.2.35. Interestingly, in the *Republic* 10.620A (in the myth of Er's visit to the underworld) Plato depicts the dead Orpheus as a misogynist. Unwilling «to be conceived and born of a woman», given his terrible death at the hands of the maenads, he opts in his next incarnation for the life of a swan, since it only sings as it dies. See my *Birth Day of Venus* cit., p. 89.

in his final seclusion «in the wilds of Thrace», and not in some arcadian golden world,[68] that he would at last become the third of the six most eminent ancient theologians of the later Neoplatonic tradition.

This future death of ours, this Orphic death even, will enable us to hear once again the lost music of the spheres that, in Milton's conceit, will dissolve us into ecstasies and bring all heaven before our eyes. «Divinest Melancholy» as Eurydice and her amplitude of judgment will unite us musically, that is, with the angelic choirs, with God Himself, «in Service high and Anthems clear». Such will be the Eurydicean bliss which is at the heart paradoxically of the black *choler adust* that had weighed so heavily on those born under the Saturn of the Renaissance night sky, and that had certainly dominated Ficino's Aquarian horoscope. In this sublime mystery, the four-stringed lyre will have now become the sacred instrument of Eurydice, and no longer of her mortal lover. Perhaps indeed its incantatory magic had never truly been Orpheus's at all, or had become so only after he had retreated, at the latter end of his life, into the great 'emptying' of the wilderness.

One more unsettling complication awaits us. The Platonic postulation of a twin Aphrodite and a twin Jupiter, and the Neoplatonic logic that extrapolated a true Hades and a true Herakles, and if I am correct a true Eurydice, along with their accompanying phantasms, must necessarily lead us eventually to postulate a true Orpheus and his pale *eidôlon*, the true Orpheus being the authentic philosopher-theologian, even as the false one is the pusillanimous singer of Plato's, and Lorenzo's, and Pico's scorn. Yet, given the 'sophistry' that has taken hold of our Platonic understanding of Hades, and given that we are dealing with three bipolarities that give rise inevitably to a complicated set of interactions between them we must at last confront the enigma of who descended into Hades and into what Hades. Was it in fact the true poet, the authentic Orpheus, or merely his wraith? Or was it both the poet and his wraith, the former descending into the true Hades, the latter, into the false? Or was it the reverse (though this is barely conceivable)? And to seek for which one of the Eurydices? For in this equivocal life-and-death here, each of us is a composite of the true and the false, of enlightened selves

[68] See Giuseppe Gerbino's marvellous study, *Arcadia: Music and the Myth of Arcadia in Renaissance Italy*, Cambridge, Cambridge University Press, 2009.

and shadow selves descending equally or in turn into the true Hades and the false Hades. In this maze of options there is no easy or apparent answer to the question: What is a truly Orphic death, or Orphic life-in-death? And what is Orpheus' propitiatory song, given the enigmatic masks of Hades and presumably of his pale consort?[69]

To conclude, we can now appreciate, certainly in this instance involving Orpheus, the Plotinian duality for Ficino and Pico of myths of descent into the underworld, perhaps of all myths and mythological figures – a duality that is not merely superficially equivocal but anchored in paradox, contradiction, and alternating polarities. For underlying their encounter with one of the most famous myths of song, of shadow, and of loss is certainly what the Florentines had come to regard as the Orphic principle of divine emanation: the unity of Venus dividing into the trinity of the Graces, of Fate into the three Parcae, of Saturn into the trinity of Jupiter, Neptune and Pluto, as Pico formulated it arrestingly in his eighth Orphic conclusion on «the right way to proceed in Orphic theology».[70] But there is also, I suspect, the presence of Plato's *Sophist* and its immense web, at least in Ficino's subtle Neoplatonic interpretation, of ontological and me-ontological propositions and its exploration of the whole realm of shadows, illusions, and images as being in a way the sublime and haunting sophistry of the God of life and of death, and of life, however shadowy, in death. All this underscores the subtle challenges for both Ficino and Pico of Neoplatonic mythography and its interpretation. It also underscores the convoluted dimensions of their notion of Platonic song and poetry, woven as it is into the story of the Thracian poet, whose journey down to Hades as poet, lover, and philosopher, was more problematic by far than the epic journeys into the underworld of Odysseus or Aeneas to converse with the illustrious dead in the Elysian fields. For the Orphic journeys – and we must think of them as several – into the ambivalent realm of an ambivalent but mighty king in the quest by way of lyre and hymn to win back an absent-present naiad (who was Justice herself) were enmeshed, for a Platonic interpreter, in a net of alternative readings that constantly spoke to an alternative world or worlds. By the

---

[69] And this is to leave aside the question of the relationship between, perhaps even in certain instances the identity of, Eurydice and Persephone.

[70] See the ground-breaking studies of Daniel Pickering Walker, Ernst H. Gombrich, André Chastel, Edgar Wind, and others; also M.J.B. Allen, *Platonism* cit., chap. 5 *passim*, and esp. pp. 123-135.

same token they embraced a profound mystery about the dualities of love and truth, about Eurydice's breadth of judgment and the intelligible Ideas, and about the life that awaits us as philosophers beyond the grave under the rule of that «perfect and accomplished sophist» in whose plutonic wealth we yearn, in dread, to partake.

PROMETHEUS AMONG THE FLORENTINES: MARSILIO FICINO ON THE MYTH OF TRIADIC POWER

ABSTRACT. – This paper explores Marsilio Ficino's several attempts over his scholarly career to engage the ancient myth of the Titan Prometheus as it appears in Plato's works, and most notably in the *Protagoras* and the *Philebus*. Its collateral aim is to explore the notion of Neoplatonic commentary and its transformative philosophical and theological agenda, given that myth, theology, and philosophy inhabit for a Neoplatonist the same intellectual system. From being a supernumerary, a lesser Mercury or a mercurial daemon, Prometheus eventually became for the Renaissance Florentine the divine dialectician. It was his dialectical fire and his foreknowledge that enabled him to see the providential plan that a benevolent Olympian Jupiter had always had in mind for us and for the world, and to serve indeed as Jupiter's beneficent messenger and intermediary rather than as a thief of heavenly fire. This Ficinian Titan reminds us of the peaks of contemplation that are ours to attain, if we avail ourselves of the supreme Platonic art or discipline that can initiate us into the nature of the Good itself. As such, he continued to play a role in Ficino's evolving understanding of Neoplatonic method, and specifically of the centrality of its exfoliating metaphysical triads.

Prometheus, the Titan son of the great Titaness Themis, has had a rich life in the Western imagination. He is the god who gave us the stolen gift of fire in a fennel stalk; he is the divine artificer whom Othello invokes to relume the light of the human soul, Desdemona's soul, with the miraculous power of his Promethean heat; but above all he is the hero in the one remaining play of Aeschylus' famous trilogy, who, having acted on man's behalf, had then to endure the torturous vengeance of a tyrannical all-powerful Jupiter. All humankind was thereafter indebted to his indomitable bravery and virtually endless suffering. Rubens, Beethoven, Liszt, Scriabin, Carl Orff, Vaughan Williams, Coleridge, Goethe, Mary Shelley, Byron, Elizabeth Barrett Browning, Carl Spitteler, Robert Bridges, André

Gide, Robert Lowell, Ted Hughes, Paul Manship,[1] Kokoschka[2] – these are just a few of the names of artists, sculptors, poets, and composers, who have explored or invoked the Aeschylian, and/or the later Romantic vision of the noble god, the god who is nailed or chained to a Caucasian crag, with his liver daily devoured by a ravenous eagle, and who is the archetypal prisoner enduring without remission the cruelties of absolute power until an entirely new world order begins.[3] The most memorably Aeschylian of them all is surely Percy Bysshe Shelley's impassioned lyrical drama *Prometheus Unbound*, which is accompanied by a correspondingly impassioned preface on the revolutionary role of poetry as itself a Promethean struggle against the punitive rigidities, the stifling authoritarianism, the tyrannical sway of the past.

Today I would like to explore a radically different interpretation as set forth by the illustrious Florentine Platonist, Marsilio Ficino (1433-99).[4] He took up the ancient myth, not by way of the accounts in Aeschylus or Hesiod or in the other poets and mythographers, including Apollodorus, Hyginus, Pausanias, Ovid, but by way predictably of Plato's own sundry allusions in the *Philebus* 16C, *Gorgias* 523D, *Statesman* 274C, and *Second Letter* 311B, and most fully in the *Protagoras* 320-321E. In turning directly to Plato, Ficino was nonetheless pursuing his own transformative philosophical and theological agenda – Platonic myth, theology, and philosophy inhabiting for him, as for any Neoplatonist, the same intellectual planetary system.

---

[1] As the creator of the gilded bronze statue for New York's Rockefeller Center Plaza.

[2] As the painter of the Prometheus ceiling for Count Seilern's house at Princes Gate, London.

[3] The bibliography is immense; see, for example, K. Kerényi, *Prometheus: Archetypal Image of Human Existence*, translated from the German by R. Manheim, New York 1963 (first published in 1946). See also L. Séchan, *Le Mythe de Prométhée*, Paris 1951; L. Awad, *The Theme of Prometheus in English and French Literature: A Study in Literary Influences*, Cairo 1963; C. Kreutz, *Das Prometheussymbol in der Dichtung der englischen Romantik*, Göttingen 1963; and R. Trousson, *Le thème de Prométhée dans la littérature européene*, Geneva 1964.

[4] For other Renaissance versions of the myth, see O. Raggio, *The Myth of Prometheus: Its Survival and Metamorphoses up to the Eighteenth Century*, «Journal of the Warburg and Courtauld Institutes», XXI, 1958, pp. 44-62; E. F. Rice Jr., *The Renaissance Idea of Wisdom*, Cambridge, Mass. 1958, pp. 93-123; J.-C. Margolin, *Le mythe de Prométhée dans la philosophie de la Renaissance*, in *Il Mito nel Rinascimento*, a cura di L. Rotondi Secchi Tarugi, Milano 1993, pp. 241-269; and E. Faye, *Le symbole de Prométhée dans la philosophie de Bovelles et en son temps*, in *Fine follie, ou La catastrophe humaniste: études sur les transcendantaux à la Renaissance*, éd. par B. Pinchard, Paris 1995, pp. 115-138. For the medieval account of Prometheus and his two children, Isis and Deucalion, and in particular for the creation of Pandora (all of which Ficino seems to have ignored), see Boccaccio's *Genealogia deorum gentilium* 4.44-47.

We must first note, however, that Prometheus is rarely mentioned by the ancient Neoplatonists, though they were the prime source of Ficino's Platonism and remained at the centre of his lifetime's concern with resurrecting the ancient wisdom. Prometheus never appears in Iamblichus' *De mysteriis*, and in Proclus's *Theologia platonica* he is mentioned just twice, in 5.24 and 5.34,[5] as the god who had taken the gifts of the arts from Hephaestus and Athena, but who could not provide men with the political art, since he could not scale the guarded heights where Zeus dwelt. In his *In Parmenidem*, Proclus adduces the *Protagoras* myth just once, though he does not mention Prometheus himself;[6] and with the interesting gloss that the «secret and unintended participation in divine goods by inferior beings is called, even by the gods, divine theft». In his *In Timaeum* 5, and by way of a reference to the *Protagoras* 320D ff., Proclus declares that just as man is enchained because of Epimetheus's attraction to the irrational, so he can liberate the Prometheus in himself when «he has corrected the circle of the Other and released that of the Same».[7] Finally, Prometheus is mentioned thrice in passing in the second half of Proclus's *In Rempublicam* in dissertations XIII and XVI;[8] but Ficino had no knowledge of this half, since a manuscript of it did not arrive in Florence until long after his death.[9]

More importantly, Plotinus, the most authoritative of all the Neoplatonists for Ficino, makes only one reference to the Titan. In the *Enneads* 4.3.14 he echoes Hesiod's *Theogony* 60-89 and 521-528 and briefly mentions Prometheus' fashioning of Pandora as «the woman whom the other gods helped to adorn»;[10] and a few sentences later he notes that Heracles

---

[5] PROCLUS, *Théologie Platonicienne*, 6 vols., texte établi et traduit par H. D. SAFFREY et L. G. WESTERINK, Paris 1968-77, V, pp. 87-88, 124.

[6] PROCLI *Commentarium in Platonis Parmenidem*, in PROCLI *philosophi Platonici Opera inedita*, éd. par V. COUSIN, Paris 1864², col. 718.27-39.

[7] PROCLI *In Platonis Timaeum commentaria*, 3 vols., edidit E. DIEHL, Leipzig 1903-06, III, p. 346.14 ff.

[8] PROCLI *In Platonis Rempublicam commentarii*, 2 vols., edidit G. KROLL, Leipzig 1899-1901, II, pp. 20.1; 53.2-12; and 304.2-5.

[9] See J. WHITTAKER, *Varia Procliana*, «Greek, Roman, and Byzantine Studies», XIV, 1973, pp. 427-428. For Ficino's engagement with the first half of Proclus's *In Rempublicam*, which has no Prometheus reference, see Sebastiano Gentile's entry number 117 in *Marsilio Ficino e il ritorno di Platone*, Mostra di manoscritti, stampe e documenti (Firenze, 17 maggio - 16 giugno 1984), a cura di S. GENTILE - S. NICCOLI - P. VITI – hereafter *Mostra*.

[10] Epimetheus then married her, we recall, despite his brother's warnings and she released all the evils from the stone jar in which they had been stored.

eventually rescued him from his agony. He concludes quixotically, however: «This interpretation is as anyone likes to think it».[11]

Nonetheless we should take cautious note of the one set of notices in the Neoplatonic commentary tradition that we know for a certainty did come to Ficino's attention even though he ignored or rejected them. These are all in paragraphs 57-61 of the ancient *Philebus* commentary – in reality a collection of lecture notes – that Ficino attributed to the sixth century Olympiodorus the Younger of Alexandria, though L. G. Westerink has since attributed it to Damascius.[12] Ficino read this *In Philebum*, along with the accompanying *In Phaedonem*, likewise attributed to Olympiodorus, in what is now the Riccardiana's Greek MS 37; and we know he read both commentaries very carefully, since we have his extensive Latin marginalia in both his more formal and his rough-copy hand; and, in the case of the *In Phaedonem*, we have his Greek marginalia as well.

The paragraphs devoted to Prometheus, *i. e.* to the lemmata in the *Philebus* at 16C, are not, however, an interpretation but a brief succession of notes unattended, incidentally, by any marginalia. Paragraphs 57 and 59 refer to the Pythagorean notion – a notion later accepted it is claimed by Iamblichus – that Prometheus reveals «the ways in which the gods proceed down into nature», while Epimetheus reveals «the modes of their reversion»; and this privileging of reversion over procession runs directly counter to Plato's privileging of Prometheus in the *Protagoras*. Paragraph 58 acutely notes that, on the authority of Proclus, there are «many aspects of Prometheus», depending on the ontological level in question: intellective, supramundane and intramundane. Paragraph 60 identifies the gift of Prometheus as more particular and thus more adapted to ordinary men: he has the providential care of rational souls whereas Epimetheus has the care of irrational souls. Finally, paragraph 61 describes the stolen fire as «elevatory existence and elevatory perfection» viewed not in

---

[11] For Ficino's response to this Plotinian passage, see note 19 below.

[12] L. G. Westerink, *Damascius: Lectures on the* Philebus *Wrongly Attributed to Olympiodorus*, Amsterdam 1959, pp. vii, ix, xv-xx; Id., *Ficino's Marginal Notes on Olympiodorus in Riccardi Greek MS 37*, «Traditio», XXIV, 1968, pp. 351-378; Gentile in *Mostra*, pp. 110-111 (*i. e.* number 86); and my *Synoptic Art: Marsilio Ficino on the History of Platonic Interpretation*, Florence 1998, pp. 157-161. Despite Ficino's extensive marginalia, Westerink finds in general very few points of contact between the two commentaries (p. 354), though he does identify three of the four unattached chapters concluding the final version of Ficino's *In Philebum* as «stray notes» on certain paragraphs in Olympiodorus. None of these four chapters mentions Prometheus, however, though the fourth one does deal with dialectic as a divine gift that was given as fire, «that is, with the same sort of power that fire has».

its upward motion but in the process of being distributed to the lowest stratum of the universe: it is stolen precisely because it is brought down: «its descent is effected by Titanic powers while its existence as form is due to other gods».[13]

In short, even with these notes on Prometheus in Olympiodorus we can appreciate the paucity if not the inadequacy of Ficino's sources: none of them provided him with a comprehensive interpretation, a truly Platonic interpretation, of the famous myth of the son of Themis, the divine friend of primitive man.

*

It is not surprising therefore that he had to make several independent attempts to interpret the «pagan mysteries» associated with Prometheus; and a brief review of his more significant references and allegorical sorties is in order before we take up what eventually emerged as his core interpretation.

In the *Platonic Theology* 14.9.3,[14] in pursuing the argument that men must be led ultimately not by a mere man like themselves but by God, Ficino alludes to Protagoras's story in his eponymous dialogue which declares: a) «that men cannot live together without law»; b) that they had been unable to receive law sufficient enough to live together from Prometheus – «from the providence, in other words, that is particular and created»;[15] and c) that Jupiter himself, «the creator of all», had ultimately despatched Mercury down to men with the law – «had despatched, that is, a prophet, an interpreter of the divine will, and a giver of both divine and human law». This is a radical recasting of the story. Prometheus is merely an aspect of providence, providence that is particular and created,

---

[13] I am citing Westerink's translation, *Damascius*, cit., pp. 28-30.

[14] M. Ficino, *Platonic Theology*, 6 vols., edition and translation by M. J. B. Allen and J. Hankins, Cambridge, Mass. 2001-06.

[15] In the first book of his *Epistolae* in a letter entitled *Lex et justitia* and addressed to the lawyers Ottone Niccolini and Benedetto d'Arezzo and others, Ficino again glosses Prometheus as signifying human providence: «those skills which relate to sustaining life were transmitted to us by Prometheus, that is, human providence». But the law of living well and happily was granted by Jupiter, that is, by divine providence, through Mercury who is angelic inspiration (Ficini *Opera Omnia*, Basel 1576, pp. 611-612: 612 = *Letters* 1.6 – hereafter *Opera*). He says the same in a letter to Francesco Berlinghieri, *Opera*, p. 827.3 (= *Letters* 6.30).

while the hero of the story at this point for Ficino is Mercury as prophet, giver, and interpreter of the law.[16] By contrast, in the *De Vita Triplici* 3.13.18,[17] Ficino briefly defines Prometheus as a creator-god who had seized life from the heavens and infused it into a clay model (*Prometheum figmento quodam luteo vitam rapuisse lucemque coelestem*). Indeed the tradition held that Prometheus was the master potter who modelled man from clay (Pausanias 10.4.4) and from bits of animals (Horace, *Carmina* 1.16.13 ff) and then animated him with the stolen fire (Ovid, *Metamorphoses* 1.82).[18] Elsewhere Ficino thinks of such modelling in terms of statue magic – of making statues and of animating them – at least allegorically.[19]

In the seventh book of his *Letters*, in an apologus entitled *Potentia sine sapientia non regnat*, Ficino muses in an oddly astrological vein that Prometheus ascended to heaven, and there he learned, among the many secrets Jupiter imparted to him, the reason why the Sun and Mercury are such constant close companions: «for the Sun goes nowhere without wise Mercury», because power and wisdom must always go together; and therefore on earth power should never be granted anyone without wisdom.[20]

The most arresting revisioning of Prometheus in Ficino's *Letters* occurs, however, in the second book's opening tract entitled *Five Questions concerning the Mind*, in the section *Immortalis animus in corpore mortali semper est miser.* Here Ficino describes Prometheus not as a god or daemon but rather as man himself who suffers grievously after his theft of fire, meaning his acquisition of reason, and who will continue to suffer until he re-ascends at last to the fire's origin and source:

> Nothing indeed can be imagined more unreasonable than that man, who through reason is the most perfect of animals, indeed of all things under the

---

[16] And he reinforces this argument by referencing Avicenna's call for a prophet as «a divine leader», though we might have anticipated rather an allusion to Moses.

[17] M. Ficino, *Three Books on Life*, critical edition and translation with introduction and notes by C. V. Kaske and J. R. Clark, Binghamton, N.Y. 1989.

[18] In a letter to Pico in the ninth book of his *Letters* – a letter composed after Pico had written his *Heptaplus* and Ficino had completed the third book of his own *De vita* «On obtaining life from the heavens» – Ficino observes whimsically that «Imitating Prometheus we are making man, you the soul and I the body»; *Opera*, p. 900.3 (= *Letters* 9.15).

[19] Cf. Ficino's comments on Plotinus' *Enneads* 4.3.13-14 where he identifies Prometheus as «a certain natural providence ruling in the vital part of the World Soul who fashioned statues, meaning natural things, from the clay, that is, from prime matter»; *Opera*, p. 1738.3. See my *To Gaze Upon the Face of God Again: Philosophic Statuary, Pygmalion and Marsilio Ficino*, «Rinascimento», II s., XLVIII, 2009, pp. 123-136.

[20] *Opera*, p. 848.2 (= *Letters* 7.14).

heavens – the most perfect I say in that he looks to that formal perfection which is bestowed upon us from the beginning – should, for the same reason, be the least perfect of all things with regard to the final perfection, for the pursuit of which the first perfection is given us. Man seems to be that most unfortunate Prometheus who, instructed by the divine wisdom of Pallas, gained possession of the heavenly fire, that is, reason. But because of this, being on the loftiest peak of the mountain, that is, at the very height of contemplation, and being continually pecked at by the most ravenous of birds, that is, the torment of inquiry, he is rightly judged to be the most miserable of all beings. And this torment will continue until the time comes at last when he is borne back to the same place whence he first received the fire. Hence, just as he is now continually prompted to seek in that one small beam of heavenly light for the whole light, so at that future time he will be utterly filled with that whole light.[21]

This is remarkable on several counts: that Prometheus can symbolize man himself, albeit man in his original divine or daemonic state; that Prometheus' torment is not inflicted by a vengeful Jupiter but rather by Prometheus on himself, being the torment of intellectual reasoning; that the fire symbolizes the gift of reason that helps to restore us to the «celestial light»; that just one small beam of that heavenly fire will eventually lead us to the whole light of understanding; and that the mountain peak is therefore not a Caucasian escarpment but the craggy summit of contemplation. Even more strikingly, Minerva has not given man the artificer's gifts. Rather, she has bestowed on Prometheus the art of finding and possessing the fire of reason. Vulcan does not figure in this reconstruction at all, nor obviously does Epimetheus, nor (surprisingly) does Mercury, and nor, in truth, do many features of the traditional – one might be tempted to say the original – core story.

Ficino's most dramatic intervention here is the suggestion that Pro-

[21] M. FICINO, *Lettere*, 2 vols., a cura di S. GENTILE, Florence 1990-2010, II, p. 19, lines 378-392 (= *Opera*, p. 680.3): «Nihil vero irrationabilius fingi potest quam hominem, qui per rationem est animalium immo omnium que sub celo sunt perfectissimus, perfectissimus, inquam, quantum ad formalem perfectionem illam spectat que tributa nobis est ab initio, ob eandem rationem esse omnium imperfectissimum quantum ad finalem illam perfectionem, ad quam consequendam perfectio prima tribuitur. Hic esse videtur infelicissimus ille Prometheus, qui divina sapientia Palladis instructus ignemque celestem, id est rationem, adeptus, ob hoc ipsum in summo vertice montis, hoc est in ipsa contemplationis arce, ob continuum avis rapacissime morsum, id est inquisitionis stimulum, miserrimus omnium merito iudicatur, donec transferatur eodem, unde olim acceperat ignem, ut quemadmodum uno illo luminis superni radiolo nunc assidue stimulatur ad totum, sic toto deinde lumine penitus impleatur». I have ventured to revise and expand the translation in *The Renaissance Philosophy of Man: Petrarca, Valla, Ficino etc.*, ed. by E. CASSIRER - P. O. KRISTELLER - J. H. RANDALL JR., Chicago 1948, p. 208.

metheus' torture of thought, that man's restless search for knowledge, will continue until the time comes when at last «he is borne back to that same place whence he first received the fire». This implies some notion of an appointed span, the end of a temporal, perhaps even an astrological cycle, a «return» to a time and place when and where he first received illumination, and where he can regain his status as the most perfect of all creatures. At that moment of conversion to his final cause, his whole being will be flooded with the light of celestial understanding, light beyond the single small beam of the reason. Ficino has in effect metamorphosed the old rebellion myth of a god into a creation-resurrection myth keyed to the return of man's reason and intellect to their pristine condition as faculties suffused with celestial, with angelic light. Even the Promethean torture is the anguish of thought and forethought and not the suffering of retribution or even of retrospection. In effect, Ficino has compiled an idiosyncratic but transformative version of the myth in order to figure forth the relationship between God and primal man, God and Adam, and to concentrate on the faculty that ultimately determines Adam's ability to contemplate God. The myth has gone from being about the gift of artisanal fire to being about the coming of the Johannine light «which lighteth every man that cometh into the world», and which eventually fills us with its radiant plenitude.

*

How then does Ficino interpret the myth in the one place we would most anticipate a full treatment, namely in his epitome of the *Protagoras*, the introduction to the dialogue which he wrote for his great *Platonis Opera Omnia* volume of 1484?[22] While it is true that he fails to elaborate on some of the transformative insights in the passage from the *Five Questions* treatise we have just analyzed, he nonetheless again appropriates Plato's account. To begin with, Protagoras does not simply tell a tale: rather, it is the ancient theologians who tell the story of how all living things once lay buried under the earth. Ficino interprets this to mean that «the seeds of things lay hidden in the world's prime matter».[23] Jupiter, «the world's

[22] This epitome is most accessible in the modern reprints of Ficino's own *Opera*, pp. 1296-1300: 1298.

[23] See his *Protagoras* epitome, *Opera*, p. 1298: «Tradunt theologi veteres sub terra quondam animalia, id est in prima mundi materia rerum semina praefuisse».

Creator god», and not just the gods as such, then used the lesser gods, glossed as the stars, by way of their astrological influences to fashion creatures from the four elements. Plato says to the contrary that creatures were fashioned from a mixture of earth and fire and the substances compounded from them. This demiurgic vision derives from the *Timaeus* of course, where the lesser gods in turn made use of the daemons' help; and Prometheus represents, says Ficino, the highest levels of the daemons and at the same time the higher providence, while Epimetheus represents the host of lower daemons and the lower providence. The higher daemons assist the incorporeal and rational nature, while Epimetheus gives aid to the corporeal and irrational nature in matters pertaining to the body.

Moreover, Ficino's epitome insists that Prometheus received (*accepit*) – and did not steal – «the principle of art and skill» (*ratio artis*), together with the gift of fire, from the workshop (*ex officina*) of Minerva and Vulcan. Ficino extracts a triad here: Minerva is the intelligence, Vulcan is the practical skill, and fire is the tool. The twin divinities, Minerva and Vulcan, are deemed to be in the Ideas themselves of the arts; they govern the powers of Mercury and Mars; and they preside finally over the daemons who watch over the arts and skills. In other words, Minerva and Vulcan remain the primary, originating dyad, and Ficino sees them as the givers of the gifts to Prometheus, and thereafter to the other daemons and eventually to men. There was no sacred theft (however resonant the notion may be for us).[24] Prometheus, defined differently now as the ruler of the rational soul, passed diligence on to man in the exercise of art (*in hominem traiecit artis industriam*).[25] «But because the divine gift was present in man, through this kinship with the divine, man worshipped God before he could either speak or practice any of the lesser arts».[26] For the divine gift through its wonderful power elevated him to the divine sphere before despatching him to human activities. Prometheus was «afflicted with pain» on account of that gift and «moved by compassion towards us»

[24] See Patrick J. Geary's fascinating study, *'Furta sacra': Thefts of Relics in the Central Middle Ages*, Princeton 1978.

[25] Again see Ficino's *Protagoras* epitome in his *Opera*, p. 1298: «Accepit autem artem ipsam una cum ignem ab officina Minervae atque Vulcani, Minerva quidem in arte ingenium, Vulcanus autem efficaciam continet, ignis denique instrumentum. Gemina vero haec numina Minerva Vulcanusque primo quidem in ipsis artium ideis excogitantur. Deinde in Mercurii Martisque virtutibus. Postremo in daemonibus gubernatoribus artium. Ab his igitur omnibus Prometheus rationalis animae gubernator in hominem traeicit artis industriam».

[26] *Ibid.*: «Quoniam vero divinum id existit donum statim, ob ipsam cum superis cognationem, homo veneratus est Deum antequam loqueretur vel artes aliquas exerceret».

(*dolore affectum [...] misericordia quadam erga nos affici*), since he knew that, by way of the very reason he had given us, we would now rationally understand how wretched our life is to be here, a life more burdened «with care and sorrow» (*vitam [...] sollicitam atque explebilem*) than that of the dumb beasts. Such a dolorous chord indeed serves as the resonant opening of Ficino's *Platonic Theology* 1.1.1.

In this *Protagoras* epitome account, which differs in many respects from the *Protagoras'* own account, Prometheus plays very much the subordinate role as the helping daemon obeying the god's commands. Notably, Ficino again bypasses the notion of retributive torture by substituting the companionate notion that Prometheus – indeed by implication all the higher daemons – felt «compassion» (*misericordia*) for us: that the spiritual beings who have been charged with caring for us did and do continually feel on our behalf.

Ficino turns at this point, however, to the *Philebus* 16CD, because from his perspective it has the most innovative things to say about the ultimate Neoplatonic art, the art of dialectic (*ars disserendi*), which the gods «let fall from their abode». It was through the agency of Prometheus, «or of one like him», that the gift, «together with a fire exceeding bright», reached the ancients, who were better than ourselves and dwelt nearer the gods. The gift was «in the form of a saying» to the effect that «all things that are ever said to be consist of a one and a many, and have in their nature a conjunction of limit and unlimitedness». They bequeathed this saying to lesser men who were then able to use dialectic, which in the Platonic tradition always transcends mere logic. For, argues Ficino, it divides universals into particulars and thus «represents» the procession (*processus*) of things down from the higher world (*ab superioribus*); and yet it resolves particulars into universals and thus indicates their return (*conversio*)[27] to the realms above (*ad superiora*). It defines and demonstrates and reveals the existence of things as being independent in the higher realms but dependent here.[28] Dialectic is a divine gift of illumination and not just a tool. In the words of the *Philebus* 58D3-7, it is «a certain faculty in our souls» which is beyond even «reason and intelligence in their purity», and is «naturally directed to loving truth and doing all for the sake of truth». As a faculty it portrays the divine order of the uni-

---

[27] I have emended the *Opera's* «controversiam» to «conversionem».

[28] *Opera*, p. 1298: «existentia rerum ostendit ibi quidem in seipsis, hic autem ab aliis dependentium».

verse which it possesses in itself. Moreover, it is given with fire, because fire too, like dialectic, divides, resolves, defines, and demonstrates; and in so doing, it illumines the intellect and ignites the will and subsumes both these principal faculties into itself.

It seems to matter little here that Prometheus was unable to bestow the civic virtues which were left for Jupiter to bestow upon us via Mercury as another messenger of the divine will. Mercury may write the laws of «civic knowledge» on our hearts along with the jovian decrees that order our communal existence and welfare, but all this seems subordinate to the Promethean gift of «the hymn» of Platonic dialectic, the «capstone» of the sciences which «alone goes directly to the first principle» – to evoke the memorable phrases of the *Republic* 7.532A, 533C, and 534E.[29]

*

In his *Philebus* Commentary Ficino goes further still:[30] In 1.26, the chapter heading reads, «How God illuminates our intelligences and how Prometheus brought us the divine light from heaven, which consists of the art of dividing, uniting and demonstrating». Note that here, in what Ficino refers to as an extended parable (*prolixiori quadam parabola*), Prometheus is now bringing light not fire.[31] More intriguing still is Ficino's exploration of the interaction of various triads, triads which had become, with Plotinus and even more so with Proclus, the fundamental key to his understanding of Platonic metaphysics and hence to his attempt to accommodate this metaphysics to Christianity. Each triad marks a descent or emanation. First, Ficino says, is the triad of the Seraphim as a single divine intelligence consisting of its head, breast, and thigh – its head gazes up towards the Good, its breast looks towards its own beauty, and its thigh reaches down to providing for and creating lower things. Second is the triad associated not just with the highest angelic choir but

[29] Cf. *Philebus* 57E ff. See my *Synoptic Art: Marsilio Ficino on the History of Platonic Interpretation*, Firenze 1998, chap. 5: «Promethean Dialectic».

[30] M. FICINO, *The Philebus Commentary*, critical edition and translation by M. J. B. ALLEN, Berkeley - Los Angeles 1975; repr. Tempe 2000.

[31] Is this light indirectly keyed to the *Philebus* 16C2-3's mention of «the instrument through which every discovery ever made in the sphere of the arts and sciences has been brought to light» (*phanera gegone*)? The obvious root is *phaos* (light) or *phanos* (bright); hence *phaneros* (visible) and *phanê* and *phanos* (a torch), and hence too the abstract Orphic deity *Phanes*.

with all the angels which in Dionysius the Areopagite's *De nominibus divinis* 4.8 are declared to have three motions, circular, straight and spiral: circular in their returning to God, straight in their «offering/extending their power» to lower things, and spiral insofar as they devote attention to themselves.[32]

Third is the ray of the Good which becomes triple in any intelligence. When it strives towards the Good, this ray is Saturn (though some say the Sky, Coelius); when it reverts to itself, it is Jupiter; and when it turns towards lower things, it is Prometheus. Accordingly, the soul in turn has three powers: one joining it to the higher, another whereby it retains its proper energy, and another joining it to the lower. The first is the light of intelligence, the second is the ability to reason, the third is the force of the phantasy and its skills. Notice that Prometheus only features here at the lowest intellectual level. Nonetheless, he is above the epistemological triad associated with soul itself: he is the last reaching out of the divine to the human – the point where the divine and the human intellects interact. But instead of being the protoplastic Man invoked in the *Five Questions* tract, he remains a heroic divinity above man. Even the slow-witted Epimetheus, who presides over nature and the natural powers that provide the beasts with protection and armor, cherishing the body and ensuring the sexual desire that perpetuates the species, represents, says Ficino, the providence of Jupiter, even though he is the providence that extends down into the world of irrational things. His brother by contrast is the other providence, the «ingenious providence of the divine Mind», that is, the providence of Jupiter as the cherisher of our artisanal, our ingenious skills.[33] In other words, both brothers are now aspects of Jupiter whereas in Ficino's *Protagoras* epitome, we recall, they had signified merely the higher and the lower orders of the daemons.

Ficino supposes Plato's statement that Prometheus took the «activity centered on the arts» (*industria artium*) from the workshop (*ex officina*) of Minerva and Vulcan to mean that the «lowest part of the intelligence» which is called Prometheus takes light and power (heat?) from the middle part, the workshop; and that this middle part looks three ways: towards

---

[32] *PG* 3, cols. 704D-705A.

[33] *In Philebum* 1.26 (ed. ALLEN, pp. 240-247). Cf. Ficino's epitome of Plato's *Second Letter* where he says that Plato has properly linked together the names of Jupiter and Prometheus [311B] because Jupiter is [divine] power and Prometheus is the wisdom that underlies God's providence.

a higher part from which it depends, towards itself as it is in itself, and towards producing a lower part. The first orientation is called Jupiter «greatest and best», the next, Jupiter «friendly and hospitable», the third, Pallas and Vulcan – Pallas is born from Jupiter's head, «because she gives to the lower power from the prime power»,[34] whereas Vulcan is lame, «because there is something wrong in what is the product of desire». We are left at this point with an intricate if not confusing framework that postulates a lower part (Prometheus), a middle part (the workshop), and the latter's «three respects», *i. e.* its triple orientations designated respectively Jupiter *maximus*, Jupiter *amicabilis*, and Pallas/Vulcan.

This provocative doubling of Jupiter[35] emphasizes the fact that for Ficino the Olympian king has become the central figure in the Prometheus myth – perhaps he had always been the central figure, given that he is the supreme giver of gifts to mankind. Following the *Philebus* 30D's reference to a double Zeus with a royal soul and a royal intellect, Ficino sees Jupiter either as Soul, or as Soul's prime manifestation as the World Soul, or as the demiurgic Mind, the Creator God of the *Timaeus* 28A ff.[36] Even in the network of the various triads, Jupiter is either a deity who looks upwards towards the Ideas as in the *Phaedrus*' mythical hymn, where he leads the host of gods and souls to the outermost rim of the intellectual heaven thence to gaze from afar at the intelligible Ideas; or he is the providential power or force that looks paternally to the lower realms, since indeed he is the universal father of gods and men.

Futhermore, Ficino is committed to positioning Jupiter with Saturn. The *Cratylus* 396B equates Cronus (Saturn) with «the mighty intellect [...] the pure and garnished mind».[37] For contemplation comes from the head that is Saturn, whereas sovereignty comes from the breast that is Jupiter, and human actions and skills come from the thigh that is Pro-

---

[34] Note that either Prometheus or Hephaestus is said to be the god who took up an axe to cleave open Jupiter's head so that Athena could be born.

[35] Cf. *Statesman* 269E: «the lord and leader» which Ficino, following Plato's *Sixth Letter* 323D, sees as designating two separate deities.

[36] And thus, for the Neoplatonists, of the Jupiter referenced in other dialogues – *Statesman* 269E, *Philebus* 30D1-3, and *Protagoras* 320C ff.

[37] Cicero's *De natura deorum* 2.25.64 derives Saturn's name from his being «saturated or satiated with the years» in the sense that he gorged upon his offspring as Time devours the ages; while Varro's *De lingua latina* 5.64 derives the name from *satum* meaning «what has been sown». For Ficino the compelling etymology was the one associated with Fulgentius: *sacer nus* meaning «sacred intellect». For the four methods of «multiplying» the gods, see Ficino's *In Phaedrum* 10 (edition and translation by M. J. B. ALLEN, Cambridge, Mass. 2008, pp. 81-93).

metheus. Hence the ray from the divine good «becomes triple in the triple divine intelligence and becomes triple in the triple soul and has revealed three abilities to the soul: philosophy to the intelligence, prudence to the reason, and skill to the phantasy. All that men know are therefore God's inventions and God's gifts, as in Ficino's readings of the *Timaeus* 47C and the *Statesman* 274CD. In this scenario Jupiter initiates and completes the bestowal of gifts, and Ficino can depict him as a loving father accompanied by and aided by Prometheus as a loving son (even though such a filial kinship is generationally as well as biologically impossible given Prometheus's birth as a pre-Jovian Titan).

In short, for Ficino the Phileban Prometheus has become an aspect or an attribute of Jupiter. With his «ingenious quickness of mind», with his dialectical powers, he is «the intermediary» and «the preparer», and he has the gift of foreknowledge – in the *Gorgias* 523D ff. Plato even says he has foreknowledge of death. Accordingly, he turns our intellect and our reason back towards the wisdom of Jupiter, a wisdom that Ficino does not confine just to the jovian art of citizenship (*civilis peritia*). This linking with Jupiter (a linking which Plato's *Second Letter* 311B passingly attributes to «primitive men») is precisely why, Ficino says, Prometheus is mentioned «most» in the *Philebus's* account, even though the gifts of the sciences derive from every single divine spirit (*ab unoquoque divino numine*), and only ultimately from Jupiter.

*

By way of further confirmation of the centrality for Ficino of the references in the *Philebus* over and against those in the *Protagoras*, let us turn to two paragraphs in the twenty-sixth chapter of Ficino's own *Philebus* commentary. These are not in the first of his three versions of the commentary and date therefore from the August of 1490 or even later:[38] they indicate that Ficino was still wrestling with the interpretative possibilities of the myth in the last years of his life. The first added paragraph describes Epimetheus as the Moon cherishing the body and ensuring the health of the species through Venus, and of the individual through Jupiter (however odd this may be). By contrast Prometheus here is the Sun cher-

[38] *In Philebum* 1.26 (ed. ALLEN, pp. 244-247 – the sizeable MS W omission: «Possumus etiam Epimetheum [...] in argumento *Cratyli*»).

ishing the rational spirit, ensuring through himself as the Sun the power to perceive, through Mars the power to divide, through Saturn the power to resolve, through Mercury the power to define, and again through himself the power to demonstrate. And since the powers to perceive and to divide are the first pair of this gift – perceiving coming from light, division from heat – Prometheus is said to give light and heat with «the brightest fire» under the prime power of the Sun and of Mars, while Saturn presides over resolution and Mercury over definition. This solar interpretation of the Titan is obviously blended with the notion of the various «powers» of dialectic, but the distribution is unique to this passage and does not appear to be indebted in any way to Olympiodorus.

In the second added paragraph, in yet another extrapolation and exfoliation of triads, Ficino introduces the Coelius/Saturn/Jupiter triad in the primary usage as the triad of God/intelligence/soul; in the secondary usage as the triad of God's creativeness/God's understanding/God's will; and in the third usage as the triad of looking upwards/looking selfwards/looking providentially downwards. In «any spirit» (*numine*) Prometheus and Epimetheus signify Jupiter's providence: Prometheus with regard to rational matters, and Epimetheus, to irrational. The specific daemons promoting the use of the reason are under Prometheus, while those promoting the natural functions are under Epimetheus, but the Titans themselves are seen once again as signifying the third aspect in the fundamental Neoplatonic orientation triad of looking upwards, selfwards and downwards.

*

To conclude. It is obvious that the Prometheus story was not the same story for Ficino as it is for us, and in particular it was not in essence the saga of Aeschylian defiance. To the contrary, our illustrious Florentine had no interest in arguing that the supreme god of Olympus did not want men to have either the fire of understanding, or even the fire that would enable them to master the art of forging iron.[39] Rather, Ficino eventually read the myth, and read it deliberately, in the context of a jovian theology that had no role to assign to the original account of a conflict between a Titan and an Olympian, between a noble thief and

[39] And with it the forging of weapons that we associate with Vulcan, the armorer?

a tyrannical judge. Even though one could interpret his gift of fire as a witness to the coming of the last age of iron in the succession of the four ages, Ficino did not link Prometheus with Vulcan and his stithy; and he did not even link him with Pallas, the goddess of wisdom, of weaving, of olive culture, of the arts of peace. Rather, following his own analysis of the reference in the *Philebus* 16C, Ficino focused on the myth as an account of the origin of the fire of «understanding» or specifically of the light, the illumination that is the goal and the mark of Platonic dialectic. Even though he made no attempt at a Christian reading, let alone at identifying Prometheus with Christ, or with some attribute of Christ, yet the light metaphysics here is intrinsic to Ficino's interpretation of both Platonic and Christian illuminationism. Nor did he make a concerted effort to transform Prometheus into a demiurge, even a sublunar demiurge, though he is potentially such a demiurge in Aeschylus' figuration of the rebellious Titan – and Ficino was certainly drawn to the notion of a sublunar demiurge, as a Proclian scholion he translated as a preface for his *Sophist* Commentary demonstrates.[40]

It is true that difficult, even repugnant myths are part and parcel of the Neoplatonic world where antitheses, polarities, and ambiguities are both cherished and reconciled. In it alternative readings are embraced on different occasions in the fervent belief: a) that the One is unapproachable with the discursive reason, or even with the intuitive intelligence; and b) that contemplating the One ultimately demands paradox and contradiction, the primary instruments of a negative, an Eleatic theology based upon the second part of the *Parmenides*. Even so, unlike Pico, Ficino shied away from the more rebarbative myths of the ancient poets, and perhaps we are coming up here against an instance of this avoidance or re-accommodation of a difficult story.

In the case of Prometheus, he was clearly concerned with interpreting the myth positively, and with exploring the part it had to play in the divine's triadic flow into the human and its subsequent conversion. Equally obviously he was not concerned with interpreting, let alone incorporating, what has traditionally been a central feature in the Prometheus story: the stealing of fire in a fennel root and the Titan's subsequent torture on the Caucuses – in some versions lasting for thirty thousand years – his liver daily devoured by a ravenous eagle or vulture, as a punishment for hav-

---

[40] See my *Icastes: Marsilio Ficino's Interpretation of Plato's* Sophist, Berkeley-Los Angeles 1989, pp. 83-116.

ing brought mankind a divine but forbidden gift. Rather, as we have seen, Ficino is orchestrating a variety of triads, where Prometheus, when he appears, is invariably the third term in a descent triad, and thus represents the emanative power that flows out of the divine realm of the gods into that of the daemonic shepherds of the *Statesman*'s myth 271DE.[41]

It would be wrong to argue, however, that Prometheus retained only a limited appeal for Ficino or that he functioned as a tangential figure, though it is true that the Titan's myth was dominated for him by Jupiter, and was intrinsically therefore a jovian myth. After all, the Jupiter of the *Protagoras* and the *Philebus* alike gradually emerged as the central mythological figure in Ficino's entire Christianized Proclian system along with the demiurgic Jupiter of the *Timaeus* 28A and the *Statesman* 269E, and the Jupiter who is the World Soul, the «mighty leader» of the *Phaedrus* 246E ff. This preoccupation with Jupiter was inevitable, given Ficino's Christian assumptions that jovian theology was a poetic foreshadowing of Christian theology and that Jupiter was a foreshadowing, however inadequate, of Christ, of Christ's benignly providential care of us and the world, and of His soteriological role as the Redeemer.

Far from being a supernumerary, a lesser Mercury or a mercurial daemon, Prometheus was for Ficino – and one is tempted to say had always been, given his youthful engagement with the *Philebus* – the arch dialectician. It was his dialectical fire and his foreknowledge that enabled him: a) to see the providential plan,[42] the order that the *Philebus* 16D says consists of the «conjunction of limit and unlimitedness» that a benevolent Olympian Jupiter had established as the fundamental ontological principle of us and the world; b) to serve, according to Ficino, as Jupiter's beneficent messenger and intermediary; and c) to remind us of the peaks of contemplation that are ours to attain, if we master the supreme Platonic art that can speak both to the ordering of the world and to the nature of the Good itself.[43] As such, Prometheus continued to play a role, even at the close of Ficino's career, in his evolving un-

[41] Cf. Ficino's *Statesman* epitome (*Opera*, pp. 1294-1296). Elsewhere, as we have seen, Prometheus is identified as the chief of the daemons and therefore as the chief shepherd.

[42] And not, ironically, what the Titan was traditionally said to foresee, namely that any son of the nereid Thetis, who was the object of Jupiter (and of Neptune's) desire, would be greater than his father and eventually depose him. By not divulging these prophecies under torture, Prometheus was able in the end to procure his liberty. Jupiter abandoned his pursuit of Thetis and arranged for her to be married to a mortal, Peleus, by whom she gave birth to Achilles.

[43] PLATO, *Republic* 7.532A.

derstanding of Neoplatonic method; and specifically of its concern with exfoliating Neoplatonic triads,[44] that is, with the ordering of the powers that emanate from the One and return to the One. In short, Prometheus is one of the golden keys to what we might call Ficino's meta-dynamics: his transformation of the traditional story of the one-time gift of fire into a quasi Proclian metaphysical account – triadic if not trinitarian – of the perpetual overflowing of power divine.

[44] See in general Edgar Wind's brilliant exposition in his *Pagan Mysteries in the Renaissance*, rev. ed., London-New York 1968.

18

RATIO OMNIUM DIVINISSIMA: PLATO'S *EPINOMIS*, PROPHECY, AND MARSILIO FICINO

The *Epinomis*, which has in the past been seen by some but not all as spurious[1], as «scanty and unsatisfactory», the product of an «inferior mind»[2], played a rather special role in

[1] For a full survey of the older competing views on the dialogue's authenticity and authorship – in Diogenes Laertius's *Lives of the Philosophers* III 37 for instance – see A.C. Lloyd's *Introduction* to *Plato. Philebus and Epinomis*, Translation and Introduction by A.E. TAYLOR, Edited and Annotated by G. CALOGERO-R. KLIBANSKY-A.C. LLOYD, Nelson, London 1956; and especially L. TARÁN, *Academica: Plato, Philip of Opus, and the pseudo-Platonic* Epinomis, American Philosophical Society, Philadelphia 1975. For more recent views, see J.M. DILLON, *Philip of Opus and the Theology of Plato's* Laws, in S. SCOLNICOV-L. BRISSON (eds.), *Plato's* Laws*: from Theory into Practice. Proceedings of the VI Symposium Platonicum*, Academia Verlag, Sankt Augustin 2003, pp. 304-11; and L. BRISSON, Epinomis*: Authenticity and Authorship*, in K. DÖRING-M. ERLER-S. SCHORN (Hrsgg.), *Pseudoplatonica. Akten des Kongresses zu den Pseudoplatonica* (vom 6.-9 Juni in Bamberg), Steiner, Stuttgart 2005, pp. 9-24.

[2] See Lamb's dismissive comments in *Plato. Epinomis*, transl. by W.R.M. LAMB (Loeb Classical Library), Harvard University Press, Cambridge 1925, pp. 424-5 (to which I shall refer in this article): «we soon become aware of contact with an inferior mind which feebly strays and stumbles among the last physical and metaphysical speculations of Plato ... [it is] the hardy attempt of a zealous but small-minded imitator». Lamb considers the *Epinomis* a spurious dialogue assembled «to meet the book-collecting zeal of the Ptolemies in the third century B.C.». But the Alexandrian scholars of that age accepted it (and the *Minos* with

the thought of the immensely influential philosopher-scholar-magus, Marsilio Ficino (1433-1499). We can immediately see this in the opening of his summary of the dialogue, or rather of his brief commentary on it, written in the 1470s, where he declares: «None of Plato's followers doubts that the treasury (*thesaurus*) of the divine Plato lies hidden away in the *Epinomis*»[3]. The accolade is primarily the result of his assumption that the dialogue was meant to succeed the *Laws* as its name suggests, and therefore to serve as the *Laws*' authoritative conclusion, its thirteenth book, and not merely its appendix[4]. Furthermore, we must always bear in mind that he regarded all the books of the *Laws*, and thus the thirteenth book too, as Plato's last body of work[5] (followed only by some of the *Letters*[6]), and as written moreover in Plato's own voice[7] and not in that of a spokesman

which it is customarily linked) as genuine and as supplementing the passage at the end of the twelfth book of the *Laws* (966d-968a7) on the mathematical and astronomical education of the Nocturnal Council. The speakers – the Athenian Stranger, Megillus the Spartan, and Clinias the Cretan – remain the same and they continue the conversation of the day before. Presumably they are still walking from Cnossus to the grotto and temple of Zeus beneath Crete's Mount Ida (as described in *Leg.* I 625).

[3] But the two greatest of Plato's followers did not subscribe to this treasure notion; see nn. 8 and 9 below. Perhaps Calcidius' *In Tim.* 128, 171.4; 254, 262.21 (ed. Waszink), was Ficino's guide here; see L. TARÁN, *Academica*, cit., pp. 159, 182.

[4] Hence a Ficinian reference to material in the *Laws* may be, and often is, a reference to material found only in the *Epinomis*!

[5] Following Aristotle, *Pol.* B 6.1264b26; cfr. Ficino's *Vita Platonis* and his epitome for *Laws* I (*Opera omnia*, pp. 766.2, 1488.2). See, J.M. DILLON, *The Neoplatonic Reception of Plato's* Laws, in F.L. LISI, *Plato's* Laws *and Its Historical Significance. Selected Papers of the Ist International Congress on Ancient Thought (Salamanca 1998)*, Academia Verlag, Sankt Augustin 2001, pp. 243-54.

[6] At the onset of the *Sixth Letter* Plato declares that he is now an old man (322d). Cfr. Ficino's epitome in *Ficini Opera omnia* (Basel 1576), p. 1533.

[7] As Ficino also notes in his *Platonic Theology* (ed. & tr. M.J.B. ALLEN-J. HANKINS, Harvard University Press, Cambridge Mass. 2001-2006, 6 vols.), IV 1, 31, XVII 4, 5-6 (citing book, chapter & paragraph).

such as Timaeus or Socrates. Plato is to be identified, that is, with the Athenian Stranger who is the principal speaker in what is in effect Plato's last dialogue.

These singular "takes" on the thirteenth dialogue of the *Laws* by the great Florentine Neoplatonist were not based, ironically, on any ancient Neoplatonic interpretation of it. Notably, he could not turn to his two most august Neoplatonic authorities, Plotinus and Proclus; for Plotinus makes not a single explicit reference to the *Epinomis*[8] and Proclus little more so, since he regarded it as inauthentic and misleading[9]. The "takes" were based rather on Ficino's own interpretation and estimation of the over-arching theme and the diverse contents of the dialogue itself. To these I shall now turn confining myself to the salient features.

1. The epitome which Ficino prepared for his Latin rendering of the dialogue first appeared along with that rendering in the 1484 *editio princeps* of his *Platonis Opera omnia*; and was then published in the subsequent Plato editions. It later

[8] L. TARÁN, *Academica*, cit., p. 158: there is «no evidence that either *E.* 981 B-C or any other passage of this work influenced Plotinus or that Plotinus [...] cites the *E.* as Platonic». The notion that at *Enn.* II 9, 9, 21-22 and VI 7, 11, 44 ff. Plotinus «may have been thinking» of *Epinom.* 983e6-984a2 and 981b-c and 984b-c respectively is simply editorial surmise. See, however, A. Linguiti's essay in this volume.

[9] Proclus makes no mention of it in his *Theologia Platonica*, and makes just one slighting mention to its daemonology in his *In Tim.* (III 108 Diehl). In the *In Remp.* 16 (II 134, 5-7 Kroll) – Ficino had no access however to this sixteenth treatise – Proclus again refers to its daemonology but expressly declares that the *Epinomis*, «filled as it is with inauthentic material and enigmatic signification, deceives any mind that is naïve and simple mind». Equally passing is his ref. in the *De providentia*, 50, 11-14. Proclus does not even credit the dialogue to Philip of Opus, the author favoured by Diogenes Laertius in his *Lives*, III 37; see L. TARÁN, *Academica*, cit., pp. 115-39; and now E. Gritti, in this volume. The situation with regard to the *Epinomis*' relationship to various ancient mathematical texts by Iamblichus, Theon, Nicomachus and others is less straightforward; see G.R. Giardina, in this volume.

reappeared as a free-standing epitome without the translation in Ficino's own *Opera omnia* of 1561, 1576[10], and 1641, along with all his other epitomes and commentary materials on Plato, Plotinus, Porphyry, Iamblichus, Psellus, and so on. Ficino was convinced that it served as an authentic window into the training of the elite philosopher-rulers of Plato's imagined Nocturnal Council; and he never branded it as spurious, or of dubious authorship, though he was aware that such imitative dialogues existed. We should take note from the beginning, however, that in his synopsis of its argument Ficino does not stick,. or stick very closely, to the order of the dialogue's material, and there are jumps, omissions and recapitulations. While summary is clearly one of his main purposes, it is interesting to see him focusing on a few Neoplatonic motifs, and by the same token ignoring or skating over other aspects of the original argumentation. What emerges in fact is a Ficinian introduction with cross references primarily to his magnum opus, the *Platonic Theology,* and, more predictably, to his *Timaeus* Commentary, since he saw the *Timaeus* as the major elaboration of Plato's cosmological, mathematical, and musical analyses. Scholars should be aware, however, that Ficino's final word on some of Plato's signal mathematical and musical speculations is to be found, not in his long commentary on the *Timaeus* important though it is, but in his commentary on the passage on the fatal or nuptial number in Book VIII of the *Republic* at 546a ff.[11]. This commentary, otherwise known by one of its titles as the *De numero fatali*, was written in the early 1490s and first published along with the *In Timaeum* and Ficino's other substantial Plato commentaries in 1496.

Traditionally subtitled "The Philosopher," the *Epinomis* requires many "devices" (*machinae*), Ficino argues, to bring its treasury of mysteries into the light. But he cannot elaborate on

[10] Pp. 1525-1530.

[11] For an edition, translation, and study, see my *Nuptial Arithmetic: Marsilio Ficino's Commentary on the Fatal Number in Book VIII of Plato's* Republic, University of California Press, Berkeley & Los Angeles 1994.

them in his epitome, he says, since the scribes and printers are pressing him to finish the summaries for the 1484 Plato edition, indeed are «wresting the summaries importunately from his hands». Nonetheless, it is clear that the main goal of law and of the *Laws* is to promote the philosophical wisdom that comes from investigating the principles and causes of works divine, but with the goal always of perceiving and worshipping their Creator; for worship contains within itself the end of all law which is religion. Ficino sees the *Epinomis* as being indeed preeminent (*praestat*) and God-inspired (*aspirante Deo*). For «having prophesied the possibility of reacquiring the mind's perfect habit» (*perfectus habitus mentis*) at the onset of this work, Plato, «in a prayer of supplication» (*supplici quadam oratione*), then begs the perfect habit from God as the crowning achievement of worship or rather as its divine gift.

In other words, the Florentine is attributing an all-encompassing religious status and aim to the *Epinomis*, even as he inteprets it as a witness to the vision of Plato himself in his autumnal years as the philosopher *par excellence*, and as the man of prayer, the *senex orans*, pleading to receive what he has already foreseen and prophesied: namely, the perfect, the angelic perfection of the mind utterly given over to, and absorbed in, adoration. In the *Platonic Theology*, XIV 10, 13, Ficino lauds the *Epinomis* precisely for its affirmation that «men possess nothing more divine than religion», and that religion consists in loving rather than in knowing God, since human knowing is created, finite, and inadequate because incommensurate, but our will to love God only comes to rest «in the first, the measureless Good alone».

Plato had faith in the notion suggested at 973c (and again at 992c) that some «rare souls» (*paucissimos quosdam*) – and Ficino refers to passages in the *Phaedrus*, *Phaedo* and *Republic*[12] – can enjoy in this life the ultimate happiness (*felicitas*) that is customarily reserved for the blessed in the life beyond. They

[12] *Phaedr.* 249c-e; *Phaed.* 80e-84b; *Resp.* VI 491a-b are possibilities.

can only do so, however, if they receive, while still on earth, the divine gift of living outside the body, of sipping the ethereal nectar, to use Ficino's own image, even in the midst of the dull Lethean waters. This is the gift of «living for God rather than for oneself» (*Deoque ipsi potius quam sibi vivant*) – a goal that is unattainable via «the powers that are merely human» (*humanis viribus*) since it requires God to breathe into us, to inspire us.

The basis of the foregoing determination of the principal theme or *skopos* derives from the Stranger's comments at 976c ff. and then again at 991e-992d at the conclusion of the dialogue. Here, as Ficino says in the *Platonic Theology*, XVII 4, 8, citing this conclusion, «the thinking soul separated from the body will spend the rest of time in the contemplation of the most beautiful of all things»[13]. Effectively, Ficino is transforming the notion of the *Republic's* philosopher-king or the *Laws*' astronomer-guardian into something proximate to that of a hermit, anchorite, or saint in solitary ecstasy.

2. The apex of the speculative hierarchy of learned disciplines (*speculatrices doctrinae*) that the *Epinomis* goes on to explore is arithmetic, which the dialogue at 976e declares is «the science which gave number to the whole race of mortals». It also declares that God not chance gave this discipline to preserve us, meaning for Ficino that God gave enumeration to the human mind to serve as the instrument we need in order to return to Him: without it our rational soul would seem to be mindless (*animus amens appareat*). Allied with arithmetic are geometry, stereometry, astronomy, and finally music as the art which is based on «the numeration of notes» (978a), and which imitates the harmony of the heavens, whose «numeration of motions» astronomy meticulously observes. Below these math-

[13] Cfr. *Theol. Plat.* XVIII 18, 8: «In the *Epinomis* he concludes with the summit of beauty when he says that the utterly purged soul [...] gathers itself entirely into its own unity, which is higher than the intellect». This is a ref. yet again to 992b-d.

ematical and scientific disciplines are the natural sciences of physics and biology; but above them – above arithmetic even – is the art, the testing of dialectic. The *Epinomis* does not introduce this "testing" – the references at 977c being to the art of enumeration – until 991c, when the Stranger speaks of the need in discussions to refer «the particular thing to its generic form», such a referring constituting «the finest and first of tests for the use of men». For Ficino, this passing mention obviously served to evoke other more explicit references to dialectic in the *Resp.* VII 532a-534e, *Epist. VII* 343d-344b, *Parm.* 135d, *Pol.* 258b-268c, *Phaedr.* 266b, 277b, *Soph.* 235b, 253d, *Phil.* 57e ff., and so forth[14].

Ficino identifies dialectic as the art, not of logic, but of metaphysical speculation, and as having theology as its crown or rather its queen, since she is the intermediary, the intercessor even, between us and God. For dialectic regards the vast multitude of things, he says, in order to discern their single common principle, what the *Epinomis* calls «the one bond naturally uniting all things» (992a). It is «that which unites all the branches of learning» and leads us to the One: it unites the mind to itself and thus enables it to be re-united with God and it enables our particular oneness to return to the One (986c-d)[15]. Anyone who knows «the divine within generation», writes Ficino, knows true number and thus holiness, "the divine within generation" meaning both the soul's inner spiritual motion or power and at the same time the single natural species which remains one in the everlasting succession of generation. For «in the movement of soul there is true number in accord, as Timaeus says, with musical proportion and harmony»; and there is true number too within a species. From the former we can deduce divine self-existence, and from the latter, eternity. This whole line of argument constitutes, predictably, a Neoplatonic reading,

[14] For Ficino and Platonic dialectic, see my *Synoptic Art: Marsilio Ficino on the History of Platonic Interpretation*, Olschki, Firenze 1998, chap. 5: *Promethean Dialectic.*

[15] Cfr. *Theol. Plat.* XII 2, 3.

adaptation, and centering of the scattered notices in the original text.

3. In turning to the daemons introduced at 977c and 984d ff., Ficino confronts several problems. He takes up Plato's inclusion of men in "the race" of terrestrial daemons, and the connected theme of the three fires: the celestial revolving fire, the sublunar fire which gives warmth rather than light and is properly called the aether, and the ordinary fire here on earth which not only warms but burns. In the Neoplatonists' "element" theory or stoicheiology, each element appears in each sphere but predominates in one: thus aether is found in an earthy form in the sphere of the earth, while earth appears in the aether in an aetherial form; and so on (981b-c). Fire and aether are treated separately by the Stranger and aether is given special consideration. But Ficino counts aether as intermediate between fire and air, being airy fire or fiery air, and preserves the traditional symmetries associated with the notion of four elements. All four elements, including the mediating aether, have «living rational creatures» dwelling in them. These are the creatures compounded of body and of a life now rendered corporeal. Each particular life depends on a triple soul: on its own; on the soul of its sphere, and on the soul of the whole world.

In elaborating on the notion of being subject to the ruling soul of a sphere, Ficino goes considerably beyond the material actually in the dialogue, and seems to be adhering to the hierachical distinctions between emperor, king, and prince. Any creature is subordinate to the twelve ruler-souls or kings of the twelve spheres, the realms of the four elements, of the seven planets, and of the fixed stars: these ruler souls are identified with the following twelve gods, beginning with the goddess of the earth: Vesta, Neptune, Juno, Vulcan, Diana, Mercury, Venus, Apollo, Mars, Jupiter, Saturn, and Uranus. These in turn are under the imperial sway of the World Soul traditionally identified with Jupiter (who is thus seen in a twofold capacity as king of his planetary sphere, and as emperor of all). But within each sphere – and in his *Platonic Theology*, IV 1, 11-16, where the whole scheme is elaborated, Ficino seems to think of this as an explicitly Pythagorean feature – there are twelve ranks or orders of souls[16]. Each of these twelve orders is ruled by a soul-prince though it contains numberless lesser souls. Looking up at the celestial fire, at the uranian sphere, that is, of the fixed stars, we can see these twelve princes as the twelve zodiacal animals or constellations or rather as their principal stars[17]. On earth at the other end of the cosmic scale we encounter under the regal soul of the earth which is Vesta the twelve kinds of earthy daemons and men, kinds which Ficino identified in the *Platonic Theology* in terms of the ways they are governed by reason, wrath, and desire, or by just two of them in various combinations[18]. By logical extension therefore with the ten other intermediary spheres each has one soul-king and twelve subordinate orders each led by a soul-prince[19]. Thus in the air (including the aethereal air) under regal Juno dwell the twelve orders of airy daemons, in the water under Neptune, the twelve kinds of watery daemons (usually characterized as nymphs); and similarly with each of the planetary spheres.

Thus each particular soul has its place in a hierarchy of souls, ordered by twelves, and all under the soul-emperor which is the World Soul[20]. Each pure soul, moreover, possesses mind,

[16] Numerologically twelve has of course always been significant: for Ficino see my *Nuptial Arithmetic*, cit., pp. 71-2.

[17] *Theol. Plat.* IV 1, 15.

[18] *Ibid.*

[19] *Ibid.* IV 1, 16.

[20] In the *Theol. Plat.* XVI 6, 3 – with reference obviously to *Tim.* 41a-42e, *Epinom.* 981c-e, and PLOT. *Enn.* IV 2, 1; 3, 1-9; 8, 3-4 – Ficino writes that «in descending from the summit, the crowd of indwelling beings always increases in number, and this is why in the highest heaven itself just one leader suffices for the number of the stars, namely the soul of the [starry] sphere, but since more and inferior beings dwell in the individual circle of the planets than at the summit, more leaders are needed; and so

a jovian mind being equally, in the famous formulation of the *Philebus*, 30d, both royal mind and royal soul and endowed with the power of the cause.

This whole Pythagorean argument about twelves may seem contorted; and it is only fully explicable if we turn to the paragraphs in the *Platonic Theology*, IV 1, 11-16 already referred to[21]. What haunts Ficino, as he will emphasize later at IV 1, 31, is the *Epinomis*' assertion at 983b-c that «It is impossible for the earth, the heavens, and all the stars and the masses they comprise, to perform their yearly, monthly, and daily revolutions with such exquisite rationality and to render all things good for all of us, unless soul is present near them or in them individually (*nisi anima singulis aut adsit aut insit*)».

Ficino connects the remark at 981e-982a that the stars are either eternal «or very long-lived» – the latter being on the face of it an indefensible notion for a Platonist[22] – with the notion found in Orpheus, «perhaps in Hermes [Trismegistus]», and certainly in Anaxagoras, Empedocles, Heraclitus, and many of the Stoics, of a cyclical and fated combustion of the world followed by a reconstitution that results in a re-creation, or a like creation, of this world. The argument of these ancients is that a cyclical notion of creation is part and parcel of God's handiwork. Ficino, interestingly, raises no objection to this contention[23]; for he sees the notion of restitution as the result of

God has established two leaders there [...] namely the soul of the sphere and the soul of the planet». These distinctions embroil us in further complications.

[21] The whole scheme for Ficino is derived from the *Phaedrus*' depiction at 246e ff. of the cavalcade of the eleven deities led by Jupiter ascross the intellectual heaven – eleven because Hestia/Vesta «remained alone in the gods' dwelling place» even though she is one of the twelve cosmic gods. See my *The Platonism of Marsilio Ficino*, University of California Press, Berkeley-Los Angeles 1984, pp. 116-21, 139-43, 148-9, and 250-3.

[22] In *Theol. Plat.* XVII 4, 6, Ficino says, in citing this passage, that the stars have as much life or length of life as suffices for them.

[23] He fully Christianizes, however, the notion of the end of a world cycle or aeon in terms of the last Judgement and the Resurrection in his

the finite nature and internal strife of creation itself, of its deficiency of form, a deficiency that God periodically compensates. «Such», he says, «is the vision of these men».

The souls of the eternal or long-lived stars are their "gods" and their bodies are their images, the stars having senses, the Stranger adds, that are keenly perceptive and much more acute than ours (984d). The daemons, however, have faculties, though superior, that more closely resemble ours: they are aware of our thoughts and feelings, and they favor the good ones and oppose the bad ones. Here, and in the *Statesman*, 271d ff. and the *Symposium*, 202e, Ficino sees Plato as regarding all daemons as good, though in other dialogues he indicates that some are evil or at least punitive or retributive, most notably those who appear in the myth of Er in the *Republic*, X 615e ff. as the instruments of the judgements and penalties meted out in Hades. The wicked are taken up by «savage beings of fiery aspect» who bear them away, carding and flaying them.

From the ancients, Ficino also derives the notion that some of the daemons are invisible, namely the aethereal and airy ones, while the watery daemons are occasionally visible «to the inner but not to the outer eye». At 985b Plato says that this watery kind is at one time seen, but at another conceals itself and becomes invisible, «presenting a marvel in the dimness of vision»[24]. Hence they visit us in our dreams, they haunt us as ominous utterancies or voices, they fill us with prophecies, and they present us with signs (cfr. 985c). They especially do so when the soul abandons the body; and for Ficino this includes the abandonment of the body that occurs in trance as well as the final abandonment at death.

analysis of the myth of Plato's *Statesman*. See my *Nuptial Arithmetic*, cit., pp. 128-135; ID. *"Quisque in sphaera sua": Plato's* Statesman, *Marsilio Ficino's* Platonic Theology *and the Resurrection of the Body*, «Rinascimento», ser. 2, XLVII (2008) pp. 25-48.

[24] As translated by W.R.M. Lamb. A.E. Taylor's version of this clause reads: «and thus perplexes us by its indistinct appearance».

In addressing the notion at 986c which declares that «the most divine principle of all has established the visible world» – an utterance he treats as as a prophecy as we shall see momentarily – Ficino is convinced that Plato at 988e is refuting the dualistic notion that there is a good World Soul and an evil one[25]. Good things proceed from the former but evil things only emerge from what «is entirely devoid of number and is therefore discordant». In that they are lacking order, these evils are overcome by good things, and by the Ideas in the divine mind; and they must assuredly be so overcome as long as the world endures, since the evil of injustice is necessarily overcome by the goodness of justice; and all things are so full of gods and spirits that we are forever supported by them, as Plato observes at 991d. In sum, Ficino sees Plato as accounting for the existence of evil by defining it, in the Neoplatonic manner, as the absence, the privation of good.

As to numbers, Ficino espouses the assumptions, again Pythagorean, that numbers are incorporeal and are nothing but unity, i.e. are the number one repeated; and that when allotted extension, number becomes first a point, then a line, then a surface or plane, and then a cube or solid with depth[26]. As a consequence, some numbers are with respect to lines, others to surfaces, and yet others to cubes and solids. One is like the point; two is like the line, two being closest to the one; four is like the plane or surface since four proceeds by way of the two from the one; and eight is like the three dimensional solid since it comes from two times two times two. This gives us the obvious primary sequence of 1-2-4-8 which is one of the two legs in the so called lambda of the *Timaeus*, 35b ff. Hence the perfect ratio, the Stranger maintains at 991a, is that of 2:1, while subordinate to it are the other two major ratios of 3:2 (the sesquialteral) and 4:3 (the sesquiter-

[25] Hinted at in *Leg.* X 896d-897d.

[26] ARISTOT. *Top.* Z 4.141b5-22; *Metaph.* B 5.1001b26-1002b11.

tial)[27]. Ficino sees these primary ratios as being derived from the first four numbers, that is, from the Pythagoreans' tetraktys, which when added together sum to ten; and he sees them as preserved, or rather observed, in a variety of spheres. First in the heavens. Here he turns to the Pythagorean theory of the musical intervals of the planetary spheres (and not we should add the distances between them). This is a technical passage that needs quoting in detail:

They compare the Earth to the Firmament and again to the Moon and the Sun, and the Sun too to the Firmament. In these comparisons the interval from the Earth to the Sun is contrasted with the interval from the Sun to the Firmament. Thus there is a sequialteral interval between the Earth and the Sun, but a sesquitertial interval between the Sun and the Firmament. From the first proportion is born the consonance of diapente, the fifth; from the second proportion is born the consonance of diatessaron, the fourth. But from both together comes the double proportion or consonance of the diapason. The Pythagoreans also want the interval from the Earth to the Moon to be a fourth, as that from the Earth to the Sun to be a fifth, and that from the Sun to the Firmament to be again a fourth[28].

Thus the interval between Earth and the Firmament, being that of the diapason, includes both the interval of the fifth between the Earth and the Sun and that of the fourth between the Sun and the Firmament (another interval of the fourth being that between the Earth and the Moon).

These ratios Nature herself observes in the actions and passivities of the elements, where the agent must be twice as powerful as that upon which it acts for the action to be ful-

[27] Cfr. Ficino's epitome of *Republic* IV (*Opera omnia*, pp. 1402-4 at 1403)

[28] *Ficini Opera omnia,* p. 1529 as translated in my *Nuptial Arithmetic*, cit., p. 111. In the *Timaeus* commentary 35 (*Opera omnia*, p. 1461.1), Ficino propounds a somewhat different system, though again based on the lambda numbers of *Tim.* 35b ff.; see *Nuptial Arithmetic*, cit., p. 111 n.

filled[29]. Just as this double ratio leads to the generating of substantial form (*conducat ad substantialem speciem generandam*), so the sequialteral ratio leads to the familiar effecting and shaping of that form[30] (*ad familiarem speciei effectionem atque figuram*), and the sesquitertial ratio leads to certain more common accidents (*ad accidentia quaedam communiora*). Here Ficino is clearly contrasting substance with accident by way of a musical terminology, and deploying the sesquialteral ratio to mediate between the two.

The key double ratio also pertains to the humoural balance insofar as there is twice as much blood in us as phlegm, twice as much phlegm as bile, and twice as much bile as black bile – again 8:4:2:1 – with the result that there are eight times as much blood and four times as much phlegm as there is black bile. Similar ratios are found in hearing (*in auditu*), Ficino says, where there are four degrees (*gradus*) of air, three of fire, two of water and one of earth, i.e. 4:3:2:1. This sequence contains of course the sesquitertial proportion and the sesquialteral as well as the double, the triple and the quadruple ratios. These, he says provocatively, «are more obvious in the affect [or sensation] of hearing» than in the others senses, meaning I take it that we can immediately identify them aurally in the harmonies of the diapason, the diapente, and the diatesseron.

Even physicians, Ficino continues, observe the sequence of ratios when they divide our perception into what is barely perceived, what is clearly perceived, what is uncomfortably perceived, and what is destructively perceived, since here too we find the double, sesquialteral, and sesquitertial ratios. «But leave this», he says, «to the medics». At this terminal point, he

[29] Cfr. THEO. *Exp.* 3, 15; MACROB. *In Somn. Scip.* II 1, 1-25; 4, 1-10; and Ficino's own *De rationibus musicae* (ed. P.O. KRISTELLER, *Supplementum Ficinianum*, 2 vols., Olschki, Firenze 1935, I, pp. 51-6). This entire system was known to antiquity and to the Renaissance as the eight-stringed lyre of Pythagoras.

[30] Or possibly «leads to the usual effects and shape a form has».

notes, Plato introduces the ampler sequence 1-2-4-6-8-12 since it contains four doubles, two sesquialterals and a sesquitertial. And he perfunctorily closes by saying that he has dealt with all these matters more conveniently in his *Timaeus* Commentary[31].

4. Despite this obvious fascination with the *Epinomis*' elaboration of Platonic ratio and harmony theory and its ramifications, material which he interpreted in light of the *Timaeus*, what was most notable about Plato's last dialogue in Ficino's Christian Platonic eyes was a reference which to us now is a mere passing mention. At 986c the Stranger refers to the order which «law, divinest of things that are» (*logos ho panton theiotatos*), has set before our eyes. Marsilio renders "law" here as *ratio omnium divinissima*, and in citing the phrase elsewhere he adds *sive divinissimum verbum*. In the *Platonic Theology*, X 7, 2 he invokes this very formula to describe God's "divine influence" and "formative power" which in flowing forth «penetrates the heavens, descends through the elements, and reaches as far as inferior matter». This is the power "perchance" which Plato calls «the reason of the divine understanding» (*divinae intelligentiae rationem*). In the *Platonic Theology*, XI 4, 6 Ficino again invokes this *ratio*: «In the *Epinomis* Plato affirms that the sensible world was adorned (*exornatum*) through this divine reason or word, which he calls the intelligible world».

In his eyes the phrasing at 986c was not a reference to law as such: rather it was a signal prophecy about the most divine Word or Reason, the Logos that was and is and will be before all things. Predictably he interpreted it in the light of the famous invocation of the Logos at the beginning of St. John's Gospel, the Word that was with God and was God, the Word by whom all things were made, the Word being, in the definition of Colossians 1:13-15, the dear Son who is «the image of the invisible God» and «the firstborn of every creature». In other words, we are looking at the key formulary phrases asso-

[31] We should recall he had not yet written his *De numero fatali*.

ciated with the Second Person of the Trinity and more particularly with Johannine and Pauline Christology.

It is obvious that from the onset Ficino had come to regard this reference at 986c as one of Plato's most memorable and inspired prophecies. Indeed, its presence in this, the thirteenth book of the *Laws* must have been sufficient in itself, I suspect, to deter Ficino from ever wishing to entertain any doubts about the dialogue's authenticity[32]. It was too profound an ancient witness to be relegated or dismissed.

In order to establish a context for understanding its status as an oracular prediction attributed to Plato himself in his old age and not to some interlocutor, however venerable, let us turn to two other prophecies attributed to the aged Plato.

For Ficino the most famous of all Plato's mysterious utterances is the knotted statement in the *Second Letter* at 312d-e which became a fundamental challenge for the later ancient Platonists and notably for Proclus to unravel. This declares that «related to the King of all are all things, and for his sake they are, and of all things fair he is the cause. And related to the Second are the second things and related to the Third, the third. About these then, the human soul strives to learn, looking to the things that are akin to itself».

The Neoplatonists had scrutinized every word, phrase, and modality of this enigma, and they succeeded in explaining it only by way of referencing it to the three Neoplatonic concepts of the One, Mind, and Soul[33]. As a Christian Platon-

[32] He was quite prepared to doubt the authenticity of other works: for instance, he attributed the *First* and *Fifth Letters* to Dion.

[33] Some modern scholars have decried the many, unconvincing readings by Middle Platonists and even more exaspiratingly it would seem by their own academic peers. In the fray they tend to ignore the consensus arrived at by the Neoplatonists that the solution to the *Second Letter's* riddle was metaphysical. Contrast, for instance, Bury's scornful comments in the Prefatory Note of *Plato. Timaeus, Critias, Clitopho, Menexenus, Epistulae*, Text and translation by R.G. BURY (Loeb Classical Library), Harvard University Press, London-New York 1929, pp. 400-1, with Saffrey-Westerink's careful analysis in *Proclus. Théologie Platonici-*

ist Ficino then transformed the whole enigma into an adumbration, albeit subordinationist, of the three persons of the Trinity; and he did so by interpreting the King as a reference to the Father, the Second as a reference to the Son, and the Third as a reference to the Holy Spirit. Elsewhere I have examined Ficino's account of the *Second Letter*[34], and also dealt, separately, with the enigma itself[35]. Clearly there are many intriguing problems, some of which at least Ficino attributed to Plato's necessarily imperfect knowledge of the Logos, given that he lived centuries before the coming of Christ, and given too his unfamiliarity with, and independence from, the Hebrew tradition and its long line of prophets. Nonetheless, Ficino revels in the idea that the enigma is a triumph of Plato's old age, being an adumbration of a central Christian truth, even as he accepts the reality that Plato could only have dimly foreseen what Christian interpreters would later see with dazzling clarity.

This is reinforced by the *Second Letter's* statement at 314a that the doctrines contained in Plato's enigma, and especially the doctrine concerning the nature of the King (312d), make no sense to the vulgar and should not be transmitted to them. Rather, they should be «refined at length, like gold, with prolonged [meditative] labour» and only by «men of refined disposition themselves» (314a), men who must always bear in mind that Plato never committed himself to writing anything down on these subjects, but only to imparting them orally. He

enne, Texte établi et traduit par H.D. SAFFREY-L.G. WESTERINK, 6 vols., Les Belles Lettres, Paris 1968-1997, II, pp. XX-LIX.

[34] *Sending Archedemus: Ficino, Plato's* Second Letter, *and its Four Epistolary Mysteries*, in S. EBBERSMEYER-H. PIRNER PARESCHI-TH. RICKLIN (Hrsgg.), *Sol et Homo: Mensch und Natur in der Renaissance. Festschrift zum 70. Geburtstag für Eckhard Kessler*, Fink, München 2008, pp. 405-20.

[35] *Marsilio Ficino on Plato, the Neoplatonists and the Christian Doctrine of the Trinity*, «Renaissance Quarterly», XXXVII (1984) pp. 555-84; this is now in my *Plato's Third Eye: Studies in Marsilio Ficino's Metaphysics and its Sources*, Variorum, Aldershot 1995.

had never written, and never would have written, he declares, a treatise on them (314c)[36].

In the *Sixth Letter* Plato ends with the exhortation, albeit delivered enigmatically and in an earnest and yet playful manner, that Hermeias, Erastus, and Coriscus should swear by «the God who is the Leader (*hegemon*) of all that is and that shall be, and swear by the Lord and Father of the Ruler and of the Cause» (323d). These enigmas Ficino likewise transformed into a prophecy of the Trinity, as his epitome for the *Sixth Letter* clearly demonstrates. «The Leader (*dux*) of all that is and that shall be» is the World Soul. The Father (*pater*) and Lord (*dominus*) is Almighty God, the Good itself. And midway between the two, he says, Plato is positing «a certain Divine Mind» (*mens quaedam divina*), since in repeating «of the Leader» (*ducis*), he adds «and of the Cause» (*subiungit et causae*).

The epitome goes on to explain that "King" often stands for the Good in Plato's writings, that "the Cause" means Mind, and that "Leader" stands for Soul, i.e. the World Soul. And here Ficino makes reference to what he takes to be the *Timaeus*' statement that Mind or Intellect is the Son of the Good and the architect of the world[37]. He then quotes the famous prophecy we are scrutinizing from the *Epinomis* at 986c: «The most Divine Reason or the most Divine Word adorned the world that we see (*Ratio divinissima sive divinissimum verbum mundum visibilem exornavit*)». A similar juxtaposition of the two prophecies occurs in the *Platonic Theology*, XI 4, 6 where, as we witnessed earlier, Ficino declares that the *Epinomis* calls the intelligible world Reason or Word, whereas the *Sixth Letter* refers to it as "God the Son", the Good being

[36] Cfr. *Epist. VII* 341c: «There does not exist, nor will there ever exist, any treatise of mine dealing therewith [i.e. with the most important doctrines]». Rather, understanding comes not from reading through a treatise, but suddenly, «as kindled by a leaping spark» (cfr. 344b).

[37] *Tim.* 28a-29a.

God the Father. Plotinus, he recalls, «refers to the intelligible as the God from God, as the light from light, and as God's reason and word»[38].

Moreover, in speaking of the Father and the Lord does Plato mean, Ficino asks, that God is the Father of Mind but the Lord of Soul? For this too would imply a subordinationist, or for a Christian, an Arian, explanation, since the title "Lord" is different from that of "Father". So perhaps someone, Ficino observes tentatively, should take Leader to mean the Holy Spirit, and Mind to mean the Son; «for when Plato says the Father he also means the Son». This would be presenting an orthodox not an Arian explanation. Were someone to assume a single essence for the three, futhermore, he would be attributing, "it would seem", a correct trinitarianism to Plato, even if the majority of Platonists would oppose such an interpretation.

Of interest here is Ficino's reference to the *Epinomis* towards the end of his epitome of *Republic* VI in the context of Iamblichus' memorably enigmatic formulations in the *De mysteriis*, VIII 2. Ficino assumed that these formulations were subsequent to, and dependent on, similar formulations in the Christian Platonism of John, of Paul, and of Paul's putative disciple, Dionysius the Areopagite; and that they were indebted in general to the orthodoxies of that Platonism. He deems it significant that Iamblichus, Julian's teacher, had rejected the Arian subordinationism adopted by his imperial pupil; and he interprets the Iamblichian "mystery" as proclaiming the notion that the Father and the Son are different in principle (*diversa quidem ratio*) while their substance «seems to be the same». And he presents the "mystery" in an abbreviated and doctored form (in all likelihood because his text of Iamblichus was demonstrably corrupt):

The first God is also the one Father of the first God whom He begets while remaining in the solitary unity of Himself. But

[38] *Enn.* V 1, 6, 8; 5, 3; 8, 1.

He is the model of the Son who is named the Son of Himself amd the Father of Himself and the Father of the One. He is the truly good God, for He is the fountain of the ideas, and from this one [fountain], God, who is sufficent in Himself, unfolds Himself in light. Hence He is called sufficient for Himself and the Father of Himself. For He is the principle, the God of gods, the One from the one, who is above all essence as the principle of essence[39].

Ficino adds that Iamblichus bears witness that this mystery of the Son's identity with the Father derives from Hermes, i.e. from such passages in the *Corpus Hermeticum* as 2, 14, 5, 9-11, and 14, 4.

However, he never grants a higher wisdom to the Egyptian sage than to Plato himself, and clearly he wants to see the enigma as a more elaborate unfolding of the prophecy concerning the Son as the living Word that was already present in the *Epinomis*, 986c. The culminating formulation, as Amelius had testified, was of course in the opening of the fourth Gospel. In the event, however, he leaves the impression in the *Republic* VI epitome that Iamblichus had arrived at the correct formulation of the dogma of the Son's relationship to the Father, if not at the full mystery of the Trinity itself, the mystery which Plato could only have intimated but which Iamblichus (c. 250-c. 325 AD) could have actually known.

5. Significantly, these three prophecies concerning the Trinity, the Son, and the Creation provide us with an arresting theological perspective on the late Plato, a perspective Ficino inherited, so far as I can tell, neither from antiquity (though doxographers such as Diogenes Laertius had addressed the notion of a Plato chronology and thus the notion of his last works), nor from the Greek Fathers, nor from Bessarion and other Renaissance Greek witnesses. It would seem to be of his own making, though the issue awaits examination.

[39] *Opera omnia*, p. 1408.

One can assert, of course, that Ficino saw quasi or proto-Christian mysteries and prophecies throughout Plato's work: witness the soteriological implications of the *Phaedrus*, the metaphysical theology of the *Parmenides*, the cosmological dimensions of the creation myth in the *Timaeus*, the eschatological mysteries of the myth of Er in the *Republic*, the mysteries of the Last Judgment and Resurrection adumbrated in the *Statesman*, the prefiguring of Christ in Socrates (and particularly in the *Apology* and *Phaedo*), the nature of the divine love explored in the *Symposium*, and so on.

Nonetheless, I would argue that these three enigmas in the *Epinomis* and in the *Second* and *Sixth Letters* constituted for him the signal achievement of Plato as a prophet and seer. Their presence elevated their three respective "works", otherwise relatively minor ones, to the level of being pivotal sacred texts in the gentile theology. They must have assuredly reminded Ficino of other dicta in the various compilations he cherished as the authentic scriptures of that theology: the *Chaldaean Oracles*, the golden sayings of Pythagoras, the various verses in the Orphic hymns and fragments, the fragmentary quotations in ancient sources of sundry pre-Socratic dicta, particularly those of Heraclitus and Empedocles.

To conclude. Far from being relegated to the margins as a doubtful or spurious dialogue, the *Epinomis* for Ficino was central to Plato's *Laws*, indeed their climactic conclusion[40]; and proximate in date to the two most important of Plato's *Letters*. All four of these works, however incommensurate in size, were the product of Plato's old age wherein, for the first time Ficino believed, he was speaking at last *in propria persona*, and thereby investing his words with his own unique authority as the culminating figure of the ancient theology. This set of perspectives is at odds with the views held by many, perhaps most, modern Plato scholars: those who sense in the *Laws* something of decrepitude – a loss or absence of internal con-

[40] Ficino's interpretation of the *Laws* awaits detailed examination.

sistency, of stylistic polish, of intellectual rigour and elan, however impressive much of the work may be[41] – or those who entertain fundamental doubts about the authenticity of the *Letters* – and in addition are unimpressed by the enigmas in the *Second Letter* and the *Sixth*; or those finally who tend to assume that the *Epinomis* is of dubious if not spurious authorship, however interesting it might be as an example of post-Platonic, epigonal imitation. Certainly no contemporary scholar entertains the notion so dear to Ficino's heart that at 986c the *Epinomis* presents us with a profound quasi-Biblical insight into the Logos which is God the Son, the Son who is both one in substance with the Father and yet the idea, the cause, the life, the perfection of all creation, the divine source of its harmony and of its sublime arithmetic[42].

Whatever its scholarly interests for us now, and they are many, the *Epinomis* itself no longer has the extraordinary allure, the theological aura it once possessed for the Florentine philosopher-priest, and therefore, we must presume, for his Renaissance readers, including the readers of his great Plato translation and its attendant commentaries. We have only to think of the Cambridge Platonists in the seventeenth century[43]. By the same token, to re-enter Ficino's *Epinomis* is to re-enter the fascinating Christian-Platonic world of one of the Renaissance's most important and influential figures, a world where this, the last of Plato's dialogues, is duly accorded a certain grandeur and pride of place.

[41] For example, W.K.C. GUTHRIE, *A History of Greek Philosophy*, V: *The Later Plato and the Academy*, Cambridge University Press, Cambridge 1978, pp. 321-2, speaks of its infelicities of style, its repetitions, and its internal inconsistencies, while attributing them to the unrevised state in which Plato had to leave the work.

[42] See my *Nuptial Arithmetic*, cit., pp. 140-2.

[43] See Ralph Cudworth, for instance, in his *True Intellectual System of the Universe*, p. 403, on the motion of the earth, and p. 789, on the vehicle of the soul: its «*Spirituous Vehicles*, seems to have been derived from *Plato*, he in his *Epinomis*, writing thus concerning a Good and Wise man after *Death*».

CORRIGENDA & ADDENDA

for the 18 items in this Variorum edition

1 (Columbia volume)

306.1.3up	forms in matter [NOT Forms]
306.2.9	Good NOT good]
307.2.9	ADD The *Platonic Theology* was first published in 1482
311.3.1up	ADD in Savoy.
312.9	his *Timaeus* had shown that [ADD shown]
312.2.2up	had been [NOT has]
314.3.8up	in the mid 17th century [NOT after mid-century]

For Ficino and musical harmonies, see now the fascinating study by Jacomien Prins, *Echoes of an Invisible World: Marsilio Ficino and Francesco Patrizi on Cosmic Order and Music Theory* (Leiden, Brill: 2014).

2 (Pico).

The most important recent work on the *Oration* is undoubtedly that by Brian P. Copenhaver, "The Secret of Pico's *Oration*: Cabala and Renaissance Philosophy," *Midwest Studies in Philosophy* 26 (2002), pp. 56–81; idem, "Magic and the Dignity of Man: De-Kanting Pico's *Oration*," in *The Italian Renaissance in the Twentieth Century: Acts of an international conference in Florence, Villa I Tatti, June 9–11, 1999*, ed. A Grieco et al. (Florence, 2002), pp. 295–320.

3 (Cantab Crit)

BIB on p.653	sub Kallendorf
	CUT 1943, reprint Gloucester, MA: Peter Smith, 1964
	ADD Hanover, N.H.: University Press of New England, 1989.
	Sub Kristeller ADD reprint Gloucester, MA: Peter Smith, 1964.

5 (Res et verba)

15.6 Every fourth year [NOT fifth]

17.9 The king [NEW SENTENCE]

27n34 This section of Ficinian commentary on the *Mystical Theology* is now in chapter XIII.1–2 of the new I Tatti edition (Cambridge, Mass.: HUP, 2015): Ficino is interpreting the opening of 1.3 (ed. Cordier, i.e. Migne's 1000BC).

6 (Cultural Icon)

250n33 4.2.2–4 [NOT 4.4.2–4]

7 (Kristeller)

We now realize the Nixon tapes began in 1971

2mid. Giuseppe Saitta [NOT Guiseppe]

8 (Education)

235n40.2: of bodily

Bynum [NOT Bynn]

Resurrection in Western Christianity CE 200–1336.

9 (Language of Past)

40n8 move IV.1 up to follow *Theology*

3 vols. should be 6

41.2.1 Count [NOT Duke]

10 (Venus)

81 title [italicize *Commento* and *Heptaplus* and un-italicize all the rest]

103.5 in a sense [ADD a]

11 (Quisque)

44.1.6up It is also quite [ADD is]

12 (At Variance)

34.10 of souls {NOT of the soul}

43n44 ADD Luke 9:28–36

13 (Achedemus)

411.1up Angelic [NO italics]

14 (Statuary)

130n10 ADD Cf. the well-known passage in the *Enneads* 1.6.9—indebted as it is to the *Phaedrus* 252D6–7—on the need to work on one's own statue until we see "self-mastery enthroned upon its holy seat" (*Phaedrus* 254B7).

15 (Saturn)

ADD This essay has also appeared in *Renaissance Averroism and its Aftermath: Arabic Philosophy in Early Modern Europe*, ed. Anna Akasoy and Guido Giglioni, International Archives of the History of Ideas 211 (Dordrecht: Springer, 2013), pp. 81–87.

25.5 complementary [NOT complimentary]

16 (Eurydice)

30.2.3up had lost: he was [NOT has ...is]

30n43.2up below. [i.e. END sentence];

33n55.2 Dombek

35.5 comma not semicolon

18 (Epinomis).

476.2.2up comma not semicolon

482.2.3up other senses [NOT others]

INDEX